SENSE-MAKING METHODOLOGY READER

SELECTED WRITINGS OF BRENDA DERVIN

edited by

Brenda Dervin
The Ohio State University
and
Lois Foreman-Wernet
Capital University
with
Eric Lauterbach

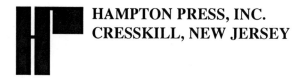

HAMPTON PRESS, INC.
CRESSKILL, NEW JERSEY

Printed in the United States of America

Library of Congress Cataloging-in-Publication Data

Dervin, Brenda.
   Sense-making methodology reader : selected writings of Brenda Dervin/
  edited by Brenda Dervin, Lois Foreman-Wernet with Eric Lauterbach.
     p. cm.
  Includes bibliographic references and index.
    1. Communication--Philosophy. 2. Communication--Methodology.
  I. Foreman-Wernet, Lois. II. Lauterback, Eric. III. Title.

P90.D466   2003
302.2'01--dc22

                            2003059550

Hampton Press, Inc.
23 Broadway
Cresskill, NJ 07626

John Jordan Dervin Sr.
Who, in small seemingly inconsequential acts, made life possible.

Richard F. Carter
Whose genius made Sense-Making Methodology possible.

Patricia Dewdney
Whose continued support and casual suggestions made this volume possible.

CONTENTS

PART I: PHILOSOPHICAL FOUNDATIONS

PART II: RESEARCH, DESIGN, AND PRACTICE

PREFACE

The approach to communication research and practice that I now call Sense-Making Methodology began in 1972 as a detour. A recent recipient of the doctorate, I envisioned my project as an academic to be the conduct of research that would enable the design and implementation of responsive communication and information systems and procedures. I wanted to be a specialist in audience studies by whatever name the audiences involved might be labeled—users, clients, customers, readers, patrons, recipients, constituencies, and so on.

This was the goal that had sent me to graduate studies. As an undergraduate I had been trained as a journalist and public information specialist. I had worked as a practitioner for seven years. While I had been schooled in an array of communicating skills, I was disappointed to learn that my employers—in the press, industry, and non-profits mandated to public service—were not interested in communication. Rather, they were interested in one-way education, usually well-intentioned, or in persuasion, and too often in manipulation.

Naively I thought graduate studies in communication would provide me the frameworks to change this dominant status quo. The communication field I entered was one bifurcated as it essentially remains today between polarized approaches—quantitative versus qualitative, administrative versus critical, and theory-driven versus applied and practical. I was not comfortable with the implications for understanding audiences of these bifurcations. I felt it must be possible to do audience studies capitalizing both on the systematizations that typify quantitative studies and the interpretive and critical sensibilities that typify qualitative studies. And I felt it must be possible to conduct theoretical research in such a way that it directly informed communication practice.

Thus began my detour. In order to develop approaches for the design of user-oriented systems and procedures and the conduct of user-oriented research, I had to become a methodologist—to invent in effect an alternative approach to audience studies and to thinking about communication practice. This journey officially started in 1972 (although I wasn't really aware that it had begun until the early 1980s) and continues to the date of this writing. The chapters in this volume consist of writings originally published over a 22 year period, from 1980 (when the Sense-Making Methodology first began to emerge as a formally labeled approach) to 2002.

Because I have explicitly set out to develop Sense-Making as a generalizable communication-based methodology, I have sought to apply it in a wide variety of contexts. Understanding this is an important aspect of understanding what I was attempting to do. I sought contexts for a variety of practical as well as theoretic reasons. Practical reasons included, for example, the availability of funding support. I have been fortunate to have received funding from a wide variety of sources, most notably the U.S. Office of

Education, the National Cancer Institute, and the California State Library. Theoretic reasons for my choices of research contexts always involved positioning research applications so that they impelled the methodological design to rise to new challenges.

Over the years Sense-Making has been applied in a wide variety of contexts—library and information science, health communication, telecommunications policy, educational pedagogy, political communication, arts policy and education, national development, peace studies, disability studies, citizen participation studies, and so on. In all cases, the focus has been on audiences (by whatever labels they are called) and the building of responsive communication and information systems to serve them. The specifics aspects of communication behavior which have been a focus have also varied widely—information seeking and use, audience reception, public opinion, system evaluations, and so on.

The diversity of these fields and phenomena of focus shows in this volume. As the diversity is encountered, it may be useful to the reader to understand that for me each specific context and specific phenomena was not an end of interest in itself. Rather, each was a vehicle for understanding how to study and respond to diversities in human sense-making in such a way that a new kind of generalizable communication theorizing could emerge, one that honors diversity while at the same time addressing human universals.

There is much that is not in this volume for those readers with a serious interest in using Sense-Making Methodology to inform their research or their communication practice. The volume is neither a manual nor even a methodologically framed guide. Rather, it is a collection of writings that mirror the development of the Methodology in various contexts and lay out in detail the philosophic frameworks which guide it. While the writings do indeed include attention to how Sense-Making Methodology informs research and general communication practice, the presentation here is neither comprehensive nor linearly designed. Readers who wish a more detailed and deliberately framed introduction to how Sense-Making informs research practice (e.g., question-framing, interviewing, analyzing, interpreting) or communication practice are invited to visit the Sense-Making web-site: *http://communication.sbs.ohio-state.edu/sense-making/* or to contact me directly.

Brenda Dervin
Columbus, Ohio
dervin.1@osu.edu
September 20, 2002

ACKNOWLEDGMENTS

Persons far too numerous to mention have aided, nurtured, and contributed to the development of the Sense-Making Methodology. First and foremost, there have been literally thousands of persons who have been involved in Sense-Making's development as participants—as students, informants, respondents, experimental subjects, and test group members. A sense of this extraordinary level of involvement can be glimpsed by visiting the Sense-Making web-site at *http://communication.sbs.ohio-state.edu/sense-making/*.

Sense-Making approaches to interviewing, research, and communication practice have yielded a continuing serendipity. They provide tools not only for conducting research, but also for a critical reflexivity that has proven valuable not only in research but in teaching and in communication practice. There has been a genuine synergy in Sense-Making's development in which the interests and involvements of these many participants have nurtured Sense-Making and according to their testimonies more often than not Sense-Making has nurtured them in turn.

Thanks are also due to a specific group of theorists-researchers-scholars whose work has significantly informed Sense-Making. Foremost credit goes to Richard F. Carter, University of Washington Professor Emeritus of Communication, to whom this book is dedicated. Without his efforts to develop a theory for communication methodology and a methodology for communication theory, the development of Sense-Making would not have been possible.

Thanks are due as well to scholars writing on both sides of the polarities which divide within and between the social sciences and humanities. From U.S. based quantitatively oriented social sciences, I owe a debt to: Jerome Bruner, whose early work on information processing charted my direction and who with his move to focusing on meaning has positioned himself between polarities serving as a model for my quest; and, William McGuire whose persistence in developing a contextualized approach to social psychological analytics has been inspirational. From American pragmatism I owe a debt to John Dewey for his conceptualizations of community as made in communication; and to Richard Rorty for interpreting pragmatism in the current postmodern frame. From the European critical-cultural traditions, I owe a debt to Paul Bourdieu whose critical focus on practice as habitus has informed my attention to social structure manifested in practice; Michel Foucault, whose writings propelled my understanding of the necessity of including power as a central concept in Sense-Making Methodology; Anthony Giddens,whose attention to structure and agency opened a door to Sense-Making's attentions to human struggles to sometimes fall in line, and sometimes fall out; Jurgen Habermas whose focus on the development of communication-based theories of social structure have provided both foil and fodder; and Hans-Georg Gadamer whose treatment of philosophical hermeneutics in its relationship to method propelled my own quest. From the Third World emphasis on critical liberatory praxis, I owe a debt in particular to Paolo Freire whose work on critical pedagogy and the concept of conscientizing informs the foundational premises of Sense-Making interviewing approaches; and my special friend Luis Ramiro Beltrán—a founding "father" of communication research in Latin American—whose lifelong project to improve life conditions of the less privileged has served as a continuing reminder to me of what this work is all about.

I must acknowledge as well the members of the disparate discourse communities in which I attempt, often faltering, to be a member: both my quantitative and qualitative, administrative and critical, philosophical and instrumental, theoretical and applied friends and colleagues deserve thanks—especially those from the Information Seeking in Context community anchored primarily in Library and Information Science; the Participatory Communication Division of the International Association of Mass Media and Communication; the fringe members (they know who they are) of the Philosophy of Communication Division of the International Communication Association; and the practitioner-theorists of the Union for Democratic Communication. I know I more often than not abrade rather than cohere but your tolerance of my schizophrenic search for the "in-between" has helped my work more than you can ever know.

I must thank those whose funding of research, practice, and design has been fundamental to the development of Sense-Making Methodology: California State Library, Los Angeles Archdiocese, National Cancer Institute, Ohio Air Quality Development Administration, Ohio Department of Health, Ohio State University Ameritech Fellowship Program, Ohio State University College of Social and Behavioral Sciences, Puget Sound Blood Center, University of Washington Graduate School Fund. In particular, I thank Gary Strong, formerly the California State Librarian, for his vision and risk-taking; and Carroll Glynn, Director of the Ohio State School of Journalism and Communication for her continuing support in small ways and large.

And, of course, I owe a debt to the many scholars world-wide who will remain unnamed here but who have used Sense-Making in their own work—sometimes borrowing from its tenets and tools, sometimes critiquing it; sometimes getting it the way I intended, sometimes challenging me with their informatively different interpretations.

Finally, I want to thank specific people giving none the attention they deserve but hopefully conveying in the remembering the fact that the importance of their contributions and challenges has not been forgotten.

*The many students who served admirably as research assistants on funded projects: at the University of Washington, Kathleen D. Clark, Benson Fraser, Carol Garzona, Edward Payson Hall, Sylvia Harlock, Ed House, Thomas Jacobson, Claudia Krenz, Colleen Kwan, Molly Martin, Michael Nilan, Jae Chul Shim, Scott Wittet, Josephine Yung; at Ohio State University, Kathleen D. Clark, Usha Hariharan, Eric Lauterbach,

Lois Foreman-Wernet, Peter Shields, Vince Waldron. Many of these students continue to use Sense-Making in their writings and/or practice.

*A host of graduate students worldwide have used (or are using) Sense-Making in some way for their dissertations and theses and have thus tested and helped me refine its contours.: Rita Atwood, Nancy Brendlinger, Andrew Calabrese, Carol Garzona, Kathleen D. Clark, Bonnie Cheuk, Angela Coco, Steven David-Mendelow, Patricia Dewdney, James Dias, Nancy Dudley, Mark Dworkin, Debbie Ellen, Regina Entorf, Benson Fraser, Lillie Jenkins, Jayme Harpring, John Higgins, Robert Huesca, Patricia Kelly, Julie Knight, Elizabeth Lane Lawley, Albert Linderman, Kym Madden, Ruth Morris, Tony Murphy, Jamie Newmeyer (Litty), Michael Nilan, Michael Ollsou, Christlin Rajendram, Mary Lynn Rice-Lively, Samantha Romanello, David Schaefer, Peter Shields, Vickie Shields, Peter Strimer, Bert Teekman, Lois Foreman-Wernet, Scott Wittet, Many of these students—now academics and/or practitioners—continue to use Sense-Making in their work.

*Other colleagues not named above who have taken a special interest in the Sense-Making project, have sometimes written formally about it or used the Methodology in explicit ways, and who have nurtured as well as challenged my own thinking include: Robert Arundale, Lynda Baker, Roberta Brody, Christine Bruce, Patricia Dewdney, Joan Durrance, Susan Edwards, Micheline Frenette, Sue Curry Jansen, Myke Gluck, Michael Harrison, John Hocheimer, Robert Jacobson, Thomas Jacobson, Astrid Kersten, Yushim Kim, Joyce Kirk, Franco Levi, Ed McLuskie, Michel Menou, Paul Nelissen, Prashant Nikam, Karen Pettigrew, Catherine Ross, Reijo Savolainen, Kimmo Tuominen, Vickie Shields, Marti Smith, Sanna Talja, James Taylor, Peter Taylor, Pertti Vakkari, Gael Walker, Douglas Zweizig.

Brenda Dervin
Columbus, Ohio
October 4, 2002

NOTES ON TECHNICAL EDITING

Preparing this collection of writings for publication has been an honor and a challenge. Being a so-called "nontraditional" (i.e., "older") undergraduate student—and studying outside the field of communication—I had little exposure to Sense-Making Methodology before accepting this assistantship. However, this task afforded me the privilege of meticulously reading Brenda Dervin's articles and deepened my appreciation for her work on both a personal and academic level. A prolific author and persuasive figure, Dervin's words and guidance have given me more insight into the processes of human communication than she knows; for this opportunity, I give her my appreciation and respect.

While I had only minimal input on what publications were to be included in this book, I did enjoy tremendous freedom of design, organization, and scrutiny. From the beginning, Dervin entrusted me to learn a series of complicated software applications on multiple computing platforms and endured my numerous "trial-and-error" failures with grace. Thankfully, the problems became less frequent and the work eventually coalesced into what the reader now holds.

Throughout this process, my goal was to align the text with APA publication guidelines. In so doing, I renumbered graphics for clarity (i.e., all tables and figures herein are numbered consecutively according to chapter organization), substituted certain terms for consistency (e.g., within the text, "vs." becomes "versus," "percent" becomes "%" when proceeded by numbers, and so forth), inserted colons before long quotes, replaced "her or his" (or "his or her") for instances of "her/he" and "his/her," and changed "article," "paper," or "essay" to "chapter." In addition, I applied APA citation guidelines to all referenced material, thereby creating a uniform system of quotations from a mélange of writing styles. Dervin herself wished to present direct quotes in italicized format, necessitating the inclusion of underlined words where an author indicated emphasis. I also used italics to designate key terms and concepts, such as *analytics*, *gap idea*, and so on.

In addition, I repaired obvious misspellings, corrected minor citation errors (e.g., page numbers, spelling of authors' names, dates, etc.), and updated references to reflect previously "in press" and "forthcoming" material that has since been published. Of course, all of these small changes were executed in the spirit of clarification and improved accessibility to scholarly readers. However, with the exception of chapter 13, I cut nothing from Dervin's original work. In the unfortunate instance of chapter 13, the published article was so replete with errors that it necessitated a thorough reworking under Dervin's careful guidance; as such, readers who compare the work within this book to the original source will notice much dissimilarity.

Because this is a compilation of many articles from many different publishers—both here in the U.S. and abroad—I opted to "standardize" the language and writings conventions in some instances. For example, the British idioms "colour" and "labelled" have become "color" and "labeled" respectively; here, I must confess my own U.S. bias in the decision to make such terms uniformly familiar.

Dr. Dervin and I also elected to retain much of the stylistic formatting present in the original article. Although this results in what appears to be a random collection of section and subheads, we felt that keeping the feel and flow of the previously published article was more important than presenting a homogenized work. In some cases, however, we were unable to maintain the presentation and forced to deviate from the model.

Finally, those who read Dervin frequently will know that her interests are wide-ranging and her writings span nearly three decades; because of this, Sense-Making does not represent a static collection of dry assumptions, but rather an evolving methodological approach. In most cases, Dervin's own words reflect this growth: For instance, the early "Sense-Making approach" eventually becomes the present "Sense-Making Methodology," and elements in her theory become progressively self-defined and recognizable (e.g., "time-line interview" shifts to "Time-Line Interview"). Consequently, the reader should understand that variation within and between the articles embody the author's maturation and scholastic reassessment, not inaccuracy. Also, as previously mentioned, some footnotes and references originally listed as "in press" or "forthcoming" have since been published; where this occurs in the text, I have substituted the published reference as needed.

All told, this work has been difficult yet enjoyable. While I am looking forward to the final printing of this book, it is not without some regret that I type these final words—Sense-Making Methodology Reader: Selected Writings of Brenda Dervin has been a friendly companion to me for some time now; I only hope those who read it enjoy its contents as much as I have.

Eric Lauterbach
Columbus, Ohio
October 4, 2002

ABOUT THE AUTHORS

Kathleen D. Clark is an Assistant Professor at the University of Akron School of Communication in Akron, OH, USA, teaching courses in public speaking, small group communication, interpersonal and intercultural communication. She has taught at the University of Washington, the Ohio State University and Denison University. Her research focus is communicative practice that attends to spirituality as a means for creating and maintaining liberating social space in areas such as interracial friendship; women, religion and spirituality; and contemplative spirituality. She uses qualitative research methodologies such as ethnography (especially participant observation and autoethnography) and Sense-Making methodologies (including communication-as-procedure) for interview instruments and to guide analysis. She holds a B.A. and M.A. in communication from the University of Washington and a Ph.D. in communication from the Ohio State University.

Brenda Dervin is Full Professor of Communication in the School of Journalism and Communication at Ohio State University where she has located since 1986. Previously, she worked on faculties in communication at the University of Washington and Michigan State University and in library and information science at Syracuse University. She has held visiting lecturer positions at numerous universities worldwide, including a Distinguished Visiting Professor position at University of Technology, Sydney, Australia. She holds a bachelor's degree from Cornell University in journalism and human ecology; a master's and doctoral degree from Michigan State in communication research; and an honorary doctorate in social sciences from University of Helsinki, Finland. Her teaching and research specialties focus on methodologies, both qualitative and quantitative; philosophies of communication; and the use of communication procedures in the design and implementation of responsive organizations and systems. She is a frequent author. A complete list of her writings can be obtained from her (*dervin.1@osu.edu*) or found at *http://communication.sbs.ohio-state.edu/sense-making/*.

Lois Foreman-Wernet is on the faculty of the Department of Communication at Capital University in Columbus, Ohio. Prior to her current position, she was a lecturer and research associate at Ohio State University. She has more than fifteen years of professional experience managing communication programs in cultural and educational institutions. She holds a bachelor's degree in music education, master's degree in journalism, and Ph.D. in communication from Ohio State University. Her teaching and research interests focus on the intersection between institutions and their audiences, communication theory, and cultural communication.

Micheline Frenette is currently Associate Professor of Communication at the Université de Montréal in Canada, where she has served since 1989. Prior to her academic career, she worked as a clinical psychologist. She holds a doctoral degree in education from Harvard University, a master's in communication from the Université de Montréal as well as a master's in psychology and a bachelor's degree from the University of Ottawa. Her research and teaching focus on mass media theory and applied communication including the design and evaluation of health campaigns and of educational technology. She also conducts research on the integration of communication technologies such as the Internet in family and school settings. She serves on different committees related to health policy and has authored several research reports, articles and chapters as well as a book on adolescents and television.

Robert Huesca is an Associate Professor in the Department of Communication at Trinity University in San Antonio, Texas where he has taught since 1994. He has a bachelor's degree in communication from California State University, Fullerton and a master's degree in Latin American Studies from the University of Texas at Austin. His research interests include alternative media and participatory communication for social change. His research on international and development communication issues has been published in *Communication Studies*, *Gazette*, *Journal of Communication*, *Media, Culture & Society*, and *Media Development*, among others. A complete list of research and teaching experience is available at: *http://www.trinity.edu/rhuesca/*.

Eric Lauterbach has been a Research Assistant, Editor, and Webmaster for Dr. Dervin's Sense-Making project since 1999. He recently graduated magna cum laude from the Ohio State University with BA degrees in sociology and psychology, and a minor in women's studies. In the near future, Eric plans to pursue a graduate degree.

David J. Schaefer is Chair and Associate Professor in the Department of Communication Arts at Franciscan University of Steubenville in Ohio, where he has taught since 1990. His research interests include sense-making processes within online environments, media competency/literacy, global/intercultural communication, and multimedia production. He has published journal articles and book chapters in several of these areas and has presented papers at numerous communications conferences. In the 1980s, he worked as a children's program writer-producer in public television and as a professional announcer and newscaster for several commercial radio stations. He teaches courses in media literacy and film history, web design, broadcast/audio production, media theory, broadcast journalism, and international communications. He currently produces an international radio program, entitled Franciscan University Connections, aired on the EWTN/WEWN domestic and shortwave radio networks. He received his PhD in communication from Ohio State University in 2001.

PART I

PHILOSOPHICAL FOUNDATIONS

Chapter 1

Rethinking Communication: Introducing the Sense-Making Methodology

Lois Foreman-Wernet

AN INVITATION TO ENGAGE

One of the defining characteristics of society today is the existence of an extreme form of self-reflexivity.[1] We—individually and collectively—are constantly looking for ways to improve. Institutions continually engage in self-monitoring in order to generate more sales, cure diseases, increase votes or audiences, be the first or the best, and so on. One only need look at the number of self-help books available to see the manifestation of this phenomenon at the individual level. This is a modern notion of progress.

We are reminded, though, in the wake of personal tragedy, corporate and political scandal, and global unrest, that progress needs to be evaluated according to qualitative—not necessarily or only quantitative—terms. We need to strive to make things better, not just more abundant or bigger or faster. We need to gauge not just the quantity but also the quality of progress.

Today, when advertising is all around us, breaking news is available day and night, telephone conversations occur in every venue imaginable, and massive amounts of information are just a mouse-click away, it is easy to take communication for granted. This volume presents us with an opportunity to rethink our daily communication practices. It invites us to engage in a different way of thinking about our assumptions of human communication on every level.

This book was initiated because of growing interest in the Sense-Making Methodology from scholars and practitioners within the field of communication as well as within related fields such as library and information science and policy studies. Sense-Making has been in development by Brenda Dervin since 1972 and has, from the beginning, sought to better understand communication from a more communicative (dialogic) perspective and to apply that understanding to the design and implementation of formal communication efforts. Until now there has been no single, widely accessible resource where those interested could readily locate the significant body of work regarding Dervin's Sense-Making Methodology. With the current volume, we hope this oversight is corrected—at least for the present time.

It often has been noted that the field of communication is a largely fractured arena where sub-disciplines such as mass communication, new media, interpersonal communication, political communication, rhetoric, critical theory, cultural studies, and journalism co-exist but seem to share little common ground. Not only do they appear to be unrelated or disconnected from each other, but also there is an acknowledged disconnection between theoretical and research-related activity and the activities of communication practitioners outside academia.

The Sense-Making project, to some extent, has been affected by this fragmentation as well. It has perhaps too often been associated with the narrower conceptualization of communication as information seeking and use. Indeed, this is an arena where Sense-Making has had a great impact, as a result of Dervin's early groundbreaking work in library and information science. But to categorize the Sense-Making Methodology in such a narrow and limiting way is both erroneous and unfortunate, because its framework encompasses the entire spectrum of human communication. While Sense-Making has much to say to those who design information retrieval systems, it is a much larger project that speaks to those interested in communication according to the broadest possible definitions.

Dervin's use of the term methodology itself reflects a broad conceptualization that refers to the relationships between the actual research methods used in any given situation and the substantive theory, or working concepts, that direct those methods as well as to the metatheory, or philosophical assumptions, on which the entire research edifice rests. Methodology in this sense embraces a broad spectrum of activity that has implications for looking at research comprehensively as communication practice. Because Dervin defines research as communication practice, the practical implications of Sense-Making Methodology have been developed to inform not only research but all communication practice.

THE SIGNIFICANCE OF
DERVIN'S SENSE-MAKING METHODOLOGY

The chapters that follow elaborate on many aspects of the Sense-Making Methodology and illustrate what I see as three major reasons for its significance. First, Sense-Making offers a thorough and convincing critique of the transmission model of communication —a model that, despite widespread agreement regarding its limitations—continues to ground most communication theory, research, and practice. Second, Sense-Making examines in an ongoing manner philosophical assumptions about the nature of reality, the nature of human beings, and the nature of observing upon which our communication theories and practices are built. And finally, Sense-Making pays explicit attention to the "hows" of communicating that occur at every level of society and that contribute to understanding not only current communication practices but also the potentials for intervention and change—for improving—those practices in the future.

Sense-Making's Critique of the Transmission Model

Ongoing discussion in this book of the transmission model of communication refers to the traditional way of talking and thinking about communication whereby the sender sends a message through a communication channel to a receiver. Dervin argues that this basic model implies that messages, or information, are things to be gotten, like dumping something into the heads of receivers as though they were empty buckets. Thus, the transmission model—no matter how we may try to fix it to mitigate its inadequacies— is detrimental to our understanding of the communication process because it portrays communication as mechanistic rather than dynamic and dialogic.

Communication research based on the transmission model tends to focus on the messages sent by senders and the resulting effects or impacts of these messages on receivers. With research related to news and public affairs, governmental services, and public information, especially, there is an assumption of message importance and the desirability of audience effects as defined, usually benignly, by sources. The objective of such research is to determine if the receivers actually received the message and responded to it as intended; and, if not, why not. Receivers who don't *get* the message are perceived to be somehow deficient or disinterested or recalcitrant. Often these receivers (at times significant portions of the general public) are simply written off as unreachable.

Communication research and practice based on the transmission model focus on messages created from the perspective of the sender with the assumption that these will lead to the desired effects. There is an assumption that receivers share this perspective— that somehow this perspective is obvious or normal or natural—and that demographic characteristics and life contexts of receivers are barriers to and mediators of message effects. Furthermore, there is a presumption on the part of the senders or sources (as well as on the part of the researchers who represent them) of what is of value or importance. This model of communication suggests that truth and reality are "out there" to be accurately observed, packaged into messages (information), and disseminated to receivers.

An alternative communication model, Dervin suggests, conceptualizes messages not as *things* to be gotten, but as constructions that are tied to the specific times, places, and perspectives of their creators. Such messages are understood to be of value to receivers only to the extent that they can be understood within the context of receivers' lives. Such a model assumes there are differences in human beings' understandings and experiences and acknowledges that social power structures, such as systems of expertise, decide whose understandings and observations get preference.

Dervin argues that continued reliance on the transmission model constrains us in our efforts to see communication as a dynamic process. Use of the model reinforces our tendency to see information/messages as things and people as static entities. As a result, our research continues to rely solely on categorizations such as demographics, psychological traits, consumption patterns, and lifestyles. Alternatively, messages/information in Sense-Making are seen not as independent of human beings but as products of human observation. All observing is relevant to both physical time-space and psychological time-space. There is a situational logic to how people construct sense, and human universals are to be found in how people respond to a variety of situations or experiences.

The conceptualization of messages/information as things leads to communication systems that are designed for transmission rather than dialogue. Such systems measure people against external standards that are assumed to have truth-value but, in fact, are created by the people who develop the systems. Information in such cases is thought of as natural, as a thing to be disseminated, but, as Dervin challenges, there is nothing natural about it; information has always been designed.

In contrast, Dervin's Sense-Making Methodology mandates that we see communication as dialogue, which requires open-endedness, or reciprocity, in an institution's approach to its receivers (audiences, clients, or publics). In order to implement a model of communication as dialogue, institutions need to learn to listen and to address differences and contests in human beings' understandings and experiences. The Sense-Making Methodology, then, is proposed as an alternative to approaches based on the traditional transmission model of communication.

Sense-Making's Examination of Philosophical Assumptions

A second reason that I see for Sense-Making's significance is Dervin's ongoing efforts to articulate the underlying philosophical assumptions upon which our understandings of communication are built. A fundamental fault line in current scholarship in both the sciences and the humanities is centered on what Dervin calls the order-chaos dualism, or the distinction between modern and postmodern views.[2] On the modern side of this polarity is an understanding of reality as fixed, orderly, and universal. In this view, knowledge is seen as isomorphic with reality such that any one person with normal faculties of perception should be able to observe and describe the same phenomenon as could any other person in a given situation. The other side of this duality, postmodernism, views all knowledge as relative and any kind of order as tyranny because it is imposed through some external source of power.

Similarly, these modern and postmodern views presume humans to be either rational and orderly or muddled and decentered, respectively. The human condition is seen either as internally driven by individual human agency or determined by external forces beyond the individual's control. These polarized worldviews play themselves out in assumptions about the nature of knowing as absolute or interpretive, with knowledge as objective or subjective, and with research methods as neutral or unavoidably framed.

We have reached a point, Dervin says, where scholars and researchers cannot, or at least ought not, proceed without conscious consideration of these fundamental philosophical contests. Thus, no matter what model we choose to base our communication theories and practices on, there remains a need to make clear the philosophical assumptions on which our chosen model rests. We need to make explicit the philosophical foundations (metatheory) of our research that provide ways of looking based on presumptions about reality (ontology), knowledge (epistemology), and power (ideology). These assumptions in turn guide methodology, or the theoretical analysis of methods, which prescribe our choice of actual methods or procedures in the sense of research techniques.

The Sense-Making Methodology carefully articulates an alternative philosophical perspective that straddles the polarities of the modern and postmodern worldviews. Sense-Making assumes: 1) that both humans and reality are sometimes orderly and sometimes chaotic; 2) that there is a human need to create meaning, and knowledge is something that always is sought in mediation and contest; and 3) that there are human differences in experience and observation. Dervin sees human difference in observing as a strength of the species rather than a weakness. Because of the human need to create meaning and to establish facts—and despite the uncertainties of our knowledge—we are able to circle phenomena from different perspectives and at different times. This circling process then provides the means for us to arrive at a more comprehensive, more fully informed, potentially more useful set of understandings of the situation.

Sense-Making assumes that through continuing dialogue we eventually can arrive at stable, although limited and tentative, observations or facts. Currently, both academic and lay conceptualizations of difference often reduce difference to cacophony. We lack a useful way to handle difference and to put it into dialogue. Sense-Making assumes that people, even experts, anchor and use facts in terms of an interplay of situational and psychological experiences. People are helped by others who see the situation as they do, but also by those who see the situation differently. They want to know how other people put the pieces of reality together. Sense-Making conceptualizes difference not according to demographics or other static categories but rather according to how people attend to phenomena differently. The focus is on how people connect: how they construct bridges and what accounts for differences in observations.

Sense-Making Methodology presents the human being in phenomenological terms, as a body-mind-heart-spirit moving through time and space, with a past history, present reality, and future dreams or ambitions. It acknowledges that humans are anchored in material conditions, but also it recognizes the utter impossibility of separating the inner and outer worlds of human existence. Another Sense-Making assumption is that humans always are potentially changing, or becoming, and that movement through time-space is an irreducible aspect of the human condition. Because humans are engaged in a never-ending quest to fix the real, to create meaning, this movement from one moment in time-space to the next is always new.

One of the fundamental tenets of Sense-Making is the discontinuity assumption borrowed from Richard Carter.[3] Because Sense-Making assumes that reality is partly ordered and partly chaotic, it also assumes that reality always is subject to multiple interpretations because of changes across time and space, because of differences in how humans see reality arising from different perspectives or positions in time-space, and because of how humans construct bridges over a gap-filled reality. This pervasive gappiness or discontinuity can be evidenced in the difference between observations of the same person at different times, between different persons at the same time, and different persons at different times. Although the specific human responses may be too numerous to account for in any systematic way, Sense-Making Methodology suggests that research can usefully look for patterns in the human condition that relate to how we make sense rather than merely at the content of our responses.

Sense-Making also assumes that issues of force and power pervade the human condition and, thus, pays specific attention to forces that assist or facilitate movement in time-space (e.g., freedom and creativity) as well as those that constrain or hinder it (e.g., structure and habit). In this view humans are seen neither as totally free nor are their actions totally prescribed. Instead, human beings are seen as being both affected by structural power and are themselves sites of power. Sense-Making assumes that no human movement, either individual or collective, can be fully instructed or determined a priori. Even if the next step (the next moment) is in conformity, it is a step made anew by the individual.

There are three ways that the methods of Sense-Making reflect these philosophical assumptions. First, Sense-Making mandates the framing of research questions such that the respondent is free to name his or her own world. In other words, great care is taken to allow the respondent rather than the researcher to describe and define the phenomenon in question and a specific theory of the interview drawn from Sense-Making Methodology explicitly informs Sense-Making interviewing practice. Second, the Sense-Making interview is designed such that the respondent is able to circle, or repeatedly engage with, the given phenomenon or situation. Drawing from psychoanalytic theory, it is presumed that redundancy is useful for allowing both the embodied and the unconscious to be articulated. Sense-Making also presumes that respondents are themselves theorists and are capable of self-reflection. Finally, the metatheoretical tenets of Sense-Making are reflected in the analytical aspects of research through the search for patterns in terms of processes or verbs rather than things or nouns.

Sense-Making as a Link Between Theory and Practice

This focus on process is the third reason I believe the Sense-Making Methodology contributes significantly to communication and related fields. Because of this theoretical understanding of process, Sense-Making helps us to understand how we might actually change our communication practices for the better. In Sense-Making Methodology, the focus is on movement and the universal array of both internal and external communicatings that people need to make meaning. Instead of focusing on static characteristics of human beings, Sense-Making looks at the *hows* of communicating (how individuals define situations, how they bring past experiences to bear, how they make connections, and so forth) in order to provide a framework that allows us to compare communicative behavior in a way that concentrating on specific contexts or static categorizations cannot.

By looking at communication as a dynamic process, from what Dervin calls a "verbing" perspective, we can look at other, often more powerful, predictors than demographics, psychological traits, and similar categorizations that remain fixed across time and space. The primary difficulty with these traditional ways of looking at communication is that they don't allow researchers to consider humans as sometimes free and sometimes constrained, sometimes changing and sometimes rigid in their responses to various situations. In contrast, Sense-Making understands the process of communication as occurring in the space where structure and agency, rigidity and freedom meet. Sense-Making assumes that under some conditions, indeed, humans do move repetitively and habitually through time-space. Models that allow only for repetition and habit, however, capture only a portion of human communicating.

Sense-Making provides a missing procedural link between the macro and micro levels of human communicative behavior, between larger social organization and individual actions. One of the key aspects of Sense-Making is the understanding that social structure is energized, maintained, and changed by individual acts of communicating. Given the law of least effort, we expect humans to repeat past responses or behaviors; we expect habits and routines. But we know that humans do create new responses to some situations. The Sense-Making Methodology attends explicitly to this juncture where repetition and innovation meet, and it pays attention to how people make sense, how they choose one or the other path or bridge.

By addressing the *hows* of communicating, the Sense-Making Methodology also lends itself to those involved in the practice of communication in applied settings. As anyone who has ever used a computer knows, even though information systems evidently fit the needs and struggles of those who design them, they often put others (users) at a disadvantage. The same is true of institutional communication in general. Because the Sense-Making Methodology looks at communication from the perspective of the receiver or user rather than the sender or source, it can serve as an important resource in the study and design of a range of different kinds of communication systems.

Finally, in her discussions of Sense-Making, Dervin invokes the notion of utopian vision. Again, because Sense-Making allows us to look at the *hows* of communication, and at the space of human response, it also allows us to consider the range of what is humanly possible. Each movement (or moment) exhibits the possibility for change and innovation as well as for habit and routine. While habits are sometimes good and sometimes not, the point is that we as a species have the capacity to reflect on these and change them. There are, for example, existing kinds of communication procedures such as brainstorming that are more dialogic in nature. Such procedures are explicitly designed to prevent us from falling back into authoritarian power structures that inhibit dialogue. Certainly it would be to our benefit to reconsider any unproductive communication habits and suspend them long enough to invent or learn new, better procedures for communicating.

Dervin argues that there are tremendous possibilities for new technologies but as long as we use them in the same old ways we will not be tapping their potential (or ours). To the detriment of the species as a whole, most procedures for communicating are derived from non-communication theories (i.e., transmission-based rather than dialogic). For humanity to genuinely handle massive amounts of information and difference in an effective manner, the invention of new communicative procedures is required. Sense-Making suggests that in order to achieve more effective democratic forms, we need to attend to the ways that power interrupts communication efforts in daily practice, and we need to develop procedures for dialogue that can transcend materially anchored differences. The Sense-Making Methodology offers one possible guide for progress toward this goal.

OVERVIEW OF CHAPTERS

The chapters in this book address in detail the various aspects of Sense-Making discussed above. Although they include writings that span more than twenty years, the chapters are not presented chronologically in this volume but rather appear thematically. Some reflect the subtle changes that have occurred over time as Sense-Making has developed from what was initially referred to as an approach to what Dervin now more formally calls a methodology. Earlier writings, for example, utilize constructivist terminology that reflects a way of talking about phenomena that later are described in broader terms.

The book is divided into roughly two parts, with the first nine chapters concentrating more abstractly on the basic assumptions that ground our understandings of communicative behavior. The remaining nine chapters address more specifically the implications of these assumptions for the research, design, and practice of communication.

In chapter 2 ("Communication Gaps and Inequities")[4], Dervin analyzes the literature addressing the concept of the knowledge or information gap, which hypothesizes
that as information becomes available, the rich get richer (more knowledgeable) and the
poor get poorer. This literature, almost without exception, is framed within the traditional transmission model of communication. Dervin discusses two challenges to this
approach, one that questions the assumed deficiencies of receivers when the message
isn't received, and one that problematizes the conceptualization of information as
absolute, as something that can be dumped into one's head in mechanistic fashion.
Dervin concludes that it would be useful to reconceptualize the notion of gaps.
Traditional transmission-model research focuses on the gap between messages sent and
impacts observed. Perhaps a more fruitful gap to address is one that focuses on receivers
and what they need to make sense and to move forward in their lives.

In chapter 3 ("Users as Research Inventions") Dervin examines how designers of
communication systems identify and categorize users in terms of demographics, psychological traits, and geography. She argues that not only are these categories of analysis not able to predict very well, they may be inherently anti-democratic in that they exacerbate already defined social inequities. As a result of such categories, the potentials of
new technologies are greatly constrained to the point that they do only what the old ones
did—just faster and over greater distances. Six alternative categories based on the Sense-
Making Methodology are presented in which the user is described at a particular moment
in time and space rather than statically perceived across time and space.

In "Comparative Theory Reconceptualized" (chapter 4), Dervin suggests that as a
field communication has failed to develop a comparative approach that can transcend the
various polarizations of qualitative and quantitative, critical and administrative, inductive and deductive, theory and practice. The difficulty, she says, is the continued use of
state or entity analytics rather than dynamic or process analytics or, said another way, in
the use of nouns rather than verbs. Current methods don't allow researchers to look at
humans as sometimes flexible and sometimes rigid. By focusing on the dynamics of
communicating we can look at patterns that reflect the *hows* of communicating rather
than the *whats*, which are static and context specific.

"Information ↔ Democracy"(chapter 5) offers a rigorous explication of the philosophical assumptions that underlie the marketplace of ideas narrative that suggests,
among other things, that given the free flow of information, truth will rise to the surface.
Consideration is given to six stereotypes related to assumptions about the nature of reality and the nature of knowing as well as about how power enters the equation. The fundamental fault line here is polarized views of reality and people as either rational and ordered
or random and chaotic. The challenge is how to deal with a conceptualization of the world
as ontologically incomplete and discontinuous while still permitting the conceptualization
of any kind of democratic order. Dervin suggests that one such alternative is to consider

communication systems from the perspective of users so that these systems would be democratic and responsive at their core. Such systems would mandate a procedural circling of the reality being made and remade by citizens from multiple perspectives. This alternative, dialogic model could offer a resolution between absolutism and relativism, acknowledging that knowledge is something that is contested and negotiated over time. Dervin proposes that if this dialogic approach is framed communicatively it can avoid the solipsism that results from trying to handle difference non-communicatively.

In chapter 6 ("Verbing Communication"), Dervin observes that communication as a field has not dealt with the issue of human difference in a substantial way, and this has resulted in weak theories and disciplinary squabbling. The field has failed to understand the role of communication in the making and unmaking of order and disorder, freedom and constraint, homogeneity and difference. The problem, Dervin says, is that we tend to think of these conditions as relatively stable—as nouns, rather than as conditions that are constantly created, maintained, and changed in communicating. She suggests the key is to look at (and theorize) communication from the point of view of process. Rather than analyzing communication as a noun, or series of nouns, the Sense-Making Methodology suggests the utility of conceptualizing communication as a verb, as the process of constructing meaning that energizes our movement through time and space.

Chapter 7 ("Context and Methodological Tools") offers an analysis of the concept of context, which while generally agreed to be important, rarely is clearly defined. Rather, it is treated in many different ways. Among those researchers who work in the more quantitative traditional social science vein, context is treated as one of many analytic factors. The problem here is that the choices of what contextual factors relate to the phenomenon in question often seem capricious. At the other end of the continuum, among those who work in the more qualitative humanistic arenas, context is seen as the intersection of a host of factors or influences that are so delicately intertwined it is not possible to consider them separately. Thus, research results are so specific or particular that comparisons across studies are impossible. For those nearer the middle of this continuum, who are addressing context theoretically and philosophically, there are some common themes but still many disagreements. Dervin presents a pictorial illustration of ten different theoretical views of context and discusses their implications for research.

"From Metatheory to Methodology to Method" (chapter 8) articulates the bridges that are built—usually implicitly—between metatheory and method. Dervin looks at how metatheory (philosophical assumptions about the nature of reality and of humans, about knowledge, and about observation) is carried through to methodology (the reflexive analysis and development of theorizing, observing, analyzing, and interpreting) and finally to method (the specific techniques used to conduct research). In an effort to make explicit the underlying assumptions of Sense-Making, fifteen metatheoretical themes are presented and the specific ways in which they ground various research methods are discussed.

Dervin and Clark argue in chapter 9 ("Communication and Democracy") that theorists often mistakenly focus on the whos and whats but not the *hows* of communication. As such they are missing the procedural linkage between the societal level and individuals in democratic communication. Borrowing heavily from Richard F. Carter,[5] the authors propose a framework for procedural communication that uses two dimensions: situation defining strategies and communicating tactics. Situation-defining strategies include the individual relating to self, to other individuals, and to a collectivity; and a collectivity relating to itself, to individuals, and to another collectivity. Communicating tactics include such behaviors as creating ideas, finding direction, mediating, expressing, and confronting opposition. By considering the daily step-takings by which humans make sense of their worlds, the Sense-Making Methodology addresses both the larger context and the individual communicative actions that mediate structure and agency.

Chapter 10 begins the second half of the book, which discusses more directly present and potential applications of the Sense-Making Methodology to communication research, design, and practice. The first three chapters in this section are pieces written for the three editions to date, respectively, of the book *Public Communication Campaigns*.[6]

"Changing Conceptions of the Audience" (chapter 10), discusses a consistent portrait of audiences described in the scholarly literature on public communication campaigns. This portrait is one based on the transmission model of communication such that those who don't get the message sent by the source are seen as somehow deficient or recalcitrant. The implicit assumption here is that campaign messages are things that can be dumped into people's heads. Dervin discusses an alternative conceptualization of information as construction, noting that messages are of value only when they are relevant to the lives of receivers or members of the public or audience. The findings of several studies based on the Sense-Making Methodology that challenge traditional notions of the audience are presented, and implications for communication practice are discussed.

"Audience as Listener and Learner" (chapter 11) examines how the conventional conception of public communication campaigns assumes that messages are truths that must be diffused to the populace. But employment of this basic transmission model of communication can have deleterious consequences, such as negatively stereotyping segments of the public and unnecessarily limiting potential audience participation. Instead, we need to look to see if it is our systems and messages that are inaccessible and irrelevant—as opposed to an assumption of deficient audiences. An alternative perspective, communication as dialogue, requires an open-endedness in the institution's approach to the audience. Several exemplars of audience studies that use the Sense-Making Methodology are discussed.

In chapter 12 ("Sense-Making and Campaign Audiences"), Dervin and co-author Frenette argue that institutions need to face both ethical and procedural questions when

approaching the communication campaign communicatively. Several calls in the literature to approach campaigns more communicatively are discussed, ranging from modest
reforms that take into account different cultural norms of audience members to more radical approaches that problematize the truth claims of experts and focus on the implications of social class and power. Sense-Making is proposed as a possible guide for
responding to these mandates to communicate more dialogically with campaign audiences. A number of examples are given using the Sense-Making Methodology and providing direction for the study and design of communication campaigns.

Most scholars and practitioners agree there is a wide chasm between communication research and practice. Chapter 13 ("Research for Communication Practice") suggests that one possible reason is because both practitioners and researchers rely on the
transmission model of communication, which prevents not only a useful diagnosis of current communication practices but also the possibility of alternative means of practice.
Another way of approaching the study and practice of communication is offered through
the Sense-Making Methodology. Dervin discusses the basic theoretical assumptions of
Sense-Making and how they differ from the normative approach. She then presents one
of the basic interviewing approaches used in Sense-Making and shows how the data collected from such interviews can yield findings useful to communication practitioners.

Chapter 14 ("Qualitative-Quantitative Methodology") also addresses the connection between theory and practice. Sense-Making is accurately understood to be both a
body of theoretical assumptions that support a particular understanding of human communication and also a specific set of methods that guide the design and implementation
of communication research and practice. It is a methodology that has been developed for
the study of all situations that involve communicating, and while its methods for data
collection are qualitative in nature, the results can be analyzed in quantitative as well as
qualitative ways. What is common to all studies informed by the Sense-Making
Methodology is that they are based on the same operational metaphor, which assumes
that humans move through time and space continually facing gaps or discontinuities
inherent in the human condition. These gaps will be bridged, consciously or unconsciously, repetitively and habitually, innovatively or perhaps capriciously. How individuals interpret and bridge gaps is the focus of the Sense-Making project. In this chapter
Dervin provides a number of examples that illustrate the use of the Sense-Making
Metaphor, the central metaphor on which the Sense-Making Methodology is based, to
systematically study human communicating.

Current uses of technology, especially computer technology, are addressed in chapter 15 ("Information as Non-Sense; Information as Sense"). The tragedy of the new technologies, Dervin argues, is that despite their enormous potential to assist humans in the
flexible handling of information processes, they are being used primarily to do more of
what old communication technologies have done. The problem is that new technologies
are still designed according to the traditional transmission model of communication

where information is conceptualized as a thing. Users of information systems are measured against standards created by those who design the system, thus determining in effect who is able to use the system (those most like the designers) and who cannot (those most unlike the designers). Additionally, the conceptualization of information as a thing removes it from consideration as situationally embedded and thus makes it less useful to its intended users. Sense-Making Methodology suggests that by reconceptualizing information from the user's point of view (i.e., understanding information as actually informing how we make sense of our worlds), research can be conducted that leads to more useful information systems. Several examples are given for the possibilities of new technologies employed according to this alternative communication model.

In chapter 16 ("Practicing Journalism Communicatively"), Dervin and Huesca argue for re-theorizing journalism practice. We need to focus on the *hows* of journalism rather than the *whos* and *whats*, they say, because it is only through the *hows* that we can attend to difference. Current attempts to deal with issues of difference tend to focus on personalities and representative perspectives (whos) or on subject matter (whats), but these efforts are inadequate because they only superficially address the issue of difference. Without putting difference into dialogue, the authors state, difference is not useful. And putting difference into dialogue leads to a focus on the *hows*—how people make sense of their worlds in different ways. Ten potential journalistic practices theoretically derived from the Sense-Making Methodology are offered to illustrate the potentials of a dialogically based journalism.

Those writing about new technology often refer to information design as a new arena of activity. In chapter 17 ("Sense-Making and Information Design"), Dervin challenges this, saying that information design is not much different from the design involved in the use of old technologies or even in non-technological communication practices. There is nothing natural about information, Dervin says; it has always been designed. What's important, she argues, is to examine how we design communication systems to make sure they are doing what we want them to do. Numerous examples of Sense-Making applications relevant to the design and implementation of communication systems are presented.

The final chapter in this book, "Peopling the Public Sphere," lays out the breadth of potential for the Sense-Making project. Dervin and co-author Schaefer suggest that there are two thrusts in current debates about the nature of communication that have important ramifications for the human species. For purposes of discussion, these are presented in their most extreme forms. One is a structural thrust, where human beings and their communication worlds are enslaved and those in power control the public sphere. The second is a postmodern thrust, where nothing is ever totally inscribed and humans have the capacity to transcend even the most enslaving of conditions. These two discourses (both scholarly and lay) are stuck between a belief that any kind of social order is somehow naturally tyrannical and any kind of free association is somehow naturally not. The authors suggest that the road out of this polarity requires the invention of procedures for communicating peacefully and democratically across differences. The Sense-Making Methodology offers a theoretically informed framework for the creation of such procedures.

It is my hope that readers of this book will be challenged to reconsider their assumptions about communication and how they use these assumptions in conducting research and implementing communication designs. I hope as well that readers will be inspired to invent procedures that have the potential to improve the quality of communication in their own lives as well as others'. The chapters that follow are intended to provoke readers' imaginations and serve as a guidebook for rethinking communication.

NOTES

1.   For useful discussions see Giddens (1991) and Taylor (1989).

2.   These positions are presented here in their most extreme forms in order to illustrate the point being made.

3.   The discontinuity assumption is an idea introduced by Richard F. Carter (1980). See also Dervin and Chaffee (in press).

4.   I have taken the liberty of abbreviating titles here for ease of reading; the shorter titles are consistent with those used at the tops of pages throughout the book.

5.   This procedural perspective draws on the theoretical work of Richard F. Carter (1980, 1982, 1989b.)

6.   See Rice and Paisley (1981) and Rice and Atkin (1989, 2001).

Chapter 2

Communication Gaps and Inequities:
Moving Toward a Reconceptualization

Brenda Dervin

COMMUNICATION GAPS AND INEQUITIES

The Ideas

In the recent literature in the communication and information science fields, one increasingly sees references to a set of terms that differ in nuance but essentially refer to the same hypothesized phenomena. The terms—*knowledge gap, information gap, information inequity, information poor*, and, most recently, *communication gap*—all have been used by theorists who have observed that when it comes to information/communication availabilities in society, there are those who are rich and those who are poor. Further, these theorists hypothesize as more information/communication becomes available, the rich get richer and the poor get poorer.

These essential ideas have been the focus of the work of a growing number of writers (Branscomb, 1979; Childers & Post, 1975; Dervin, 1977a; Dervin & Greenberg, 1972; Donohue, Tichenor, & Olien, 1975; Galloway, 1977; Genova & Greenberg, 1979; Parker, 1978; Rogers, 1976; Smith, 1975; Tichenor, Donohue, & Olien, 1970; Tichenor, Rodenkirchen, Olien, & Donohue, 1973).

Some writers have focused primarily on the static portrait—the observation that there are those that are information poor. Perhaps the most comprehensive treatment came with Childers and Post's 1975 book, *The Information Poor in America*. But the idea has been the focus of many. In their work on the communication environments of the urban poor, for example, Dervin and Greenberg (1972) referred to the "information void" within which they saw the urban poor as living (p. 221). In the same line, Smith (1975) expressed a concern for the ". . . uneven distribution of information and commu-

This work originally appeared as: Dervin, B. (1980). Communication gaps and inequities: Moving toward a reconceptualization. In B. Dervin & M. Voigt (Eds.), *Progress in communication sciences: Vol. 2* (pp. 73–112). Norwood, NJ: Ablex. Reprinted by permission of Greenwood Publishing Group, Inc., Westport, CT.

nication" and suggested that some groups in society ". . . have little access to our primary resources. They have no control of information, communication, production, or anything" (p. 17). Along with these observations came an increasing concern for rectifying the situation. An example is Branscomb's question in her 1979 *Science* article:

> *Food and energy challenge us because they are in short supply . . . . Information is quite different. It is in quantitative surplus . . . the yawning chasm is between what some people have learned, yet others have not put to use . . . since so many individuals are information poor, how do you use the surplus of information in society to overcome the scarcity of information available to individuals? (p. 143)*

Other writers have been more concerned with the impact of the growth of information societies, the so-called communication revolution, on these inequities. They are the ones who hypothesized that the poor get poorer while the rich get richer, a process now referred to with the label "the knowledge gap hypothesis." The best known, and first fully formalized presentation of the hypothesis was presented by Tichenor et al. (1970): "As the infusion of mass media information into a social system increases, segments of the population with higher socio-economic status tend to acquire this information at a faster rate than lower status segments, so that the gap in knowledge between these segments tends to increase rather than decrease" (pp. 159–160). While in early formulations the inequity idea focused primarily on information inequity or knowledge gaps, Rogers (1976) expanded the focus to the "communication effects gap" suggesting that the idea

> *. . . should deal with the attitudinal and overt behavioral effects of communication as well as just 'knowledge'; thus, I propose calling it the 'communication effects gap' hypothesis. (p. 233)*

The purpose of this chapter is to review the formulation of the communication gap and inequities ideas—their origins, their logical foundations, and how recent theoretic trends in the communication and information science fields are not only changing the nature of the ideas but, in some cases, making them no longer useful or appropriate.

The Context Within Which the Ideas Were Conceived

In understanding the nature of the inequity ideas, it is important to note that they came to the fore at the very same time that social scientists were becoming increasingly disenchanted with the traditional assumptions that suggested that communication of information into society was a powerful force. These traditional assumptions are typified well by Donohue et al. (1975): "A traditional viewpoint is that resolution of social problems is related to inputs of information. If a system is sufficiently saturated with information, according to this view, a general understanding of the topic will develop within the system" (p. 3). As Donohue et al. (1975) point out, these traditional assumptions rested on two premises. One is that information availability leads to understanding. The second is, in their words:

> . . . *that higher levels of information input lead to general equalization of knowledge throughout the system. (p. 3)*

The inequity or gap ideas were, of course, striking at the heart of the second assumption. It was no longer assumed that the presence of information served as an equalizer. In the mass media context, Tichenor et al. (1970) stated in support of their knowledge gap hypothesis ". . . the mass media seem to have a function similar to that of other social institutions: that of reinforcing or increasing existing inequities" (p. 170). Röling, Ascroft, and Chege (1976) provided a similar statement in the more general context of development. Diffusion processes, they said, "are imperfect equalizers" (p. 160).

More general than the strike at the equality idea, however, was the challenge to the root premise behind the idea—that information availability leads to use. This challenge was coming from a host of specific studies showing, for example, that mere availability of, or even exposure to, information did not necessarily bring about awareness or information gain (Allen & Colfax, 1968; Greenberg, 1964; McLeod, Rush, & Friederich, 1969; Robinson, 1972; Spitzer & Denzin, 1965). This challenge was also based on a growing number of reviewers who concluded from their own assessments of the literature that the power of communication campaigns was vastly overrated. It was the time, for example, of Bauer's (1964) "obstinate audience" seemingly impervious to the most persistent efforts of communications; and of Klapper's (1960) "limited effects" statement suggesting that communication campaigns have effects only under limited conditions, for some of the people, some of the time.

The context was one, then, of disenchantment with the results of research, not with the research itself. It was assumed that the results showing the "obstinate audience" with "limited effects" were useful and accurate pictures of audience behavior. It was time for trying to isolate the conditions within which one could not find effects. It was a logical time for the introduction of gap or inequity ideas as one explanation of why only limited effects were available. It was not yet a time for challenging the very premises that lead to the research that concluded that only limited effects were possible.

The Traditional Logic Supporting the Ideas: Receiver Deficits

The literature which posits gaps and inequities as existing is generated, almost without exception, within the frame of an explicit or implicit use of a traditional model of communication—a source is seen as having a message which he or she wishes to send to a set of receivers. The research then attempts to see whether the receivers got the message—which receivers didn't, which did, and how well. This description is a fitting summary of communication research of the 1950s, 1960s, and most of the 1970s. It is still estimated, in fact, that it is still a fairly standard perspective although one that is receding as alternate perspectives emerge (Dervin, 1978).

Within the frame of this traditional perspective, two questions have been "answered" with such a massive amount of evidence that the power of the generalizations seem almost irrefutable. One question is whether gaps exist. The second is why they exist. When one looks at research generated within the conceptual frame posited above, the evidence is clearly in agreement. Gaps do exist, according to the evidence. They exist, the evidence goes on to suggest, because some people are less able and less willing to take in information than others. While there is evidence that contradicts these conclusions, almost without exception that evidence comes from research using a different model of communication. These alternate models and their supporting evidence will be reviewed in later sections of this chapter.

When researchers using the traditional perspective of communication have gone out to ask whether some members of the audience are not receiving the sources' messages, they have done so primarily using a structural or sociological framework, or with what Galloway (1977) calls a *substratum approach*: "Substrata are sectors of a social system which function to mediate distribution of communication effects, resulting in what are termed differential effects between substrata" (p. 381).

An important part of this approach is the attempt to isolate identifiable subgroups of the audience who are receiving or not receiving messages. In the early stages of the work, the groups were identified primarily in terms of socioeconomic variables (race, income, and education). In the latter stages, they were identified more by what Galloway (1977) called "information-contextual variables" such as media exposure, social participation, or contacts with experts (p. 383). In actuality, the literature is such that the distinction between these two classes of differentiators has not been terribly important. What has emerged is an almost tautological portrait of connection between the socioeconomic and information-contextual variables. Certain groups of people are identified as information poor. They are also identified as being those with less education and income and less able and willing to intake information both because of lower ability as well as less opportunity to gain and use information.

In their comprehensive review, for example, Childers and Post (1975) said that the same groups of individuals who suffer from economic poverty also suffer from information poverty. They identified these groups in the United States as Mexican American, Puerto Ricans, other Spanish, American Indian, Eskimo, poor Black and White, Appalachians, poor farmers, migrant workers, aging adults, prisoners, and the blind and deaf (pp. 78–79). The groups they identify are those groups in the U.S. who have less education and lower incomes.

The Childers and Post (1975) emphasis is not unique to them. When research is conducted using the traditional communication model, the results consistently show that those with less education and lower incomes are less likely to be information seekers, use expert information sources, be informed generally, have informed interpersonal contacts, expose themselves to high information content print media, be aware of information sources, have organizational ties, have information processing skills, have sufficient background information that would allow them to become aware of and understand informational messages, or trust establishment and organizational sources. This portrait emerges clearly from reviews (Childers & Post, 1975; Dervin, 1976b; Dervin & Greenberg, 1972; Ettema & Kline, 1977; Greenberg & Dervin, 1970) and from the intersection of many articles (Block, 1970; Caplovitz, 1963; Hiltz, 1971; Hsia, 1973; Hurwitz, 1975; Key, 1961; Levine & Preston, 1970; Mann, 1973; Mendelsohn, 1968; Parker & Paisley, 1966; Rieger & Anderson, 1968; Smith, 1975; Spitzer & Denzin, 1965; Tichenor et al., 1970; Udell, 1966; Voos, 1969; Wade & Schramm, 1969).

Making the situation worse, according to these studies, is the evidence that showed that as with the vicious cycle of economic poverty which seems difficult to escape, information poverty has the same traplike quality. Studies, again using the traditional communication model, suggested that an information alienation can become established such that once an individual has failed in finding appropriate information for a problem he begins to believe that relevant information can never exist for him (Bowes, 1971; Rotter, 1966; Seeman, 1966).

Within the framework of the traditional communication model, the findings above have been extended to a wide range of contexts. Rogers (1976) gave essentially the same portrait of the findings from diffusion of innovation research. Higher status individuals, he said, were less likely to be receptive to change messages, more likely to be nonhomophilous (different from the sources of the messages), and less likely to have the tight, informed interpersonal networks that allow change messages to "trickle down" (p. 234).

Similar findings have emerged from the field of education. Here, myriad studies—looking at contexts ranging all the way from learning from *Sesame Street* broadcasts (Bogatz & Ball, 1971) to school achievement and intelligence testing (Fells, Davis, Havighurst, Herrick, & Tyler, 1951; Hess, 1970; Ireton, Thriving, & Graven, 1970; Quay, 1974; Willerman, Broman, & Fiedler, 1970) to the development and use of language (Bernstein, 1961; Deutsch, 1965)—have confirmed, using the perspective of the traditional communication model, the presence of socioeconomic status-related gaps.

In summary, then, what appears in the literature that has emerged from those using the traditional communication model, is a strongly supported view of a phenomenon which is talked of as being real. As findings in the social sciences go, this phenomenon is one of the more supported ones. These studies say: Yes, the gap is real; yes, it is caused by the fact that some groups within society are less able and less willing to take in information. In their recent review of the literature on cause of the knowledge gap, Ettema and Kline (1977) termed this the "deficit" explanation of gaps (p. 82).

The Appearance of Contradictions

When one looks at this set of findings, there are two interesting things about them. The first is the sheer extent of the support behind them. This support has come in terms of both quantity and time. As early as 1947, Hyman and Sheatsley were offering a similar set of conclusions to explain "why information campaigns fail?" The second interesting thing about the findings is that there began to emerge in the mid 1970s, with spurts of activity prior to that, increasing evidence suggesting that the communication gap hypothesis is more idea than reality.

These contradictions came first in the form of descriptive evidences from studies which started out to replicate gap findings and found either no gap, gap reversals, or narrowing gaps (e.g., Galloway, 1974, 1977; Shingi & Mody, 1976; Tichenor et al., 1973). A call was issued for isolating the conditions under which one could or could not expect to find gaps (Ettema & Kline, 1977; Tichenor et al., 1973).

With this call, the theoretic circle became complete. Recall, the gap idea was one that emerged when research conducted within the traditional communication model found it had to explain why communication was not as powerful as expected, why direct effects could not be found, why only limited and indirect effects from information campaigns could be found. The call, then, was to isolate the conditions under which information impact occurred or did not occur. The gap research emerged as one thrust in that effort to isolate conditions. One condition seemed to be the existence of subgroup deficits—some people, it was assumed, just were not able or willing to process all the information that the information society made available. Yet, now, a call was out to explain the conditions under which the condition operated.

The response to this call came in two forms. The first was a more traditional reaction, an attempt to hang on to the hypothesis and explain the contradictory evidence. This took the form of what has become termed the "ceiling effects" explanation. Ettema and Kline (1977) ably review studies relating to this explanation (Cooke, Appleton, Conner, Shaffer, Tamkin, & Weber, 1975; Donohue et al., 1975; Galloway, 1977; Katzman, 1974; Kline, Miller, & Morrison, 1974; Shingi & Mody, 1976; Tichenor et al., 1973). Basically, the idea is that there are conditions under which some kind of ceiling prevents the informationally/communicatively rich from acquiring more, giving the poor a chance to catch up, or, in some cases, reverse the gap. In this line of reasoning, the "ceiling" is seen as taking on several forms. One is a kind of saturation whereby the rich have all they want of a particular message/innovation so the poor have time to catch up. This kind of ceiling was seen by Galloway (1977) as the major reason why he found narrowing gaps resulting from message dissemination: "The most important influence lead-ing to narrowing gaps appears to have been the operation of ceiling effects. . . . Restricted room for better-off segments suggests that other segments were able to catch up to reduce the differentials" (p. 382). The second form of the "ceiling" idea has been more interventionist. The idea here is to give the poor an advantage by encouraging their exposure and planning information campaigns with them in mind. It is this kind of ceil-ing which Shingi and Mody (1976) referred to when they said:

> . . . *the communication effects gap is by no means inevitable.* It can be avoided if *appropriate communication strategies are pursued in development efforts. (p. 189, emphasis in original)*

While the ceiling idea has taken on other interpretations, the two reviewed above form the major ones. What is important about the ceiling idea, however, is that it was a response to the call for explaining why the hypothesized gaps were not always present and, in particular, a response that arose within the frame of the assumptions which gen-erated the gap hypothesis to start with. In essence, the ceiling idea accepted the source-receiver model of communication and continued to try to identify those conditions under which one could assure that receivers received the source's message.

But there was a second set of responses to the call for understanding the conditions of message receipt and, in this case, the conditions for the existence or absence of gaps. These responses, while not always identified as such, were generated from different mod-els of communication. Because they were generated from different models, they were not concerned about explaining whether the gaps really exist or not. Rather, they say, if you start with the kind of assumptions the researchers using the traditional model did, you are bound to find the brunt of your evidence supports the gap idea. What is common to all the literature in this second set is that the authors agree that the traditional gap research (what Ettema & Kline, 1977, called "classical") has been asking the wrong questions.

Because the responses in this second set are, in essence, challenging the very frame-work within which most communication research is conducted, and thus, are relatively new in focus, the literature reporting them is not as organized. Essentially, though, the responses appear to be of two different but complementary types which come up with dif-ferent explanations of why gaps or inequities occur, explanations with their roots not in empirical evidence but, rather, in conceptual perspectives. The first challenge to the tra-ditional "deficit" explanation of gaps is one that changes the point of focus from receivers to sources. Here, rather than the receivers lacking, it is the sources who are seen as lack-ing, particularly in their responsiveness to the needs of receivers. The second challenge is, in actuality, a more fundamental challenge, for when pushed to its extreme it suggests that any data available on the presence of inequities and gaps is nothing more than numer-ic myths created by the use of inappropriate assumptions about the nature of human infor-mation seeking and use. Each of these challenges will be reviewed in turn below.

THE FIRST CHALLENGE:
SWITCHING THE EXPLANATION TO SOURCE DEFICITS

This first alternative way of approaching the gap phenomena originates primarily through the efforts of Latin American and other Third World communication researchers. The essence of this thrust is its call for turning attention from receivers to sources/systems. Ettema and Kline (1977) summarize it as a turning ". . . away from characteristics of the individual and toward the social system in the study of the factors which originate and maintain SES-related differences" (p. 184).

The fact that this thrust is identified primarily with Third World researchers does not mean there is a complete absence of the focus in the literature authored by U.S. researchers. An example of the U.S. emphasis is a series of studies which have suggested that the system is at least in part to blame for the existence of gaps. These studies suggest, for example, that the information systems within which citizens attempt to inform themselves are disorganized, overly bureaucratic, frequently humiliating in treatment of clientele, often unresponsive to more difficult needs, and uninformed about the lifestyles of their users (Dervin & Greenberg, 1972; Dervin, Zweizig, Hall, Kwan, & Lalley, 1977; Furman, Sweat, & Crocetti, 1965; Greenberg & Dervin, 1970; Grunig, 1972; Kurtz, 1968, Levin & Taube, 1970; Levine, White, & Paul, 1963; Mendelsohn, 1968; Pratt, 1969; Scott, 1967; Sjoberg, Brymer, & Farris, 1966). There has been a turning of attention to media structure as a possible explanation with a concern for the fact that the most-used U.S. medium (television) places far less emphasis on disseminating helpful information than does the least-used medium (newspapers) (Dervin & Greenberg, 1972; Wade & Schramm, 1969). Katzman (1974) made the point explicitly when he said that gaps may exist because of unequal access to communication technologies. This, he suggested, would be a gap resulting not from receiver characteristics but channel characteristics.

Despite the presence of some U.S.-authorized research focusing on source behavior as a possible explanation of communication gaps, the emphasis by Third World researchers is different both in magnitude and kind. For U.S. researchers, the focus is simply one more possible explanation in addition to explanations rooted in the focus on receivers. For the Third World researchers, in contrast, the focus is not simply central and pervasive but also the obvious consequence, in their eyes, of their concern for the development of their countries and for the fact that until very recently the only research perspectives available to them were those they learned during their U.S. training (Beltrán, 1976; Diaz Bordenave, 1976; Röling et al., 1976). These perspectives, they challenge, do not meet the development needs of their countries. Rogers (1976) summarized it when he said that the traditional (now called "classical") approach to development research started with the assumption ". . . that poverty was equivalent to underdevelopment. And the obvious way for less developed countries to develop was for them to become more like the developed countries" (p. 217).

One aspect of this acceptance was an acceptance, the researchers challenged, of a persuasion-oriented focus on receivers and getting them to accept messages from sources. In Beltrán's (1976) view, the research tradition which guided the early years of development research placed ". . . a high emphasis on the receiver so that research could determine how the commercial or political persuasion was effectively exerted on him" (p. 108). Diaz Bordenave (1976) made the same observation when he suggested that up until recently in development research:

> Communication was seen still as the long arm of the government's planners, and its main function was supposed to be that of obtaining people's support for, and partici-pation in, the execution of development plans. (p. 137)

Essentially, then, these writers challenge that the communication context that guided development research until recently was the source-sending-messages-to-receivers model which has traditionally guided communications research in the U.S. generally. They see this research paradigm as being a product of the U.S. which is not useful in the Third World context because it has embedded within it some assumptions about the nature of social systems which, they feel, either do not apply in the Third World or ought not to have been applied. More generally, they see these same assumptions as having pervad-ed all the U.S.-generated social sciences. As Beltrán (1976) puts it, the U.S. has created:

> . . . sciences for *adjustment*—essentially addressed to studying conformity with the pre-vailing needs, aims, values, and norms of the established social order, so as to help its ruling system to attain "normalcy" and avoid "deviant" behaviors. (p. 115)

These writers see, then, the focus on the receiver that has been traditional in U.S. communications research generally and in the gap research in particular as being tied in with the emphasis in U.S. research on attaining source goals and trying to manipulate receivers to those ends. Further, the authors see that research emphasis as being a reflec-tion of the society which has generated it. In the severest form of criticism, for exam-ple, Beltrán (1976) challenged that the research paradigm is a product of:

> . . . a society where individuality was predominant over collectivism, competition was more determinant than cooperation, and economic efficiency and technological wis-dom were more important than cultural growth, social justice, and spiritual enhance-ment. (p. 115)

From the point of their agreement that U.S. communications research has empha-sized source goals in its focus on the source-sending-messages-to-receivers paradigm, these researchers then suggest that a central focus of taking this perspective is the blam-ing-the-victim syndrome which they see as pervading U.S. communications research. In essence, this idea suggests that what U.S. researchers do is go looking at receivers to see if they got the source's message. When groups of receivers have not, it has been assumed, these writers challenge, that the receivers are deviant. As Rogers (1976) terms it, what has been operating is a kind of "intellectual ethnocentrism" or a "contemporary intellectual extension of social Darwinian evolution" (pp. 217–218). In fact, Rogers suggests that the very idea of "underdevelopment" when seen in the context of the U.S. research paradigm is also a blaming-the-victim idea. In this context, Rogers notes, underdeveloped nations are seen as deviant but always with the "hoped-for potential of catching up" (p. 218).

This idea—that the receiver has been blamed for gaps—is one that has been mentioned by a number of writers, both non-U.S. and U.S. (Beltrán, 1976; Dervin, 1977a; Diaz Bordenave, 1976; Elliott, 1974; Hsia, 1973; Mann, 1973; Mathiason, 1970; McAnany, 1978; Nordenstreng, 1977). Increasingly, the authors agree that a major consequence of the use of the idea has been the development of communication programs which have led to greater rather than less development equity in Third World countries. This is not an unexpected result given the fact that evidence shows the same impact in the U.S. as a result of communication campaigns guided by the same research paradigm. As Röling et al. (1976) explained it, the development research drew conclusions that reinforced the focus on progressive farmers who were more ready to change, more like the change agents to start with. As a result, the research generated development programs in which:

> The current practice . . . is to provide intensive assistance to a small number of innovative, wealthy, large, educated and information-seeking farmers, and to expect that the effect of such assistance will reach other farmers indirectly by autonomous diffusion processes. (Röling et al., 1976, p. 159)

The result, Röling et al. charge, is that inequities emerge and increase. Beltrán made the point more strongly when he suggested that "communication . . . often works against development . . . in favor of the ruling minorities" (p. 159).

Based on this reasoning, these writers come to primarily two conclusions. One is that much more attention must be placed on changing the structural conditions which lead to the potential for or actuality of inequities in the first place. Again, Beltrán (1976) makes the summarizing point: "Communication itself is so subdued to the influence of the prevailing organizational arrangements of society that it can hardly be expected to act independently as a main contributor to profound and widespread social transformation" (p. 111). A consistent theme that runs through these writings, then, is the idea that sources and systems must be changed and that these changes in the social structure are fundamental prerequisites for attaining development or equity.

The second conclusion is a corollary. It is that the agencies and individuals who launch development programs and information campaigns much change their communication strategies. As Röling et al. (1976) put it: ". . . it is not the characteristics of farmers as much as the characteristics and deployment of government development services which are the prime determinants of diffusion efforts" (p. 168). In the process of calling for this change, these writers agree that what is needed is a changed conception of the role of communication in development away from source-oriented message transmission to self-development (Diaz Bordenave, 1976; Havelock, 1969; Rogers, 1976; Rogers & Adhikarya, 1979; Röling et al., 1976). This change is, perhaps, best summarized by Freire's (1970) call for a move away from the "transmission mentality." Diaz Bordenave (1976) sees it as a need for a more liberating type of communication education based on dialogue. Havelock (1969) suggests that what is needed is to start with the needs of users, the ways they diagnose their problems, and the changes they want to initiate. Röling et al. (1976) call for obtaining "preventive feedforward" about the needs for innovations and the conditions of receivers (p. 165). In particular, they suggest that sources should learn not only about the "average" receiver but about the range of characteristics across all receivers. As they put it in the development context: "The profile of the intended utilizer should reflect not only the characteristics of the average farmer, but also those of the farmer with the smallest resource base" (Röling et al., 1976, p. 165).

With this call, the literature of the first challenge turns full circle back to a focus on receivers. The difference, however, is that in the deficit explanation literature, the focus is on source goals and receivers are blamed when they fail to get the message. In the challenge, the writers suggest, the focus should be placed on receiver goals with sources blamed if they fail to communicate and respond.

It is at this point that this literature tradition, authored primarily by Third World researchers, collides with a far more fundamental communication issue than the question of who is to blame for gaps and inequities. Rather, the issue becomes how can one design communication programs so they can be receiver-initiated and deal with the uniquenesses of the full range of receivers. While the literature reviewed in this section makes a call for turning away from the source-sending-messages-to-receivers model to a model where receivers are the initiators, as a body of literature it has not generated a cohesive theoretic way of looking at receivers so as to avoid the very pitfalls of the model it abhors. Atwood (1980a) agrees when she suggests that the avant garde of Latin American communication research is as plagued by the very same conceptual weaknesses that have been troublesome in traditional communications research. As she puts it: "The most serious flaws evident in Latin American communication research are related to conceptual weaknesses which transcend cultural barriers, and cannot be attributed solely to culturally-based viewpoints" (Atwood, 1980a, p. 2).

Atwood (1980a) sees these flaws as rooted in how it is that the researcher looks at the communicating of both sources and receivers. It is telling that when one looks at the literature reviewed in this section, one sees much mention made of the need for alternative communication strategies in general terms but very little mention made of the "how" of that communicating. At the most, one sees case examples of one particular kind of receiver-initiated effort or another (Röling et al., 1976).

It is this focus on the development of a cohesive theoretic net for looking at receivers that forms the second challenge to traditional foci on communication gaps and inequities. The second challenge is represented by a large and growing body of literature that, like the literature of the first challenge, suggests that the traditional blame-the-receivers deficit explanation of gaps and inequities is conceptually wrong. This literature, too, calls for communication programs that are genuinely receiver-oriented.

What differs, however, is that the literature of the first challenge is, at root, less concerned with the nature of communicating and more concerned with the nature of power. It is in this context that the literature of the first challenge posits essentially a series of "mal-intent" charges suggesting that the sources-sending-messages-to-receivers paradigm was a product of a particular kind of society which then attempted to impose the paradigm on different kinds of society. The literature of the second challenge, in contrast, but not in contradiction, is concerned more fundamentally with the idea that no matter who is in power or what their goals, the nature of communicating is such that the problem of communicating will remain. At root, the second challenge is concerned not only with a changed conception of the role of communications, as the literature in the first challenge is, but more generally with a changed conception of the nature of man, his information seeking and use.

In a sense, the literature of the second challenge begins where the literature of the first challenge leaves off. It is ironic that, for the most part, the two literatures have existed independently of each other. It has been issues such as those raised by the literature of the first challenge that has generated much of the purpose and direction for the literature of the second challenge. And, it is the literature of the second challenge which will make the aims of the first challenge possible.

THE SECOND CHALLENGE:
MOVING TOWARD COMMUNICATION FUNDAMENTALS

Any observer of the literature in the communications field with an interest in reading between the lines, and, particularly, between the lines of the voluminous quantitative results which still mark the field, can readily see that for the first time since the field became established in its own right, the literature of the field is beginning to be as typified by profound conceptual discussion as by the evidentiary results of observation. Further, at this juncture of time, the conceptual discussion is taking primarily the form of confrontation in efforts to tear the field away from what are seen as the unuseful paradigms of the past to the useful paradigms of the future.

These conceptual confrontations are themselves taking on numerous forms, sometimes implicit, sometimes explicit; sometimes embedded in a mire of seemingly irrelevant data, sometimes brought out for crystallized view. Further, the confrontations can be found taking place at different points of location within the field. It does not seem to matter if one focuses on traditional topical divisions (e.g., interpersonal communication or mass communication), geographical divisions (e.g., Midwestern schools, Eastern schools, or Western schools), or conceptual divisions (e.g., those focusing on process, rules, or information). No matter where one looks in the literature the same evidence can be found of important conceptual discussion cast as confrontation.

In one sense, one can see much of the literature of the field of communication as being in a conceptual cyclone. No matter where one looks into the center of the cyclone, one sees the literature increasingly focusing on fundamental issues dealing with the nature of communication. When looked at with this distance, it can be seen that the literature that has received the label as being focused on gaps and inequities is but one of a series of literatures that are being challenged in the communication field. Yet, it is appropriate to see the gaps and inequities literature as being more central in the conceptual confrontations that are occurring for the gap and inequity literature focuses, by definition, on evidence showing that some people, some times, under some conditions just don't get the source's messages. When one looks at the nature of the conceptual confrontations occurring in the field, one sees that they are also dealing with this same issue. The question has become whether one should believe the evidence or see it as an artifact of a series of assumptions that have been made about the nature of communication.

The basic assumptions about the nature of communication are nested symbolically in the phrase "sources-sending-messages-to-receivers." The image the phrase conjures is very much one of sources-sending-messages as if messages can be tossed like bricks to receivers. This analogy is a brief description of a host of assumptions which are being torn down as the result of the conceptual confrontations now going on in the eye of the cyclone. While the literature focuses on these confrontations in a variety of forms, for purposes of this chapter it is useful to present them in two major categories. The first category deals with different perspectives on the nature of the message that the source is sending—whether it can be looked at as a "brick" or as something quite different. The second category deals with the nature of receivers and whether they can be looked at as catchers of messages or as something quite different. Each of these categories will be reviewed in turn.

Observer Versus User Constructions of Information

While the various gap or inequity statements differ in terms of whether they are focusing primarily on information/knowledge gaps or on a wider variety of assumed message effects (e.g., adoption or attitude change), they all assume implicitly or explicitly that they are concerned with the impacts of messages or communications. And, without exception, they implicitly or explicitly concur on the widely accepted idea of traditional communications research that information exchange or transfer is at the center of the communicative act or ". . . the stuff of communication" as Schramm (1973) puts it.

In essence, then, the gap or inequity idea has been one that comes from an observer looking at the world to catch in his or her vision some hoped-for-impacts of message or information transfer, whether those hoped-for-impacts be greater knowledge gain, greater self-development, or greater adoption. The idea of looking for impacts requires that some standard be established. It requires that an observer be able to look across a large number of receivers and measure each of them against the standard. In the gap and inequity research, as in communication research generally, the standard has been implicitly assumed to be the message. The sources send the message. It is then seen, traditionally, as existing much as a brick exists. One then looks for impacts from the existence of the message.

This line of reasoning has embedded in it a host of assumptions. It assumes that messages cause impacts, that they exist independent of sources or receivers, that messages have lives of their own. More fundamentally, however, these assumptions are tied to a host of assumptions about the nature of information, the thing that is said to be the "stuff of communication." Actually, it is not so much the message that is seen as having a life of its own but the information it imparts. It is this conception of information that provides the standard against which observers can judge whether some people suffer from communication gaps.

It is also this conception of information that is at the root of most of the confrontations going on in the conceptual cyclone. So, while the cyclone manifests itself in the form of a variety of arguments pro and con, the arguments that focus on the nature of information are the most fundamental ones.

Dervin (1977b) summarizes the traditional assumptions that have been made about information in her critique of how the communication and information science disciplines have used this concept:

> *Information is essentially seen as a tool that is valuable and useful to people in their attempts to cope with their lives. Information is seen as something that reduces uncertainty. As the individual moves through . . . the time-space continuum that makes up life . . . it is assumed that information can both describe and predict that reality and thus allow the individual to move more effectively. (p. 18)*

This suggests that traditionally, information has been seen as a valuable resource, something that describes reality, reduces the uncertainty about it, and allows people to cope more effectively. Like most underlying or fundamental assumptions, proof of their use abound but are found between the lines rather than stated explicitly.

These assumptions about information have behind them a set of even more funda-mental assumptions. Dervin, Harlock, Atwood, and Garzona (1980) summarize them as "the absolute information" or "objective information" assumptions (see also Dervin 1976a, 1977a, 1977b.). Essentially, these assumptions are the very assumptions that have been most often associated with logical positivism or positivistic science. The idea here is that the world can be seen as discoverable, describable and predictable and the purpose of information is to so describe it and predict it. As Dervin (1976a) says: "If we assume that we are discovering reality, then the acquisition of more and more informa-tion about reality will make a better fit" (p. 327).

What is important about this complex of assumptions is that they all rest on one fundamental assumption—that information can exist independent of the observer. When brought out for a stark examination like this, the fundamental assumption, of course, runs counter to the basic relativity tenet in the communication field that: ". . . an accurate understanding of the human communication process must begin from the recognition that persons subjectively perceive their world—a principle now accepted as a truism in virtually every communication text" (Stewart, 1978, p. 198).

Despite the presence of the truism, ideas about absolute information persist. As Dervin (1976a) suggests, it is a symptom of a kind of "disciplinary schizophrenia" that has yielded a flood of confusing and contradictory results not only about gaps and inequities but about communicating in general:

> *We are at the same time, and sometimes almost in the same breath, both communica-tion relativists and communication determinists. On the one hand, our research data and our practitioner experiences say "relativism" loud and clear. Meanings are in people. Messages sent do not equal those received. The same person is different across time and space. On the other hand, we commit ourselves to research and action efforts which seek deterministic answers. We continue to look for normative, nonvari-ent rules. (p. 324)*

Other examples of recognition of this confrontation exist in the literature. Clarke and Kline (1974), for example, challenged that most communication research "adopts a strictly normative definition of 'knowing'" (p. 228).

What appears to have happened in the gap and equity literature, in particular, and in communications research generally is that researchers unknowingly accepted absolute information assumptions and imposed them on their respondents. It has been suggested by several that the assumptions themselves were derived from positivistic science with its belief in a deterministic world that could eventually, given enough effort, be fully described. Increasingly, these same positivistic assumptions are seen as being the root source of limited progress not only in the communications field where the concept of information and how it is defined is so central but to all of the social sciences. What seems to be happening, then, is that fundamental changes are occurring not only in the way the conception of information is viewed but in the way social scientists look at man and his use of information. In reviewing psychological research, for example, Allport (1960) warned that:

> *The designs we have been using in our studies of motivation, of symbol and hence of the foundations of moral behavior are not . . . sufficiently iconic with our subject matter. Addiction to machines, rats or infants leads us to overplay those features of human behavior that are peripheral, signal-oriented or genetic. Correspondingly, it causes us to underplay those features that are central, future-oriented and symbolic. (p. 65)*

Weimer (1978), in reviewing the use of psychological models of man in communications research, made a related charge:

> *A conceptually adequate approach can result only if the positivistic conception of science found in logical empiricism and related philosophies of science is recognized to be inadequate and abandoned, and if the behavioristic-information processing model of man is recognized to be inadequate and replaced by an adequate cognitive psychology. (p. 57)*

Weimer concludes that the confrontation between positivistic views and those that are not is a major confrontation facing the communications field and social science generally and fears "polarizations." A merging can occur, he suggests, but the dominant models of ". . . both *methodology* and *man* . . ." must be abandoned to achieve it (p. 57).

Brown (1979), reviewing communication theory, agrees with Weimer but sees little reason for optimism when he says:

> *. . . contemporary social science seems content in its search for absolutes and ultimates, confidently proclaiming itself in the forefront of scientific thought while at the same time standing mired in the metaphysics of a previous epoch. (p. 64)*

The conflict that emerges in these comments is an interesting one. First, it suggests that the charges made by the literature reviewed in the first challenge may be too simplistic. It is one thing to suggest that too much attention is paid to source goals and too much blame placed on receivers. It is another to challenge the very meaning of the term "information" and to suggest that the term has been used deterministically rather than relativistically. It is also a different kind of challenge to suggest that this deterministic treatment of the information concept has roots that extend beyond the confines of a given country's approach to the study of human behavior.

Interestingly, the challenge to social science takes its roots from science, what might be termed the relativistic sciences of the 20th century. It is from this that the idea of information takes on a new form. All observation is inherently biased, we are told. No observation can be made as a statement of "absolute truth." Information is a construction, a product of observer and observation. Myriad authors have made the point:

Information is necessarily about fragments of the cosmos and history . . . . At any time a man has some collection of pieces of information fitted into various systems of thought or accepted stereotypes of experience. He cannot know, except in regard to the most immediate physical effects, whether his information is all that exists which bears on his choice of action. (Schackle, 1974, p. 10)

. . . information is associated with the <u>relation</u> between message and receiver. (Conant, 1979, p. 179)

. . . the objective world is, it does not happen. Only to the gaze of my consciousness, crawling upwards along the life line of my body, does a section of this world come to life as a fleeting image in space which continuously changes in time. (Weyl, 1963, p. 216)

In general terms, then, what is happening in the literature is that conceptions of information are moving from observer constructions to user constructions. The essence of the reasoning is that any piece of information is merely the product of the observing of one or more humans that has been made public and shared (Wilson, 1977). The observations of one or more humans are always constrained. First there are the obvious constraints of human physiology; man's perceptual equipment is limited. But even beyond these constraints, there are others. There are the constraints of time; no person can observe from every point in time. There are the constraints of space; no person can observe from every possible vantage point. There are the constraints of change; observations of one moment do not fit the next.

It has been reasoning of this type that has propelled what is being called the "phenomenological" thrust of the communications field. In his review of some of the phenomenological literature, Stewart (1978) summarizes the main conclusion drawn from the reasoning presented above: ". . . the accurate study of human phenomena, specifically the study of human communicating, not only may be subjective and experiential but *must be*" (p. 198).

There is a major implication of the reasoning that goes beyond Stewart's phrases "subjective" and "experiential." The implication is that human communicating—in terms of this chapter, the use of information—cannot be seen as a passive process where the receiver catches messages thrown by sources. Rather, information use is inherently a creative process. Given the observational constraints of time, space, change, and physiological limitations, no amount of information provided by another can provide an individual with the instruction he or she needs to cope with even the limited reality of a personal existence. This is, in Gorney's (1972) terms, a human imperative; in Bruner's (1964, 1973) terms, the human necessity of "going beyond the information given;" in Carter's (1972, 1973, 1974a, 1974b, 1975; Carter, Ruggels, Jackson, & Heffner, 1973) terms, the mandate of "gap-bridging" or "construction" necessitated by the absence of "instruction"; in Dervin's (1979b, 1979c) terms, the mandate of "making sense when none is given"; in Schackle's (1974, p. 2) terms, the need for origination rather than calculation. Two quotes, one from Dervin and one from Schackle, catch the essence of the idea:

> *Humankind's information is some unknown combination of information about reality and information that is the creative product of people. Since both adaptation and creation are simultaneous and continuing human activities (in the collective sense), no amount of "objective" information can possibly describe reality. Indeed, humankind's creations of today make maladaptive the adaptive behavior of yesterday. Given a picture of the universe that allows for the possibility that "objective" information cannot completely describe reality, the avoiding of accidents . . . is not a matter of simply getting more "objective" information. Rather, it is a matter as well of humans being able to create and operate with their own instruction and understanding. (Dervin, 1976a, pp. 325–326)*

> *. . . the sequel of an action chosen by one man will be shaped by circumstance, and its circumstances will include the actions chosen now and actions to be chosen in time to come by other men. If, therefore, choice is effective, it is unpredictable and thus defeats, in some degree, the power of choice itself to secure exact ends. (Schackle, 1974, p. 2)*

This idea—that human information processing is inherently creative—has one additional implication. This implication has to do with the issue of whether anything in a message can cause the behavior of a receiver and is best summarized by Stewart (1978): "This insight into the nature of the most fundamental human process, perceiving, can also be seen as the grounding for the rejection by many communication scholars of causal models of communications" (p. 199). One sees in the literature, thus, a significant movement away from traditional causal assumptions about communication behaviors to assumptions that place the control of outcomes of communication situations in the hands of receivers. As Berlo (1977) states it: "We have begun to move away from the hypodermic metaphor of communication as something a source sticks in a receiver, and moved toward concentrating on relationships other than the relationship of causally dependent change" (p. 11). Others have not been so optimistic but have made the same call (Atwood, 1980a; Carter, 1974b; Grunig, 1975, 1978a, 1978b; Grunig & Disbrow, 1977). Others (Blumler, 1979; Katz, Blumler, & Gurevitch, 1974, McQuail, Blumler, & Brown, 1972; Swanson, 1979) have not spoken to the causality issue directly but have spoken indirectly in their growing body of work in the "uses and gratifications" tradition. One of the major premises of the tradition is that the receiver takes "initiative in linking need gratification and media choice" (Katz et al., 1974, p. 21). This quote from McQuail et al. (1972) states the position:

> *. . . the relationship between content categories and audience needs is far less tidy and more complex than most commentators have appreciated. It is not just that most popular programmes are multidimensional in appeal. It is also the case that we have no*

single scale by which we can reliably attach a value to any given content category.
Given the heterogeneity of materials transmitted over the broadcast media, not only is
one man's meat another man's poison, but one man's source of escape from the real
world is a point of anchorage for another man's place in it. (pp. 162–163)

In summary, then, a core of arguments against traditional assumptions about the nature of information and information use are emerging from the literature. These arguments suggest that the very notion of communication-produced gaps and inequities rests on the assumptions that the informational content of messages exists independent of either sources or receivers and can have impacts on receivers independent of any intervention by receivers. The analogy of sources throwing bricks at receivers aptly summarizes the traditional assumptions. Information existing independent of sources and receivers is set up as a standard against which all receivers are measured. Those receivers who do not catch the message are then labeled as being in gap or inequity.

In the context of the arguments that are attempting to tear down traditional assumptions about the nature of information and its use, the idea of using a conception of "absolute information" as a standard for assessing the success or failure of messages is both a theoretically unsound idea as well as a self-defeating one. It is a theoretically unsound idea when juxtaposed with our understanding of the nature of human perception and its inherent constraints. It is a self-defeating idea because it means that when assessed in absolute information terms most information campaigns will necessarily fail. And with such a standard, one will find the most failure when sources attempt to send messages to those people most different from them. Logically, any source's messages will be least useful informationally to members of the audience who observe the world from points in time-space most different from those with which the source observes the world.

It is possible to posit the use of "absolute information" assumptions as an alternative explanation of why gaps have been found. Unlike the deficit explanation discussed earlier, this explanation is more a product of conceptualization than evidence. This explanation suggests that the ideas of gaps and inequities are ". . . not so much summary of human communication behavior as summary of things observed using these paradigms" (Carter et al., 1973, p. 36).

More specifically, one can see that what has happened in the gaps and inequities literature as well as communication research generally is that researchers have accepted absolute information assumptions and imposed them on their respondents. Since absolute information is unobtainable, what has really occurred is that researchers have imposed their views of what is informing (and, thus, to them "information") on receivers and called it "the" information. Clarke and Kline (1974) make this observation:

. . . most research . . . adopts a strictly normative definition of "knowing." To be
informed means to grasp the kind of facts about public events that usually interest edu-
cators. The identities of statesmen, dates of events, and awarenesses of sanctioned

viewpoints figure prominently . . . . Most often these kinds of cognitions are measured concerning public events that are salient to researchers, who are educators themselves—whether or not the events are relevant to mass publics. (pp. 228–229)

Dervin (1979a) makes much the same point:

One begins to understand that much of the social sciences is based on mythical data collected by asking people to care about and make sense of things that have nothing to do with their own lives as they see them. (p. 11)

When one looks at the literature dealing with human information use, its one most outstanding characteristic is how little it has told us about when, how, and why people use information. This observation has been made by many (Brittain, 1970; Carter et al., 1973; Dervin 1976a, 1976b; Dervin, Zweizig, Banister, Gabriel, Hall, & Kwan, 1976; Donohew, Tipton, & Haney, 1978; Hollis & Hollis, 1969; Rees & Schultz, 1967; Warner, Murray, & Palmour, 1973; Zweizig & Dervin, 1977).

In fact, if one were to believe the literature, one would think that people used information hardly at all. Yet, the evidence runs counter to the nature of human existence. The evidence has been produced primarily in the context of absolute information assumptions. Several authors (Moore & Newell, 1974; Rees & Schultz, 1967) have challenged that the reason that so much literature has yielded so little worth is that the literature has been constrained by its acceptance of the research techniques valued in logical positivistic science. More specifically, the challenge has been made (Carter et al., 1973; Dervin, 1976a) that the literature has rarely focused on the constructing of information and, instead, has implicitly assumed, contrary to relativistic assumptions, a kind of isomorphic relationship between external reality and the ideas that people construct about it and then share as information. This assumption is a logical outcome of a belief in absolute information. Swanson (1979) states this well: "For only if we assume perception to be a passive process of registering unproblematic content are we relieved of the necessity of investigating meaning created in perception" (p. 42). As the literature moves into the 1980s, research is beginning to emerge that looks at information as a user construct rather than an observer construct. Clarke and Kline (1974) describe the transition away from normative or absolute information assumptions:

One remedy is to inquire how people become informed about issues that are important to them. A corollary need is to measure "knowledges" about those issues that are of value to respondents, as well as the researcher. This calls for respondent-centered and open-ended measurement techniques. (p. 229)

In their study of what they called "information holding," Clarke and Kline tapped the thoughts respondents articulated about issues of interest to them. Dervin et al. (1980) took a similar approach when they defined information as the answers respondents created to their questions in situations they personally faced. Edelstein (1974) used the same approach when he had his respondents identify problems of personal interest and then articulate their thoughts on possible solutions and how the problem compared to other problems.

In each case, the researchers have defined "information" as a user construct or, in terms of Hollis and Hollis (1969) as "personalized information." In each case, the researchers created a context within which respondents could report on how they informed themselves for their unique worlds.

As one looks at the assumptions about information that have guided social science, they seem like the tip of an iceberg. Yet, more properly, they should be seen as the foundation of an iceberg. With each step that is taken in understanding the implications of having used absolute information assumptions additional implications emerge. A key set of implications focus on the ways that information behaviors can be predicted.

Linking issues of how information behavior can be predicted back to a root in absolute information assumptions is something not generally done in the literature. Exceptions are found in the articles by Dervin (1976a, 1977a, 1977b) and Dervin et al. (1980) who see the efforts at predicting information use as being a direct reflection of the nature of the assumptions being made about information. While no other authors were found who made the same explicit connection, numerous citations were found in which writers have been wrestling with the issue of how to best predict information behaviors.

The very fact that prediction of information use is necessary is, in itself, proof of the failure of the absolute information assumptions. The hypodermic model was a direct manifestation of these assumptions. It is assumed that the presence of information was both a sufficient and necessary condition of information use. When it was found that the hypodermic model only fit some of the people, some of the time, a variety of predictive structures were introduced to attempt to explain why this was so. Basically, these structures have traditionally assumed that when a person does not get a message, this person can be seen as prevented from getting the message by a series of barriers that stand between the person and the message. Since absolute information was assumed, the only possible explanation of why these barriers existed was that they were barriers the individual had attached in some way to his or her person. The barriers were all seen as standing between the individual and "the" information that existed in an orderly, well-described world, a world in which the use of absolute information was an assumed necessary and sufficient condition of existence.

In this description, then, the traditional use of "deficit" explanations for explaining why some people attend to media information while others do not can be seen as a result of a blame-the-victim syndrome, as charged by those writers reviewed in the literature of the first challenge, or as a result of a more fundamental error in thinking—assuming that information describes an orderly world that is knowable in an absolute sense.

From Dervin's (1976a, 1977a, 1977b) point of view, there is a definite parallel between conceptions of information and attempts to predict impacts of communication.

She sees the communication literature as having started with absolute information assumptions that do not require a concern for the conditions of information use. Rather, one can look at information as being able to drop into receivers like bricks into buckets.

The absolute information assumptions did not work, however, and evidence of their failure was all too apparent. As has been the pattern in the field, the attempts to explain the contradictions and contrary evidence then focused not on the assumptions behind the evidence but on trying to isolate the subset of receivers who were not behaving like buckets. Only when persistent efforts in the line failed has attention been placed on changing the underlying assumptions.

Not surprisingly, the change was one that moved from attempting to predict information use, first, as a straightforward, unchanging, mechanistic process to a process that is now beginning to be seen as occurring at specific points in time, space, and as changing over time and space.

In broad perspective, then, the moves in attempts to predict information use have paralleled the ways in which information has been defined. And, in particular, the move has been toward incorporating the very constraints of time, space, and change that were so crucial to the move away from observer to user constructions of information. This movement in approaches to predicting information use will be reviewed below.

Observer Versus User Constructions of the Predictors of Information Use

In the 1960s, when it became clear that the hypodermic model of communication did not hold, the first response was, as suggested above, to assume that the model held for some people and not for others. This assumption opened the door to essentially two decades of attempts to predict information use, specifically, and communication behavior, generally, on the basis of individual traits. The traits ascribed to receivers were of two types: (a) personality traits, with the reigning definition being that of Allport (1960) as relatively stable, highly consistent attributes of people that exert widely generalized causal effects on behavior; and (b) demographic traits, generally defined as accepted indicators of a person's "station" in life (e.g., education, income, socioeconomic status, age, race).

Commonly, the trait approach was based on the idea of cross-situational consistency. This meant that the traits were assumed to predict behavior regardless of time, space, or change. As Bem and Allen (1974) stated, the assumption of cross-situational consistency is "virtually synonymous with the concept of personality" (p. 506).

Given the logic presented in the last section of this chapter that unravels the absolute information assumptions, it is not surprising that the trait approach has simply not worked. At this juncture in the literature, many writers are trying to come to grips with this failure. While the postures shown in the literature vis-à-vis the cross-situationality issue vary, there is clear and growing agreement that the idea of cross-situationality in its current form does not work. The challenge has come from many quarters (Bem, 1972; Cappella, 1977; Carter, 1974b; Clarke & Kline, 1974; Davis, 1977; Dervin, 1976a, 1977a, 1977b; Dervin et al., 1976, 1980; Endler & Hunt, 1969; Grunig, 1973a, 1973b; Grunig & Disbrow, 1977; Hewes & Haight, 1979; Miller, 1963; Mischel, 1968, 1973; Rotter, Chance, & Phares, 1972). Typical statements include the following:

> ... *empirical evidence obtained over a wide variety of constructs does not support this [cross-situational] assumption. (Hewes & Haight, 1979, p. 262)*

> ... *behaviors appear to be "idiosyncratically organized in each individual." (Endler & Hunt, 1969, p. 20)*

> *When it comes to dealing with individuals as individuals . . . [trait] attributes are but labels imposed by the outside world. The attributes may or may not be relevant to the individual. Furthermore, whether they are relevant or not, attributes are not the reason an individual may intersect with [a message] . . . at a given point in time. (Dervin, 1977b, p. 27)*

> *Response patterns even in highly similar situations often fail to be strongly related. Individuals show far less cross-situational consistency in their behavior than has been assumed by trait-state theories. The more dissimilar the evoking situations, the less likely they are to produce similar or consistency responses from the same individual. Even seemingly trivial situational differences may reduce correlations to zero. (Mischel, 1968, p. 177)*

The extent of the challenge is best shown by the statements made by Mischel (1968, 1969, 1971, 1973) that suggest that regardless of improvements in measuring instruments the amount of variability that personality variables can predict across situations is never likely to exceed 10%. Even without the limitation suggested by Mischel, there is growing agreement that a shift from cross-situational predictors to situationally-bound predictors should greatly improve the prediction situation. As Grunig and Disbrow (1977) suggest, a cross-situation approach may work some of the time because individuals with common demographic characteristics and common personality traits often are found in similar situations. But, such traits are too far removed from the actual situations in which information use occurs. Dervin (1977b, p. 19) makes this point when she suggests that the irony of the use of cross-situational approaches as a means of trying to improve the prediction of individual behavior is that it is, in itself, a normative response ". . . attempting to correct the damages . . ." of a normative, absolute information approach. She continues: "In the normative approach, the individual is treated as irrelevant to the situation. In the use of across time-space demographic predictions, the situation is treated as irrelevant to the individual . . . " (Dervin, p. 19).

It is clear in the literature that the move away from cross-situational approaches and toward situationally-bound approaches came first as post hoc explanations of why expected results did not occur and then as piecemeal, primarily atheoretic attempts, to obtain better predictability. Long before the concept of situationality was bantered about, researchers were introducing variables such as "level of importance" and "degree of interest" and "life situation context" into their predictive statements. And, consistently but still out of the collective research consciousness, these variables—bound to the perceptions of situations at given moments in time-space—proved to be powerful predictors. Study after study showed significant relationships between interest or relevance and information seeking and use (Adams, Mullen, & Wilson, 1969; Atkin, Bowen, Nayman, & Sheinkopf, 1973; Bishop, 1973; Clarke & Kline, 1974; Donohue et al., 1975; Fitzsimmons & Osburn, 1969; Genova & Greenberg, 1979; Hanneman & Greenberg, 1973; Johnson, 1973; Levy, 1969). Other studies have shown a strong relationship between the presence of receiver uses for information and actual information seeking and use (Dervin et al., 1976, 1980; Edelstein, 1974; Grunig 1975, 1978a, 1978b; Grunig & Disbrow, 1977; Sears & Freedman, 1967). Other studies have focused specifically on the presence of interpersonal uses for potential information and have found relationships between the presence of such uses and information seeking and use (Chaffee, 1970, 1972; Chaffee & Atkin, 1971; Clarke, 1965; McLeod & Wackman, 1967; Milbrath, 1965).

This move toward situationally-bound approaches on the basis of post hoc explaining and piecemeal predicting was characteristic of the communication field generally and characteristic specifically of the gaps and inequities research. The first sign of the move came with the introduction of a gaps and inequities explanation that was presented as an alternative to the "deficit explanation." This alternative—called the "difference" explanation—was presented by Ettema and Kline (1977): "The major thrust in the difference interpretation is . . . that persons from different social strata and/or cultures manifest their abilities in different circumstances and, further, that these circumstances are predictable and reasonable given the differences in status and culture" (p. 187). In this statement, Ettema and Kline are explaining why gaps occur and, while still adhering to the cross-situational use of social strata and culture, they show the first signs of using situational explanations.

The second sign of the move toward situationality came in the face of contradictory results that disproved the existence of gaps or even found gap reversals. As had been the pattern in communications research generally, attempts were made in the gaps and inequities research to isolate the conditions of these variations in the gap phenomena. The studies of Donohue et al. (1975) and Tichenor et al. (1973) are best known for this attempt. They isolated a variety of conditions that related to reduced or dampened gap effects in communities. Prominent among these conditions were degree of community interest, presence in the community of social conflict, and degree of community homogeneity. Each of these conditions attempts to capture some of the uniquenesses of the specific points in time and space and, in particular, the points in time and space when there would be reason to expect that media messages would have broad general interest and use in a community.

It was research such as this that led to what might be called a situational reinstatement of the gap hypothesis:

> *As the infusion of mass media information into a social system increases, segments of the population motivated to acquire that information and/or for which that information is functional tend to acquire that information at a faster rate than those not motivated or for which it is not functional, so that the gap in knowledge between these segments tends to increase rather than decrease. (Ettema & Kline, 1977, p. 188)*

In sum, then, both in communications research generally and gap research specifically, the first move toward situationality was primarily an inductive one. At some point a critical mass of evidence was reached and one began to see explicit statements calling for situational theory. Typical examples of the call are shown below in quotes by two psychologists, Mischel and Rotter, and one communication scholar, Cappella:

> *It is the position of [our theory] . . . that most predicative instances require an adequate description of the situation before useful predictions can be made. To rely solely on internal determinants or states results in either highly general predictions or else inaccurate ones. (Rotter et al., 1972, p. 4)*

> *Given the overall findings . . . on the complexity of the interactions between the individual and the situation, it seems reasonable . . . to look more specifically at what the person* constructs *in particular conditions, rather than trying to infer what broad traits he generally* has, *and to incorporate in descriptions of what he does the specific psychological conditions in which the behavior will and will not be expected to occur. (Mischel, 1973, p. 265)*

> *Situational factors seem to act as catalysts or attenuators so that relationships hypothesized and validated in one context are modified or perhaps reversed in other contexts . . . personality traits can no longer be expected to predict communication behaviors . . . unless situational factors are accounted for. (Cappella, 1977, p. 44)*

The nature of the calls obviously varied. For some (e.g., Cappella, 1977; Hewes & Haight, 1979), the introduction of situational approaches was part of an attempt to find ways in which to retain cross-situational ideas. In these cases, the idea of situationality is, in actuality, simply one more case of the cross-situational idea. It is assumed that somehow the observer can judge the nature of the situation and that these observer-ascribed situational attributes will be helpful in the predictive realm. In actuality, however, given the perceptual constraints within which all communicative activity occurs, observer constructed ideas of situationality can be no better than observer constructed ideas of demography or personality.

The stronger theoretic call for situationality is typified by the quote by Mischel (1973, p. 265) with its emphasis on "...what the person constructs in particular conditions." Mischel makes his call for the field of psychology. Dervin et al. and Grunig have made the same call for the field of communication when they suggest that in the context of the situationality assumption:

> . . . *predicting and understanding how people use information and cope with events must be based on their perceptions of how they see the situations they are in. (Dervin et al., 1980, p. 592)*

> . . . *a person's perception of a situation is the best explanation of when and how he or she will communicate about that situation. (Grunig, 1978a, p. 42)*

Edelstein (1974) reflects the same underlying assumption in his definition of the situational approach:

> *What is significant about the approach is that it takes the point of view of the individual who is attempting to cope with problems he defines for himself. He deals with a problem as it affects him at a particular time. He is thus defining a situation in his own terms. (p. 242)*

With this call for a situational approach came a series of explicit tests pitting a variety of situational measures against more traditional cross-situational demographic or personality measures. With few exceptions—these exceptions being explained by the fact that researchers mistakenly used observer assessments of situations—the situational predictors proved more powerful than cross-situational predictors (Chaffee & McLeod, 1973; Clarke & Kline, 1974; Dervin et al., 1976; Donohue et al., 1975; Genova & Greenberg, 1979; Grunig & Disbrow, 1977; Hewes & Haight, 1979; Stamm & Grunig, 1977; Tichenor et al., 1973). Typical results show, for example, that message discrimination (respondent recall of messages voluntarily exposed to) was a stronger predictor of information holding than education (Clarke & Kline, 1974); personal interest was a better predictor of knowledge than education (Genova & Greenberg, 1979); situational measures were more powerful predictors of information seeking than across time-space attitudinal measures (Stamm & Grunig, 1977). Relevant studies in this roster, of course, are the explicit tests of the impact of situational measures on gap effects (Donohue et al., 1975; Tichenor et al., 1973).

With these tests, the beginning of coherent ideas about situationality began to emerge. Yet, strangely, most of the emerging ideas still lacked a generalizable base. This was due, in part, to the fact that there seemed to be in some quarters a sense of disbelief about what was happening. An example can be found in this statement by Hewes and

Haight (1979): "If we fail to circumvent the cross-situational problem, a major reassessment of communication research priorities and paradigms must be forthcoming" (p. 265). What seemed more crucial to coherent development of a situational approach, however, was full recognition of the need for user-constructed perceptions of situations and, more fundamentally, full recognition of and allegiance to the ideas of user-constructed information. Because the root assumptions about information are so frequently implicit, confusions over these issues abound in the recent situational literature. Yet, like most confusions tied to implicit assumptions, there frequently isn't enough direct statement to ferret out the confusions.

It is clear in the literature, though, that while more and more researchers are accepting user-defined situational assumptions, they frequently attempt to do so while retaining observer-defined information assumptions. Interestingly, it is those studies that have moved fully out of old observer perspectives into user perspectives that have made the most progress in developing a coherent situational perspective.

The core issue in developing a coherent perspective is how to select the situational variables. Some writers have suggested that the task is impossible. Dervin et al. (1980) summarizes the dilemma:

> *The enigma, of course, is that each situation is seen by each participant uniquely. The research problem becomes how to tap this uniqueness in a way that allows it to be dealt with and, yet, at the same time, does not revert back to noninstitutional, absolutist assumptions. The task is one of tapping variable classes . . . in such a way that the resulting measures can be seen as existing in all situations while at the same time tapping the very elements of uniqueness in specific situations. (p. 593)*

It is this juncture that a solid hold on user-defined information assumptions has proven helpful. It is the constraints of time, space, and change that mandate the requirement of user-defined information and, in turn, user-defined situationality. It is these very same constraints that provide the basis for developing a coherent approach to situationality. The theoretical work of Carter (1972, 1973, 1974a, 1974b, 1975) and its applications suggests that what is common to all situations is that the individual can be seen as moving through time and space. In Carter's terms, the individual has a mandate—to construct sense of the world in order to move through it. Sense is not seen as being "out there" but rather as being something that the individual constructs. The individual operates on available sense—the ideas made in the process of experiencing life, being educated, listening to others—only as long as available sense works. Since life is inherently unmanageable, available sense frequently runs out and the individual must ask questions and seek answers in order to design the next movement.

This viewpoint provides a conceptual context within which to hypothesize when people will seek to inform themselves. It is the point of the need for gap-bridging, when old sense has run out. It is the point when, for some reason, movement straight ahead through time and space cannot continue unfettered.

A number of researchers have made profitable use of this theoretic base. This use has taken three forms. One is predicting the "when" of information seeking; the second is predicting the nature of the situations in which the seeking occurs; the third is predicting the "what" of information seeking.

In terms of predicting the "when" of information seeking, the "gap-bridging" perspective suggests, quite simply, that individuals will move to inform themselves at the point of need, when old sense has run out, when there is a missing piece in a picture of a situation (Dervin, 1976a, 1977b; Grunig, 1975). Using this line of thinking, a number of researchers have found visible evidence of active information seeking by audience members where other researchers have found little or none. Chaffee and Choe (1978), for example, isolated political information use where others found little by isolating those points when citizens do their deciding; Stamm and Grunig (1977) did the same on environmental issues by isolating citizens in situations where they had gaps to bridge; Dervin et al. (1976) compared their respondent references to information as traditionally defined in absolute terms to their references to need for sense-making and found that while only 6% of their respondents indicated they needed some form of objective, absolute information while facing a recent everyday, troublesome situation, 42% of them reported reading something relevant to their situations, and 75% or more spent time thinking and talked to someone.

The second use of the moving through time-and-space perspective has been in isolating the kinds of situational measures appropriate to studies of information behaviors. Here, the "gap-bridging" idea suggests that these situations should be those when the mover sees movement as somehow deterred or fettered. Grunig (1975, 1978a, 1978b) and Grunig and Disbrow (1977) have applied these ideas in the development of a situational typology which, in its simplest form, juxtaposes a respondent's perception of the existence of a problem with his perceptions of the existence of constraints limiting movement. Grunig predicts, and the evidence shows successfully, that, for example, those people who recognize problems and don't see themselves as constrained will be active information seekers for they are ready to move on a recognized problem. Dervin (1976a, 1977b) and Dervin et al. (1976, 1980) develop a related situational typology although their explicit predictions differ from Grunig's. In the Dervin typology, movement through time and space is looked at in terms of whether the respondent is stopped from moving because he or she sees more than one road ahead (decision situation), sees no road ahead (worry situation), sees the road blocked by something or someone (barrier situation), or sees self as being propelled along a road of someone or something else's choosing (problematic situation). This typology has also been highly successful in predicting information use.

The third use of the moving through time-and-space perspective in developing coherent situational theory has focused on the "what" of information seeking. The basic idea here is that since informing behaviors are rooted in situations, the focus of these behaviors should be predictable based on assessment of these situations. The research cited above by Dervin provides an example of this application. Dervin (1979c) lists the kinds of questions people try to get answers to in situations as: "Where am I? Where am I going? How can I get there? Where have I come from? Am I alone? How can I control me?" (p. 20). She hypothesizes a direct connection between the kinds of situations people see themselves as being in and the kinds of questions they ask. Dervin et al. (1980) gave an explicit test to this hypothesis in their recent study of sense-making by patients and found clear and significant relationships between how a person described his or her situation and the questions asked. They found, for example, that patients who saw their health situations as "barriers" frequently asked questions on why things were happening while, in contrast, patients who saw their health situations as decisions more frequently asked questions focusing on the how of getting to where they wanted to go.

The important thing about these theoretic developments is not so much their specific characteristics or their results, but the fact that for the first time hypotheses are emerging, predicting the conditions of information use rather than assuming it will be used and then trying to comprehend why it isn't. More important than this, however, is the fact that these hypotheses are highly generalizable because they speak, in the terms of Dervin et al. (1980) to the uniquenesses of situations that can be applied across situations; or, in Grunig's (1975) terms to conditions that apply across systems. In a sense, it can be said that these hypotheses speak to the imperatives of the human condition, generated as they are by an understanding of the constraints on human experience of time, space, and change.

CONCLUSIONS

This chapter has attempted to track through time a number of related but relatively isolated themes in the communications and information science literature and set them in the context of the fundamental assumptions upon which they rest. It has been concerned with communication gaps in the most generalizable sense. First, the "gaps" seen by observers between potential message receivers and the hoped-for-impacts of those messages. Second, the "gaps" seen by receivers between the pictures they now have in their heads and the sense they require to design movements for their lives.

Both types of "gaps" are communication gaps. In the former, it is assumed that communication occurs when sources throw messages at receivers. In the latter, it is assumed that communication occurs when receivers reach out to use input useful in their lives. The contrast between the traditional view of "gaps" and the recent, phenomenological perspective, is not idiosyncratic to research focusing on gaps per se. The "gap" idea is central in any concern for communicating. For this reason, a review of literature dealing with the idea is, in itself, a review of the trends of the literature in general.

In looking at the movement toward reconceptualization of the "gap" idea, this chapter has reviewed two significant challenges to traditional conceptualizations. The first of these—expounded primarily by Third World researchers—sees communications research as having primarily blamed receivers for being in "gap"—for not becoming informed, innovating, developing as a result of exposure to messages. In this view, research has been blaming the victim rather than focusing on the nature of systems which create gap conditions and the nature of communication campaigns which reinforce the rich while letting the poor fall further into gap. This first challenge draws two conclusions. One is that communication itself is limited in its power to change structural inequities in systems, that this requires a specific focus on system changing. The second is that communication campaigns must become receiver-oriented.

It is at this point where the first challenge leaves off that the second challenge enters. This challenge sees communications research as having been led astray by inappropriate assumptions about the nature of information, the thing that it is assumed is transmitted by messages. In this view, communications research is seen as having dealt with mythical gaps—those seen when an observer measures a receiver against a standard not relevant to that receiver—while ignoring the kinds of gaps that are crucial in communication—gaps that individuals see in their pictures of the world and sometimes try to fill with input from messages.

While these moves toward reconceptualization often seem cast as if they represent marked polarizations between points of view, this appearance is, in itself, more myth than reality. The literature of the first challenge does deal more with power while the literature of the second challenge deals more with fundamental premises. Yet, both call for a move to a more receiver-oriented social science and both call for more receiver-oriented communication programs. And, both contribute to the move toward reconceptualization in different but not contradictory ways.

The literature of the first challenge can be called the pragmatic literature. It presents the problems that need addressing in the arena of the sternest test, the arena of Third World development where there is little disagreement about the enormous gaps that need bridging, individually and collectively, economically and informationally.

The literature of the second challenge can be called the philosophic literature. It presents the reasoning that supports the philosophic leap that is required if new power structures, no matter how responsive to citizens in intent, are not merely to supplant old ones, leaving the worlds of citizens as isolated from the mainstream of power as ever.

Chapter 3

Users as Research Inventions:
How Research Categories Perpetuate Inequities

Brenda Dervin

By reifying conceptual systems that set up market-based disparities, we allow the new technologies to do only what the old ones do and blame the user for the failure of the system. Those who manage and design communication systems have confidence in their abilities to identify and categorize users;[1] vast marketing and academic research enterprise rests on this assurance. Users are described demographically, psychologically, and geographically. They are examined in terms of what they own, what they have access to, what they control, how they live, and what they are able to do, use, or think. They are located in networks. They are seen as more or less likely to use certain kinds of communication channels or certain kinds of technologies. And, for the bottom line, they are examined in terms of whether and how often they use the system of interest. Sometimes they are asked to evaluate it: Did they like it? Were they satisfied?

This set of what I call here "traditional categories of users" is presented more formally in Table 3.1, along with specific examples of factors or variables typically addressed by researchers. Beyond providing examples, Table 3.1 shows that the same categories are applied at all levels of analysis—the individual, group, organization, institution, or nation.

Both researchers directly involved in the marketing enterprise and those tangentially involved overwhelmingly concur with this set of categories. Probably 95% of the available studies on users of communication systems rely on these categories, and much the same emphasis has been placed in system design.

The literature for the most part presents these categories as if they are real, as if they offer objectively truthful descriptions that provide a solid basis for system operation and design. It is a major assumption of this chapter that categories of users are inventions or constructions, the by-product of the particular kind of microscope that observers bring to the observing task.

This work originally appeared as: Dervin, B. (1989). Users as research inventions: How research categories perpetuate inequities. *Journal of Communication, 39* (3), 216–232. (ERIC Document Reproduction Service No. EJ 400 429). Reprinted by permission of Oxford University Press, Oxford, UK. Contains material presented as: Dervin, B. (1989, January). *Categorizations of users in telecommunications research: Perpetuating myths, reifying inequities.* Paper presented at the 11th annual meeting of the Pacific Telecommunications Council, Honolulu, HI.

The traditional categorizations of users that now dominate views of communication systems have far-reaching consequences. First, they reify systems that create disparities between the haves and the have-nots. Second, in providing no basis for system design to resolve these inequities, they intensify them. Finally, they result in our relegating the immense potentials of new communication technologies to existing design functions. Thus the new technologies are allowed to do only what the old technologies did—but at greater speed, with greater search capacity, and at greater distances (Rice, 1980).

The categories in Table 3.1 are all rooted in essentially the same mechanistic, transmission-oriented, objectivity-oriented model of communication (Dervin, 1980). Sources are seen as creating, storing, and retrieving messages and disseminating them to receivers, who are judged in terms of demographic characteristics, access to technology, literacy, networks, and a variety of other characteristics. Although the model's details vary as it moves from the level of individual to the level of group, organization, and nation, the implicit assumptions remain the same. The message is "thrown" via a communication channel, and the question asked is "who catches it?"

The questions asked about the user are based on observer perspectives rather than actor perspectives. They are external to the inner worlds of users, where most of the important acts of communicating—interrogating, planning, interpreting, creating, resolving, and answering—are performed. They can be seen, in fact, as the system's response to the fact that communication processes are not always one way and their outcomes are not always predictable. Systems designed don't necessarily get used; messages sent don't necessarily get read. Asked "why doesn't the process work?" systems (and the research that supports them) have answered "because people are different." The categories in Table 3.1 represent the attempts to describe *how* they differ—demographically, psychologically, and so on.

This chapter argues that traditional user categories lead us to a view of communication systems that makes haves and have-nots inevitable. To track this argument, we must look at five major generalizations that have emerged from all varieties of research on communication systems and their users:

> *1. The one who "catches" the message or service offered by a communication system is the one who is able to (has the resources, time, skill, and access). This is true both of systems that are searched for particular things, such as libraries and databases, and those that are searched more generally, such as the mass media (Bureau of the Census [BOC], 1987; Dervin & Dewdney, 1986; Gandy, 1988; Guttman, 1980).[2]*

> *2. The one who is able to "catch" the message is most like the sender: more educated, wealthier, more literate communicatively in all spheres, and more embedded socially. (Mass popular entertainment provides an exception.)*

TABLE 3.1
Traditional categories of users of communication/information systems

Criteria groupings	Individuals	Groups, organizations, institutions	Nations
Demography	Marital status Family size Age Race Ethnicity Income Socioeconomic status Education Occupation Gender	Aggregated statistics of some kind: Size Demographic profiles Gross income	Aggregated statistics of some kind: Size Demographic profiles Gross national product
Personality/psychology	Cognitive flexibilities Apprehensions Cognitive styles	Aggregated profiles	Aggregated profiles
Communication literacies/abilities	Computer Reading Language Interpersonal Analytic Cognitive Able-bodiness	Aggregated statistic of some kind	Aggregated statistic of some kind
Access to technology	Radios TVs Newspapers Telephones Computers	Aggregated statistic of some kind	Aggregated statistic of some kind
Role in communication transaction	Source Receiver Seller Buyer Co-participant	Same	Same
Location of transaction	Home Work Entertainment center Retail outlet Library	Own versus other turf	Own versus other turf
Nature of communication controls	Maternal Paternal Democratic Child-centered	Centralization Privatization Status rigidities Openness	Centralization Privatization Status rigidities Openness
Lifestyles	Hobbies Interests Culture	Aggregated profiles	Aggregated profiles
Network setting	Group memberships Network size Network strength	Information flows within and between	Information flows within and between
Content focus of system used	Topic	Same	Same
Affective evaluation of transaction	Liking Satisfaction	Aggregated profiles	Aggregated profiles

3. The introduction of different, more elaborate, more flexible technologies has done little to improve the situation and actually may have made it worse. That is, the informationally rich get richer, the poor get poorer (BOC, 1987; Computer and Business Equipment Manufacturers Association, 1985; Dervin, 1980; Gandy, 1988; Guttman, 1980; Hunter & Harman, 1979; Kozol, 1985; Steinberg, 1985).

4. The differences among technologies have had relatively little impact on the central organizing characteristics of peoples' lives or of institutions. For example, those removed from the mainstream remain removed and, some say, get more removed; organizations whose decision-making is highly centralized tend to remain that way (Colton, 1979; Gandy, 1988; Guttman, 1980; Robey, 1977; Strassman, 1980).[3]

5. The traditional categories allow researchers to confidently predict who gets access or exposure to information/communication systems. They also allow practitioners to use repetitive design principles to perpetuate or exacerbate the same patterns of use and exposure. These categories do not, however, provide a basis for explaining how to use technology innovatively or how to design systems that will change patterns of use and exposure. Nor do they guide policy decisions concerned with equity issues.

Traditional categories have documented the differential access and effectiveness of communication systems for differing subpopulations, organizations, and nations. Those who "have-not," economically and politically, have less access; when they do gain access, they get less value. In the "information society," essentially these same subgroupings of society become the informational "have-nots" (Dervin, 1980; Gandy, 1988; Kozol, 1985).

Traditional categories are also assumed to have marketing utility and are used in the design of campaigns intended to entice new users to systems. But since traditional categories of users offer no assistance in system design, design descends to appeals to sensationalism, homogenized entertainment, and the lowest common denominator. The impact of marketing-based entertainment television continues to spread geometrically faster among the informationally poor.[4]

By providing data on who is able to use the current systems, traditional categories guide entrepreneurs about where to target their developments. Since both those who run the systems and those who successfully use the systems are "haves"—like talks to like, plans for, and markets to like. The "have-nots" must somehow get more of what they lack—education, money, literacy, motivation to read news, computer skill, cognitive complexity, etc.—so that they can become like the "haves" (Dervin, 1980; Gandy, 1988). They must become culturally homogenized in order to get into the communication "fast lane" (Gandy, 1988; Webster & Robins, 1986; Woodward, 1980).

But the informational have-nots are not a small minority of U.S. citizens. In many respects the *average* U.S. citizen is informationally and technologically a have-not. Evidence shows, for example, that as many as one-third of U.S. adults are illiterate, that

50% or more are uninvolved in any democratic processes (e.g., voting), and that entertainment TV viewing outstrips informationally oriented media use by a ratio of at least ten
to one. A large proportion of U.S. citizens can be conceptualized as information poor, and
clearly some citizens are much poorer than others (BOC, 1987; Hunter & Harman, 1979;
Kozol, 1985; National Advisory Council on Adult Education, 1986; Steinberg, 1985).

**The role of traditional categories in causing, maintaining, or exacerbating these dis-
parities has not received much attention.** More often the literature focuses on the
technology per se. The naysayers see technology as exacerbating already defined societal inequities; the yeasayers dream of a variety of technologically driven positive outcomes that will lead toward more just, more democratic societies (Bell, 1973; Dupuy,
1980; Gandy, 1988; Hyde, 1982; Mosco, 1982; Rice, 1980; Rogers, 1986; Toffler, 1980;
Webster & Robins, 1986; Woodward, 1980).

But the categories themselves are what drive both system design and the research that
underlies that design. Based as they are on population segmentation and marketing principles, the traditional categories thus can lead only to conclusions that reify systems based
on the same categories. Such systems may be inherently antidemocratic (Gandy, 1988).

Those who are attempting to design systems for more than entrepreneurial ends
(e.g., databases with democratic access) are thus caught in a series of seemingly
inescapable binds. Either they pay the "rich get richer" price, or they descend into lowest common denominator homogenization. As an alternative they can pursue market
segmentation, but that approach quickly leads to infinite regress. Taking demographic
characteristics alone, twenty such characteristics, each defined with only two values each
(e.g., rich and poor, north and south, educated and not), would require more than one million different kinds of system designs. Beyond the fact that this kind of marketing segmentation has been found not to reach those who lack access, the necessary resources
are simply unavailable. Trying to make the have-nots more like the haves so they can
use the systems designed for the haves does not work either.

Some observers believe that information system design should not play a role in
issues of equity; if society is the source of the difficulty, corrections must occur there.
Others, however, suggest that information system design must be addressed directly if
systems are not to become less just over time, regardless of the goodness of the intentions of those who run those systems (Dervin, 1980).[5]

This latter is a foundation for academics who are proposing supplements or alternatives to the traditional categories. Rather than limit new technologies to doing more
of the same, faster, from more distant points, they emphasize that the crucial flexibilities
allowed by new technologies should open up systems for fundamental redesign.

**The option of fundamental redesign, which either remains invisible or is deemed
unnecessary within the framework of traditional categories, becomes both visible**

and necessary when one refocuses on new categories. The alternative categories of users listed in Table 3.2 all involve entering the world of users from actor's perspectives, from the inside.[6] A number of researchers have attempted to categorize users in terms that address the fundamental nature of their intersections with the system—that is, in situational, informational, functional, and strategical terms (Belkin, Oddy, & Brooks, 1982a, 1982b; Belkin, Seeger, & Wersig, 1983; Dervin & Nilan, 1986; Dervin, Nilan, & Jacobson, 1981; Lievrouw, 1988; MacMullin & Taylor, 1984; Taylor, 1984, 1985). Most of these researchers build on a common metaphor of people using various tools (e.g., systems, information, or sources) in constructing cognitive bridges across gaps. The intent is to address "universals" of the human experience, using categories that are valid for all users in all situations but can be measured in specific situations. If these universals could be built into systems, more people would get more use from those systems.

People acting as intermediaries in systems informally categorize in related terms. A librarian will remember a book that gave someone solace after a family death and recommend it to a patron in a similar circumstance; a teacher will remember a paragraph that helped the last student who seemed blocked in a particular way, a database access intermediary will remember what goals a user had in her last search; a writer reaches for a situation with universal human understanding. Further, it is well documented that people frequently expose themselves to new media products based on peer recommendations. Even highly educated scientists look first to their closest colleagues for citation suggestions and most profitably track citations offered by those with compatible views.

We have always required that people do this kind of categorizing independent of system design, yet we are surprised to learn that most information "transfer" occurs informally, between friends and colleagues, where the important collaterals are exchanged—information that means something, that is interpretable, that is culturally relevant. And we perpetuate the problem by conducting research embedded in traditional assumptions.

In fact, we can trace in the literatures of the professions (e.g., education, journalism, social work, medicine, and education) a kind of schizophrenia. On the one hand, the professional who interfaces directly with the patron, client, student, user, or reader is expected to "empathize." On the other, the mass of detail about individuals is overwhelming without a theory of what to attend to, and those people who intuitively emphasize burn out. The riddle that plagues systems persists: How can professionals empathize systematically?

At the group, organizational, institutional, and national levels we have done somewhat better. Thus, social science perspectives focusing on collectivities have been based far more on alternative categories, either implied or explicit, than have perspectives focusing on individuals, in part because it is difficult to find in collective descriptions a single source of action or agency. However, although alternative categories have been applied to collective behavior in a number of contexts, they have seldom been applied in

		Groups, organizations,	
Criteria groupings	Individuals	institutions	Nations
Actor's situation	Nature of barrier Complexity Power Barriers Specificity	Same, applied collectively	Same, applied collectively
Gaps in sense-making	Questions asked Understandings missed Confusions faced Anomolies faced	Same, applied collectively	Same, applied collectively

Actor-defined purpose	To get ideas
	To find direction
	To surveil
	To acquire skills
	To connect with others
	To get support
	To be happy
	To achieve goals
	To belong
	To design
	To discover
	To stimulate
	To be heard
	To get diverse input
		Same,
		applied collectively:
		   To surveil
		   To educate
		   To interconnect
		   To achieve consensus
		   To raise morale
		   To anchor culturally
			Same,
			applied collectively:
			   To surveil
			   To educate
			   To interconnect
			   To select goals
			   To socialize
			   To control

Information using strategy	Browsing Formatting Grouping Highlighting Indexing Formulating Citing Connecting Networking Interpreting Transmitting Skimming	Same, applied collectively	Same, applied collectively
Information values	Timeliness Depth Breadth Adaptability Specificity Quality Accuracy Touchability Moveability Newness	Same, applied collectively	Same, applied collectively
Information traits	Quantitative/qualitative Hard/soft Single point/options Precedence/futures Clinical/consensus	Same, applied collectively	Same, applied collectively

TABLE 3.2
Alternative categories of users of communication/information systems

the study of communication/information behaviors. Communicating, the most situated of behaviors, ironically remains cast primarily in nonsituational terms, whether the focus is individuals or groups, organizations, institutions, or nations. As a result, just as the professionals who communicate with individuals do so mostly based on personal experience and hunch, professionals who advise and plan for collectivities also operate primarily on personal experience and hunch.[7]

Recent attempts to answer the question of how to empathize systematically have been made primarily in the field of information science by researchers drawing on insights from European-based advances in social theory. Their common mission was to find a way to formalize into system design (e.g., aspects of system structure, access points, procedures) universal aspects of the human experience.

The use a person makes of an information or communication system can be understood in terms of the universal human mandate to make meaning. Without information systems that effectively support meaning making, a number of theorists charge, effective individual, community, organizational, national, and world life is impossible.

The groupings in Table 3.2 can be described in terms of the six major categories common to this genre of studies. All of these characterizations describe the person at a particular moment in time and space, rather than across time and space.

The actor's situation. This grouping of categories attempts to assess why in a given situation a person tries to use an information or communication system (e.g., database or mass medium). Dimension of attention includes, as examples: situation complexity (the embeddedness in a complexion of other situations; the diversity of elements involved; the clarity of the situation; the number of people involved); power and constraints (the actor's perception of his or her freedom to move and his or her own force); and barriers (what the actor sees as standing in the way—self, others, bureaucracies, timing) (Dervin, 1983a; Dervin & Nilan, 1986).

Gaps in sense-making. Theoretically, all communicating is seen as responding to some gap. When this gap is articulated as a question, "information" or "messages" serve as fodder for constructing the answer. One set of gaps includes: gaps regarding the characteristics, aspects, or dimensions of self, others, objects, events, timing, spacing, causes, consequences, and what-ifs (Dervin, 1983a; Dervin & Nilan, 1986).

Actor-defined purpose. What must people do in order to take steps and move through situations? Various schema differ, but generally the categories are defined both from the mover's point of view and at an abstract level, allowing a relatively few categories to offer large gains in generalizability. Categories in Table 3.2's "actor-defined purpose" grouping are not unrelated to those in Table 3.1's "observer-defined purpose" grouping, but the latter are conceptualized in a way that is removed from human action and movement. Further, they assume that all uses of a given system are related. One exemplar set of "generic" actor-defined purposes includes: getting pictures (cognitions), finding direction, gaining skills, getting motivation, avoiding bad places, getting out of bad places, getting support, getting connected, achieving goals, getting happiness, and getting rest (Dervin, 1983a; Dervin & Nilan, 1986).

Information-using strategy. These categories include the strategies for seeking and using information that are preferred by the actor at a specific moment. Examples include: browsing, formatting, grouping, highlighting, indexing, citing, digesting, abstracting, formulating, transmitting, interpreting, connecting, and skimming (Hall, 1981; MacMullin & Taylor, 1984; Taylor, 1984, 1985).

Information values. The criteria by which the actor evaluates information include timeliness, breadth, adaptability, accuracy, specificity, touchability, movability, and newsiness (Hall, 1981; MacMullin & Taylor, 1984; Taylor, 1984, 1985).

Information traits. The specific characteristics of how the user would like the information presented are assumed to respond to the "needs" captured by all the above groups. They include quantitative or qualitative, hard or soft, single point or options, precedence or futures, and clinical or census (Hall, 1981; MacMullin & Taylor, 1984; Taylor, 1984, 1985).

The research that has guided the generation of these alternative categories represents a fundamental transition to a new perspective on users; some would call the transition a paradigm shift (Belkin et al., 1982a, 1982b; Belkin et al., 1983; Brookes, 1980; Dervin, 1981; Dervin & Nilan, 1986; Levitan, 1980; Wilson, 1981, 1984). Regardless, while eclectic in its foundations, the research fundamentally rests on an array of assumptions very different from those that undergird the categories in Table 3.1.[8] The core set of assumptions is seen as applying equally well to all communication situations—media use, database use, use of interpersonally based transactions, and involvement in organizational life. In all cases, the model rests on the idea that communicating is at root a cognitive and behavioral event occurring within a cultural/societal system that is itself primarily the product of past and present cognitive/behavioral events. Because the categories focus on the making of meaning or sense, they are seen as generalizable across contexts (e.g., they describe the circumstances of a sitcom viewer as well as those of a database user).

Further understanding of the traditional versus alternative categories of users comes from comparing and contrasting the two sets and examining potential relationships between them. The traditional categories describe users and some aspects of their communication situations in static terms; the alternative categories are process-oriented. The traditional categories predict aspects of information seeking and using that are constrained by societal structures, that is, by the very aspects of people and situations that the categories tap. They predict, for example, that only a small elite use libraries regularly and that, as income goes up, so does use of print media and databases. Essentially, they predict access and potential for contact: "if . . . then." The alternative categories, on the other hand, predict what people do communicatively at specific moments in time and what they would like to have done but couldn't: "then . . . then." Research has shown the greater power of "then . . . then" predictions (Atwood & Dervin, 1981; Dervin, 1983a; Dervin & Nilan, 1986).

It is difficult to relate the categories in Table 3.1 and Table 3.2 because, as research shows, the latter are not well predicted by the former. Theoretically, this means that behavior bound to situations and based on cognitive events is best predicted by characteristics of those events, not by a priori characteristics of the participants.

The exceptions to this, of course, are specific structural or personal rigidities. An example of the former is the intercorrelation of the categories in Table 3.1. For instance, demographic characteristics are generally strong predictors of source use (e.g., poorer nations import and export less information). Different national media structures yield different media contents (e.g., the U.S. media structure produces a greater emphasis on entertainment than the British media structure). Another example is the way particular organizational structures (Table 3.1 categories) tend to relate to particular situation profiles (as tapped by Table 3.2 categories). For instance, at the level of nation, poor countries are more likely to face situations over which they have little control. At the individual level, poorer, less educated people are less likely to use libraries or read (Table 3.1 categories); they are also more likely to face situations over which they see themselves as having little power (Table 3.2 categories).

In theory, if society were entirely open, there were no specialization, and people were never hurt or oppressed, Table 3.1 categories would predict and relate to each other; Table 3.2 categories would predict and relate to each other. The categories in Table 3.1 would relate to those in Table 3.2 only if they referred to genuine changes in life conditions that pertain to information/communication. One example would be the situational changes that come with aging (Atwood & Dervin, 1981; Dervin, 1983a).

The more a communication situation can been seen as arising from cognitive events (either individual cognition or the meeting of minds that is somehow produced by members of collectivities), the less relationship we should find between Table 3.1 and Table 3.2. Thus, for example, at the individual level we find that people who share demographic characteristics are more likely to also share certain situational conditions as tapped by Table 3.2. Yet, they will be less likely to actually process and make sense of information in the same way, because they see and define their situations very differently.

Communication and information behaviors naturally respond to the inherent discontinuities of existence (Carter, 1980; Carter, Ruggels, Jackson, & Heffner, 1973). Situations change, usually rapidly. People need to create new understandings with each change. Categories that do not directly describe the changes cannot predict them well, as several studies have documented (Atwood & Dervin, 1981; Dervin, 1983a; Dervin & Nilan, 1986).

Communication and information behaviors ought to constitute the most flexible behavioral realm—the realm most responsive to discontinuities. Therefore, anything that constrains this flexibility (beyond the influences of necessary specialization) limits human potential, whether in the case of the individual person who uses media only to escape or a media structure that yields a media diet high in escapist fare.

The highly constrained models and little flexibility our media and communication systems exhibit generally is rationalized as specialization; but it is specialization removed from communication practice, because it is based primarily on Table 3.1 categories. Further, since system design and general policy pay little attention to Table 3.2 categories, such specialization lacks the communication savvy that would give it power.

In the end, we must conclude that both Table 3.1 and Table 3.2 categorizations are essential components of a repertoire.[9] Political realities and a long heritage of market segmentation approaches necessitate the use of Table 3.1 categories. Communication theorists are beginning to suggest that effective communication necessitates the use of Table 3.2 categories.

The trade-off between traditional categories and alternative categories of users can be illustrated by features of system design. Because research on which the alternative categories is based is barely fifteen years old, and because traditional categories are so pervasive, there are few examples of systematic applications of the alternative categories in system design. Some possibilities and a few actual applications can be usefully reviewed for features designed to improve access via intermediaries, via networks, and via software.

An *intermediary access* approach sees intermediaries as responsible for making the system appealing and useful to larger numbers of diverse people. Research suggests that the practice of these intermediaries can be both more efficient and more effective if it is based on the conceptual assumptions that undergird the alternative categories. This result contradicts a long-held assumption of communication systems: that effective communication with users of systems takes more time.

Applying alternative user categories to intermediary access changes the procedures by which intermediaries operate. For example, librarians and database intermediaries would ask users about their life situations and what brought them to the system rather than pose the traditional questions that attempt to specify what portion of the system's resources are relevant to the user's needs.[10] Media systems would ask their users what gaps could be bridged by media coverage—what questions viewers have regarding current events, what happenings in their communities seem troublesome, and so on.

Networking access encourages users to address the system, using electronics, in terms of the alternative categories that have proved relevant to past users. In a library, the ways in which books served purposes for past users would be recorded in an electronic reader's advisory service. In a governmental information system, a current user's question would be linked to the most closely matching questions of past users. The user could then call up the materials and sources that had helped those past users.

A *software access* emphasis builds the alternative categories into the information system as central design features: as keywords, search mechanisms, coverage categories, and so on. Authors might describe what gaps they saw themselves bridging in writing articles or their motivations for writing; users could then elect these as search categories. Alternatively, user-defined gaps might be matched via computer with computer produced portraits of a particular resource's potential for addressing these gaps (see, e.g., Belkin et al., 1982a, 1982b; Belkin et al., 1983).

These design potentials are now available only on a limited basis, though alternative categories are used informally by many interpersonal intermediaries. In the long run, however, the new communication technologies may allow alternative templates to be laid on top of those already used to collect, store, retrieve, and disseminate information. Evidence shows that very little has been done to tap this potential.

The policy applications of alternative categories can be compared to those of traditional categories in the context of three specific policy issues: (a) deregulation, (b) privatization, and (c) vertical and horizontal integration of communication industries. All three policy issues can be treated for our purposes as conceptually related. All decrease the diversity of communication system ownership and management by making market forces the primary criterion by which development proceeds. As a result, people who share particular demographic, psychological, sociological, and situational traits control communication and information systems, and certain kinds of rules and procedures dominate their operation. The resulting systems necessarily reflect this homogeneity.

How can we offset this impact? Traditionally, diversity in our communication systems has been assumed to be handled by market forces; all who wished to gain access as communicators (message senders and receivers) could do so. That this has never been true was not considered to be a problem, because it was also assumed that one communicator, if trained well, was as good as another. It was not the lack of diverse ownership and management but the lack of diverse users that was troublesome.

The problem is thus moved from source to receiver, and the policy solution is to try to provide access to the users—making sure, for example, that economics don't stand in their way by providing them with hardware or free or low-cost access. The categories in Table 3.1 identify those who lack hard resources, like money and shelter. If one focuses only on the hardware through which our systems operate (phones, televisions, radios, newspapers, computers, and VCRs), then those categories provide clear policy direction.

However, having physical access to a piece of communication hardware whose content lacks meaning or relevance is equivalent to having no access at all. The frequently heard call for "media education"—training our citizens to be critical consumers of media—again shifts the problem from source to receiver. Programs that attempt to bring computer literacy to the "illiterate" with hardware grants do nothing to alter the fact that equitable distribution of hardware is not the only measure of communication/information equity.

One might conclude that sufficient diversity in ownership and management would produce diversity among the categories in Table 3.2. This might be true at the individual level, but communication systems are highly constrained by procedures that are themselves ideologically driven and rooted in historic practices, which leads us to two problems. The first is whether diversity in ownership and management is possible given current market forces and the moves toward deregulation, privatization, and integration. The second problem is whether such diversity can solve the access problem when the problem is defined in communication terms.

The communication solution to the problem of access involves building nontraditional categories into system operation. For purposes of illustration, here are some *extreme* examples: Journalists would be trained to present reports not "objectively" but by facilitating the observations of a variety of observers; for example, those in "power" and those "out of power." Abstracts and keywords in databases would be built in part on alternative categories. Television fare would maximize diversity of utility rather than competitive edge based on sheer exposure. The mere existence of multiple viewpoints in the marketplace would not be considered sufficient; rather, we would require that multiple viewpoints be presented at the same time and place.

In essence, what is proposed is moving away from diversity guaranteed by multiple ownership, not because market forces are not guaranteeing multiple ownership but because multiple ownership does not itself ensure communication access. What is proposed is a new kind of diversity—diversity based on communication processes.

In some realms, little stands between our current system and a new kind of diversity, other than a mandate to invent and test alternatives. In other realms, there are major constraints. In the United States, for example, the definitional structure of First Amendment rights makes the idea of requiring diversity of perspective clearly alien to newspaper practice and a matter of grave contention in broadcasting. These difficulties notwithstanding, the important point is that alternative categories make communication-based solutions available to communication policy, system design, and practice.

The traditional categories are insufficient means of addressing equity issues because the contents and systems of access in most communication systems lack relevance and meaning except to an elite. What is needed are categories that are communication based—situated and relevant to actors. Such categories provide more useful assessments and provide entry points for both policy decisions and system design features that will enable greater access (Taylor, 1984).

NOTES

1.   This chapter is based on extensive literature reviews and a 17-year programmatic series of studies focusing on problems and potentials of communication system design. References given here are suggestive and representative rather than comprehensive. For detailed background see Dervin (1980, 1981, 1983a); Dervin and Dewdney (1986); Dervin and Nilan (1986); and Dervin et al., (1981). Readers may contact the author for as yet unpublished work.

2.   The data on who uses our existing communication and information systems has remained relatively stable over the past 10–15 years, with sharp demarcations shown between more educated, higher income people and less educated, lower income ones. But the fact is that many systems designed specifically to help more educated populations are vastly underused. Practicing teachers do not, for example, make heavy use of ERIC even though it was designed for them (Dervin, 1983a).

3.   Gandy (1988) reviews literature that documents the growing isolation of certain population subgroups; Rice (1980) reviews literature directly pertaining to technology impacts of computer mediated organizational and interpersonal communication and concludes that the impact of technology usually mirrors prior patterns while it escalates work demands, places more constraints and routines on lower echelon workers, and, in some cases, reduces both understanding and interpersonal communication.

4.   A detailed discussion of why use of TV entertainment is so pervasive is relevant to but beyond the scope of this chapter. There is, of course, the normative system view—that entertainment is what the people want. Some (Dervin, 1980, 1981) argue that it results in part from allowing entertainment to be the only human element in our communication systems, while others (Woodward, 1980) conceptualize mass entertainment use as an act of political rebellion. For our purposes, the important point is that traditional categories of users lead system design to rely on homogenized entertainment approaches.

5.   The treatment of equity issues in this chapter acknowledges and rests on critical perspectives but does not explicitly review them. One critical perspective would suggest, for example, that all attempts to provide more "access" in contexts that afford individuals little true power will be to no avail. An alternative critical view would predict that providing such "access" will inevitably increase tensions between different status groups and be resisted by those who now have more power. For a review of some of these issues, see in particular Dervin (1980) and Gandy (1988).

6.   The work of the theorists who propose alternative user categories is presented here as if from one mind. This is clearly not true, as an examination of one review of the literature (Dervin & Nilan, 1986) shows. The major demarcation between writers is the extent of their reliance on "objective" information assumptions. Of the three research approaches most cited here, work by Taylor (1984, 1985; MacMullin & Taylor, 1984) and his colleagues ascribes far more reality to messages than does that of Belkin (Belkin et al., 1982a, b; Belkin et al., 1983) or Dervin (1980, 1981, 1983a; Dervin & Dewdney, 1986; Dervin & Nilan, 1986; Dervin et al., 1981) and her colleagues.

7.   This chapter does not pursue the difficulties of audience and public opinion research, both of which have been based primarily on traditional categories of audience members and have low predictive power. For a review of the use of alternative categories in audience research see Dervin (1981). Some academics have pursued approaches to public opinion research based on alternative categories (e.g., Edelstein, 1974).

8.   No attempt is made here to trace in detail the genesis and logic of these assumptions. They include: conceptualizing communicating, information seeking, and information using as acts of meaning making that are necessary to the human condition; asking respondents about their acts in real situations; and using both qualitative methodological approaches and giving more than equal weight to the qualitative.

9.   This point is made by theorists working from a myriad of ideological orientations. Arbib (1985), for example, referred to the need to focus on personal as well as social dimensions; Habermas (1979) called for a focus both on psychoanalytic frames and critiques of ideology.

10.   A number of librarians in the United States and Canada have been trained in and use this alternative approach (Dervin & Dewdney, 1986).

Chapter 4

Comparative Theory Reconceptualized:
From Entities and States to Processes and Dynamics

Brenda Dervin

As the field of communication copes with its many polarities (e.g., qualitative vs. quantitative, critical vs. administrative, and inductive vs. deductive), the term *comparative theory* is used in many guises, referring to comparisons across entities, theories, methods, ideologies, and so on. The references come from many quarters, even from those that reject the term *theory*. They come in many forms: in calls for statistical significance, clarity, utility, impact, and social significance.

Even though the argument presented here is seen as applying to all definitions of comparative, the particular problematic that is the focus of this chapter is that of the comparison of entities (e.g., groups, subgroups, cultures, and nations), particularly cultures and subcultures. For purposes of this article we start, with Tehranian, with a conceptualization of comparative theory as standing between universalist theories that search for invariant laws and contextualist theories that search for uniqueness. How can we compare entities without imposing on them ethnocentric assumptions about human constancies and at the same time without abandoning all hope of discerning anything universal about communication?

This polarization—the search for the universal versus the unique—perhaps more than any other marks our field. It appears most obviously in our struggles between approaches (e.g., qualitative vs. quantitative, inductive vs. deductive, and practice vs. theory). But it shows as well in the struggles within: as, for example, when an ethnographic researcher worries about imposing an order on the chaotic confusion of ethnographic material or when a quantitative researcher seeks qualitative exceptions to generalizations or when an experimentalist emphasizes limited variance accounted for.

This chapter suggests that we have indeed failed to develop powerful approaches to comparative theory and that this failure accounts for many of the divisions that are now apparent in our field. Even our field's now fashionable rejection of the idea of uni-

This work originally appeared as: Dervin, B. (1991). Comparative theory reconceptualized: From entities and states to processes and dynamics. *Communication Theory, 1* (1), 59-69. Reprinted by permission of Oxford University Press, Oxford, UK.

versal theory (or, in some quarters, the rejection of theory per se) can be seen in part as a by-product of this failure.

For purposes of this chapter, I propose that we face a major barrier in our search for comparative strength in the very nature of the analytic we are now using. Many would argue that we are not now using one analytic, that in fact we are using so many we have chaos. What I propose here, however, is that our current, common analytic is hidden from us because we are framing our conceptualizations of communication in ways inappropriate to the essence of communication phenomena. The result is that we know a lot about communicating entities—different cultures and subcultures—but what we know is like random marks on pages. It seems to have no strength or endurance: in quantitative terms, it accounts for very little variance; in qualitative terms, it seems easily changed by time or place or perspective. We go searching for the pattern we expect to find in heterogeneity and find cacophony instead. In essence, we lack a basis for developing comparative theory.

COMPARATIVE THEORY RECONCEPTUALIZED: FROM ENTITY TO PROCESS, FROM STATE TO DYNAMIC

One root of this situation is our field's emphasis on state or entity analytics rather than dynamic or process analytics. I use the term *analytics* to avoid some of the difficulties we are having in our field with the word "theory." Theory, for some, is what results from our work. For others, it is what allows us to talk across our work; for still others, it is what guides our work (Carter, 1989a). Each of these positions requires framings, assumings, idea makings, implementings. The term *analytics* refers to all these strategies. In terms of the meanings of theory described above, analytics pertain primarily to the latter—what guides our work. It would be wrong, however, to construe this as a preference for deductive over inductive theorizing.

Briefly, what this chapter proposes is that our quest for comparative theory will be usefully advanced if the field moves at least some of its theorizings and observings from its current focus on entity or state conditions to process or dynamic conditions; from descriptions, predictions, and/or explanations of how entities are to descriptions, predictions, and/or explanations of how entities make and are made; from a focus on beginnings and endings to a focus on connectings between and movements from here to there.

At one level, our field almost universally accepts the idea of the active, constructing, meaning-making human as fundamental to communication phenomena. This implies a focus on processes and dynamics. Yet, in actuality, we seem beset by a disciplinary schizophrenia. We talk about process ideas but rarely implement them methodologically. Usually, these ideas receive their strongest emphasis in contextual work focusing on uniqueness. But even here conclusions focus not on process or dynamics but on states and entities.

Our schizophrenia manifests itself most clearly in how we conceptualize the nature of the communicating human. On the one hand sometimes we see our human as consistent or even rigid and recalcitrant—held in place either by personal rigidities (e.g., fear and closed-mindedness) or the rigidities imposed by others (e.g., norms, rules, oppressions, or obstacles). On the other hand, we sometimes see our human as creative and changing and responsive—somehow empowered by personal action and/or the freeing actions of others. Frequently, we end up unable to examine how individuals are enabled by structures as well as constrained by them and how humans form structures to serve human needs and sometimes succeed. Our analytics rarely allow us to treat our humans as sometimes changing, sometimes consistent, sometimes rigid, sometimes chameleon-like, sometimes bowed down by barriers that seem to exist only internally, other times by external barriers, sometimes free despite formidable obstacles, sometimes freed by obstacles, sometimes pitted against structure, sometimes served by structure, sometimes serving structure.

Our difficulty has a marked impact on the utility of any work that calls itself comparative. The question is, where does one find pattern in communication phenomena? Traditionally, approaches in our field—critical as well as administrative, qualitative as well as quantitative, micro as well as macro—have looked for pattern not in the hows but in the whats and whos, not in the moving from here to there but in the beginnings and endings, inputs and outputs. Clearly, there are patterns to be found in all these locations. But, what must be asked is, are these the only locations? Are they the most useful locations? Are they the locations with the most comparative potential?

In terms of our focus on cross-cultural comparison, the difference between a state/entity focus and a process/dynamic focus means implementing an analytic that attends more to verbs (e.g., how culture is created, maintained, contested, destroyed, or allowed to decay) than nouns (e.g., what traits or situations distinguish cultures). This would mean, for example, focusing on meaning making as well as meanings made, on the struggling to achieve order or destroy it as well as on order achieved or destroyed.

THE GAP IDEA

In order to implement the direction set above, we need an analytic that allows us to focus on dynamics. The exemplar developed here is the *gap idea*. The gap idea is a fundamental assumption (sometimes usefully called a fundamental metaphor) about the nature of the human condition. This formulation rests primarily on Carter's (1980, 1989b) discontinuity assumption as well as on ideas suggested by Giddens (1984) and others. Its essence is the assumption that there are persistent gap conditions in all existence—

between entities (living and otherwise), between times, and between spaces. Accompanying this assumption is the idea that communicating is best isolated, studied, and generalized by focusing on these gap conditions.

Communicating is best isolated by utilizing a gap perspective because gap is where communicating dynamics are found. Gap is not to be seen as some earth-shattering event, rather, an everyday occurrence—an axiomatic mandate. There are gaps between reality and human sensors, between human sensors and mind, between mind and tongue, between tongue and message created, between message created and channel, between human at time one and human at time two, between human one at time one and human two at time one, between human and culture/society/nation, between human and institution, between institution and institution, between nation and nation, and so on. Given that there is no static order in the universe, no isomorphism between "reality" and observation, no sharing of ideas between communicating entities without some behavioral effort, and no necessary equivalence between messages intended and messages received, gappiness is an assumed "constant" of the human condition.

Communicating is best studied by utilizing the gap perspective because if communicating is the bridging behaviors with which we deal with gappiness then a perspective based on the gap idea is a powerful organizing perspective for zeroing in on communicating phenomena. This is assumed both at the microlevel for individual behavior and the macrolevel for collective behavior. In gap bridging the communicating entity (individual or collective) engages in behavior: observings, thinkings, idea creatings, comparings, contrastings, rejectings, talkings, sendings, agreeings, disagreeings, and so on. These behavings are the material of the gap bridging. Many of these behaviors are necessarily repetitions of those performed in the past. Some are mindless repetitions; some are newly created. Fundamental here is the idea that it is by focusing on these behaviors that we make available a powerful perspective for understanding communication.

Finally, communicating is best generalized via the gap idea because it focuses on communicating as constructing, as gap bridging, offering for comparative analysis and application a perspective that is both fundamental and applicable across situations while at the same time pertinent to specific situations. Regardless of situational or historical context, all communicating entities (e.g., cultures and individuals in cultures) bridge gaps.

There are vitally important aspects, of course, that are unique to each situation but the general idea of gap bridging is proposed as applying to all. Some gaps are harder to bridge than others. Sometimes the communicating entity exerts a lot of force or power. Sometimes, the communicating entity is acted upon and constrained by forces and powers emanating from others. Some gaps are treated repetitively. Some seem brand new. The ideas of meeting gaps, bridging gaps, moving against gaps are all proposed as highly abstract framings of communication that are pertinent in their abstract colorations to all situations and yet can be enriched with situated and contextualized uniqueness in given situations. The gap idea provides a way of framing these uniquenesses so they may be talked about specifically but at the same time be made available for generalization.

THE GAP IDEA VERSUS
COMMUNICATION RESEARCH PAST AND PRESENT

Most communication research has conceptualized the human being, the human condition, and communication with metaphors very unlike the gap metaphor. Before proceeding with an example of the implementation of the gap idea, it is important to review these differences, organized for purposes here along five dimensions, most of which represent arenas in our field where our assumptions do not align with our implementations (Dervin, 1989b; Dervin & Nilan, 1986).

The Field Still Retains the Transmission Metaphor. Despite formidable protestations to the contrary, the transmission idea of communication still pervades much of our work whether macro or micro, critical or administrative, qualitative or quantitative. We ignore for the most part the constructions that are necessarily fundamental to the communicating process: human beings draw on their understandings of the world and make observations that they construct into ideas and then encode into messages that they then "send" out where other human beings use their understandings of the world, and so on. The entire process is a chain of constructings; communicating step-takings. Each step-taking involves a communicating entity coping with gappiness. One major difficulty for us in our implicit and explicit use of the transmission assumption is that we often end up confusing communication as process with communication as product. An example of this is the competing formulations that assume that communication is always sharing or always an exercise of power. In essence, we have observed inputs and outputs and have made assumptions about what stands between them—the constructing dynamics—rather than studied them.

The Field Assumes Communication Structures Have Lives of Their Own. Again, most of our ideas about communication involve conceptualization of communication structures (including cultures, societies, systems, and institutions) in static terms without recognition that procedures are what energize structures. A structure that is not energized via procedure necessarily dies. It is the communicatings of communicating entities, individual and collective, that maintain and transform structures. Because there is never complete isomorphism between structure and communicating entity, the entity is never completely guided by structure. Each use of a procedure is the behaving by one or more communicating entities in the process of coping with this gappiness. Because we have not emphasized the procedures we lack a dynamic conception of structures.

The field is divided into levels of analysis—interpersonal, intrapersonal, mass, small group, organizational, societal—as if these levels were not all part of a whole and as if there were no connections (i.e., communicatings) linking the levels. It is from such a framing that we end up polarized: macro versus micro, structure versus individual. It is from such a framing that we end up forgetting, while protesting that we do not, that communicating individuals make and unmake society/culture/institutions.

The field is divided into contexts—political communication, health communication, telecommunication, and so forth—as if the fundamental nature of communicating differed simply because these contexts are assumed by observers to be organizing tools for categorizing situations relevant to actors. Because of this we miss what is common as well as uncommon across communication situations, creating instead a whole plethora of artificial categories pertinent to this or that context.

The field attempts to predict and explain communication behavior based on across time-space static conceptualizations of communication rather than time-space bound, dynamic, situated conceptualizations. Where "situation" is invoked, it is situation as seen by an observer, which may or may not be relevant to an actor. This framing presents itself in many ways. What is common however, is that most of our work has been based on the idea that the entity (e.g., culture or individual in culture) moves from situation to situation in the same state condition. Looking for such regularities, we end up missing that which is changeable or creative about the behavior of human entities, collective or individual. Indeed, we find regularities, but they seem too obvious or unimportant, as if we have succeeded in focusing on only the most rigidified aspects of the human condition. We have assumed that there are no regularities to be found in the changings and the creatings that are so characteristic of the species.

The problematic of comparing cultures or subcultures is an excellent one for displaying the impact of our field's assumptions. Borrowing from anthropology, we have conceptualized culture primarily as a static structure embodying rules, norms, positions, rituals, and so on. The culture-structure is seen as exerting transmission-like force on the individuals within it. Our understanding of cultures focuses on differences in these structures, which results have shown are at best modest and at worst highly changeable.

A THEORETICAL IMPLEMENTATION OF THE GAP IDEA

In order to illustrate how the ideas presented above apply to the study of communication, particularly cross-cultural communication, a specific implementation of the gap idea will be described. The implementation presented is called the Sense-Making approach (Dervin, 1983b, 1989b; Dervin & Nilan, 1986). It is a microlevel implementation. However, the resulting theorizings and observings are not limited to the microlevel.

The most fundamental assumption of the Sense-Making approach has to do with the locus of communicative essence. While Sense-Making assumes there is no "neutral" observing (i.e., observing that is time, space, and mind-free), human observing is not seen as capricious nor is variation in human observing seen as necessarily cacophonous. At different moments in time and space, communicating entities arrive at different understandings of reality. Reducing the cacophony of individuality requires, however, abandoning the current conceptualization of the individual as a state entity—*the* individual. Rather, in the Sense-Making formulation, the individual is the constructing, creating, sometimes repeating carrier of communicatings—the maker of ideas of situations, the doer of communicating moves. The strategies of situation-defining, the tactics of communicating moves are the focus of attention—the *hows* of communicating. Sense-Making assumes that it is from this entry point that we can as a field begin to make progress in reducing the cacophony we now find in heterogeneity.

In the Sense-Making formulation, communicating consists of in-the-head as well as physical acts of gap-bridging (making ideas, using strategies, connecting sources, choosing words, etc.). Since no moment in time-space has ever occurred exactly in the same form before, given no constraining conditions, the communicating entity (e.g., the culture or individual in the culture) is capable of responding to new aspects of a situation as well as to those aspects seen as equivalent to elements of old situations. Even when constraining conditions exist, they exist in a specific moment in time and space. Thus, communicating is conceptualized as situated both in time and space. Communicating is seen as situated in at least four senses. It is enmeshed in structures; occurring at specific moments in time-space; anchored on a time line linked to the past; and conceived by humans capable of constructing and utilizing historical sense.

The focus mandated above suggests that the "essence" of the communicating moment is best addressed by determining how the actors in the moment interpret that moment when conceptualized in gap terms and act to handle the gappiness of that moment. It is important to note here that this does not mandate an acceptance of purposive, coping, or linear models. Rather, facing and bridging gaps is conceptualized as human mandate—sometimes handled with robot-like repetitions of the past, sometimes by checking out or tuning out, sometimes by cyclical constructions, sometimes by making plans, sometimes by linear thinking.

Since the gap is essence, it can be assumed that the factors that will predict and explain communicating will themselves be derivations of the gap idea: That, for example, the ways in which actors see themselves as stopped in their situations will better predict their use of news, their information seeking, or their acceptance of external power than will across time-space descriptions of actors such as demography, personality, access, networks. However, anything that restrains or limits the freedom of the communicating entity will make it more likely that across time-space factors will predict and explain communicating behavior. Across time-space rigidity, found in a species assumed to be situationally responsive, is assumed then to be a special case of situatedness. Thus, for example, human use of communicating systems is highly constrained by resources so we would expect demography to predict channel use. What the entity makes of the symbolic material carried on the channel, however, is not necessarily likewise constrained.

Whether a given communicating entity (e.g., an individual in a culture or a culture) is constrained or free in a given situation is accounted for by some combination of how that entity constructs that situation and the forces that others exert on that situation. At a given moment in time, a communicating entity may be more or less "conscious" of internal and/or external constraints. The entity is assumed to be theoretically capable of such consciousness.

While the gap idea applies equally well to collective and individual entities, when implemented for the understanding of collective entities it is assumed that there is no collective mind. Rather, it is communicating that energizes the collectivity. Collective gap defining and gap facing are the complex result of individual communicatings. It is not assumed that the behavings of the collectivity are predictable or explainable solely based on some extrapolation of individual behavior. It is assumed, however, that individual communicatings have something to do with collective comunicatings, at a very minimum in the fact that a collectivity lacking a mind cannot act. Individuals act and the collective presence is produced communicatively.

The assumptions above are seen as applying to all situations that involve communicating. They are implemented in the Sense-Making approach with a simple metaphor applied to the individual: Assume a human being taking steps through situations; for each moment, a new step. Assume a moment of discontinuity in which step taking turns from a free-flowing journey to a stop in the road. Focus individuals on those moments of discontinuity. Determine how they define the gaps and act to bridge them. How do they see the situations that interrupt their journeys? How do they conceptualize the discontinuities as gaps? How do they bring to bear past experiences? How do they construct bridges over the gaps? How do they start their journeys again? How do they proceed after crossing? To what use or help do they put the bridge they built?

This abstract Sense-Making metaphor is seen as applying at all levels (e.g., intrapersonal, interpersonal, small group, organizational, mass, telecomm, or societal) and to all contexts (e.g., health, political, instructional, and developmental). It directs attention to the steps the actor takes as defined on his or her own terms to address the gaps faced as defined on his or her own terms. It can be used to focus on how individuals move when they see themselves as individually empowered as well as how they move when they see themselves as collectively enmeshed or entirely constrained. It allows a basis for focusing on both the constraining and freeing aspects of culture as well as the constraining and freeing aspects of individuality.

One example will illustrate many of these points. U.S. researchers expect to find differences in communication behaviors between subcultures, for example, ethnic groups. A series of Sense-Making studies (Dervin, 1983b) has set out to focus specifically on this issue—comparing subcultural differences in how respondents saw themselves as stopped in everyday situations; what questions they asked; and what sources they used to try to get answers. Interviewing approaches and content analyses have drawn on the central gap metaphor. The typical study has coded situation-defining in terms of whether the respondent saw self as stopped on a road with two or more roads ahead (decision), a barrier blocking the one road ahead (barrier), or one road ahead controlled by someone or something else (problematic). Question asking has typically been examined in terms of whether the gap implied by the respondent's most important question focused on a need to create ideas about events or objects (whats); skills, directions, and moves (hows); reasons and causes (whys); or timing (whens). Source use has been categorized in traditional terms: media, books, professionals, peer-kin network. All of these measures have been seen as tapping constructings: situation-defining, source-using, question-asking.

In the context of the above discussion, we would expect these studies to show ethnic differences in the kinds of gaps faced and in the communication channels used as information sources. The reason for this expectation is that both these behaviors are constrained by societal conditions. Race is an indicator of societal placement. As expected, across Sense-Making studies blacks have been more likely to report facing survival situations than whites and are more likely to report seeing these situations as problematic or barrier situations. They are less likely to use communication channels legitimized by the system and more likely to use their own countercultural networks.

Yet in the studies that have explicitly tested these ideas, even these societally constrained communicating behaviors can be related to the different strategies individuals used to define their situations. The results contrast markedly with traditional studies of the relationship of race to source-using behaviors, which have shown straightforward results: minorities use more entertainment media and interpersonal networks; whites use more newspapers and books. In Sense-Making studies there are frequently complex interactions between race and situation-defining suggesting that source using is responsive to subcultural group awareness of its positioning in society. A typical pattern suggests, for example, that minorities are more likely to reach out for "mainstream" informational input when situations impinging on them are seen as externally imposed. For other situations, however, culturally relevant sources are more useful.

When, however, these studies have focused on how individuals defined their information needs in their gap-bridging situations—behaviors less constrained by external conditions—race is no longer a significant predictor. Rather, situation-defining is the strong predictor across all studies. In the typical study, for example, respondents who saw themselves in decision situations, regardless of race, asked more what and how questions; those in barrier situations, more when questions; those in problematic situations, more why questions.

In this set of Sense-Making studies, then, entering into the data framing, collecting, and analysis from a dynamic gap perspective and conceptualizing individuals as carriers of gap-bridging allowed both subcultural and dynamic situational differences to emerge. Further, the results have directed attention to the communicative forces underlying subcultural relationships in society.

ADVANTAGE OF THE GAP IDEA FOR COMPARATIVE THEORY

The assumptions and implementations above are seen as moving toward a new kind of comparability—a comparability at a more abstract, more powerful level but at the same time a level more pertinent to specific moments in time-space. In terms of the fundamental problematic of comparative theory, the gap idea focuses on transcending elements that bear only artificial relationships to communicating (e.g., level of analysis, context as observer defined, or across time-space descriptors) in order to focus on and analyze elements that bear directly. In the exemplar presented here—Sense-Making— these elements are defined as the hows of communicating: for example, how actors see situations as stopping them, how they define gaps, devise strategies to bridge gaps, continue journeys, create ideas to bridge cognitive gaps, bring ideas of the past to bear on the present.

Because the gap approach aims for what is core and central across levels and contexts, it allows for meaningful comparisons to be made in all situations for which we now mandate comparative analyses. Cross-cultural examples of such comparative problematics include focusing on two cultures in one study, one culture when viewed by a researcher from another culture, one culture at different times, one culture in different contexts, one culture at different communicative levels, one culture when studied using different methodologies. In all cases, the relevant differences in cultures, in levels, in contexts, in discourses are not buried by focusing on the gap idea but rather allowed to emerge.

The emergence will take on a different character, however, displayed not only in terms of states and entities but dynamics and processes. In this formulation, communicating behaviors—dynamics—are an essential point of focus. This does not mean that there is no pattern in the communicating behaviors of individuals or cultures. Rather, a focus on communicating behaviors allows these patterns to emerge. Some of these patterns will be very changeable across time and space while others will be very rigid.

What is important about focusing on dynamics, however, is that such an analytic allows patterns—both responsive to changing conditions and rigidified across conditions—to emerge. This contrasts with our current analytics—implicit and explicit— which look at the entity and the entity's inputs and outputs and not how the entity got from here to there. If what is patterned about communicating is behavior, then searching for pattern in entities or states by comparing individuals or the groups to which they belong (i.e., cultures) will miss all but the most rigidified traces and simultaneously yield the kind of cacophony that now plagues our attempts to understand human heterogeneity.

The gap idea is suggested as an analytic that directs our attention to the general conditions to which process adheres. As such, the idea focuses on the hows of communicating and on the situatedness of these hows. This focus provides us an entry point for freeing comparative research from the trap of using one element being compared (e.g., culture) as a standard by which the other element(s) are defined and measured. In doing so, it provides an example of a framework that can potentially yield a more powerful comparative base.[1]

NOTES

1.   The author owes a debt to Carter (1980, 1989a, 1989b), Craig (1989), Geertz (1973), Giddens (1984, 1989), Habermas (1984, 1987b), Hall (1989), Krippendorff (1989), and Tehranian (1990) whose work have been enormously useful in developing the formulations presented here.

Chapter 5

Information ↔ Democracy:
An Examination of Underlying Assumptions

Brenda Dervin

THE INFORMATION ↔ DEMOCRACY NARRATIVE[1]

When we bring the two concepts "information resources" and "democracy" together, we become, wittingly or unwittingly, enmeshed in a widely accepted, weblike narrative based on these premises:[2]

- *That access to "good information" is critical for the working of "good democracy";*

- *that when information is allowed to flow freely in a free marketplace, "truth" or "the best information" naturally surfaces much like cream in fresh whole milk;*

- *that the value of "good information" is such that any rational person will seek it out and that, therefore, availability equals accessibility;*

- *that "good information" ought to be available to all citizens in a democracy, that there should be no information inequities; and*

- *that it is unfortunate that some citizens have fewer resources, and that we must there- fore provide means of access to "good information" for these citizens.[3]*

Taken together, these assumptions form a narrative with near-mythic cultural sta- tus. Maintaining and strengthening the assumed "free marketplace of ideas" has become both justification and excuse for all manner of social engineerings: the protection of an increased array of messages by the First Amendment; the call for the extension of the telecommunication network infrastructures to rural and impoverished areas; the distribu- tion of computers in low-income schools; the highly visible practices of recent presiden- tial candidates in courting the citizenry through devices with such historically rich and resonant names as "town meetings."[4] It is not the purpose of this chapter to suggest that

This work originally appeared as: Dervin, B. (1994). Information ↔ democracy: An examination of underlying assumptions. *Journal of the American Society for Information Science*, *45* (6), 369–385. (ERIC Document Reproduction Service No. EJ 488 232). Reprinted by permission of John Wiley & Sons, Inc.

any of these social actions are in themselves inappropriate, but rather to suggest that they are engendered based on unexamined assumptions and, thus, cannot when tested by the forces of power or expediency or necessity, sustain their reach for the well-meaning equities they envision. More generally, it is the purpose of this chapter to suggest that the set of unexamined assumptions—the narrative woven around normative views of the relationships between information ↔ democracy—are based on other unexamined assumptions, assumptions about the nature of information and the nature of communication.[5]

It is the purpose of this chapter to unpack the set of premises that constitute the information ↔ democracy narrative by examining the foundational ontological and epistemological assumptions on which the narrative rests. Alternative sets of assumptions will be set forth and the current assumptions will be reexamined in terms of the consequences of operating under one or another set of assumptions for the design of information/communication systems serving democracy. In the ensuing discussion, it is the term "information" not the term "democracy" that is problematized.[6] Throughout most of the chapter the term "democracy" is taken in its most general sense as applying to collectively produced actions and/or policies, in any setting, designed in some way by constituent members, either directly or through mediation by representation.

A further caveat on the following discussion is required: The rapid spread of new communication technologies into every aspect of human life has permitted monetary resources to be sped across the globe electronically, reconceptualized as information. This conceptualization of information, which assuredly has relevance for the discussions at hand, is not included as an aspect of the discussions. However, whether we are informed—you and I—about how these new financial arrangements work and whether as a result we reconceptualize our own finances or challenge these arrangements are examples of some of the kinds of "informational" concerns which this chapter is intended to address.[7]

SIX SETS OF UNDERLYING ASSUMPTIONS

The discussion of normative and alternative assumptions as presented here is necessarily brief; six different versions of underlying assumptions, presented in Table 5.1, in six rows.

The purpose of Table 5.1 is to give us a framework for examining the ontological and epistemological assumptions underlying the information ↔ democracy narrative. To do this, a set of six stereotypes are drawn from a variety of literatures.[8] Each stereotype consists of a set of ontological assumptions (about the nature of reality and the nature of human beings); epistemological assumptions (about the nature of knowing and the standard of judgment for defining the results as informative and, thus, calling it "information"); the ideological bridge (how power enters the equation); and shorthand label(s) for the stereotype.[9] Table 5.1 also suggests that the six sets of assumptions are

TABLE 5.1

A selection of six different stereotyped sets of ontological and epistemological assumptions underlying discussions on the information↔democracy relationship

Stereotypic label	Ontological assumptions		Epistemological assumptions		Ideological bridge	Chronology
	Reality	Human beings	Knowing	Standard of judgment		
authority dogma positivism-accused	orderly fixed continuous	orederly fixed conscious	isomorphic and universal	none needed truth assumed	open bridge	earliest presence in literature
naturalism empiricism positivism	orderly fixed continuous	tendency to: disorderliness decentered unconscious	tendency to: constraint bias error	accuracy expert standard	expert authority as judged within episteme	
cultural relativity	orderly fixed continuous	orderly centered conscious within cultures	isomorphic and universal within cultures	none needed, within cultures	authority, as appointed within cultures	
constructivism	orderly fixed continuous	orderly centered conscious within each person	constructed by each person	none needed, each person is own standard	personal authority	
postmodernism poststructuralism postparadigmatic	chaotic floating discontinuous	chaotic decentered unconscious	chaotic no systematic knowing possible	none possible	open bridge power inherent in *all discourse *the episteme	
communitarian dialogic verbings	orderly fixed continuous and chaotic floating discontinuous	orderly centered conscious and chaotic decentered unconscious	constructed and deconstructed by structure, culture, person in mediation and struggle	recursivities consequentialities contiquities intersubjectivities	power, bracketed power, exposed	most recent presence in literature

laid out in a rough chronological order from assumptions with earliest presence in our episteme to those most recently emerging.

In this fashion, the six different "stereotypes" are presented: (a) authority, (b) naturalism, (c) cultural relativity, (d) constructivism, (e) postmodernism, and (f) communitarianism. These positions are presented deliberately as "stereotypes," in the manner of Weber's (1963) ideal-types, representing no single position but rather a conceptual pastiche of approaches often referred to by stereotypical labels. Scholarly discussions of philosophic assumptions are rarely if ever framed in terms of one of these stereotypes. On the other hand, it is fair to say that secondary sources often reify the approaches in these stereotypical ways. In this sense, the stereotypes presented here may be said to be more stereotypical of positions rather than by positions.

Further, if one tried to identify the perfect exemplar for each stereotype in the literature, it would be impossibly challenging in two senses. First, the elements of any scholarly project—the assumptions, the substantive discussions, the empirical forays— rarely fit together in one time, not to mention across time, without strain. Second, the attempt to find exemplars would yield instead a geodesic dome of possibilities—the six rows and seven columns and some 30 different concepts in Table 5.1 thrown into space with lines of connections forged between each combination somewhere by someone.

The purpose in presenting six stereotypes is to extend our reach beyond the usual dualistic discussions of these issues that one finds in the literature, where, for example, absolutist assumptions regarding information are pitted against constructivist, or constructivist assumptions are pitted against the postmodern. The purpose is also to suggest that there are complexities to this discussion that cannot be captured here. However, by marking our examination in terms of six major disjunctures (albeit stereotyped) we can get a better picture of the variety of positions being brought to bear on these issues.

Order Versus Chaos—The Fault Line

The primary organizing concepts in Table 5.1 rotate around a central dualism—order versus chaos. Recent discussions of communication and information processes in all fields are peppered with dualisms. It might be said that dualistic argument is the primary rhetorical strategy of our time. Among the many dualisms to which we attend, all of them relevant to the discussion at hand, are: structure versus agency, individual versus situation, qualitative versus quantitative, normative versus critical, modernity versus postmodernity, diversity versus homogeneity, science versus humanities, subject versus object, local versus global, and contextual versus universal.[10]

For purposes of this chapter, it is assumed that one particular dualism is foundational to the others—order versus chaos. Further, it is assumed that the ricocheting of our models between concepts of order and concepts of chaos poses the greatest challenge to our conceptions of information and, thus, of the information ↔ democracy relationship. If, for example, the most radical postmodern ideas are accepted, then the concept of information as implied in the information ↔ democracy narrative is destabilized and the narrative falls into disarray.

For this reason, Table 5.1 is ordered primarily by focusing on issues of order versus chaos and how they are conceptualized in various ontological and epistemological positions. Furthermore, in line with Hayles's (1990) portrayal of both the sciences and humanities in the last half of this century as destabilized by the order-chaos dichotomy, Table 5.1 is developed on the assumption that this destabilization and the dialectical discourses surrounding it drives our movement from row 1 assumptions to row 6 assumptions, with each successive row modifying and contesting those preceding. Hayles encapsulates this view succinctly when she calls the destabilization of the order-chaos dichotomy—a central dichotomy in Western thought—a "major fault line . . . in the episteme" (p. 16), one that has a magnetlike attraction and that therefore points to places of pervasive contradiction and contest in scholarly literatures.

The Ideological Bridge

Finally, before proceeding with the discussions of the six sets of assumptions, a note is in order on the column in Table 5.1 labeled as the "ideological bridge." As used here, ideology refers to modes of thought which stem from, and conceal, social contradictions.[11] Most discussions of ideology, informed as they are by classical Marxist thought, anchor themselves primarily in examinations of economic structures and the forces they exert on the constitution of daily life. In contrast, the discussion here tries to ferret out how the spaces left by different ontological and epistemological assumptions allow the forces of power, however defined, to build bridges—platforms from which to exert force. While usual discussions might ask, for example, how an ideology focused on the reification of an uncontrolled capitalism might use a particular ontological or epistemological view to serve its end, this discussion asks how a particular ontological-epistemological view lays itself open to this cooptation.

In asking this question, this chapter is concerned with two dimensions of ideology. One of these is the question of who gets to decide what reality is called: in Freire's (1970) terms, who names the world. The second dimension is more subtle and elusive and focuses on the principles and criteria embedded in rules, procedures, and other institutional forms. Here, in the domain of taken-for-granted institutional forms, power more often runs silently and unrecognized (Shields, personal communication, September 23, 1993).

When this discussion is applied to the design and implementation of information/communication systems, it involves the naming, designing, and maintaining of every aspect and nuance (apparent or hidden, of recent origin or lost in antiquity) of the collection, storage, retrieval, and dissemination of whatever that system (and the society in which it is embedded) calls information.

Authority

The row 1 assumptions labeled "authority," "dogma," and "positivism-accused" are conceptualized for this chapter as the most pervasive and persistent assumptions underlying the information ↔ democracy narrative.[12] Authority is defined, in *Webster's New World Dictionary*, as the power to command, enforce, decide. Dogma, traditionally defined as the formulation of belief based on the scriptures (Owen, 1967, p. 410), is used in the more generally accepted meaning, again per *Webster's*, of any belief or opinion. The use of positivism-accused is explained below.

In this version of the narrative, information is conceptualized as statements with truth value arising from isomorphic knowings about an orderly, fixed, and continuous reality emitted by orderly, centered, and conscious human beings. Ontologically, the sense-of-being implied by the narrative is that there is a reality "out there" that is fixed and continuous—definite entities exist in definite places with definite patterns of relationships that transcend moments in time-space. This fixedness and continuity is captured in something called "information." Setting aside the issue of how reality gets captured in "information," it can be logically concluded that any such "information" must be instructive about the nature of reality, it must point to what is real, and therefore, it must reduce the uncertainty in reality. This reasoning is a fundamental aspect of the use of statistical metaphors which depict information as uncertainty reduction, even though statistical approaches to uncertainty were developed for a far different problematic.[13] Information, in this sense is whatever reduces uncertainty. The more information, the better; the reduction of all uncertainty is the implied goal.

From this perspective, the human's willingness and ability to observe reality and accept information is unquestioned. In an ironic way, observing is not even questioned. The assumptions do not leave room for any kind of gap between the observer and the observed so a conceptualization of knowing is in fact extraneous to the discussion. Given the nature of these assumptions—ordered world, ordered observers, ordered information—any human who did not seek to secure information could certainly be described as seriously out-of-touch.

Using these assumptions, a standard for judging information would be unnecessary—observation should produce good information. Good information should be informative. With all citizens so informed, the collective should operate better. The information distribution problem becomes one of mere transportation and availability. If transportation and availability are privately controlled and economic systems marginalize some people, alternative mechanisms can be found to offset these unfortunate inequities.

It is important not to cast attention to row 1 assumptions aside too hastily as too out of date. As Giddens (1989) emphasizes, while positivism has become ". . . sort of a scare term" (p. 53) and few scientists exist that would now call themselves positivists, if we examine the purposive use of the terms "dogma," "positivism-accused," and "authority" in row 1, we can capture the intended flavor. While the term *positivism* was first used to designate the scientific method, it came to designate a powerful philosophic movement in the Western world whose ". . . characteristic theses . . . are that science is the only valid knowledge and facts the only possible objects of knowledge" (Abbagnano, 1967, p. 414). As a scientific philosophy, positivism has been outdated since the 1920s. However, the term has come to stand as a stereotypical label for any practice of what might be called *dogmatic science*, based on an ontological realism with little or no philosophic or material intercourse with the environment beyond its confines.

In actuality, the issue of what comprises knowledge within science has been the subject of enormous and continuing philosophical and methodological debate. And, as Hayles (1990) demonstrates, it is possible to argue that science itself has as much of a stake in the move away from positivist theories as have the various branches of the humanities. In Hayles's terms, the move is part of the fracture in the episteme.

However, when it comes to what might be called an ideology of science in the world of practice and policy, the philosophic arguments and even the elaborate corrective mechanisms of science within its own ontological-epistemological frame are often left behind. The evidence is seen in current contests between calls for tolerance and acceptance of diversity, on the one hand, and totalizing beliefs anchored in prejudice and dogma (including a modern version of dogma—the mindless application of unexamined "findings" generated by a brute or misused science), on the other.

The important point here is that row 1 assumptions incorporate neither concepts of diversity nor error nor chaos. By implication, any voice that is not authorial is in error and chaos. In such an ontologized arena, the ideological bridge—where power plays its role— is entirely open. Epistemology—the question of knowing—is in effect a moot question. Power does not have to make a space for its exertion or protect a space once made.

In the context of assumptions anchored in ontological completeness, there is no procedural or even philosophic role for compromise, negotiation, intersubjectivity, or dialogue. Some kind of external standard must be brought to bear to eliminate difference. In the context of row 1 assumptions, power will necessarily be whatever force is largest and loudest and has been around the longest. In this worldview, authority as the source of ontological truth is unquestioned. There is no basis for questioning in the theoretic assumptions.

The homogenizing of difference can, of course, be accomplished in overt as well as covert ways. One of the difficulties of the free marketplace of ideas narrative is that it assumes that power is either nonexistent or is obvious. However, when power is assumed to be at least in part hidden, and to have at least in part an interest in being hidden, then it does not readily follow that open exchange will reveal it. Our most recent understandings of the play of power in human affair suggests we must consider the possibility that power works in pervasive and myriad ways—in the very ontological and epistemological worlds of our times, in the discourses by which we constitute and by which we are constituted, in the values we apply to judging appropriateness, in the design of our communication/information systems, and in the procedures we call democratic.

Naturalism

Row 2 of Table 5.1 has the stereotypical labels of "naturalism" and "positivism."[14] *Naturalism* refers to an approach that assumes ". . . whatever exists or happens is *natural* [sic] in the sense of being susceptible to explanation through methods which, although paradigmatically exemplified in the natural sciences, are continuous from domain to domain of objects and events" (Wollheim, 1967, p. 448, emphasis in original). *Positivism*, defined in the preceding section, implies an extension of scientific ideas to the study of society and an emphasis in that context on facts as the only valid objects of knowledge (Abbagano, 1967). Both naturalism and positivism are offshoots of empiricism— ". . . the theory that experience rather than reason is the source of knowledge" (Hamlyn, 1967, p. 499).

The importance of presenting these definitions is not to anchor our discussions in any essential view of what naturalism is or is not but rather to give us a starting point for examining row 2 assumptions. The dominant scientific approach to the social sciences in the United States for at least the last half-century has been a naturalistic empiricism based on beliefs that science should generate the same kind of knowledge of the social and psychological world that it has been assumed science generates of the physical and natural world.[15] Implementing these beliefs has typically involved an elaborate set of methods—for example, operationalization, reliability and validity checks, use of reproducibility standards—to identify and control sources of so-called errors, biases, and constraints. In line with their ontological assumptions, these social scientific beliefs have also incorporated narrow views of the potential relationships that might be observed in reality, limiting the possibilities to what can be modeled by using causality statistics that are assumed to map reality in isomorphic ways.[16]

What is most definitive about row 2 is that it is here that epistemology begins to take on a major role. The important change between row 1 and row 2 assumptions is that in row 2 our human is conceptualized as being something less than an orderly, centered, conscious observer. Knowing becomes potentially biased, constrained, and erroneous. Introduced is the idea, widely accepted in the social sciences and in common parlance, that not all humans see the same things when they observe and that some humans are "better" observers than others. For example, in this context, it is assumed that humans have physiological limitations, both as a species (e.g., humans cannot hear some sounds dogs can) and as individuals (e.g., some people are nearsighted). It is also assumed that there are psychological limitations (e.g., the selectivity processes well-known to social psychology: selective attention, retention, and recall) and psychoanalytic limitations (e.g., illusions and delusions).

Using the "orderly-humans" assumptions of row 1, the human is conceptualized as an open and waiting receptacle for information; with the "propensity-toward-disorderliness" assumptions of row 2, the human is conceptualized as a potentially faulty receptacle, either leaky (with holes that information somehow leaks through) or recalcitrant (with stubborn lid that refuses to open either because of self-interest or disinterest). In either case, it is assumed that there is much misinformation about. Therefore the marketplace of ideas must be kept free so that "truth" (good information) will surface in open exchange and argument. Drawing on a long heritage dating back to Plato, it is assumed that truth will emerge in the clash of ideas.[17] Likewise, in this context, it is assumed that some humans can be made more orderly by education and training. Accuracy of observation becomes the implied standard for judging information value and expert authority takes on collateral.

Also, at this point another metaphor emerges that is applied pervasively to discussions of information ↔ democracy: the metaphor of the manufacture and transportation (transmission) of information. In this idealized scenario, the best (least-distorting) human observers collect good observations—called information—which are then sent via various means to other humans. Again, we are still assuming that information captures something real and instructive with universal applicability about reality. Within the context of such an assumption, it must likewise be assumed that all reasonable humans will be eager to possess information.

The ideological bridge in row 2 is similar to that in row 1, but with a slight difference. Here, power must put forth credentials of accuracy and expertise. In order for power to put forth credentials, the standards for judging expertise must be widely accepted. This is an important difference between row 1 and row 2. In row 1, power—whether benign or brutal—is more likely to be materially derived from heritage or strength. In row 2, power is as likely to be interpretively derived. This requires wide acceptance of similar standards and values, and commensurate investments by power in the development and maintenance of symbolically based hegemonies. This has implications for the design of information/communication systems. With historicized power, the authorial voice is sufficient; with expert power, the authorial voice must invoke procedures and structures which confer the right to speak based on expertise. With this turn, the definition of good information in the information ↔ democracy narrative must necessarily reify not only particular observers but particular modes of observing. What is introduced is the possibility of inflexible methodologies for the design and implementation of communication/information systems—methodologies which outlive and transcend any particular human observer or human source of power.

Cultural Relativity

While the introduction of the ideas of bias and constraint in observing in the "naturalism" stereotype point toward at least a theoretic acceptance of diversity, the retention of assumptions of a complete ontology and the ideal of an orderly human required that the idea of accuracy—a new kind of authority—be introduced. In effect, this still privileges a single voice. Yet, perhaps the dominant characteristic of our experience of the last century has been the continuing rise in the variety and volume of voices of difference which refuse to accept externally imposed standards. In terms of the information ↔ democracy narrative, there have been two different alterations introduced. One of these still essentially (and ironically) upholds the basic narrative; the second begins to topple it to the ground.

Upholding the narrative is the set of assumptions detailed in row 3 of Table 5.1—labeled "cultural relativity." In essence, it duplicates row 1 with one essential difference: Culture is privileged and order is seen as sensible only within or relative to cultures.[18] Our human observers are now embedded in cultural discourses and their observations constitute and are constituted by this embeddedness. Observations have only contextual, cultural generalizability and the standard for judgment is still an external standard anchored in that context. Reality is still seen as fixed and continuous, but bounded within its own context and time-place. This applies not just to making sense of the social world, but of the natural and physical worlds as well. The result is a mandate for pluralistic participation, with each constituent group in the plurality adhering to its own standard. This set of assumptions is a major impetus of the original call for a "New World Information Communication Order" and for the rebirth of that call in recent months.[19]

In this set of assumptions, we begin to see a fracture, a destabilization, of the tautological tidiness of the assumptions in rows 1 and 2, which so cleanly uphold the prevalent information ↔ democracy narrative. On the surface, it appears as if the different viewpoints arising from different contexts have something to share with each other. But since each is anchored in an assumption that its version of fixed and continuous reality is the one reality, no amount of well-meaning acceptance of difference will allow the different constituent pluralities to travel anywhere together where differences require comprehension or amelioration. There is neither an agreed-upon allegiance to an external standard nor a procedural capacity for compromise and negotiation; these flexibilities are not required by the ontological basis of the assumptions.

What is most interesting about row 3 assumptions is that, in fact, they revert to a nonepistemological view of information. Cultural difference is a sufficient explanation and within cultures homogeneity is assumed. Hence, the ideological bridge is open to power, in whatever form of authority the culture mandates. Since authority mandated in one culture is not necessarily mandated in another, the ideological bridge is open across cultures unless one culture has the upper hand. This is, of course, the challenge made by those who point to the far-reaching impacts of Western media on virtually all citizens of the world.[20]

In the context of such assumptions we have seen highly contested anthropological descriptions of cultures emerge: for example, emergent feminist voices in a culture challenging the authorial male voice.[21] For the information ↔ democracy narrative, this row of assumptions requires that attention be paid to differences in the information needs and seeking of different cultural groups. However, the narrative has no way of philosophically, thus, theoretically, handling incommensurability between cultures. Furthermore, this version of the narrative is prone to infinite regress as each new group steps forth to claim status as a culture and demands its share.

Constructivism

With row 4—the constructivism perspective—the emphasis on order in the information ↔ democracy narrative faces its most serious challenge. The move from cultural relativity to personal relativity assumes that each person constructs understandings of the world in interaction with her or his own symbolic, social, natural, and physical worlds. In the stereotyped version presented here, we find an orderly reality and an orderly human with each individual human conceptualized as different. When pushed to these stereotyped extremes, the assumptions make any kind of information-based approach to democracy impossible. The juxtaposition of overbearing individual uniquenesses, bound in an orderly personal context, makes any kind of procedural negotiation logically unnecessary.[22]

Theoretically, with such a set of assumptions no standard of judgment for knowing is necessary beyond each individual. In an ironic way, this set of assumptions reverts back to a wide-open ideological bridge. It implies that personal authority will be the exerted power, but since power dynamics do not work through atomized individuals, this view in fact leaves the way open for the forces of power anywhere and everywhere. It is often suggested that this set of assumptions is particularly attractive in the United States where our liberal democratic ideas have privileged individual over collective action and have mythologized that privilege as the pervasive Horatio Alger myth, where power is often assumed to be either nonexistent or plainly visible. One often sees this assumption operating in information technology studies where a single incident of up-by-the-bootstraps success (e.g., a poor citizen finding help over a computer network) is reified as if it stood for persistent and enduring systemic change.

Postmodernism

While on the surface it might seem that the row 5 stereotype—postmodernism—presents a sterner challenge to assumptions of order than those in row 4, in fact row 5 assumptions are no test at all. Instead, they abandon the possibility of any kind of systematic knowing.[23] Here, we have chaotic reality, chaotic humans, chaotic knowing, and no possible universal standard of judgment.

Different postmodern/poststructural theorists employ these assumptions in different ways so it is more useful to talk of postmodernisms than postmodernism. Most theorize that all knowing—all information—is defined by and within an episteme and the discourse of that episteme. Ontology as a central question is thus, in some senses, set aside. Rather, ontological reality is assumed to be manifest solely through interpretation—through discourse. There is no direct route to reality nor any methodological correction for indirect routes, as offered, for example, by some constructivists and some phenomenologists. Humans, when centered and ordered, are made so within and by the episteme. Humans are naturally chaotic, decentered, and unconscious.[24]

While the term "postmodernism" and its frequent companions "poststructuralism" and "postparadigmatic" are used in a bewildering variety of contexts with a bewildering variety of meanings, for our purposes the thrust of the movement is its intent on destabilizing all sources of truth, all grand narratives, whether assumed to be created by God, or science, or the enlightened reasoning human being.[25] In an extreme version, the deconstruction called for by many labeled as postmodernists/poststructuralists warns us that ". . . nothing, whether deed, word, thought or text, ever happens in relation . . . to anything that precedes, follows, or exists elsewhere, but only as a random event whose power . . . is due to the randomness of its occurrence" (deMan, 1979, p. 69).

If such a set of assumptions were used to construct a social world (a project which could be challenged as a contradiction to the very premises of many postmodernists), in such a deontologized world, there would be no ideological bridge—no places where power could get a hold—for it would be acknowledged that all systematic modes of knowing are capricious impositions.[26] On one hand, it would be assumed that no standard of judgment for knowing is possible; on the other, it would be assumed that if we find anything that might be called systematic knowing, power has been the sole standard used. One of the main thrusts of the postmodern project has been to deconstruct the discourses that encapsulate power, to unravel the episteme. Thus, while ideally, in a postmodern world no power could gain a footing, postmodernists typically posit power in practice as operating everywhere, in all discourse, and therefore in all systems which pretend to elicit and share anything called information. In essence, anything that orders human affairs is assumed to be imposed.

It is important to mention that the row 5 assumptions are presented, as were those above, as a stereotype—more what is said of postmodern positions rather than by postmodern positions. However, as a stereotype, it is a useful stopping point for it displays the consequences of the interplay of tensions, particularly within and between rows 3 and 4. With each step down the rows in Table 5.1, we move away from totalizing views of order, and therefore, of information. If, however, it turns out that cultural relativity is merely another kind of totalizing perspective heralding a never-ending clash within and between cultures, and if constructivism descends into overbearing solipsism or capricious tyranny with no communicative mandate, then what is left? Some would assert: only the postmodern abyss of total chaos.[27]

But this is a far too facile stereotype for there is another theme here as well. In row 5—postmodernism—we have the first genuine introduction of an acceptance of a chaotic, decentered, unconscious human.[28] Row 2—naturalism—identified the tendency but did not accept it as a proper state of being. Row 3—cultural relativity—suggests it by alleging that people differ across cultures, but does not handle the difficulty of differences within cultures, and therefore does not fundamentally deal with difference. Row 4—constructivism—points to the possibility but in fact deals primarily with the difficulties of understanding how humans know, given the constructivist view of human beings conceptualized as conscious, centered, and orderly, albeit different from each other in potentially infinite ways.

One way in which the projects of the various postmodernist theorists can be understood is in their calls for social theories to incorporate theories of the subject that allow humans to be seen as less cognitive, less centered, less purposive, less conscious than theories which have their roots in naturalism. They reconceptualize the reach of power from that which constrains our material, informational, and symbolic worlds to that which interrupts and disturbs as well our very decenteredness. In this sense, postmodern projects provide a useful challenge as we attempt to move out of an episteme that privileges order toward an episteme that privileges chaos as well.

Communitarianism

There are a variety of communitarian perspectives emerging in the literature. Most of these are, in fact, derived from of a combination of cultural relativity, constructivist, and postmodernist positions. Most are focused in some way on the idea that it is in communication that humans make and unmake order, self, community, and society and that it is only through adopting deliberately communitarian perspectives that there is any hope for peace and justice in the world.[29]

There are, in fact, relatively few communitarian perspectives offered in the literature and we can in no way suggest that it is possible to extract a stereotype as such. Instead, this discussion will rely heavily on the communitarian position that is emerging in the development of the Sense-Making approach, which calls for a methodological refocusing of attention in attempts to understand the nature of information/communication processes from entities and states to processes and dynamics; from nouns to verbs; and from noun*ings* to verb*ings*.[30] It is argued that these moves are necessary in any communication theory of information/communication processes. Further, it is proposed that communication theorizing is essential if we are to find a way out of the dualistic traps inherent in the row 1 to 5 assumptions. The stiltedness of the terms "nounings" and "verbings" all the more reinforces a fundamental assumption—that all modes of theorizing information are consciously or unconsciously procedural.

In essence, this communitarian position formally incorporates both order and chaos as ontological and epistemological assumptions. It assumes both construction and deconstruction as aspects of knowing. It assumes that the standard for judgment of knowing focuses on recursivities, consequences, contiguities, and intersubjectivities rather than external immutable standards. It assumes that knowing is made and remade, reified and maintained, challenged and destroyed in communication: in dialogue, contest, and negotiation. In contrast to the other positions, it focuses on hows, rather than whos and whats.

The position proposed in row 6 is one which accepts that humans sometimes implement assumptions of an orderly reality with useful outcomes, but also that the imposition of this as a universal assumption defies experiential and scientific understandings of the nature of human affairs. Chaos, accident, necessity, and contingency are as useful, in some circumstances more useful, explanations of events in both the natural and social worlds as are mechanisms, systems, and causalities. All explanations are assumed to be assumptions—potentially useful fictions—and the question is what different assumptions allow in terms of actions and possibilities. Notice that this approach does not negate any way of knowing on essentialist grounds, even totalizing modes of knowing. Rather it acknowledges that both the knowing and the standards of testing the knowing are made and contested in communication. Further, in assuming both ontological as well as epistemological incompleteness, it provides not only epistemological justification for a view of democracy as made in communication but an ontological mandate as well. An epistemological mandate merely requires tolerance of difference; an ontological mandate suggests interdependency. It is in this way, in particular, that the communitarianism perspective goes beyond the constructivist assumptions of row 4.

The most significant aspect of row 6 is the introduction of the privileging of process. It is assumed that by focusing on the process by which humans individually and collectively make and unmake both order and chaos a basis for systematic study can begin to emerge out of what has been a dysfunctional ricochet (as exhibited in rows 1 through 5 of Table 5.1) between order versus chaos. In this sense, this perspective incorporates all the perspectives which preceded it. Each element becomes a verb in a set of verbings: the hows by which humans make and remake order and chaos. Among the verbs: factizing, reasoning, observing, truthing, totalizing, challenging, averaging, exampling, authorizing, culturizing, evidencing, generalizing, personalizing, imagining, experiencing, resisting, relating, picturing, trusting, centering, decentering, and so on. This particular set of verbings is listed here without any particular order in order to emphasize the enormous gap between noun conceptualizations (nounings) and verb conceptualizations (verbings). There are, of course, a host of attendant concerns in making this conceptual move, such as breaking down conceptions of situation as a concept frozen in a particular time-space, and breaking down conceptions of people as different only between each other and not within themselves.

Acknowledging the incompleteness of this presentation, the important point here is the call for reconceptualizing how information is made, reified, and challenged—a call for reconceptualizing by enlarging, by encompassing all prior perspectives into a view allowing a more comprehensive vision of human possibilities—possibilities realized, destroyed, restrained, and envisioned; possibilities that comes to good ends and those that come to bad.

Presented in this way, the communitarian perspective opens itself up to the possibility of utopian perspectives. Some might set the approach aside for this reason, as if utopian perspectives are theoretically unuseful. To do so is to operate with far too narrow a definition of theory. Utopian perspectives can become a framework to work within and toward. In this context, the ideological bridge offered to power in the communitarian perspective is either one of bracketed authority or disclosed authority. What this suggests is the possibility that power can be made a central focus of attention, either by bracketing (i.e., deliberately setting it aside) or disclosing (i.e., incorporating postmodernist deconstructing along with modernist constructing into the informational frame).

INFORMATION ↔ DEMOCRACY REDEFINED

In its purest form, the information ↔ democracy narrative rests on some combination of row 1 and 2 assumptions in Table 5.1. In essence, the key assumptions of the narrative are built on a framework which assumes an orderly universe peopled by humans who are ideally at least orderly as well. In such a world, it can be assumed that a free marketplace of ideas would allow good information to surface—good information defined as that which is most isomorphic to reality. In such a world, it can be assumed that rational people will and must seek good information for it is only by being so instructed on the nature of the real world that they can act effectively and properly within it. In such a world, it can be assumed that the theoretic difficulties introduced by poverty where some citizens have fewer resources and thus less access to good information can be corrected merely by improving resources and availability. In such a world, it can be assumed that the systems that collect, store, and retrieve information are equally useful from person to person. Availability will therefore be accessibility.

Of course, we see many practical and policy implementations which employ row 3–4 assumptions as corrections on row 1–2 assumptions. One such correction is to posit that some citizens lack access to information resources. This presents an obvious paradox: if some citizens lack access to information, this contradicts the basic premise of the information ↔ democracy narrative, which assumes that availability is universal and that availability equals accessibility. There should be no need for such corrections.

The design of information/communication collection, storage, retrieval, and delivery systems which account for the needs of different cultural groups is another such correction, seen, for example, in the attempts by presidential candidates to hold town meetings in different ethnic neighborhoods, the attempts by media and information systems to assure that representatives of diverse ethnic origin are involved in collecting and processing information, and the creative uses of new technologies to allow system users more entry points for searching information structures.

The difficulty with such corrections is that they assume that the order of the world as given by systems (e.g., in the categorizing and observing systems of media, academics, and libraries) exhausts the important possibilities. They assume that finding order is the primary focus of information use and, thus, exclude alternatives such as creating, resisting, and deconstructing order. Further, the corrections embody the relevant differences between people and cultures as static categorizations into ethnic/cultural and other group memberships which are assumed to have ontologically isomorphic status. If difference cannot be tapped by these frameworks, it is left untapped, for it is, in effect, assumed to be irrelevant. There is no mandated reflexivity that would allow, for example, for emergent or silenced voices to speak.

Taking the last problem as an example for further elaboration: Studies show that when it comes to information and communication behaviors, diversities within cultures are as great or greater than those between cultures. The lack of theoretic fit between assumptions, as outlined above, and practice can be seen when attempts are made to account for the needs of smaller and smaller subsets of cultural groups—for example, young female Hispanics. As a theoretic principle which provides potential guidance for information delivery and system design, this is almost as useless as no guidance at all. Evidence suggests that very little variance in information seeking and use is accounted for by such externally imposed categorizations of people. And, even if such categorizations were useful, a mere 20 cultural-demographic characteristics, given only two values each, would yield more than one million different possible design structures.

There are also what we would call row 4 (constructivist) corrections applied to the core information ↔ democracy assumptions. Examples would include efforts to adapt information services to the specific needs and worldviews of individual users and patrons. Typically, such efforts involve mediaries trained to empathize with users. There are two difficulties with this approach when generated solely from within row 4 assumptions. One is that reality is still assumed to be orderly in and of itself; the knowings that humans construct are what vary. Without any kind of theoretical link between ontological and epistemological assumptions, we are left with the conclusion that individuality is overbearingly unique. This solipsism is no more amenable to the idea of systematic design than, in fact, is the postmodern position. We necessarily conclude that individuality is chaos and system is order and the former must give way to the later.

Such theorizings can perpetuate practices that lead to problems such as mediary burnout. In the absence of any guiding theory of individuality other than its sheer existence and diversity, the presence of individuality places an inordinate demand on human resources. A major difficulty with this approach—when seen from the perspective of row 6—is that there is no theory of the hows of constructing activity.[31] Further, there is no ontological mandate for dialogue, negotiation, contest.

The discussion above suggests that attempts to implement both row 3 (cultural relativity) and row 4 (constructivist) assumptions, as corrections for the totalizing forces of row 1 and 2 assumptions, face internal contradictions. Lacking accompanying theoretical premises that assist in dealing with emergent and persistent diversity, the only remaining alternatives are either a retreat to row 1 and 2 assumptions or a collapse into row 5 assumptions. From the perspective of the design and implementation of information systems for democracy, retreat is preferred, because row 5 assumptions require that the exercise be altogether abandoned.

What are the potential consequences if we retain row 1 and 2 assumptions with the occasional need to resort to row 3 and 4 assumptions? A potential set of consequences is suggested by taking a vantage point from within row 6 assumptions. In essence, we are asking: What if it is more useful to assume that humans are both orderly and disorderly, but we pretend they are only orderly? What if it is more useful to assume that reality is both orderly and chaotic, but we pretend it is only orderly? What if it is more useful to assume that knowing consists of both constructings and deconstructings but we only examine the constructings? What if it is more useful to assume that knowing occurs in mediation and struggle but we pretend it results from independent and isomorphic observings, albeit constrained or potentially biased? What if knowing is more usefully assessed based on recursivities and contiguities, but we pretend it requires standards of truth and essentialisms? What if it is more useful to assume that power exerts forces on information processes at all levels and of all kinds, but we pretend power is either non-existent or self-evident?

The most comprehensive answer to these questions for the purposes of this chapter is to conclude that in effect everyone is information poor, not just those who seem to lack access by current standards. In this framework, the very fabric of our information world would be built on premises too narrow for the richness, complexity, and elusiveness suggested by the alternative assumptions. A brief list of possible consequences follows:

   • *Diversity is necessarily defined as chaos; the system as order. The system has no way of incorporating diversity within its framework. Efficiency becomes defined as a trade-off with effectiveness. Communication is said to be a trade-off between efficiency, on the one hand, and empathy-effectiveness on the other. Efficient empathy is a contradiction in terms; informative chaos an impossibility.*

   • *In such a context, standards of order need to come from somewhere. Power, whether unperceived or unacknowledged is free to determine the contents, structures, and procedures of information systems. Science and expertise become the ontological-epistemological servants of power. Good information becomes expertise as defined by power. Information systems further reify these relations by adopting "expert" standards (e.g., use of the noun-oriented keyword systems of dominant disciplines) for the storage and retrieval of scholarly work. The standards imposed by power persist despite intentions to the contrary because the assumptions mandate no procedural space for recursivity or dialogue. Challenge and contest, from whatever source, must be marginalized. Alternative voices must resort to louder, sometimes violent messages in attempts to be heard.*

   • *Even if they are selected deliberately based on their cultural diversity, persons who implement information/communication system design become socialized to these authorial standards of judgment and necessarily replicate them. In essence, systems become designed to serve the needs and uses of the people who design them, again often despite well-meaning intentions to the contrary.*

   • *Information is defined as that which instructs and so despite efforts to the contrary, information systems are designed as transmission systems, not participation systems. This is as true for formal systems (e.g., newspapers, and libraries which codify, store, and retrieve materials) as for informal procedures (e.g., town meetings run by presidential candidates as platforms for arguing their points of view rather than as opportunities for hearing other points of view).*

• *When introduced into system design and operation, diversity exists in isolation without any theoretical guidance for contrast or comparison. Diversity degrades into a Babel of voices. From the vantage point of row 6 assumptions, diversity is strength; it is ontologically and epistemologically essential for making and remaking order/chaos. However, in rows 1–4 assumptions diversity is weakness. From this vantage point, even when different perspectives are acknowledged, they are ultimately seen as either error or inconvenience—a necessary but troublesome barrier that must be overcome on the way to essences and truth.*

• *Because perspective is therefore conceptualized as error or inconvenience there is little systematic attention to how perspectivity, rooted in time, space, experience, memory, and visions, can be brought to bear on dialogue. Dialogue becomes conceptualized as a throwing around of differences because differences get conceptualized as static states of being rather than aspects of the larger human enterprise of making and unmaking, ordering and chaosing.*

• *The users and audiences of such system-oriented systems who cannot or will not be recipients of the intended information get defined as in error, as chaotic factors in the system. They become the culprits—explanations of system inefficiencies and ineffectivenesses. They must be provided with what they lack—resources, skills, knowledges, attitudes. Because they are seen as out of step with the system, they are assumed to be out of line.*

• *At the same time, the Babel of voices—differences with no theoretical links between ontology and epistemology—makes information availability and accessibility contradictory. Difference remains incomprehensible and the sheer quantity results in cacophony: More availability of information increasingly becomes less accessibility.*

• *Finally, the enormous and flexible capacities of the new communication technologies are used to extend old modes of information collection, storage, and delivery—to do more of the same in larger quantities, faster, and at greater distances.[32]*

A particular example may help illustrate how the assumptions play out their role in everyday discourse. One of the many issues in the debate over national health care reform is whether and to what extent it will provide coverage for what are termed "alternative health approaches" (e.g., naturopathy, herbalism, acupuncture, chiropractic, homeopathy).[33]

This is a challenging example for our purposes because there is probably no other arena that better exemplifies the persistent human striving for "perfect" information (i.e., information that would permit the absence of disease). This is also a useful example for our purposes because it is an arena within which there is a clear normative voice, a voice of expertise. This is the voice of allopathic medicine, the dominant form of medical care in the United States. Yet, as has been widely publicized recently, some 30% of U.S. citizens turn to natural alternatives at least some of the time despite a formidable set of "facts" countered in opposition. This 30% is attempting to enter the current debates but clearly the medical establishment has the upper hand.

This is not, however, merely the clash of two interpretive communities. That clash is only one symptom of a web of institutional forms which assure that resources (e.g., tax dollars, energies of the scientific-medical community) and innovations (e.g., the development and uses of communication technologies for telemedicine) will maintain (and perhaps extend) the power of dominant interests in the pharmaceutical-medical establishment and at the same time maintain (and perhaps extend), in the medical domain, established ways of producing and sharing knowledge, established ways of developing and implementing institutional forms, and established ways of including some voices and excluding others in these processes.

Clearly, there is much money at stake in these debates—questions of where resources will go: To surgeons providing liver transplants for elderly patients? To naturopaths educating their patients about detoxifying dietary regimes? To chiropractors treating middle-aged patients whose testimonies agree that their painful backs are finally improving even after decades of nonproductive allopathic treatment? The issues are enormously complex and this brief overview is not intended in any way to diminish their complexity. However, it is clear that practitioners and citizens who advocate and use alternative medical approaches are being marginalized. In the typical media portrayal, the establishment voice is represented by credentialed spokespeople and the alternative voice is represented by isolated patients and controversial doctors. There are few references to contradictory voices either within the U.S. establishment (e.g., allopathic doctors with impeccable mainstream credentials who have doubts about the efficacy of invasive allopathic treatments) or from other national medical establishments (e.g., Britain where alternative medicines, in particular, homeopathy, are widely accepted).

At a higher level of abstraction the question becomes one of who has a valid right to name and design the world. When science is implemented as dogma in public/professional affairs, even its own built-in corrections for bias, perspective, and constraint are ignored. Truth becomes the one and only truth, implemented by an expert standard, which itself is a standard supported and reified by both scientific and economic power. In such a context, anorexia becomes defined as a psychological aberration of young, usually affluent teenage girls rather than as product of a society which imposes unrelenting standards of appearance on females while encouraging an open-ended freedom of choice in how to construct (or deconstruct) a diet. In such a context, the constellation of symptoms which are now called diabetes were once labeled mental illness with the attendant justification for isolating the doubly victimized sufferer. In such a context, cancer is primarily attributed to lack of individual discipline (e.g., refusal to exercise, failure to eat less fat) rather than to the rise of impurities in the ecological system.

At an even higher level of abstraction, we find the species left bereft of its potentials for knowing: unable to systematically share how we make and unmake sense while struggling collectively and individually through time-space. It is only when one assumes a world that is ontologically incomplete and discontinuous that one must also assume that the humans in that world may need to hear each other not only to comprehend their differences but more importantly to get a more comprehensive, albeit always in flux, always incomplete, and always elusive picture of what reality might be about.

THE ALTERNATIVE:
CHAOS FROM ORDER, ORDER FROM CHAOS

On the surface, the alternative assumptions—as represented by row 6—seem to offer no safe haven. This is most clearly illustrated in the move from Figure 5.1 to Figure 5.2. Figure 5.1 is a diagram suggestive of the ontological and epistemological assumptions regarding knowing, represented by authority, naturalism, and cultural relativity. It is a portrait of simplicity. There are multiple perspectives present but one dominant authorial voice is privileged. This one dominant voice is assumed to speak accurately of a clearly defined reality. Figure 5.2 is suggestive of the ontological and epistemological assumptions regarding knowing represented by communitarianism. Here, multiple voices in multiple times and multiple spaces attend to an elusive reality. Figure 5.1 represents order; on its surface, Figure 5.2 represents chaos.

The question is whether any kind of order—order of a different kind than that conceptualized in the past—can either be found hidden within this chaos or emerging from it.[34] Part of the difficulty, of course, is that this set of alternative assumptions is just beginning to launch its contest. Another difficulty is that row 6 (communitarian) assumptions require a genuine philosophical leap. This is not just a matter of conceptualizing that there is diversity out there between persons and cultures. Rather, it is a matter of conceptualizing the diversity within—within people, within cultures. Further, it is a matter of conceptualizing this diversity as two-pronged in its origins.

One prong is the incompleteness of reality—our ontological world could not, even if able to speak to us directly without the intermediaries of language, discourse, and power—fully instruct us. If we accept this assumption, then we must conclude that humans need to tap diverse perspectives, not merely to make peace across their differences, but as ontological necessity. This conclusion requires that we jettison the baggage of our old assumptions—the belief that anything but "expert" observations are suspect. We must find a way to think of diversity of views as a step toward never-reachable ontological completeness and as a step away from the tyranny of epistemological completeness.

The other prong is to assume the incompleteness of the person—that we are not always centered, always conscious, always ordered; that we are sometimes unconscious, sometimes decentered, sometimes disordered; that we are in a constant state of moving

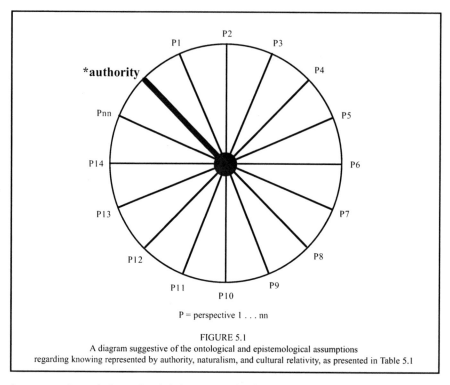

P = perspective 1 . . . nn

FIGURE 5.1
A diagram suggestive of the ontological and epistemological assumptions
regarding knowing represented by authority, naturalism, and cultural relativity, as presented in Table 5.1

between order and chaos; that it is just as much of a struggle to fall in line (i.e., to make ourselves fit our surroundings, our cultures, our societies), as it is to fall out of line (i.e., to resist and challenge our surroundings, our cultures, our societies). As individuals we constitute and are constituted by our societies; our societies constitute and are constituted by us. This work is never done, never complete. To remain muddled, to refuse to choose, to dream instead of seek facts—these can all be as informative, and therefore as gap-bridging—as what traditionally has been thought of as information-seeking and use (e.g., fact finding, evidence collecting, deciding, source connecting).

What would be the consequences for the design, implementation, and distribution of information systems in a society which adopted such a perspective? As utopian as the alternative is in its formulation, it provides a point of focus. Alternative systems would be recursive and responsive at their core. Incorporating users would not be an after-thought, a focus of feedback and accountability studies, or even of formative evaluation studies. Users and all relevant constituencies would be defined into the heart of the system. In the medical system, for example, this would include physicians (who could be seen as among the least powerful voices in the medical establishment because their own

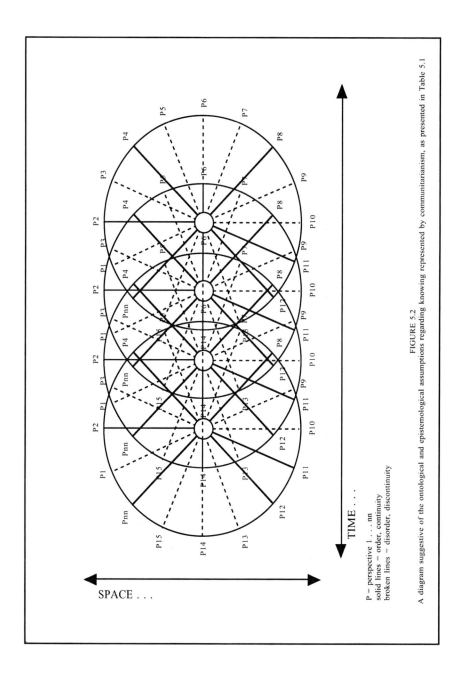

P = perspective 1 . . . nn
solid lines = order, continuity
broken lines = disorder, discontinuity

FIGURE 5.2
A diagram suggestive of the ontological and epistemological assumptions regarding knowing represented by communitarianism, as presented in Table 5.1

SPACE . . .

TIME . . .

95

assessments and judgments are marginalized in favor of research evidence) and nurses as well as patients, families, and members of the community. The multiple, constructed and deconstructed knowings would all be potential input for the information system. The task for designers, practitioners, and the researchers who assist them would be to ask questions of a different order than have been asked before.

To wit: What are the different strategies people use to construct and deconstruct their worlds? What are the different ways in which humans conform to and resist order? Where are the important contests right now? Where are the weakest voices? How many alternative voices must speak to provide a framework within which people can make their own sense? How can journalistic, scientific, and other systematic products be designed so speakers speak from the experiential and phenomenological contexts of their own world—so that their voices are not ripped out of context and made uninterpretable? How can humans learn to accept challenges to authority and power even on a small scale, even in well-intentioned contexts so that alternative voices may speak? Is it possible to bracket power? Can the deconstruction of power be systematically incorporated in systems, or is "systematic deconstruction" an oxymoron? How does one present a diversity of voices without sinking into solipsism? How does one use incompleteness informatively?

All of this requires that we develop theoretical and methodological tools very different from those we use now. It is these tasks for which the communitarian approach offers promise. It is a promise founded on the possibility of incorporating chaos into our understandings of information/communication processes and on the possibility of a new kind of order arising from or hidden within—an order based on the verbs by which people make and unmake ordered/unordered worlds.

We can begin to envision a different kind of information system for democracies— an information system that is truly multiperspectival, which mandates a procedural circling of the reality being made, maintained, destroyed, and remade by humans as they struggle individually and collectively through their lives. We can also begin to envision information systems for the postmodern age which evidence suggests is already marked by three major unprecedented trends: (a) the decline of the relevance of the nation-state in people's lives; (b) the emergence of all kinds of spontaneous and recursive democracies that cut across old conceptions of boundaries and forms; and (c) the remarkably inventive use of new communication technologies to support these new forms (Giddens, 1993).

The communitarian perspective, then, offers a tentative resolution of our difficulty of being caught, informationally, between a rock and a hard place, somewhere between the relativism of "no-truth-only-interests" and the absolutism of "truth-and-it-is-mine." The middle course suggested here is that information is something we are forever seeking, humbly and tentatively, in struggle and mediation and contest. The nature of the struggle is at least as informative as the resolution and more likely to serve diverse groups of citizens as they try to make community of their diversity. The question at hand is how shall we build this tentativeness, this struggle, this elusiveness, this humility into our information systems?

This article raises this question but does not answer it.[35]　Rather, this chapter attempts to answer a different question: whether we must reject the information ↔ democracy narrative? The answer this chapter offers is both a yes and a no. Yes, as conceived in totalizing, essentialist form. No, as reconceptualized in communitarian, recursive, dialogic form. This article is a mandate to rewrite the narrative.

NOTES

　　1.　The author thanks Sam Fassbinder, Leah Leivrouw, Tony Osborne, and Peter Shields, in particular, for their insightful and useful comments on the draft manuscript, and is grateful to Robert Huesca, Priya Jaikumar-Mahey, and Peter Strimer with whom discussions have been of enormous assistance in the development of these ideas. A very much abbreviated version of this chapter was presented under the title "Debating different approaches to studying the organization of information—the communication paradigm," at the annual meeting of the American Society for Information Science, Columbus, Ohio, October 1993.

　　2.　This chapter focuses on the dominant narrative which the author extracts primarily from U.S. discourses relating to the design and operation of information/commmunication systems for democracies. As such, the narrative is anchored in market-based conceptions of societal arrangements and accompanying assumptions of liberal pluralism regarding the nature of citizen participation in the state. The narrative has wide reach, however, and becomes increasingly pervasive in most, but not all, Western treatments of the issues. Further, the market-based narrative increasingly spreads beyond the West. However, it is not just market-based models of society that strive for "perfect" information. Planning-based models (e.g., socialistic arrangements) do so as well. What differs between them is the ". . . relative merits of centralized and decentralized mechanisms for dealing with information" (Shields, personal communication, September 23, 1993). Regardless of these differences, both models privilege an ontological center.

　　3.　This premise has been prevalent in the information ↔ democracy narrative in different ways since the founding of the United States. Recent events (e.g., the decrease of tax revenues to public education and librarianship) suggest the premise is in jeopardy.

　　4.　For comprehensive treatments on issues relating to information inequities and the role systems play in alleviating or exasperating them, see Dervin (1980, 1989b), Gandy (1988), and Shields, Dervin, Richter, and Soller (1993).

　　5.　In this chapter, the terms *information*, *knowledge*, and *truth* are used in different ways at different times. It is a major point of this chapter that most of the conceptual edifices constructed to distinguish between these terms in fact posit truth, defined as statements isomorphic to reality, as the best criterion for knowledge and information. The exercise becomes one, therefore, of explaining away any information/knowledge that does not meet that standard.

　　6.　In a later section of this chapter, the term *democracy* will be problematized briefly in the context of current discussions of the potentials for and characteristics of democracies in our postmodern era.

　　7.　The term *informational* is put in quotes here to remind the reader that the term is problematized in this chapter, and that the specific example of what might be "informational" given in this sentence is but a trace of the larger meanings that this study intends to put forth.

　　8.　It is not the purpose of this chapter to pursue extended discussions of various philosophic positions underlying the abbreviated portraits presented in Table 5.1. Suffice it to say that the author has been helped greatly by works addressing the philosophical challenges within and between science, critical/cultural studies, and that amalgam of thought now elusively called the *postmodern*. Particularly helpful references are cited in pertinent sections. In addition, this chapter rests on an understanding of the treatment of the concept of information in the fields of communication and information/library science. For recent comprehensive literature reviews, see Dervin (1980; 1989a, 1989b, 1991b), and Dervin and Nilan (1986).

9.   Given the choice of inventing entirely new labels for each stereotype versus using labels to which readers will bring both intended and unintended interpretations, the latter road was chosen in the interest of dialogic connectedness.

10.   Overviews of some of the debates in the field of communication include Delia (1987), Dervin (1993), and Rosengren (1989).

11.   The definition comes from Bottomore (1983) who actually used the term *distortions* rather than *modes*. The latter term has been used here in keeping with the premise that distortions anchors itself on the idea of an external standard. The communitarian position which is the focus of this chapter requires in its most general frame a more general term. The procedure—anchoring to an external standard—would be an instance of the possibilities. Works particularly helpful in developing this section include Freire (1970), Gramsci (1988), Hall (1989), and Lukes (1974).

12.   The reader needs to read both this section and the next one, "Empiricism," in order to understand the distinction between "positivism-accused" and "positivism".

13.   The information as uncertainty reduction idea can be traced back to the use/misuse of a single theoretic formulation developed by Shannon and Weaver (1949). However, it has become pervasive. Taylor (1993) has been particularly helpful in developing this section. It is also of interest to note that Hayles (1990) argues that information theory, the tool used to develop the edifice of information as that which reduces uncertainty, opened the way for theories of chaos.

14.   Giddens (1989) has been particularly helpful in developing this section; the foregrounding of naturalism here follows his lead.

15.   It is, of course, well-accepted that this is a far too narrow view of science as practiced today. See, for example Bronowski (1973), Hayles (1990), and Zukav (1979).

16.   The same has been true in the natural and physical sciences, as Hayles (1990) points out when she describes chaos theories as moving science in general beyond linear causal models.

17.   Others who build their discussions directly on notions of the clash of ideas in dialectical processes include Dewey (1933), Freire (1970), and Habermas (1984), each of whom extends his reach in different ways toward communitarianism. Their efforts have been enormously useful in constructing the arguments in this chapter.

18.   Particularly helpful in developing this section have been the following, none of whom should be held responsible for the stereotypical presentations presented here: Clifford (1986), Geertz (1975), and Rorty (1991). It needs to be emphasized that there are numerous approaches to scholarship that call themselves "cultural." Some would be clearly recognized if one applied the cultural relativity stereotype used in this chapter as a map. Others would be more readily recognized using the constructivist or postmodern stereotypes.

19.   See, in particular: Gerbner, Mowlana, and Nordenstreng (1993).

20.   See, in particular, Nordenstreng and Schiller (1993).

21.   For recent relevant works, see Gonzalez and Peterson (1993), and Rakow (1992).

22.   The reader is again reminded that we are deliberately stereotyping here based on dominant themes in applied communication/information science literature. In fact, among the many complex strands in the philosophical movement called *constructivism* was a position based on a mathematical rule that said that when the existence of something was mentioned, it should be accompanied by a statement of the method of finding or constructing that thing (Parsons, 1967, p. 204). This was not merely a kind of operationalism but rather a step toward procedural interface of the sort discussed in the communitarianism perspective. There are, of course, many other variations on approaches, called *constructivism*, including some which in terms of the stereotypes presented here might be called *postmodernism* and others which might be called *naturalism-corrected*. Further, most of those who now are working on communitarian perspectives, tarried in and/or moved out from constructivist perspectives. This includes the current author. Helpful to this section have been Berger and Luckmann (1966), Bruner (1973), Delia (1977b), Krippendorff (1989), and Luckmann (1983).

23. For overviews of postmodern work, see Best and Kellner (1991), Lather (1991), Mukerji and Schudson (1991), and Rorty (1985). Particularly useful to this discussion were, Barthes (1985), Foucault (1972), and Lyotard (1984). Sam Fassbinder (personal communication, September 9, 1993) provided comments which challenged, and therefore were particularly helpful in thinking through this section.

24. From one perspective it can be challenged that most postmodernists are in fact not positing ontological chaos but rather an ontological order created amd held in place through discourse and the power that is assumed to run pervasively through discourse. The implication at a higher level of abstraction is that there is no order given by reality. Hence, the characterization in this chapter of postmodernism as positing a chaotic reality.

25. See, in particular, Best and Kellner (1991), Lather (1991), Lyotard (1984), and Mukerji and Schudson (1991).

26. The term "deontologized" is used here to refer to a setting aside or bracketing of ontological concerns. This use is becoming more common and relates to but is not equivalent to the dominant current usage in philosophy in reference to a deontological [sic] theory of ethics which ". . . holds that at least some acts are morally obligated regardless of their consequences for human weal or woe" (Olson, 1967, pp. 343). Etymologically, deontology means the science of duty.

27. It must also be noted that the charge can be made, as Hayles (1990) does, that postmodernism/poststructuralism is reaching for ". . .a new globalizing imperative in its insistence that there can be no global theories" (p. 26). Lyotard (1984) acknowledges this when he speaks paradoxically of postmodernism as the master narrative to end all master narratives.

28. Particularly helpful in this section have been Deleuze and Guattari (1987), Gallop (1985), Holland (1988), Lacan (1977), and Theunissen (1984).

29. It is important to emphasize that these approaches cannot be rejected as "touchy-feely"—if only everyone would communicate, everything would be fine. In fact, these approaches deliberately contest any view of communication as an idealized remedy for human ills. For examples of the spate of recent books focusing on communitarian approaches to the construction of democracies, see Dahlgren and Sparks (1991), Fishkin (1992), and Peters (1989). For examples of developed theoretic approaches to society constituted in communication, see Dewey (1933), Giddens (1984), Habermas (1984, 1985, 1987a), Laclau and Mouffe (1985), Mouffe (1992), and Tehranian (1991, 1992). For discussions of the concept of dialogue, see Agger (1991), Buber (1970), Christians (1988), Dervin, Osborne, Jaikumar-Mahey, Huesca, and Higgins (1993), Johannsen (1971), and Stewart and Thomas (1990). For helpful related discussions, see Barthes (1985), Bruner (1990), Calinescu (1991), Corradi Fiumara (1990),Craig (1989), and Williams (1976).

30. While this chapter's version of the communitarianism approach rests on the assumptions used in Sense-Making, this chapter does not present Sense-Making as such. For methodological discussions of Sense-Making, see: Dervin (1989a, 1992), and Dervin and Nilan (1986); for development of the communitarian ideas on which Sense-Making is based, see Dervin (1991a, 1993). For an application to the constitution of democracy in communication, see Dervin and Clark (1993). For another example of a communitarian approach with a strong theoretical and methodological focus, see Carter (1989c, 1991), and Carter, Ruggels, Jackson, and Heffner (1973). Sense-Making owes a debt to Carter's project.

31. Although the development of such principles were mandated for some of the developers of constructivist perspectives.

32. This is not to suggest that the use of new communication technologies is not having qualitative impacts. Computer databases are used to codify and surveill myriad aspects of our lives (Gandy, 1993). These databases are not only used as marketing frameworks but also to make all manner of decisions—where to build, whom to tax, whom to fund, and so on. The point here, however, is that in fact the ontological and epistemological assumptions driving these changes are fundamentally the same. This issue is discussed in somewhat more detail in Dervin (1989b).

33. Statements in this section do not come from systematic observation as such but rather from the author's continuing project since 1972 to stay informed of the contests between conventional and alternative medicines. Giddens (1991, 1993) has been useful for thinking theoretically about these issues and in suggesting some relevant examples. A recent discussion focusing on allopathic medicine's body part approach to medicine and its possible consequences is found in Kimbrell (1993). A recent compendium of commentary by allopathic doctors who have turned to alternative medicines is found in Janiger and Goldberg (1993). A reader who wishes to tap into this alternative discourse could

consult recent issues of two magazines, readily available in health food stores: *New Age Journal* and *Natural Health*. In addition, *The Nation* runs regular commentary on the issues (e.g., Fugh-Berman, 1993).

34. Hayles (1990) reviews the two major themes in chaos theories in terms of two metaphors—"the figure in the carpet," where pattern is found hidden in the complexities of chaos; and "something out of nothing," where pattern results from chaos.

35. See Dervin (1989a, 1989b, 1992) and Dervin and Clark (1993) for discussions that address this question directly.

Chapter 6

Verbing Communication:
Mandate for Disciplinary Invention

Brenda Dervin

Most of the polarities that divide our field—universalist versus contextual theories, administrative versus critical research, qualitative versus quantitative approaches, the micro versus the macro, the theoretic versus the applied, feminist versus nonfeminist— are symptoms, not the disease. They are shallow indicators of something more fundamental. Because that which is fundamental eludes us, we see both tolerance (a comfortable acceptance of theoretical pluralism) and dissent (ideological and methodological contests) everywhere. It is as if we are all studying a very large elephant. Without addressing the question directly, we seem to assume that we are studying the same elephant, while comfortably relegating ourselves to our own parts. But every once in a while we bump into each other.

Our contradictions are used both as a measure of our tolerance (after all, she does *x* while I do *y*) and a measure of our dissent (but she is doing *x* the wrong way, or her work has these negative consequences). While caught in these ricochets between tolerance and dissent, we can pontificate on why media effects remain a black box or why our research seems irrelevant to practice or why disciplinary status eludes us. It's because "they" use the wrong methodology, wrong theoretic perspective, wrong ideology, wrong . . . . They should become more like "us." What we have is dissent mythologized as tolerance.

At root here is the issue of difference—both the differences between different sectors of our field and the differences that are at the heart of what we study—the differences that characterize human beings, their symbolic lives, and their symbolic products. I would propose that it is how we treat the latter differences that confounds our own differences.

Our field and the social sciences in general have for the most part handled difference in ways that are not fundamental. Because of this, our theories are weak and we

This work originally appeared as: Dervin, B. (1993). Verbing communication: Mandate for disciplinary invention. *Journal of Communication, 43* (3), 45–54. (ERIC Document Reproduction Service No. EJ 466 763). Reprinted in M. R. Levy and M. Gurevitch (Eds.). (1994). *Defining media studies* (pp. 53–62). Oxford, UK: Oxford University Press. Reprinted by permission of Oxford University Press, Oxford, UK.

end up attending with much energy to artificial, symptomatic differences, squabbling over turf and status. We end up trying to use the summation of the products of our current work as if they showed the way out. In our periods of tolerance, we call for meta-analyses, hoping these will point to ties that bind. When they don't, we move into one of our periods of dissent. Being unable to deal with difference in a way that fundamentally makes a difference, we make no difference.

Ironically, in grappling with their own substantial and/or illusive polarities, most of the other social sciences point to the phenomenon of our field—communication—as the way out (e.g., Giddens, 1984; Habermas, 1987a). Bruner (1990) clearly does this when he suggests that it is the making of meaning that is the "proper study of man [sic]" (p. 1). One sees calls for the study of communication everywhere. In a recent speech at Ohio State University, an anthropologist publicly challenged our field. Anthropology, he pronounced, has found communication and will do it better.

The anthropologist is optimistic. And, some in our field are too pessimistic about the potentials of our field for disciplinary coherency (e.g., Beninger, 1990; Schramm, 1983). There is no reason to expect that the other social sciences will change easily, cast as they are in unresponsive disciplinary frames. Nor is there reason to expect that we, upon confronting our own disarray, cannot do something about it if we can recognize that in fact we have yet to capitalize on our strengths. In one sense, it might be said that we can never be a discipline because when the disciplinary frames fall, what must rise are process-driven alternatives based on fundamentals. Clearly, communicating is a fundamental. Everyone may rightly claim it. But, in a second sense, it can be said that if we were not so busy modeling the very disciplinary structures that blind us, we might find our strength. Our field does no better than other academic fields concerned with human beings in bringing the practical together with the theoretic. Yet no one contests the bounty of practical wisdom embodied in our ranks. Even some of our most theoretic and critical scholars are called upon to make practical judgments in arenas ranging all the way from media design and practice to policy and legal considerations to the conduct of everyday personal, relational, and organizational lives. More often than not there is at least a disparity and sometimes an enormous discontinuity between the guiding academic project and the practical wisdom offered. The gap is filled with the consciousness of the individual communication academic. We call this the theoretic versus applied contradiction and accept it as a given of our field. What we don't seem to understand is that this contradiction may mask our greatest strength. It is not that our work ignores theorizing for practice. Rather, we subordinate it to the more pressing academic mission. To theorize the practice of communication would require that we focus on communication theorizing of communication. We focus, instead, on other kinds of theorizing—sociological, psychological, anthropological, and so on. This chapter asks: What if we were able to develop communication theory for communication practice—if we could bring our practical and our theoretical activities together?

The immediate response—from within the many caves in our field where our contests are waged—is that theory for practice is not possible. The reasons would themselves form an array of contradictions. On the one hand, for example, theory for practice would be challenged as too oppressive, prescriptive, modernist, and/or totalizing, or erroneously universalist, leaving important cultural, contextual, and personal factors behind. On the other, it would be challenged as too ambitious and/or too removed from experimental control.

This listing does not exhaust the challenges that can be mounted. Reacting to each would require an essay in itself. The important point I wish to make here is this: These challenges rise out of the same kinds of theorizing about difference that currently beget the unproductive dualisms that encumber our field. Our field's hidden strength is that our phenomenon of interest—communication—is positioned at the very cutting edge of the study of the human condition. We already know much of what it would mean to develop a communication theory of communicating. To capitalize on that strength, we must let go of the theoretical strategies that prevent other fields from looking at communication communicatively and look to our hidden strengths, our foundational interest in how communicating is done.

We already have within our grasp a variety of coherent theories of communicative practice, but the clarity of our vision is clouded with debris we have imported from other fields. If we can clear this debris away, we may be able to reach for a core that in no way will eliminate our contests, but will give these contests productive meaning. Our differences would become informative.

METAPHORS FOR DIFFERENCE: NOUNS AND VERBS

The debates in our field and in the social sciences generally rest on a rotating axis of polarities. The polarizations have between them something common and something uncommon. Thus, for example, the universalist versus contextualist debate focuses on positions that adhere to and challenge the idea that universal theories of human situations can be developed. In contrast, the quantitative versus qualitative debate rages between those who accept and reject quantification. Those who accept quantification are also more likely to accept the quest for universalist theory while those who use qualitative approaches are more likely to accept the quest for context-bound theorizing.

Because academics use normative narrative practices to make advances by first defeating enemies, there is some utility in looking at how innovative theoretical and methodological work is often built on fortresses of critique. This is as true of advances within literature genres—where, for example, one postmodernist tears down another, or one quantitative study proceeds by challenging another—as it is between genres—as, for example, in the critiques of so-called positivist approaches by advances in qualitative research, ethnomethodology, and cultural and postmodern studies (e.g., Hall, 1989; Lather, 1991).

Having identified an enemy is not, however, the same thing as having diagnosed a disease. Unfortunately, the metaphors get mixed and intertwined. If the enemy is called positivism, anything that has any related symptoms (i.e., quantification, analytic methods, or statistical tools) is automatically also called enemy. As a result, the polarizations on the rotating axis of contest proliferate. At one end of the polarity we most often find fundamentalism, totalization, modernism, authoritarianism, structuralism, and master narratives. At the other end of the polarity we most often find relativism, postmodernism, contextualism, culturalism, and poststructuralism. "Isms" proliferate, and in the context of the debate (and the publish-or-perish mandate that fuels it) words get used so facilely and glibly that it becomes difficult to understand what all the fury is about, particularly when the results of the fury do not seem to advance significantly our individual or collective projects.

It is a simplification, but one useful for purposes here, to suggest that at the center of all these contests is the issue of difference—where to locate it, how to define it, what to call it, and how to look at it. In our field—and, it appears, in most of the social sciences—difference is most often defined simply as that which is not the same. The approach is not to identify what difference will make a difference but rather to identify a difference that is not yet claimed as another's turf, thereby claiming it as one's own. It would be unfair, of course, to relegate all of this solely to turf war, for it often represents a genuine concern for untapped difference. It is in this context that scholarship of the disenfranchised have had such important force, for each has impelled a new voice to the fore as a voice relevant for scholarly attention, a voice heretofore ignored or marginalized.

It is not my purpose here to trace the treatment of difference in our literature. The intent is to be suggestive of our history and pertinent to our present. To do this, I shall focus on the methodological moves involved in locating something we define as *difference*. This is a methodological concern that embodies within it acts of defining, labeling, and looking. It constitutes a fundamental methodological construction, resulting from a synergy of moves.

Our projects are ultimately about difference. We search for pattern and for deviation from pattern regardless of whether we define ourselves as in the business of description, explanation, or prediction or whether we reject, as I do, this too facile division of labors. Some of us search for pattern in a straightforward prescribed manner—via statistical tools, for example, or authoritative readings, or master narrative theorizings. Others of us suffer qualms of uncertainty for fear our search for pattern disrespects difference. As we get more sophisticated in understanding discourse, we begin to understand that even the methodological act of locating difference—the act of differencing—is itself an imposition of pattern.

In short, when we difference, we must put difference somewhere. In our field right now there are two primary sites—one is in culture; the other is in agency. On the surface these look like quite different methodological moves. But from the standpoint of this chapter they are construed as being fundamentally identical. They both deal with difference without dealing with difference.

Culture is a wonderfully rich term, "warmly persuasive" in the sense that Williams (1976) characterized *community* in his useful archeological dig into the term (p. 66). When efforts to describe, explain, and/or predict human communication proved alarmingly limited using structuralist frameworks (e.g., class, organizational, personality, language, and text structures), scholars reached for nonstructuralist ways of embodying the differences that were implied by but eluded earlier efforts. Culture has in effect become one of the latest catchalls. Difference resides elusively there. This is manifested, for example, in quantitative work when cultural factors are added to predictive formulations. It is manifested in qualitative work when, for example, discourse is analyzed as at least culturally anchored if not culturally prescribed.

The culture metaphor for difference is quite simple. Culture becomes a box into which groups of entities (i.e., people and texts) are slotted. The relationship is part-whole. Culture is the whole. Humans and texts are the parts. Culture is frozen at least for that moment, conceptualized as noun. The humans and the texts are also conceptualized as nouns. Pattern is framed in these terms, as is deviation from pattern. Difference becomes defined as discrepancies between entities conceptualized statically. Culture is at one moment homogenizing structure, at the next resistant difference. Individuals are positioned as homogenized or discrepant.

The structure versus agency distinction is most often identified with Giddens (1984). My use of the term here addresses the amalgamation that has become prevalent in our field—an amalgamation that has captured some of the substantive emphasis in Giddens's project but has failed to bring forward as well the important aspects that attempted to avoid a structure-agency dualism. Most of the references in our field have not sidestepped this difficulty.

As it is commonly used in our field, the structure versus agency distinction is a step forward in that it does not on the surface define agency as a deviation from structure. It is important, however, to note that structure still is for the most part conceptualized as static. Structure is noun: agency is verb. Constraint and homogenization rest in structure; freedom and variation rest in agency. Although it is often acknowledged that there are contradictions and spaces within and between structures, at any given level of analysis the structure-agency dualism serves as a rigid methodological blinder constraining formal theoretical work.

CRITIQUING FALSE DICHOTOMIES

The difficulty with both of these sites for locating difference—culture and agency—is that they still invite the ricochet between fundamentalism and anarchy, authoritarianism and relativism, modernism and postmodernism. They still posit structure as noun and thus are discursively static. Anything that is fluid must thus be in opposition: culture versus individual, structure versus agency, power versus freedom. These ricochets allow the methodology of the moment to advertise itself cloaked in false dichotomies. These ricochets confuse method with methodology and theory with ideology. They assume, for example, that those who prefer qualitative approaches don't observe or analyze while those who use quantitative approaches don't think (Bruner, 1990). They resort to a technological determinism in assuming that methods are entirely constrained by ideology.

Even when we attempt to move away from these false dichotomies or to move away from the very strategy of polarizing as a way of defining our regard for each other, our contests bind us to a brute portrait. Difference is free; homogeneity is bound. We deny it, often vigorously, but at one end of our axis of polarities is structure, constraint, power, homogenization, order, subject as object; at the other, freedom, variety, chaos, subjectivity. We are forced to choose our entry point. Even in the most recent efforts to bring together different viewpoints—as, for example, the critical with the postmodern—the choice usually remains (e.g., Best & Kellner, 1991). We are unable to stop taking sides and start moving toward multiple perspectives that might inform each other in a dialogue of differences.

There are many avenues for critiquing the false dichotomies that bind our field. Most damning for us is that these dichotomies often lead us away from the study of communication. Pattern gets located in society (sociology), culture (anthropology), individual (psychology); political and economic processes are defined as homogenizing, serving pattern; and interpretive freedom is defined as the only place where difference can safely reside. This narrative structure is as dominant in administrative work as it is in critical work.

Because we continue to embody difference as that which is in opposition to structure, we fail to fully capitalize on (even though we give lip service to it) our understanding of the role of communication both in the implementation of order as well as disorder, structure as well as agency, constraint as well as freedom, homogeneity as well as difference. In forcing ourselves to choose one end of the polar axis or the other, we allow our own phenomenon of interest to elude us. Because we define both constraint and freedom essentially as nouns, we fail to see that both are made, maintained, reified, and changed in communicating. We fail to fully conceptualize difference as differencing, as a communicating move, as a fundamental condition of human experiencing.

The irony of this situation manifests itself most clearly in the current debates on theories of the subject. The question at hand is: How shall we conceptualize our human being? Shall this human entity be cognitive, emotional, spiritual, physical, desiring, unconscious, conscious, discursively created, empowered, disempowered, or some combination? This listing does not exhaust the possibilities nor does it represent any single corner of the debate. Rather, it is designed to represent the diversity in the array and suggest that here again we are focusing on choosing a particular static way (or set of ways) with which to characterize humans. The characteristics are defined as adjectives, attributes of the human nouns.

We have begun to discuss the ever-changing subject, but for the most part, we posit the subject as moving from one state to another. The emphasis is on the states, not the moves. Given the nature of the polarities from which we come, this avoidance is understandable. How does one explain a subject that is ever-changing if one has only the conceptual tools of structure (homogeneity) or freedom (difference) with which to work? How can one focus on the moves when all one has is nouns with which to work?

What the idea of the ever-changing subject has accomplished is that difference is now being conceptualized as both across time (e.g., one entity differing across time) as well as across space (two entities being different at the same time). What is important about difference across time is that it begins to force us to attend to difference as fundamental, not as noun but as verb, as differencing. In doing that we can begin to genuinely capitalize on the study of communication. With such a change, our field might come into its own—because difference makes a difference *in* communication; differences come into existence *in* communication; differences rigidify *in* communication; differences are bridged *in* communication; and differences are destroyed *in* communication. Likewise, structures that attempt to homogenize difference as well as those that attempt to display it come into existence *in* communication; maintain, rigidify, and disappear *in* communication.

Homogenizing and differencing are reconceptualized as communicatings. Among other possible communicatings are: idea makings and idea repeatings, thinkings and emotings, listenings and arguings, positionings and vacillatings, cooperatings and contestings, polarizings and nuancings, categorizings and hierarchializings, nounings and verbings, and a host of other ways in which we humans individually and collectively make and break order. The clumsy verbings of nouns are intentionally used here to make this point: Our strong suit is our understanding of communication as process in myriad contexts. But our understanding of process has been relegated to second-class status— we do that when we testify, when we consult, when we teach. When we do our scholarship, we focus primarily on entities, not processes; on nouns, not verbs.

My major point is this: If our field can refocus on communicatings instead of communication, we can begin to conceptualize in such a way that we can find more relevance (which does not imply more agreement) in each other's work. Further, the move will allow us to begin to transcend the false dichotomies that prevent us from theorizing communication as practice, as the verbings that humans, collectively and individually, use to construct bridges across gaps—self and other, self and community, structure and individual, self at time 1 and self at time 2, one aspect of self at time 1 to another aspect of self at time 1, chaos to order, order to chaos, homogeneity to difference, difference to homogeneity.

Even through we tend to be ashamed of our pervasive and foundational practical side, our field is the field that has always dealt with difference *in communicating* and that has always accepted both structure and difference and conceptualized communicatings as that which energizes the in between. We already have the theoretic potential for which this chapter makes a call. Sometimes this potential shows clearly, sometimes through a fog. Sometimes this potential has been a point of major emphasis (e.g., Carter, 1991; Craig, 1989; Dervin, 1991a).

In short, we know a lot that we don't know we know. Communicating is where the micro becomes the macro, the macro the micro. It is the in between, the doing, the making, the experiencing. No matter what stripe the scholars in our field wear, at some point all of them can be heard talking *communicatings* rather than *communication*, verbs rather than nouns. We are where structure and agency meet, both implemented in communicatings. It might be more useful to say we are where structure and agent meet, both implemented in the agency of communicatings. We are where individual as object and individual as subject meet, both implemented in communicatings. We are where the conscious and the unconscious meet, both implemented in communicatings. We are where hegemony and resistance meet, both implemented in communicatings.

DENOUEMENT:
WHENCE THE SPECIES

Our field has already done more to move the social sciences from noun theories and methodologies to verb theories and methodologies than any other field. One difficulty here is that our contributions to other social sciences have been more methodological than substantive. In essence, we have propelled a communicative way of looking at things. This is a double problem. First, the social sciences—particularly U.S. social sciences—don't value methodology per se. Second, the social sciences journals are organized substantively. Our contributions get hidden in the cracks. We are also so busy taking potshots at each other and valuing those in other fields that we have not garnered our strengths or resources. Our progress is impeded by extant disciplinary structures, so our movement toward the verbs of communicating is not refined, gracious, or easy. It is being propelled in contradiction and failure. It is impeded by structures heavily in place (e.g., publish-or-perish) and made worse by the economic and ideological encroachments on the academy that characterize our time.

But the bottom line is this: From the beginning we have stood more in between—the humanities and the social sciences, the social sciences and the physical sciences, the fields within the social sciences—than any other field. While other fields worry of long-time fractionalizations, our disarray is characterized more by often disarming fluidity. Cast in the mirror of current disciplinary structures, all this makes us appear weak. But more than any other field we have been unable to escape the mandate of difference. Psychology can find stable patterns in individuals across time; sociology can find stabilities in societies; anthropology can characterize culture as entity. But we are left with the sternest test of all—what happens in the elusive moments of human communicatings.

While others may be rushing in to claim the ground we have tread, from the beginning we have had to deal with theory and practice, micro and macro, structure and agency. And from the beginning we have had to deal with process. We have praised process, we have even offered it to the world as practical wisdom. We have only recently begun to acknowledge it and develop it intellectually. It is process, however—the verbs of communicating—where we have something to offer that is, if not ultimately unique, at least for now ahead of the others. Because of this, we can lead the way, if only we will.

Chapter 7

Given a Context by Any Other Name:
Methodological Tools for Taming the Unruly Beast

Brenda Dervin

> Context is ". . . the pattern that connects . . . all communication necessitates context . . . without context there is no meaning." (Bateson, 1978, p. 13)

> "The first step in taming the apparent wildness of context is distinguishing the various kinds of contextual factors." (Dascal, 1989, p. 243)

> Context is ". . . a spatial and temporal background which affects all thinking and a selective interest or bias which conditions the subject matter of thinking." (Dewey, 1960a, p. 90)

> When Justice Holmes asked John Dewey why his later writings were less clear than his early writings, Dewey replied: ". . . I was digging down three inches; now I'm trying to dig three feet." (Dewey, as quoted in Postman, 1974)

INTRODUCTION:
THE UNRULY BEAST

Our focus is on the study of information needs, seeking, and use in different contexts. However, this chapter spends little time on this focus as such. Instead, this chapter asks the question "What is context?" on the assumption that to ask a question that is so little asked may prove useful. This chapter looks for possible answers in the literatures of the social sciences generally, both philosophical and observational, focusing particularly on literatures in the communication fields on the assumption that the phenomena of our interest are most usefully defined as communication phenomena.

This work originally appeared as: Dervin, B. (1997). Given a context by any other name: Methodological tools for taming the unruly beast. In P. Vakkari, R. Savolainen, & B. Dervin (Eds.), *Information seeking in context* (pp. 13–38). London: Taylor Graham. Reprinted by permission of Taylor Graham Publishing, London, UK. Contains material presented as: Dervin, B. (1996, August). *Given a context by any other name: Methodological tools for taming the unruly beast.* Keynote address delivered at ISIC 96, Conference on Information Needs, Seeking and Use in Different Contexts, Department of Information Studies, University of Tampere and Finnish Association of Library and Information Science, Tampere, Finland.

One answer to the question—what is context—is both good news and bad. The good news is that context is hot. Everywhere one turns in literatures of the social sciences and humanities focusing on how humans make sense of their worlds one sees increasing references to context. The bad news is that the very question turns out to be almost embarrassing, and certainly a question leading to a quest that demands extraordinary tolerance of chaos. After an extended effort to review treatments of context, the only possible conclusion is that there is no term that is more often used, less often defined, and when defined defined so variously as context.[1]

There are three aspects of this confusion that stand out. The first is that the term *context* has become "almost a ritualistic invocation" (Slack, 1989, p. 329). The importance of context is rarely an issue although there are some writers who still decry what they see as the lack of generalizability that attention to context introduces while others see attention to context coming too little and too late. Mostly though, context is evoked but rarely with detailed treatments and even more rarely philosophically or theoretically.

The second trajectory that runs through this literature is one of paradigmatic isolation. It is an oversimplification but useful to note that treatments of context are plagued by the polarities that otherwise divide those of us involved in the academic study of human beings and their societies. The divide is better seen as a continuum. At one end are those who give allegiance to what is commonly referred to stereotypically and erroneously as more positivist science. At the other are those focused on more qualitative, humanistic science or critical/cultural science. There are interesting positions which are not so easily categorized about which I will speak below. In the main, however, those at the extremes of this divide appear to know little of the comings and goings of those on the other end.

At one end of the continuum, there is a great deal of work which evokes context as another analytic factor among many. Context, it is said, must be taken into account along with other factors such as structure, culture, person, situation, behavior, and so on. From this conceptualization comes a lengthy and bewildering array of possible contextual factors. Virtually every possible attribute of person, culture, situation, behavior, organization, or structure has been defined as context. Thus, for example, if the researcher focuses on the meaning of texts, then the perspectives and behaviors of sources or receivers or channels can become context. If the researcher is focused on relationships between people, then factors describing the situation can become context. In this logic, context has the potential of being virtually anything that is not defined as the phenomenon of interest. Context is conceptualized, usually implicitly, as a kind of container in which the phenomenon resides. The trick appears to be to pinpoint exactly what aspects of the container impact or relate to the phenomenon. Mostly, at this end of the research continuum, the choices seem capricious.

At the other end of the continuum lies a context that is assumed to be a kind of inextricable surround without which any possible understanding of human behavior becomes impossible. In this view, context is the carrier of meaning and research must be contextualized. Further, every context is by definition different, an intersection of a host of nameless factors. Because of this, research can only be particularized and generalization in the traditional scientific sense is impossible.

The third trajectory that emerges is that those writing at both ends of this continuum as well as those in the middle all admit that there is an inexhaustible list of factors that are contextual. At one end of the continuum, there is a mandate to build conceptual systems which would provide guidance for the selecting. At the other, the issue is set aside as irrelevant because the many factors are seen as so intertwined that systematic unraveling is unwarranted.

The two ends of this continuum as I have described them here are, of course, stereotyped. Part of the good news about context is that in the last few decades—and particularly in recent years—a variety of well-developed philosophic and theoretic positions regarding context have emerged. Most of these positions do not fall neatly at either end of this stereotyped continuum; nor do they fit easily into camps. All of them provide challenging illumination for our struggles with context. What is interesting is that writers at each end of the continuum stereotype the other end precisely as I have here even though a more useful assessment of what is going on shows many strands of common struggle. It can be said with some irony that scholars invoking context in one way or another as important to the study of their phenomena are unwilling to invoke context in their attempts to understand scholars who define context differently. This is one of many contradictions which pervade discussions of context. I will speak more of these below.

What is apparent, however, is that context is a label for a site of struggle. In this struggle, the species is reaching for a new kind of understanding. Not everyone, of course. And, not in the same way. But the intensity of attention and confusion is suggestive of a shift in the episteme, a shift that is occurring haltingly and dialectically. Context is the focus of attention for those working within a wide variety of perspectives. To name but a few: symbolic interaction, pragmatics, systems theory, qualitative studies, cultural studies, hermeneutics, political economy, phenomenology, constructivism, interpretive anthropology, transactionism, contextual psychology, ethnography, perspectivism, situationism, and postmodernism. Given that every one of these perspectives in one or another version is in contentious opposition to at least one of the other of these perspectives, this common call to context can be interpreted in two ways. One is good news—perhaps this is the road that will eventually free us from the polarities that drive us apart. The other is bad news—perhaps there will emerge a plethora of contexts, adding to what already seems overwhelming confusion.

Whether this movement toward context is called a *shift in the episteme* (as in Foucault, 1972) or a *faultline* (as in Hayles, 1990) or the *reach for a new mode of won-*

der (as in McGuire, 1986), what all the instances have in common is a move away from research that does not account for the here and the now (i.e., time and space) to research that does. Other than this common agreement, some of the approaches I examined have little else in common. But this one commonality provides at least a modest anchor across the divide.

If, however, one focuses not on the perspectives which are struggling with context at the ends of the polarized continuum, but rather with those struggling in the middle an entirely different picture emerges—a portrait of common themes and common challenges. To build this portrait, I have not relied on any particular treatment of context but rather have sought out conceptual and methodological treatments which are self-reflexive and explicitly struggling with premises which have been left unstated by the more implicit approaches at the ends of the polarized continuum.

Other writers have done extensive lineage descriptions and comparisons of approaches that call themselves contextual (e.g., Adams, 1997; S. C. Hayes, 1993; McGuire, 1986; and Rosnow & Georgoudi, 1986b). That is beyond my purpose here. What I want to do is tease out my own sense of the primary agreements and disagreements orienting specifically on issues which have methodological implications. Thus, this exercise is not to be construed as a "faithful" reading (even if such a thing were possible) of these sources but rather as my personal attempt to identify common themes of continuity and discontinuity within and between and to illuminate my own approaches.

This last statement gives the reader some guidance for the reading. I will not be discussing my own approach to research on information needs, seeking, and use in this chapter. However, obviously my own work informs my journey here. In my own work I have chosen to adopt a contextual perspective but at the same time have taken a position "in between" regarding methods for studying context, admitting both quantitative (which some label as positivist) and qualitative approaches to my repertoire and rejecting the idea that there is any necessary technological determinism embedded in method. However, philosophically I position myself closer to the qualitative end of the continuum.[2] In a sense, then, it can be said that I am attempting to be systematic about something which some scholars see as unsystematizable, either because (as at one end of the continuum) context is defined as chaos, enemy of order and generalization; or because (as at the other end of the continuum) context is defined as amorphous and fragile, fractured by the artificial imposition of method.

Several important points before I begin the search for themes. I am using the terms *contextual approaches* and *contextualist* in this chapter to refer to a variety of perspectives which under a variety of names make similar assumptions regarding something that is frequently referred to as context. The scholars referred to do not necessarily refer to themselves or their approaches by these same labels. It is my interpretation that binds them and I have intentionally reached out for theorists and philosophers operating in unconnected discourse communities. Second, my extracting of themes is of course limited to the literature of which I am aware. Given the complexity of the issues and given that context is referred to with myriad names, there are no doubt important sources of which I remain unaware. Third, in most of these discussions the terms *situation* and *context* are used interchangeably.[3] For purposes of this chapter, I will operate in that definitional framework.

COMMON THEMES

Clearly, for those who are addressing context theoretically and philosophically, there are common themes which mandate a particular approach whether their approaches are called interactionist, transactionist, contextualist, pragmatist, perspectivist, or by any other label. These common themes are:

Knowledge is partial and temporary. What is common is an anti-foundationalist position, a rejection of the idea that there is a bedrock reality that can be captured in knowledge. Any knowing is assumed to be partial and temporary, bound into context. Some posit this assumption as pre-contextual—that is, one of few assumptions necessary in contextualized approaches. Others prefer to posit it simply as axiomatic assumption admitted to up front as part of a mandate of self-reflexivity. In either case, the criteria by which knowledge and action are warranted are embedded in the doing, in practice, in workability, in consequences, not in epistemology or axiology. Also fundamental to this assumption is the conclusion that, as McGuire (1986) states it, "To admit that knowledge is intrinsically erroneous is not to imply that we should forgo it" (p. 274). One thing most of these thinkers have in common is their efforts to build a new and radically different kind of science. This new science does far more than acknowledge epistemological fallibility or diversity on the part of knowers. Rather, it challenges that it is impossible to extricate epistemological fallibility and diversity from ontological uncertainty and fluidity.

Reality is discontinuous, gap filled, changeable across time-space. This assumption aligns with the first. Reality is seen as accessible only (and always incompletely) in context, in specific situated historicized moments in time-space, in what Altman (1986) terms the ". . . spatial and temporal confluence . . ." of people, settings, activities, events that is context (p. 25). Drawing on the work of Pepper (1942), many refer to contextual approaches as based on the same root metaphor—that of the historicized, situated event. But even within this event, contextualism posits a gappiness which is both ontological as well as epistemological in root. All we have is "scraps" and "fragments" (Said, 1983a, 1983b) which come potentially from elusive origins and there is a tendency to treat these as if they are whole. McGee (1990) suggests that we should refer to contextual formations (in his terms, the convergings of texts and contexts) as "fragments" because of their inherent incompleteness and inseparability.

The knower-and-the-known are inextricably bound. Foundational to the calls for contextual approaches is the epistemological assumption that knowing is a product of some inextricable combination of human action, human predisposition, and that elusive thing called reality. Whatever fallabilities and diversities exist in human interpretation, these are inextricability bound and situated in context. As Gadamer (1975) puts it: "all understanding inevitably involves some prejudices" (p. 239). These are a pre-condition of experience. Common to the contextual theorizings which I have reviewed is the assumption that this pre-condition is neither good, nor bad. It is, rather, necessary.

Context is not usefully conceptualized as independent entity. As Ellis (1981) states: "Context is conceptualized most often as an artificial entity, invariant in time, and independent of human interaction" (p. 226). This entity is most often portrayed as a surround that in enclosing things (e.g., persons, structures, events, situations) becomes in essence an attribute imposed on these things but yet at the same time independent of these things. This kind of separation of context makes it too easy to reduce context to simple parts, and, to reduce the things onto which context attributes are imposed to these parts. A living breathing struggling person becomes merely a person in a job context. A message with history and contradiction becomes merely factual or entertaining. Extrapolating from these kind of inside-outside ideas about context (e.g., context enclosing other things and context inside other things) is a related idea which also is challenged by those who are theorizing context—the idea that somehow context is in an opposition relationship to other things. An example is the not infrequent idea that context is that which ruins the purity of purpose encoded in so-called factual messages. All of these ideas—inside, outside, opposition—are made possible only when context is conceptualized as independent.

Context requires a focus on process. While implications and implementations drawn from this assumption vary greatly, most of those who theorize context mandate attention to process, to change over time, to emergent and fluid patterns. In the terms of Dewey, considered by some one of the philosophic grandfathers (along with Hegel, Marx, Pepper, and others) of contextual approaches, this is a mandate to focus on "action verbs," on acting, doing, talking, thinking (Dewey & Bentley, 1949). This emphasis on process is usually considered another of a few pre-contextual mandates, an "irradicable" (Rosnow, 1986) necessity. In this framework, reality is in a continuous and always incomplete process of becoming. A distinction between process manifestations and product manifestations of reality is helpful here. Product manifestations only seem to have stability across time-space. Sometimes their time-space fixedness is quite wide. But, ultimately, those who address context as central see this stability as mere illusion, as a static manifestation of that which is ever changing. As Weick (1979) challenged: There is no such thing as organization. There is only organizing. As Garfinkel (1967) suggests, our accounting practices impose substance and form on otherwise indeterminate flows of activity.

Focus must be placed on the dialectical relationships between product and process. While there is even more variability in ramifications resulting from this assumption, most of those calling for contextual approaches call for attention to an inherent dialectical relationship between product and process, noun and verb, context and action, structure and agency. Bateson (1979) says it best: Context is a "dance of interacting parts . . . a zigzag ladder of dialectic between form and process" (p. 13). Form is constituted by process and is constitutive of process. Process is constituted by form and is constitutive of form. In Giddens's (1979) theory of the "duality of structure" this is stated as seeing structure as ". . . both medium and outcome of the reproduction of practices" (p. 5). Schutz (1964) was getting at the same idea when he said: "When an action is completed its original meaning . . . will be modified in the light of what has actually been carried out, and it is then open to an infinite number of reflections . . ." (p. 11).

Focus must be placed on multiple interdependencies. The assumptions above intersect on another—that there are multiple potential interdependencies. Some theorists who conceptualize context draw on systems theory for this assumption (Rapoport, 1968; von Bertalanffy, 1968) while others draw on various forms of dialectical theorizing such as that manifested in the works of Dewey and Marx (Gavin, 1988b). In both cases, ideas of linear progressions are either rejected or tempered and patterns are seen as potentially exhibiting themselves in every possible temporal or spatial direction. Further, the idea of the summation of parts, so ever-present in traditional causal thinking, is rejected in favor of views that assume either that things will be less or more than the parts, or that this kind of part-whole thinking is alien to the very nature of contextual theorizing.

Context is a necessary source of meaning. Obviously, fundamental to this line of thinking is the idea that context is a necessary source of meaning. For some, context is also sufficient for meaning but this rigid idea usually comes from those who do not attend to the subtleties of potential dialectical relationships in the analysis of context. The most subtle, and I think useful, treatment, comes from Gadamer (1976) who is interrogating a common struggle pertaining to context—that of the relationship between context and text—as he challenges traditional hermeneutic approaches. Morris (1993, p. 140) provides some helpful background. The text, he says, has traditionally been revered (a legacy, some suggest, of the Judeo-Christian reference to the Biblical text). In essence, the text has been seen as encompassing essential truths and because of this, Morris challenges, the "silences" that are thus invited are ". . . grotesque, untenable, and fundamentally anti-intellectual." This reverence of text made context into con-text, something apart from text and often something with impure impacts on text. The struggle in the humanities to theorize this relationship marks the development of interpretation and criticism literatures and, of course, remains a hotly contested issue in discussions of the value of a canon. Even in the 1990s one can still find, for example, studies which ask whether students should be allowed to take context into account when they write or when they interpret.

In Latin root, both context and text refer to connectings, weavings, unitings. Gadamer (1976), in opposition to the privileging of text over context, asks if meaning is not in the text (as accessed traditionally with semantic approaches), then where is it? He acknowledges that meaning can be individuated, unique to the person as interpreter. But, he reasons, if meaning were only individuated there could be no communication. In essence, then, Gadamer shifts attention in hermeneutics from the context of production to the context of interpretation and mandates in line with assumptions such as those detailed above attention to the circular dialectic of interpretation in which he sees a mandate for analyses of an almost endless continuum of factors (e.g., intentions of speakers, authors, interpreters; history, culture, psychoanalytic digs). In theorizing this way, Gadamer denies any basic ontological status to the subject and any ontological distinction between subject and object, a position he shares with many labeled as "postmodernists" (e.g., Bourdieu, 1989; Derrida, 1988; Foucault, 1972; Lyotard, 1984; and Rorty, 1985).

CONTESTED THEMES

If one can designate three major camps of scholars most actively theorizing context, those most apparent in the literature are (a) those grounded in hermeneutics or the analysis of texts (e.g., Branham & Pearce, 1985; Gadamer, 1981; McGee, 1990; Pearce & Cronen, 1980; and Ricoeur, 1981); (b) those grounded in Batesonian pragmatics and systems theory (e.g., Adams, 1997; Bateson, 1978, 1979; Ellis, 1981; and Fisher & Adams, 1994); and (c) those grounded in contextual psychology (e.g., Altman, 1986; Gergen, 1985; Hayes, Hayes & Reese, 1988; S. C. Hayes, 1993; McGuire, 1986; and Owen, 1996) with its emphasis on Pepperian (1942) contextual worldviews. As noted earlier, in the literature one finds some comparisons between these camps and these inform my discussion below. But my purpose is broader for I bring to bear on this discussion treatments of contextual ideas that fall outside the network of citations in these three camps: for example, those from scholars labeled as postmodernists, symbolic interactionists, and so on. Again, my intent is to inform my own use of context so the trajectories of discontinuities I tease out here owe allegiance only to my own interpretative framework. Further, my discussion attempts to dig deeper than the contests thus far explicitly identified in comparisons. Most of the contests in treatments of context involve subtleties at play within common themes. Thus, for example, while all these theorists accept the idea of the necessity to study communication processes in context and all accept that context is social, there are some marked differences in how the social is conceptualized. What is most striking to me is that the common themes described above are usefully seen as a kind of worldview (again McGuire's, 1986, term a kind of "wonder" seems to fit). While this worldview mandates certain methodological moves in common, in fact methodological differences most often are accounted for by undiscussed differences. Whether the lack of attention to these contests is by omission or commission is often not clear. It is also telling to note that even though these theories share a common contextual worldview, among the issues which divide them are issues commonly associated with polarizations between those who adhere to contextual views versus those who do not. This suggests that our discussions of what divides us are often based on superficialities that serve as markers. Thus, much is made of the contests between so-called quantitative versus qualitative work and this has become stereotyped as the absence versus presence of variable analysis and use of numbers. However, the differences in how context is conceptualized seem at root to have far more to do with the divide. This, in turn, suggests that the bridge between meta-theory, theory, and methodology is too infrequently addressed.

It is difficult to find an order in which to present these contested themes because they are so very intertwined. The reader may find it most helpful to start by skimming the entire set. Further, while each of these themes has direct implications for methodology, I will delay attending to these until the final section of this chapter.

Width of history: Now versus then. While all those theorizing context refer to the historicized event as context, what is meant by history differs. For some (Altman, 1986; S. C. Hayes, 1993), the term *historicized* seems to refer to an anchoring in the here-and-now as opposed to the kind of trans-situational theorizing that has traditionally characterized a more positivist social science. In contrast, historicized to others (e.g., Foucault, 1972, 1979; Gadamer, 1981; and Ricoeur, 1970, 1981) means anchored in the time-space of both the present and a potentially infinite past, with the limitation, of course, that interpretations of the past are necessarily contextualized in the present.

Play of power: Present versus absent. In the most overt way, this contest involves a difference between those contextually-oriented theorists who are informed by Marxist scholarship and those who are not. For the former (e.g., Bourdieu, 1989; Foucault, 1972; Gramsci, 1988; Hall, 1989; Lukes, 1974; and Ricoeur, 1981) power is itself accepted as pre-contextual—as direct or indirect force which pertains to or permeates all phenomena. In contrast, we find McGuire (1986) drawing a distinction between epistemological ways of knowing (those focusing on the nature of knowledge and the language in which it is expressed); power-inscribed ways of knowing (those focusing on issues of power in actuality or image); and perspectivist or contextualist ways of knowing (those focusing on bridging the gap between the knower and the known). In between, we find, for example, various scholars working in the transactional pragmatics tradition (e.g., Adams, 1997; Fisher & Adams, 1994) who attend to power as observable in ongoing human interactions and not in the sense of the historical dig that is mandated by critical approaches.

Nature of the dialectic: Mediation versus constitution. The subtlety involved here is one of whether the theorist emphasizes openness or constraint. Thus, while contextually-oriented scholars generally attend to the tensions between nouns and verbs, product and process, proximity and distance, some refer to the practices which form this dialectical middle as *mediations* while others refer to them as *constitutions*. Some make much of this (e.g., Sigman, 1990) charging that the former term rests on vestiges of fixed reality ideas. Ultimately this tension may arise more from language limitations because whether it is called mediation or constitution, contextualists generally focus on the duality of acting on and being acted upon. Sigman agrees in spirit when he calls for the development of ". . . vocabularies that recognize both . . . relative stability . . . and . . . change" (p. 562).

Relationship to non-contextual approaches: Opposition versus dialectic. At an abstraction level up from the preceding theme is another—that of how contextualists view the utility of the work of non-contextualists. It is perhaps a mark of our time that most contextualists present themselves in polemical contrast. This can itself be interpreted as a contextualized move of the kind that Gadamer (1976) emphasizes when he says "No assertion is possible that cannot be understood as an answer to a question . . ." (p. 11). For Gadamer this is the "most clear-cut evidence of the unsaid [i.e., context] revealing itself in the said" (p. 89). While few speak of it, it is obviously possible to look across the divide of contextualist versus non-contextualist dialectically. Lana (1986) makes the point when he calls for a kind of transcendent dialectic. Even the extreme differences between positivist science and contextualized science can themselves be considered as necessary dialectical forces. To consider one without the other, in an ironic sense, is itself a decontextualizing move. To consider them jointly would, Lana suggests, produce useful explanatory syntheses while leaving the methodological elements of the dialectic intact.

Nature of the subject: Transcendental versus decentered. Perhaps the trickiest issue, the one that draws more passion and protest, is the issue of how to conceptualize the human being. The transcendent human with an essential constancy across time-space is, of course, a fundamental tenet of the Judeo-Christian tradition. The trait-described human, boxed in by demographic, personality, and other attributes, has been a constancy of positivist social science. Despite the core contextual belief that context and person (when assumed theoretically as separable) constitute and are constituted by each other, some contextual approaches appear to retain efforts to find human constancy across time in space. Thus, for example, in distinguishing interactionist approaches from contextualist approaches, Veroff (1986) sees the former as looking at personality as stable but complex and impacted differentially by contextual factors. In contrast, Veroff asserts, the latter assume that what is stable about humans is not their personalities as these change with experience but human orientations to change.

Gadamer (1976), as was noted earlier, is an exemplary contrast to these efforts to retain a conceptualization of the human as constant across time-space when he denies any basic ontological status to the subject. Colapietro (1988) draws the same kind of emphasis from his efforts to connect the works of Marx and Dewey. Both, he says, replaced the free, conscious individual of classical liberalism with the situated, divided, conscious, unconscious subject. In essence both Dewey and Marx abandoned the isolated individual as the foundation of social order for the situated, contextualized subject bound into a matrix of human subjectivity. From these moves, of course, it is not too far to the positions of various scholars labeled as postmodern pointing to the decentered subject. One example is Foucault (1979) with his emphasis on socialized "docile bodies." Another is Derrida (1988, p. 8) for whom the subject disappears entirely and what remains is text (often referred to popularly as discourse formation) and the "essential drift" in interpretations and uses of that text over time.

Focus on behavior: Interpretation versus observable action. To exemplify this contest, I will attend to two approaches to contextual work that are both labeled discourse-analytic. One of these is more heremeneutically-based and focuses on surrounding contextual interpretation utilizing all possible sources of edification. Gadamer's (1975) anti-method method is a primary example with his emphasis on spiraling and never-ending successive interpretations approaching but never reaching a "fusion of horizons." In contrast is the transactional pragmatic approach (e.g., Adams, 1997; Fisher & Adams, 1994) which focuses only on observable behaviors in order to identify patterns of relationships between, for example, content of talk and relational/temporal structures. Proponents of the latter approach sometimes explicitly state that they see a focus on interpretation or sense-making as antithetical to what they understand as contextualism.

Choice of method: One versus many. Necessarily it follows that the various contextualists differ in allegiance to method. Some (e.g., Gadamer, 1976; McGuire, 1986) call for a multiplicity of approaches although Gadamer, while calling for a multiplicity of surrounds is explicitly anti-method. McGuire is more typical of the method pluralists in his call for psychologists to go beyond their traditional reactive methods and incorporate case studies, text analyses, and a host of alternative analytic forms as well a variety of creative uses of logical and statistical analyses. McGuire has done more to connect contextual philosophy to specific methods than any other scholar I identified. Contrasting with the pluralists are those (e.g., transactional pragmatists) who focus much more narrowly on developing and perfecting methods which allow them to analyze observable behaviors in on-going interactions.

Use of method: Bias versus illumination. This contest reflects the ends of the polarized continuum which I used as a tool in the opening section of this chapter. Within the spirit of contextualism, as well as between contextualist and non-contextualist approaches, is a divide. On one side are those who are anti-method. On the other are those who see the absence of method as concomitant with the absence of systematic scholarship. Those on the "anti-method" side call for holistic approaches that create narratives or accounts bringing together multiple strands of attention. They eschew anything that is analytic in the variable analytic sense. At the other side are those who see the dangers of reification and the freezing of the fluid as necessary concessions in the service of their goals to conduct research with consequence. L. J. Hayes's (1993) discussion is useful, referring to two contextualisms—descriptive and functional. The former with its emphasis on holistic description stays true to contextualism's root metaphor but remains isolated from practical goals. The latter borrows more mechanistic methods to serve practical ends but in the process threatens its own philosophic roots. Gadamer (1975) is, of course, most identified with the anti-method stance because of his assertions that anything that is methodical is reductive and necessarily suppresses those aspects of experience that do not fall within the methodical range. At a more abstract level here, however, is not the issue of method. Even Gadamer points not to possible step-takings (e.g., psychoanalytic digs, cultural analyses, etc.) but rather the impact of the constraints of reciped methods. The contest here is with mindless method not method per se. Only the most extreme qualitative perspectives call for the absence of analysis (e.g., an autobiographical account presented without analysis). The issue is not analysis but brutal decontextualizing analysis. Ultimately, the contest here pertains to the reduction of methodology to reciped method.

Depth of the dig: Surfaces versus dark depths. Necessarily related to the above is a difference in how much attention various contextualists pay to the depth of their digs. While all seemingly accept that what is involved in inquiry is not as straightforward as positivist social science assumes, what differs is the intensity of the mandate to pursue dark and hidden depths in a dig for which the archeological metaphor seems apt. This difference seems to relate primarily to the extent to which different theorists emphasize power. Those who do are more likely to assume that power does not play out on surfaces but rather in often hidden depths requiring, for example, psychoanalytic digs or multiply intersecting spirals of cultural and historical interpretation. Attention to power alone does not fully account for this division, however. Another aspect seems to be the pursuit of refined and narrow methods versus the pursuit of multiple methods. McGuire (1986), for example, does not emphasize the power dimensions of context but does imply in his call for innovative approaches a need to attend to deeper and deeper complexities.

Nature of interdependence: Hierarchy versus infinite regress. This contest relates to the issue of depths. Some contextualists relying more heavily on systems theory roots place privileged attention on the notion of hierarchies of contextual factors. Bateson (1979) is one example although clearly Bateson's hierarchy is more, as he puts it, a "dance of interacting parts." This very emphasis on parts in any kind of systematic order is, however, antithetical to the more descriptively and holistically oriented contextualists. Again, at issue here is the extent to which analytic moves are seen as invading the root contextual metaphor.

Role of the researcher: Contextualized versus decontextualized. All those who move toward contextual approaches concur that the researcher being involved in communicating (and, thus, both in observing and being observed) is theoretically contextualized. What happens in research practice is quite another matter. There is a general call for reflexivity—as Morawski (1986) puts it, the act of turning back on oneself. But the closer the contextualist moves to methodical reciped method, the less likely one is to find reflexivity in practice although there is no reason to believe that this is a given. Also at issue here is the extent of the demand placed on the theorist to move between the parts of their theorizing in strictly methodical logical steps. Thus, the method of theorizing is called to account as well. Gavin (1988b) in his comparison of Marx and Dewey teases out the idea that any allegiance to a non-foundational position implies a necessary involvement of value and subjectivity on the part of the theorist. The spirit of this idea appears in S. C. Hayes's (1993) assertion that all theories of truth are illusory but the contextualist admits to valuing a utility-based theory of truth. In the same volume, L. J. Hayes (1993) develops the same kind of an idea when calling for a goal-oriented contextualism because in the absence of a stable foundation effort can only be evaluated against goals which are themselves value decisions. In the absence of such explicit statements of goals, L. J. Hayes warns, there is a danger of creeping dogmatism.

Purpose of research: Intervention versus transformation. Little discussed but in many ways most obvious is the difference in various contextual approaches in their emphasis on interventionist versus transformatory potentials of research. What is involved here seems to be more of a contest over whether the scholar's focus is on serving policy and planning needs as currently defined or on critiquing and reconceptualizing the nature of society. The former perspectives are typically labeled as administrative and the latter typically as critical but in actuality the dividing lines are not so clear. As a group, scholars focused on contextualism seem more likely than most to be worried about issues of ethics and fears of imposition and more concerned about assisting society in change for the better. These attentions are in essence mandated by the premises of the contextual worldview and its anchor in situated purpose as criterion. Clearly, though, there are marked differences in how different contextualists talk about change.

Some contextualists (e.g., L. J. Hayes, 1993) discuss in some detail the conditions under which the contextualist can produce outcomes which allow useful interventions in planning and policy processes. L. J. Hayes speaks quite explicitly, for example, of the need to manipulate context because one can not impact human action directly. This is a sleight of hand move, of course, and Hayes recognizes it when later she mentions this paradox: If context is only realized in action and if I am part of context, what is it that is being manipulated and with what justification? Perhaps what we have here is in part vestiges of old mechanistic vocabularies. The word "manipulation" in itself raises a red flag.

A different kind of discourse is found with other contextualists who focus on utopian ends. What they all have in common is a debt to philosophical perspectives which imbue a self-reflexive attention to societal transformation. Dewey (1960a), for example, emphasized philosophy as a tool for reconstruction. In describing Dewey (along with Heidegger and Wittgenstein), Rorty (1979) saw Dewey as starting out as a foundation-alist but later warning of its dangers. Dewey's later work, Rorty says: ". . . is therapeu-tic . . . edifying . . . designed to make the reader question his motives for philosophizing" (pp. 5–6); and, designed as well (Rorty, 1982) to offer greater alternative perspectives and options for future action, to challenge worldviews.

Inherently involved in this kind of a move is the idea of unmasking the "potency" of interpretation and how interpretation serves the order of things (Sigman, 1990, p. 560). This kind of methodological attention is popularly labeled as deconstruction although what various scholars do when they deconstruct varies markedly (e.g., Derrida, 1988; Foucault, 1965). The very premises of contextualism (e.g., that humans constitute their worlds and are constituted by them) suggests for scholars such as Douglas (1986, p. 127) the mandate for a different kind of moral philosophy to serve research. Gadamer (1976) approaches this point when he speaks of the virtues of "translation"—allowing the for-eign to become one's own in a fusion of horizons which does not neutralize any con-tributing perspective (p. 94). The ". . . hermeneutically enlightened consciousness," he says, "seems to me to establish a higher truth [and] . . . draws itself into its own reflec-tion" (p. 94). Slack (1989) and Marvin (1989) point in the same direction when they emphasize that in contextualized scholarship relating to technologies attention shifts from decision-making and choices to how technologies may contribute to conditions of self-knowledge. Sontag (1966) also points in the same direction when she refers to the con-sequences of this deconstructing process as an awesome responsibility for inherently it involves "modifying consciousness and organizing new modes of sensibility" (p. 59).

Of course, the line between such self-reflexive, consciousness-raising goals and imposition of dogma or tyranny is easily crossed. In his often quoted statement (Gavin, 1988a), Marx called for philosophers to do more than interpret the world: ". . . the point is to change it." While this statement was embedded for Marx in a complex theory of human subjectivity and human need, in fact the complexities of his project have often been overlooked (Heller, 1974). Clearly, whether critical or administrative in orienta-tion, research informed by contextualist worldviews is challenged to a new kind of schol-arly self-reflexivity and humility.

Potential for universals: Nouns versus verbs. As Taylor (1989) puts it: ". . . dis-tinguishing human universals from historical constellations and not eliding the second into the first so that our particular way seems somehow inescapable . . . is the greatest intellectual problem of human culture" (p. 112). The issue of whether there are any uni-versal understandings possible from contextualized approaches remains contested but really more so at the ends of polarized continua. Those who are theorizing contextual approaches most often operate in an elusive terrain in between where they are not easi-ly categorized and most explicitly hold out the promise of universals of one kind or another. Thus, for example, Colapietro (1988) says of Marx and Dewey that their attention to historical context does not preclude attention to universals.

As one traverses this body of work, there seems to be four different kinds of attention to universals which are rarely simultaneously present. What they have in common, however, is that they are all methodological. The first three have to do with methodology as theory of method—here providing guidance for step-taking in observing. One is the idea that more complete understandings emerge from contextual approaches. McGuire's (1986) comment is representative: The perspectivist (contextualist) does not deny the "imperfections of knowing" but instead exploits them by ". . . using the fuzziness and internal contradictions of knowledge representations dialectically to create additional knowledge, until a holographic image emerges from the convergence of multiple fuzzy representations of the known seen from different perspectives" (p. 274). Gadamer (1975), operating out of a very different discourse, approaches the same idea with his often-used phrase "the fusion of horizons."

A second reach for universals focuses on the moral consequences of the unraveling of processes of interpretations for human self-knowledge. Here, in essence, the utopian idea gets implemented as a universal in the sense of becoming a mandated methodological move. The issue is not whether one can make utopias but rather the value of pointing in utopian directions. A third reach for universals is the mandate to bring to bear a greater variety of methods, that this kind of method plurality is an inherent mandate of the contextual worldview.

Finally, the fourth reach toward universals is a bit different in that it points more toward methodology as theory for theorizing or a theory of method for theorizing. The universal implied here is the call in contextualism for theorizing focusing on both verbs or process manifestations and on noun or product manifestations, and on dialectical bridges between. This, in turn, mandates the kind of emphasis on practice and action which characterizes much of this work. It is, in essence, a reach for a new kind of understanding of the human condition—not an understanding of what that condition is or even was or might be, but rather an understanding of its becoming, its struggling, its transforming. One implication of this kind of change in focus is the possibility that process approaches focusing on verbs will engender a new kind of knowledge about the human condition, a knowledge including some of those elusive universals, which pertains not to substance but to process.

Inherent paradoxes: Decontextualized or contextualized context. One theme permeates the discussion above but needs separate attention. Virtually every contextualizing theory points to things which are considered pre-contextual. These essentially axiomatic propositions are often described as a minimalist approach to ontologizing because, of course, contextualizing perspectives mandate against positing ontological existences across time and space. Thus, for example, Gadamer (1976) deontologizes the human subject but mandates that ". . . depending on the situation is not situational" (p.

66). Others, as noted above, speak of the idea of context being in itself pre-contextual and of the inherent difficulty of talking about context when one is part of it. Others refer to the contradiction of having to rest research on human-established goals in the absence of a stable foundation while being party to the constituting of the very context that is being studied.

L. J. Hayes (1993) talks of these contradictions as a permanent ambiguity which must be tolerated. If not, contextualism would have to be abandoned. Hayles (1990) in speaking of the impact of chaos theories on both the sciences and the humanities refers to the inherent paradox in assertions of this kind: "there is no absolute knowledge" or "everything is contextualized." Everything is thus false except this; or everything is true except this. As has been suggested above, this tension can be looked at as unbearable constraint or welcoming opportunity.

METHODOLOGICAL IMPLICATIONS

In recent years the term *methodology* has been used as a substitute for methods when it is more usefully referred to as *the theoretical analysis of methods*. In essence, methodology is theory for research step-taking, including theory of the methods of theorizing as well as theory of the methods of observing and analyzing. This is an important point to hang on to for, in fact, there is very little useful discussion of methodology in the social science literatures and methodologists (in this sense of the term) are typically under-appreciated.

The many ways in which the themes of context described above play out in the move from theory to method and method to theory—that is, in methodology—is extremely hard to trace at this stage. Clearly, this work is richer in the theory of method for theorizing then in the theory of method for observing and analyzing. The work has generated ideas about context which give direction for theorizing potential.

Figure 7.1 attempts to picture using an analogic spatial language the relationships between reality, information, person(s), structure(s), context(s) and actions/practices implied in a series of 10 theoretic treatments of context, organized in rough chronological order of their appearances in social science literatures.[4] The set of 10 pictures is not intended to be exhaustive, nor representative of any particular single or body of work. Rather the intent is to show how over time conceptualizations of context have changed. In pictures 1 through 4, for example, there is no context. First there is reality from which information mysteriously emerges (picture 1); then there is reality from which information emerges mediated either by persons (picture 2) or structures (picture 3); or by the actions of persons or structures (picture 4). In picture 5 we find the relationship between reality and information mediated now by persons or structures in context (in culture, in episteme, in historical formation) and in picture 6 we see structure and person now

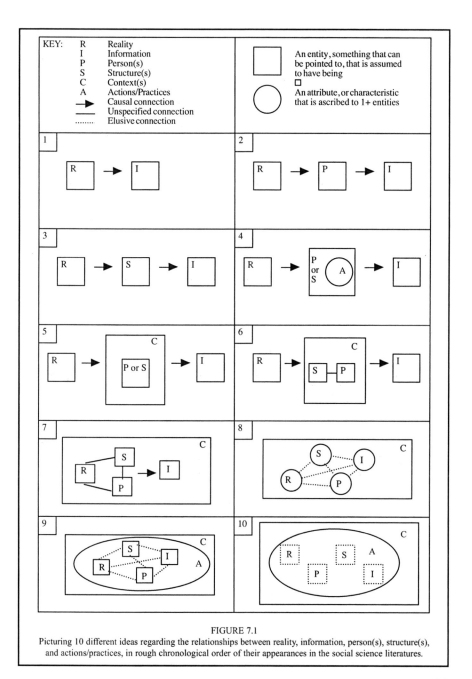

FIGURE 7.1
Picturing 10 different ideas regarding the relationships between reality, information, person(s), structure(s), and actions/practices, in rough chronological order of their appearances in the social science literatures.

explicitly but intertwined in context as mediator between reality and information. With picture 7, something radically different happens. Neither reality nor information exists now outside of context—this is the first contextualized picture. With picture 7 we see an intertwined but unspecified relationship between reality, structures, and persons which yields that which is called information. With picture 8 the relationships become not only unspecified but elusive with two important changes: Information is no longer seen as separate consequence, and the elements—reality, person(s), structure(s), information—become attributes of context rather than entities in context. In picture 9 structures, reality, information, and persons become but instances of actions and practices which characterize contexts. This is another more radical ideational move pointing toward perspectives which are frequently labeled "postmodern." Finally, in picture 10, we see reality, structure, persons, and information as themselves disappearing—as merely noun manifestations of the situated actions/practices which are attributes of context.

The purpose of this brief ideational journey is to provide some flavor of the profound implications of these differences in ideas for theorizing and ultimately research conduct. We move, for example, from a focus on embodied transcendental individuals to fractured decentered elusive subjects. Even more difficult, perhaps, is the idea that seemingly immutable structures are usefully conceptualized as having the same kind of temporality. It is these kinds of changes in fundamental ideas that have led to near agreement among theorists of context that what is called for in contextualized research is a ". . . radical new position regarding the aims and methods . . ." of the human sciences (Rosnow, 1986, p. 309). Further, if we were to really do this, as Shotter (1986) says, we would ". . . find ourselves in a world that is utterly strange to us, even though it would still be the world of our own everyday life" (p. 227).

But what lessons can we extract for step-takings in our own research efforts. Each reader will hopefully draw their own conclusions from the review of common and contested themes above. My own list follows, informed most usefully by Branham and Pearce (1985), Carter (1989c, 1991), Carter, Ruggels, Jackson, and Heffner (1973), Gadamer (1975, 1976, 1981), Gavin (1988a, 1988b), and McGuire (1986). The reader will no doubt ascertain that my position is one of comprehensiveness. I see lessons to be learned from most of the discussions above.

This is not to imply that I do not see incommensurabilities. For example, I mandate that power be a consideration in all my research both because of my interest in critical approaches and because of my conceptualization of movement (and process) as inherently involving forces and, thus, power. Because I make this choice, however, does not necessarily mean that there is nothing for me to learn from acritical work. This goes back to the idea of whether I will see work completed outside my perspective as in opposition and thus irrelevant or as in dialectic and thus as inherently relevant.

In essence, my list of implications can all be summarized in one statement: I must learn—and, I believe we must all learn—to walk the in between:

1. To be concerned about the coherency of our conceptualizations as we move from metatheory to theory to methodology to method and back, but to acknowledge that there is no foundational stable logic that can bridge all these gaps. To understand that there is, as Gavin (1988b) suggests a "will to believe" (borrowing from James, 1927) in between.

2. To find a balance over time between more particularized approaches to research (such as case studies and participant observation, accounts, and narratives) and more systematized approaches to research (such as systematic interviewing and statistical analyses). To understand that I must reach for a variety in methods if I am to implement the contextual mandate to surround. To pursue alliances across bridges with colleagues so that cooperatively we can apply the full range of possibilities to our study.

3. But at the same time to understand the necessary tension between more holistic, narrative-based accounts and more systematic attempts to tease out patterns. To explicitly put these differences into contest with each other. To understand that there is a marked difference between merely incorporating context and being contextual and to put these ways of moving into contest with each other allowing one to inform the other.

4. To posit (as McGuire, 1986 suggests) every contradiction, every inconsistency, every diversity not as error or extraneous but as fodder for contextual analysis. To ask and re-ask what accounts for this difference or this similarity and to anchor possible answers in time-space conceptualizings. To search for and develop a variety of creative ways for bringing multiple sources of evidence to bear on theorizing.

5. To seek out not only multiple approaches but multiple voices. To no matter what research approach I use learn from qualitative researchers the necessity of including myself as a subject of my own examination, and to check with the actors who are the subjects of my focus how they interpret my interpretations. But, at the same time, to not marginalize my own voice. To take seriously what contextualized multi-method, multi-perspective means.

6. To unearth and invent approaches to interviewing and listening to others that are explicitly dialogic and explicitly invite others to theorize about their worlds. But, at the same time, to understand that surfaces and depths, textures and strands, nouns and verbs require different research approaches and that the research interview and even the invitation to multiple voices is but a slice of the spiraling circle. Other, often stereotyped as more determinist approaches, such as political economy or statistical analysis, necessarily inform and enrich. To avoid grasping too firmly to the popular idea that the way to tame the unruly beast of context is to (as suggested by Nofsinger, 1996) focus on context only as relevant to actors in that context. This move is too bound by non-contextual views of the human subject and ignores, for example, the possibility that there is something to be learned from marginalized and protest voices, or from the search for the hidden and silenced.

7. *To risk and own up to my own choices, including the choice to be a contextualist, by defining reflexivity as an ever-present, ongoing mandate. But, at the same time, to not be frozen into inaction or by the fear that every word I speak is potentially a tyranny. To utilize utopian ideas as methodological moves.*

8. *To avoid the temptation of dabbling which seems to beset the human sciences and pursue a programmatic program of scholarship aimed at surrounding my project philosophically and observationally.*

9. *To simultaneously attend to constraint and freedom, finitude and openness, limitation and changeability, flexibility and inflexibility, proximity and distance, historical formation and everyday resistance and invention. To posit that the possibility that a new kind of transsubjective knowledge will emerge from focusing on process, verbs, and dialectics.*

10. *To use the mysterious depths and contradictions of context as methodological tool. In the absence of any kind of essentialist external foundation, it is comparisons and contrasts, discontinuities and bridges, struggles and accomplishments which provide analytic frameworks. The infinite regress of context mandates a constant circling in and out of frameworks which becomes in itself methodological guidance.*

CONCLUSION

Context is something you swim in like a fish. You are in it. It is in you. A contextual view mandates a new way of being as scholar and researcher. The journey, the inventions have just begun. To implement a contextualist methodology implies in essence what Blumenberg (1983) terms not method as planning but as "the establishment of a disposition: the disposition of the subject, in [her] place, to take part in a process that generates knowledge in a transubjective manner" (p. 30).

Admittedly in this discussion I have refused to be cowed by the polarized arguments of either the more postmodern contextualists who see nothing but tyranny in systematization, or the more modern contextualists who see nothing but chaos in a fully implemented contextualism. Rather, I have explicitly chosen the "in-between" as an appropriate position for a contextualist worldview which mandates dialectical attention.

What I have been unable to do is provide reciped guidance for how to tame the unruly beast. In one sense, a contextualist approach requires that we understand that the beast is inherently wild. In a second sense, a contextual approach requires that we be wilder, accepting the inherent absolute unattainability of our quest while pursuing the journey. In a third sense, the taming is of us, mandating a walk toward complexity, toward as Dewey (1960a) proposed, digging deeper.

NOTES

1.   This chapter is based on references obtained from a search of the 75 journals of the communication fields indexed by Comserve. From these, additional references were extracted from bibliographies. Some 200 possible sources were identified but only the 100 most useful are listed in references. (Most of these works are cited within the text; however, helpful sources not cited in text include: Altman & Rogoff, 1987; Ang, 1996; Barthes, 1985; Bruner, 1990; Buber, 1965; Chandler, 1993; Corradi, 1991; Damico, 1988; Freire, 1970; Galgan, 1988; Geertz, 1983; Georgoudi & Rosnow, 1985; Habermas, 1987a; Lacan, 1977; Lannamann, 1991; McCurry, 1993; McDermott, Godpodinoff, & Aron, 1978; McGuire, 1973, 1983; Mishler, 1986; Moores, 1990; Mouffe, 1992; Rosnow, 1981; Sarbin, 1993; Schegloff, 1987; Sontag, 1982; and Woodward, 1993.) The author is grateful to Sam Fassbinder and Kathleen D. Clark, both of whom assisted with literature review; and to Peter Shields with whom continuing discussions regarding philosophic issues guiding the social sciences have been most helpful.

2.   See Dervin (1991a, 1992, 1994).

3.   Pettegrew (1988) is an exception—positing situation as always contained in contexts but his container approach to context is one which ultimately I would label as non-contextual.

4.   The notion of "picturing" was developed by Richard F. Carter (1974a). This version used here was adapted by Dervin (1975).

Chapter 8

Sense-Making's Journey from Metatheory to Methodology to Method:
An Example Using Information Seeking and Use as Research Focus

Brenda Dervin

> *Theory constructs its evidence, and values and faith construct what constitute theory. (Maines & Molseed, 1986)*
>
> *To admit that knowledge is intrinsically erroneous is not to imply that we should forego it. (McGuire, 1986)*
>
> *Theory constructs its evidence, and values and faith construct what constitute theory. (Maines & Molseed, 1986)*
>
> *It is not enough for theory to describe and analyze, it must itself be an event in the universe it describes. In order to do this theory must . . . tear itself from all referents and take pride in the future. Theory must operate on time at the cost of a deliberate distortion of present reality. (Baudrillard, 1988)*

MEGA GAPS:
METATHEORY, METHODOLOGY, AND METHOD

The purpose I have mandated to myself for this chapter is to explore the implications of articulating the bridges that are built, usually implicitly, between metatheory and method, and between these and their ultimate interests, the doing of research. In brief, the purpose is to articulate the uses of methodology. To chart this as a mandate is to assume, in

Reprinted in part from: Dervin, B. (1999). On studying information seeking methodologically: The implications of connecting metatheory to method. *Information Processing and Management, 35,* 727–750. (ERIC Document Reproduction Service No. EJ 601 992). Reprinted by permission of Elsevier Science, Oxford, UK. This version includes a section on "Mega gaps: Metatheory, methodology, and method" not included in the published journal article but presented as: Dervin, B. (1999, May). *Sense-Making's journey from meta-theory to methodology to method: An example using information seeking and use as research focus.* Paper presented at the annual meeting of the International Communication Association, San Francisco, CA.

contradiction to most texts on methodology and methods, that: (a) the journey has not yet been fully mapped; and (b) in fact there are multiple and ever-changing ways of bridging these gaps with no one agreed upon set of criteria by which the results can be evaluated. Above these assumptions is a higher level assumption that impels this journey—that taking an explicitly and self-consciously methodological approach is necessary to the improvement of the enterprise of systematic study. The grounds for this necessity are one of the major themes set out in what follows.

Although the discussion could apply to the systematic study of any phenomenon, for purposes of this chapter the context will be narrowed to the study of human beings and their personal, cultural, and societal structures and practices—specifically, information seeking and use.[1] The context will not be narrowed, however, to only the social sciences for reasons that will become clearer below.

To begin our journey, we must start with two sets of understandings. One provides a background framing of the multiple fault lines facing those who purport to study human beings and their worlds. The second provides a definitional ground for the terms *metatheory, methodology, method* and the focus of their interests, *substantive theory*.

Fault Lines in the Study of Humans and Their Worlds

It is beyond the purpose of this chapter to provide an in-depth overview of the crises which face both the sciences and the humanities in their approaches to the systematic study of humans and their worlds. Suffice it to say, the terrain is highly contested and the subject of a great deal of attention albeit far too little dialogue. In brief, the crises involve a set of polarities that pertain to disagreements about the capacities of, approaches to, and outcomes expected from systematic study.[2]

What is most interesting is that when examined from the highest level of abstraction, the same polarities do their dancing within the sciences and within the humanities, as well as between. All except those who have reduced their study to the most recipe-like robotic activity are struggling. What is the nature of reality—fixed and orderly? Chaotic and fluid? What is the nature of humans—rational and orderly? Muddled and decentered? Are human beings better characterized as transcendent personalities or situated meaning-makers? What is the nature of knowing—mappings which can be tested for validity and accuracy? Interpretations impacted by time, place, experience, and history? What is the best way to think of the human condition—impelled by external forces? Internally driven and motivated? Chaotic and muddled? Searching for universal laws and essences? Searching for interpretations and meanings? What is the role of human language—tools for creating knowledge or frameworks which bind and direct knowledge? What is knowing—can there be "objective" knowledge? Is "non-objective" knowledge useful? What is method—is there neutral method? Do all methods distort? What suffices as an explanation of how reality works—a focus on external causality? Human intention? Historical patterns? Homeostatic, self-regulating conditions? Simultaneity? Narrative? Metaphor? What are viable criteria for evaluating research work—accuracy and validity? Usefulness and vision?

There are, of course, stereotypic debates that mark these struggles—sciences versus humanities, structuralist approaches versus hermeneutic, positivism versus phenomenology, classical Marxism versus cultural studies, realism versus critical realism versus postmodernism, through a seemingly endless list. It is true that within the social sciences foundationalism still holds dominant sway, but not without challenge from a host of counter-approaches (e.g., feminist, phenomenological, interpretivist, cultural, linguistic, ethnomethodological, and interactionist). It is also true that in the humanities the idea of a core canon of cultural products which provide special vision for what it means to be human still holds sway, but it does so amid rising voices of diversity now occupying formalized spaces in the cultural academy.

Clearly there is a force afoot that has been unstoppable, a force that interrupts what might best be called the arrogance ascribed to scholarly knowledge. The force is too often reduced to a single term—postmodernism—and too often marginalized as that which seeks total chaos and denies the species capacity for knowing and for providing order, hence making science and systematic knowledge impossible.[3]

These marginalizations reduce a complex and varied set of debates to seeming silliness and they miss the main point. The fundamental thing that the unstoppable force is about is the challenge to systematic scholarship from the ideas that there is no neutral, objective knowing and that all knowing is implicated in the time, place, tools and histories of its making. Postmodern approaches talk about the downfall of totalizing theories and grand narratives. Translated into the world of everyday experience, the force becomes a mandate for the human species to humble its knowledge, to respect the diversity of knowers, and to find a way to use knowledge without arrogance. The mandate has invaded every aspect of human existence; even for those who reject the mandate, its force impacts their practices.

While the force has been brewing in the philosophical, spiritual, cultural, and scientific discourses for many centuries, as a force it has come to an apparent apex in our time and place. The implications for those of us who aim to do systematic study of the human condition with the goal of achieving some manner of useful understanding is that our work can no longer be conceptualized unproblematically. No matter what our answers to the questions set forth above, we can no longer proceed unselfconsciously whether we would like to or not. We work in a context where no matter how loud the protestations there is no longer one scientific method and one acceptable approach to studying the human condition. At the least, the resulting debates force us to a defensive accountability; at best to a reach across discourse barriers.

This call manifests itself differently in scientifically-driven versus humanistically-driven studies of the human condition. Stereotypically, scholars in the former terrain have focused on a belief that they sought knowledge that mirrored reality and were as observers capable of producing that knowledge with a tool kit of unifying methods labeled scientific; while scholars in the latter terrain have interrogated the positivist and foundationalist assumptions of science with deep metatheoretic explorations while at the same time calling for a plurality of humanistic methods and decrying the specific methods of science as anti-human. Given this portrait, it is useful to think of scientific approaches as having historically been strong on method and weak on metatheory and methodology. In fact, an examination of books on methods and methodology which are primarily written by those coming from the sciences show that they have collapsed methodology into method and built few explicit links to metatheory. On the other hand, for the humanists it may be said they have been stereotypically strong on metatheory and weak on method and methodology. By their own description, they have collapsed methodology into metatheory.[4]

In the midst of these debates, it is not surprising that we find scientific scholars turning to metatheory and humanistic scholars turning to methodology and method. Their journeys are defined within the discourses from which they arise, so not unexpectedly we find warnings among the scientists that they ought not become too philosophical, and warnings among the humanists that they ought not be taken in by the instrumentalities of science.[5] In turn, we find the more interpretive of the scientists being accused of being antiscientific, and the more systematic of the humanists being accused of being too rationalist.

Metatheory, Methodology, Method, and Substantive Theory

One has to examine the writings of only a few scholars on each side of these divides— science and humanities, and their turns to metatheory and methodology—to understand that the journey to inventing new ways of talking about the project of systematic study of the human condition has only just begun. On the surface, the definitions of these four terms seem commonly agreed upon even while uses in practice markedly differ.[6] This set will suffice for purposes here:

> *Metatheory: Presuppositions which provide general perspectives or ways of looking based on assumptions about the nature of reality and human beings (ontology), the nature of knowing (epistemology), the purposes of theory and research (teleology), values and ethics (axiology), and the nature of power (ideology).*

> *Methodology: Reflexive analysis and development of the "hows" of theorizing, observing, analyzing, interpreting.[7]*

*Method: The specific "hows"—techniques, guided implicitly or explicitly by methodological considerations.

*Substantive theory: Inductively and/or deductively derived concepts (which define phenomena) and propositions (which suggest how and under what conditions concepts are thought to be connected); sometimes called unit theory.[8]

What differs between those approaching these terms, however, is which aspect they privilege and how they conceptualize issues of discourse as impacting their efforts. At one extreme, we find some science-based researchers referring to metatheory as orienting strategies and maintaining a separation between the concrete and the abstract, the discursive (i.e., argumentational and rhetorical) aspects of their work and their practices assuming a transparency to their discourse. At the other we find some humanities-based scholars arguing against scientific methods in a technologically determinist way that defies their own theorizings about the capacities of humans to appropriate and reinvent, at least in part, structures (including research technologies and tools) to their own ends.

For my purposes, the extremes of these arguments are less interesting than the moves toward each other. What is encouraging is the variety of efforts emerging that can best be described as "in-between" the polarities, as trying to bridge the gap between more objectivist (i.e., structural, realist, universalist, and quantitative) and more subjectivist (i.e., hermeneutic, interpretive, contextualist, and qualitative) approaches to study. Most prevalent are critiques of the polarities as artificial and illogical; but one also finds explicit calls for so-called "objectivist" studies to attend to the ways in which their work rises from unwitting assumptions embedded in discourses and histories. At the same time, one finds calls for the exploration of statistics as tools in research genres where they were formerly verboten.[9] Most encouraging of all, however, is the emerging call to bridge the polarities with explicit attention to the full and reasoned articulation of methodology.[10]

Despite this encouraging activity, most thoughtful observers agree that the bridges between metatheory, methodology, method, and substantive theory have been little explicated primarily because the terrain to date has been charted by a set of foundationalist assumptions which assumed a knowable orderly human reality and a capacity for creating isomorphic knowledge of that reality. In the midst of such assumptions, the bridges between metatheory, methodology, method, and substantive theory can be flimsy or non-existent, and have traditionally relied on formal logic and statistical theory. Hence, one sees methodology reduced to method in most method texts; and one sees a prevailing absence of metatheoretic talk in most science-based social science journals. The result is that we lack a vocabulary for talking about methodology, a vocabulary which attends to the philosophic mandate in the term, the way in which it might build a bridge between metatheory and method and, thus, make more obvious the impacts of these on research and its theory-constructings. The task is made more difficult because attending to issues of methodology implies a self-conscious a priori choice of method which in turn implies an awareness of at least some of the array of contested possibilities. This, in turn, mandates being informed by and drawing upon understandings from seemingly incommensurate discourses. One of the difficulties with the current moves toward metatheory and/or methodology in both the sciences and the humanities is that most of the moves are ironically insular, concerned far more with self-definition and demarcation of turfs than with building bridges across discourses.

SENSE-MAKING:
A METHODOLOGY BETWEEN THE CRACKS

My intent is to illustrate the implications of forging explicit bridges between metatheory and method, for the practices of research and theorizing. I do this using information seeking and use as phenomenon and the Sense-Making Methodology as metatheoretic tool. Since my intent is exemplification, it is beyond my purpose to provide an in-depth introduction to Sense-Making and its lineages.[11] This section starts with a brief description of Sense-Making, its historical roots and its uses, and then reviews the approach's metatheoretical propositions and how they are explicated methodologically. In a final section of the chapter, implications are drawn, using the phenomenon of information seeking and use as a specific research focus.

Sense-Making has been in development since 1972 by Dervin and colleagues although the label was applied for the first time in 1983. Sense-Making was first developed as an approach to studying information needs, seeking, and use communicatively.[12] What this meant back then and still does is that Sense-Making rests itself on a massive body of evidence regarding the nature of human communicating and concludes that the dominant models used in formalized communication, education, and information systems do not work either efficiently or effectively because they are based on transportation/transmission (sometimes also called *banking*) rather than communication metaphors.[13] Sense-Making Methodology from the beginning has mandated itself to the design of methodology for the communicative study of communication. Information seeking and use are defined as communicative practices. So too are the practices of researching information needs and seeking.

It is important to emphasize, however, that from the beginning Sense-Making has been concerned primarily with theorizing of the metatheoretical sort. Theory as a term is used loosely in scholarship sometimes referring to that which results from and is tested by our work (substantive or unit theorizing); sometimes to that which guides our work (metatheorizing). Sense-Making's mandate has been focused primarily on the development of philosophical guidance for method, including methods of substantive theorizing and of conducting research

From these beginnings, Sense-Making has evolved into a generalized communication-based methodology seen as useful for the study of human sense-making (and sense-unmaking) in any context.[14] As of 1999, some 100-plus persons are actively using Sense-Making as a tool for metatheoretical critique, as methodology for research, as theory about communication, as research method, and/or as guidance for communication design and practice. Much could be said about the uses and misuses of Sense-Making. Some people use it primarily as method, stripping away its metatheoretical intentions. Some refer to it as substantive theory and find it wanting. Others have extrapolated from its metatheory approaches to theorizing and studying a variety of phenomena in a variety of research genres. These include not only library and information science but, as examples, journalism, media studies, cultural studies, critical theory, education and pedagogy, communication campaigns, health communication, citizen-government communication, doctor-patient communication, and telecommunication policy.

There are understandably many different interpretive freezings that can be developed to make "sense" of an enterprise some 26 years in duration involving this many people. For purposes here, I have extracted 15 major metatheoretical themes which I see as permeating the enterprise.[15] One of the difficulties in presenting these assumptions is that they are inherently intertwined and would be best presented in a hypertextual way. For example, Sense-Making's assumptions about the nature of human beings are necessarily related to assumptions about the nature of reality, and the nature of knowing. No one linear order of presentation works best because the linearity of the discourse can only but grasp fragments of what Sense-Making assumes is the complex, analogic, elusive, lived human condition.

The Human Subject, Embodied in Materiality and Soaring Across Time-Space

Perhaps most fundamental of Sense-Making's metatheoretical assumptions is the idea of the human, a body-mind-heart-spirit living in a time-space, moving from a past, in a present, to a future, anchored in material conditions; yet at the same time with an assumed capacity to sense-make abstractions, dreams, memories, plans, ambitions, fantasies, stories, pretenses that can both transcend time-space and last beyond specific moments in time-space. This portrait of the human subject is central to Sense-Making. It mandates simultaneous attention to both the inner and outer worlds of human beings and the ultimate impossibility of separating them. It also mandates positing as possible fodder for sense-making not only thoughts and ideas, observations and understandings, but emotions and feelings, dreams and visions, pretenses and illusions, connections and disconnections.

The Ontological–Epistemological Divide, the In-Between: The Gap

Sense-Making describes itself as methodology between the cracks, as addressing the in-between. This metaphoric self-portrait is a short-hand way of addressing the read of philosophy on which Sense-Making rests. Sense-Making thrusts itself between chaos and order, structure and person, facts and illusions, external worlds and inner, universals and particulars. Sense-Making posits reality as ordered in part, chaotic in part, evolving in part. Sense-Making assumes a human being that is also ordered in part, chaotic in part, evolving in part. Given this joint problematizing of both ontology and epistemology, Sense-Making assumes that the quest of human beings to fix the real faces a never-ending riddle. The real is always potentially subject to multiple interpretations, due to changes in reality across space, changes across time, differences in how humans see reality arising from their differing anchorings in time-space; and differences in how humans construct interpretive bridges over a gappy reality. In attempting to fix which of these explanations is best, we have ricocheted through a series of philosophic all-or-none answers, placing the explanation entirely in reality or structural condition or culture or person or chaos or society, and so on. Instead of choosing all or none, Sense-Making focuses on some, assuming all potential explanations might hold under some conditions.

Time-Space, Movement, Gap: Fluidities and Rigidities

Sense-Making positions time-space conceptualizations as a mandate for theoretic attention. However, unlike many approaches that call themselves situational and/or contextual, Sense-Making does not methodologically mandate attention to substantively based characterizations of situation or context. Rather, it focuses on movement through time-space. What this mandates, in turn, is the description of every human as potentially static across time-space (as manifested in inflexibility, habit, rigidity, stability) or fluid across time-space (as manifested in flexibility, randomness, innovation, creativity). What is important here is not that Sense-Making denies across time-space characterizations of human beings (e.g., culture, demography, structural routine) but rather that Sense-Making mandates empirical attention to the conditions which foster flexibility, fluidity, and change as well as those that foster rigidity, stability, and inflexibility. In Sense-Making, it cannot be assumed in advance that across time-space characteristics are what account for human individual and/or collective sense-making. Nor can it be assumed that any manifestation of human sense-making (e.g., knowledge, learning) remains static. Rather, it is assumed that humans are involved in a constant journey through sense-makings and sense-unmakings.

The Verbing as Primary Ontological Category

Inherent in the explanation above is the idea that the subject, the sentient human being, is no longer given absolute ontological status; nor are the institutions human subjects create and maintain given absolute status. It is assumed that humans and their worlds are constantly evolving and becoming, sometimes decentered, sometimes centered, sometimes fluid, sometimes rigid. It is assumed that structures are energized by structurings; organizations by organizings; human beings by sense-makings and sense-unmakings. Sense-Making refocuses attention from the transcendent individual or collective human unit to the verbing. It is by focusing attention on practices rather than persons that Sense-Making's mandated attentions to time, space, movement, gap are systematically addressed. Sense-Making assumes that movement is the one irreducible of the human condition and that in the face of endlessly multiple interpretations a focus on verbings offers a different entry for the search for systematic understandings of the human condition. Instead of focusing on elusive, ever-changing and constantly challenged nouns, Sense-Making mandates a focus on the hows of human individual and collective sense-making and sense-unmaking, on the varieties of internal and external cognizings, emotings, feelings, and communicatings that make, reinforce, challenge, resist, alter, and reinvent human worlds.

In Sense-Making, the same framework is applied to both structures and agents. Each is seen as potentially changeable across time, sometimes orderly, sometimes disorderly; sometimes centered, sometimes decentered; sometimes flexible, sometimes rigid. The fact that structures change more slowly does not impact the generality of the framework. As a metatheory, then, Sense-Making refocuses our attention away from nouns and substances to verbs and processes, In doing so, Sense-Making assumes that it is only by focusing on changes across time and space and on the flows of events that we can search for and study patterns in the human condition without fixing them tautologically and a priori. The patterns that emerge may pertain to noun aspects of the human condition (e.g., a structure or person moving through time-space in repetitive ways)—the very kind of understanding which has been the almost sole quest of scholarly studies to date. Or, the patterns that emerge may pertain to fluidities in sense-makings and unmakings opening up a new kind of theorizing.

Where the Real and the Interpretive Meet: The Verbing Between

Sense-Making further assumes that it is not necessary to privilege either realism-based or interpretative-based methodologies. Rather, Sense-Making reconceptualizes factizing (the making of facts which tap the assumed-to-be-real) as one of the useful verbings humans use to make sense of their worlds. Factizing, of course, is not the only verbing that creates what we call knowledge. There are a host of other verbings involved (e.g., consensusing, negotiating, power-brokering, defining, hunching, muddling, suppressing). By focusing on the verbings by which sense is made and unmade, Sense-Making frees research from the implicit assumption that there is one right way to produce knowledge. Emoting, for example, usually marginalized as a non-useful strategy for sense-making takes equal footing along with factizing. Sense-Making conceptualizes every verb of collective and individual human sense-making as useful under some conditions and methodologically mandates research to unearth those conditions.

The Role of Power, Energizing the In-Between

A focus on movement across time-space implies the idea of energy. Energizing is central to Sense-Making's focus. Sense-Making mandates attention to forces that both impel, assist, and facilitate movement as well as those that constrain, hinder, and limit movement. In Sense-Making a variety of terms are used: *constraints, barriers, facilitation, motivation, personal power, societal power*, and so on. Sense-Making assumes that issues of force and power pervade all human conditions; that humans are impacted by the constraining forces of structural power (both natural and societal) and that as individuals in specific situations they are themselves sites of power, to resist, reinvent, challenge, deny, and ignore. Again, we see the assumed-to-be-real structure meeting the assumed-to-be-interpretive agent. Sense-Making mandates attention to this meeting in verbings, anchored in time-space. This enables attention to be refocused from the polarized questions which dominate research approaches to human studies (i.e., which is it, the real or the interpretation, the structure or the agent?) to conditional analyses. Sense-Making mandates asking not what questions but what if questions—under what conditions does something ensue with what consequences. The term *consequence* is used here not to imply causality as the only outcome but rather as con-sequence, pointing to all possible outcomes.

Horizons, Past, Present, and Future

In keeping with the focus on movement through time-space and coupled with the assumption that humans have the capacity to be both anchored materially in time-space and soar across time-space, Sense-Making mandates attention to time horizons, past, present, and future. Every sense-making instance is seen as arising from a past in the present and moving toward a future. In this way, then, the sense-maker is assumed to be simultaneously situated and transsituated. This implies simultaneous attention to the interplay of history, presence, and movement as a focus of empirical attention.

Ordinary Human Beings as Theorists

Extrapolated from the above is a central assumption that ordinary human beings are theorists, not just potentially theorists, but theory-makers. Sense-Making posits that theory-making is a mandate of the human condition given pervasive discontinuity. This discontinuity manifests itself in multiple ways: in the gappiness of the human condition with its gaps between external worlds and internals, time, and space; in the gaps between human mind, tongue, heart, body; in gaps between people at the same time; in gaps in a person across time; in gaps between structure and person, structure and structure. The assumption of pervasive discontinuity leads to the assumption that no human movement, collective or individual, can be fully instructed or fully constrained a priori. The next step may be a repetition, or an invention; by design or by caprice; in conformity or resistance; a muddle or a thrashing about. Whatever the next move, whether it be a move by a single person, or a move by one or more persons on behalf of a collective, that move is made without complete instructions or constraint. The very idea of this incompleteness presents the possibility of considering these moves as at least in part designed (consciously or unconsciously, repetitively or innovatively). Being in part designed, they can be conceptualized as practices that are in some way theorized even if that theorizing appears mute and inarticulate or dominated and constrained. It is in this space that Sense-Making mandates the positioning of humans as theorists and the study of communication as dialogic.

Talking the Embodied and Unconscious into the Cognitive and Conscious

Given its complex theory of the human subject, Sense-Making draws on the metatheoretical underpinnings of a variety of psychoanalytic theorizings to posit that humans potentially have the capacity to, at least in part, and often in struggle, translate knowings from the unarticulated realms of their beings (emotional, spiritual, embodied unconscious) to the articulated. This is an important assumption because it is what allows Sense-Making to posit that ordinary human subjects have the capacity to dialogue with us about how they make and unmake their worlds, how they see and struggle with the forces of power in their worlds, how they sometimes stumble about innocent of these forces, and how they sometimes collide with them. It also allows us to ask what they might do if not so constrained, to tell us of their dreams and wishes. To pursue method in this way does not mean that Sense-Making assumes all humans have clear visions of themselves. Rather, it assumes that the struggle to see self, others, reality, the social world is a struggle with moments of confusion and insight, with observings that turn out to be factually useful and ones that do not, with events amenable to factizing and some that are not. Sense-Making posits that across human beings we can ascribe this kind of trust to the capacity for human articulation even if in a given moment a single human or across moments all humans seem mired in confusion or illusion or delusion. Sense-Making also posits that humans can and will talk about their confusions and stumblings if the dialogic interface is conducive to trust.

A Utopian Imagination

Sense-Making may be described as an inherently critical methodology in the sense that it has mandated itself to the redesign of communication procedures and systems to better serve human beings. This mandate is inherent in its development, resting as it does on assumptions that the theories of communication that guide communication systems and practices are usually transportation/transmission theories and not theories of communication and dialogue. Indeed, Sense-Making assumes that the invention of communication-based alternatives to the design of organizations, governments, systems, and, indeed, society, is a mandate for the species as we face a future caught between tyrannies of imposed dogmas and Towers of Babel of ever-increasing multiple interpretations. To say this, however, does not mandate Sense-Making-guided research as ideological. It posits a utopian focus not as an end, but a methodological move. And, it acknowledges simultaneously that all research on the human condition inherently impacts the design of human worlds. To, for example, assume that human behavior is propelled by across time-space characteristics such as demography and to then produce research results that only pertain to that assumption will necessarily reify demographic-foci as design principles. By explicitly focusing on potential redesign and invention as a methodological move, Sense-Making intends to free the research it guides from assuming and then reinforcing without explicit test any particular assumptions about human rigidities, inflexibilities, and incapacities for change. Sense-Making makes the issue of human flexibility versus inflexibility (resistance and creativity, habit and fluidity) foci of empirical investigation. Further, Sense-Making assumes that research such as in the genre focusing on information seeking and use whose intent is to inform system design and operation must adopt a utopian methodology for it is only in this way that the research can break free of unstated assumptions embedded in the normatively accepted defining discourses of the system.

The Researcher as the Researched: A Dialogic Humility

Sense-Making also explicitly positions the researcher as humbled and dialogically involved. This implies that the researcher must be involved in a new order of research verbings to serve a mandate of self-conscious self-reflexivity. This requires even more than a concern for the potential tyrannies of interpreting the worlds for others. It requires the positioning of self as a focus of investigation, as an exemplar of the human condition. Further, it implies a use of self as a site and tool for the bridging of discourses and the development of dialogic procedurings that make this possible. This does not imply that researchers suppress their own interpretations, or the access to understandings that the privilege of their chosen life paths gives them. Rather, it implies that these are humbled and tested in dialogue and that the researcher become a vehicle of dialogic practice. Further, it implies that just as Sense-Making assumes that ordinary human sense-makers struggle with multiple verbings in myriad conditions with myriad outcomes and uses, researchers as human sense-makers are likewise involved.

Searching for Patterns: Multiple Connectivities

Sense-Making assumes that there are myriad ways that human beings have individually and collectivity verbed their worlds, in adaptation, response, resistance, creativity, challenge, and invention. This, in turn, implies that in attempting to understand the human condition Sense-Making admits all manner of connectivities and patterns, not just causalities but spontaneities, simultaneities, temporalities, collaboralities, and so on. This includes not just connectivities that imply anchorings in the real (e.g., factizings, experiencings, or structurings) but those that imply soarings beyond (e.g., narratings, fantasyings, or imaginings). In essence, Sense-Making mandates that the connectings between entities and events that have been traditionally called theorizing and traditionally relegated to the researcher's superior tools and training become themselves a focus of study. A causal assumption would, for example, become an interpretive focus not merely an outcome of statistical testing or researcher extrapolating. By positioning ordinary persons as theorists, Sense-Making mandates that ordinary persons be asked and that the patterns—the connectivities—not be imposed by assumption. Where there are different "readings" (and Sense-Making assumes there always will be) these must themselves be put into dialogue rather than making one reading central by caveat and homogenizing or marginalizing the rest.

Metatheory as Deconstruction

Implied by the assumptions above is the idea that metatheory must be an inherently deconstructive enterprise. In Sense-Making, it mandates the freeing of theorizing about human patterning from a priori imposition by assumption. It becomes theorizing for the opening up of and pointing to ways of looking. It mandates, for example, attention to verbings of the structure-agency relationship, to verbings for how the forces of structural power intersect with the forces of human creativity and resistance, and to verbings of how humans struggle to balance fluidity and constancy, flexibility and habit, anchorings and growth as they move across time-space. Sense-Making does not mandate particular research questions as much as a way of looking at all research questions. It reaches for a more generalizeable way of looking as a methodological framework that can be applied in particular phenomenal contexts. In this way, Sense-Making aims to interrupt (or at least trouble) the too often tautological connections between method and result.

Standards of Explanation: The Dialectic Dance of Contest and Commonnesses

Fundamentally, what Sense-Making mandates is a moving from a focus on nouns to a focus on verbs. This, in turn, permits a way of looking at nouns which is free of nouns in several senses. In one sense, it allows the researcher to be freed of the riddle of understanding one noun-based interpretation through the lens of another noun-based interpretation. When noun-based theorizing (usually substantive or unit theorizing) is used as the sole basis for extracting understandings what happens is that the standard for analyzing is inherently bound into the phenomenon. The conclusions become too readily tautological. It is as if we were mandated to describe an orange by calling it not-apple, or second-class fruit. Instead, Sense-Making mandates that the nouns be compared to each other outside a noun framework. This is what is meant when Sense-Making is described as a verbing methodology. Further, Sense-Making frames a series of mandated dialectical considerations. A particular phenomenon is explicitly positioned as potentially and systematically variable across time, across place, across perspective, arising out of differing ways of verbing sense-making and sense-unmaking. Because of potentially multiple interpretations, Sense-Making mandates not a single explanation but a series of explanations anchored in a series of dialectical considerations focusing on commonnesses and contests. This mandate is a methodological move necessitated by the very metatheoretic premises on which Sense-Making rests. It does not deny the possibility of multiple perspectives finding places of convergence. At the same time it does not tautologically impose this concept by relegating all divergence to error.

A Quadruple Hermeneutic

Sense-Making has been designed, from the beginning, to serve as a methodology for communication practice. Research practice is conceptualized as a subset of communication practice, different in some of its specific qualitative mandates and patternings but not different in any important metatheoretic way when looked at communicatively. In essence, then, it could be said that what is substantively theoretical about Sense-Making is its emphasis on practice because its intent is to be a theory of communication practice. In being a theory of communication practice, Sense-Making faces some challenges which in the context of how we have traditionally looked at theory and methodology seem almost paradoxical. A theory of practice is, for example, inherently methodological; it is a terrain where methodology elides into substantive theory. Sense-Making focuses on the making and unmaking of sense, the practices and procedures by which individuals and collectives make and unmake their worlds. It focuses on verbs, not nouns. It stands between traditional foci on structures and traditional foci on persons. It is inherently then a methodology between the cracks and at the same time a theory of practice. If it remains true to its intent, Sense-Making cannot freeze itself in order to become the many things which are demanded by approaches that focus on nouns. By definition, Sense-Making focuses on movement and fluidity, even when that movement and fluidity involves repetitions and habits. This web of connections is elusive and inherently paradoxical because it mandates theorizing (which has been traditionaly thought of as freezing) something which is inherently fluid—process. At the same time, Sense-Making, in line with a variety of chaos theories, sees a new kind of understanding made possible by attending to seemingly disorderly processes. What this means is that there is a kind of quadruple hermeneutic operating in Sense-Making's enterprise. Any methodology involves interpretations (hermeneutic #1). In the case of studies of human beings, the focus is the interpretations of interpretations made by researched human beings (hermeneutic #2). But Sense-Making is self-consciously focused not on interpretations per se, but on interpretings, those of researchers-interpreting interpretations (hermeneutic #3) of human-beings-interpreting interpretations (hermeneutic #4).

Sense-Making assumes that this mandate to attention to verbings is a new kind of mandate for scholarly attention, a mandate which offers ground for a new kind of theorizing, a theorizing that focuses on verbings. But the theorizing involved in Sense-Making is cast primarily as metatheorizing which presents itself as guidance or method for theory-building (i.e., substantive or unit theorizing) and at the same time as theory for method. It is at this juncture where we can see most clearly the inherent elusivenesses in the margins between metatheory, methodology, method, and substantive theory. At the highest level of abstraction, Sense-Making's metatheory impels a particular kind of substantive theorizing. When implemented in a particular phenomenal context (e.g., information seeking and use), the particular implementations will be unique to that discourse and certainly be framed in the modes of empirical working relevant to that discourse whether qualitative or quantitative. But at the highest level of abstraction, metatheory and substantive theory elide into each other. Substantive theory in this sense falls out of the metatheory-methodology-method fusion. Its potentials are residual of that fusion. This is so whether the bridge between metatheoretic assumptions and the practices (i.e., methods) which propose and test substantive theorizings are fully explicated or not. One of the difficulties facing both humanities and a social science-based study of humans and their conditions is that the bridge from metatheory is rarely explicated into method. Researchers assume one set of things at the highest level of abstraction and implement another in method. The point being made here is that our work is in desperate need of more articulated methodological bridges.

IMPLICATIONS FOR THE STUDY OF INFORMATION SEEKING AND USE

There are three ways in which Sense-Making's metatheory is implemented in method: (a) in the framing of research questions; (b) in the designing of interviewing; and (c) in the analyzing and concluding processes of research. It is fair to say that Sense-Making's metatheory has never been fully realized either in research or in explication of method. Despite this, one does find growing convergence regarding the guidance Sense-Making gives to the research process. The purpose of this section is to tease out how the metatheoretic assumptions of Sense-Making have been or might be implemented in studies of information seeking and use.

This is done through a series of provocatively designed propositions which interrupt in some way the assumptions about information and its use made normatively in research on information needs, seeking and use. It is important to note before proceeding that in fact the genre of research focusing on information needs, seeking, and use has recently attracted diverse and sophisticated treatments that fall outside the dominant portrait. In fact, there are so many emerging perspectives that it is difficult to find coherence or points of potential convergence even while the eclecticism and flourishing bode well.

In this context, comparing the explicit mandates of Sense-Making to the usually implicit mandates of "normative" or "traditional" approaches to studying information needs, seeking, and use is a rhetorical move to emphasize stark contrasts and permit a more straightforward execution of the use of Sense-Making as exemplar of the journey from metatheory to methodology to method. The comparison is not intended as a critique of research in information needs, seeking, and use studies. It is fair to say, however, that the normative approach to information as presented below still dominates most research on information needs, seeking, and use and certainly most designs of information/communication practice.[16]

"Information" as a Disappearing Category

Fundamentally, Sense-Making mandates the disappearance of the term *information* as a static, absolute, ontological category. This is so for two reasons. First, because the quadruple hermeneutic always stands between an observing and the observed. Second, because it is assumed that anything that might be called information can provide only a partial and temporally tenuous factizing potential of the observed. In method, then, Sense-Making never imposes the term "information" and rarely uses it. The typical study defines "information" as sense-made and asks actors such questions as what questions they had, what muddles they struggled with, what conclusions they reached. When Sense-Making attends to the term "information," its metatheory mandates that the term be qualified with a phrase like "information as defined by the expert." The metatheory would mandate as well attention to challenges and resistances to this "information."

"Information" as Inherently a Structural Term

Thus, Sense-Making mandates attention to the term "information" as inherently a structural term. Information is typically used to describe the observings of experts—their factizings, their concludings, their evaluatings, and so on—which have been given the imprimatur of the consensus through the actions of empowered collectivities and enterprises (e.g., professions or science). Most information seeking and use research constrains itself to this realm. Sense-Making mandates attention to this realm and beyond. The intent is to reach for the most general understanding that incorporates the idea of information as structural representation and at the same time as something that the human species, because of the discontinuity mandate in the human condition, makes and then challenges and unmakes and remakes as events move forward. In method, Sense-Making attends to this in three ways: (a) by bringing work done by political economists, deconstructionists, and other structural analysts to bear on its studies of information seeking and use; (b) by privileging the actor as a theorist of her world, both constructing and interrogating understandings and making observations on the impacts of power on their worlds; and (c) by assuming that challenges to whatever is unworkable about the "information" currently classified as expert or knowledgeable exist at the margins and must be sought out by invoking procedures such as searching for maximum diversity and maximum contest. Thus, Sense-Making mandates attention to the power and authority forces that impact those who make and use information. In a specific study, this might be accomplished by asking actors what barriers stood in their way, what struggles they had, and how power and authority played a role. Further implementations would involve bringing to bear outside deconstructions of the power arrangements in the particular context on these responses; and, as well, putting the responses into contest with each other. A typical approach would be to ask, for example, how actors from different class conditions differed in their responses even if in traditional quantitative senses the variance accounted for by such structural attributes was low.

"Information" Made by Heart, Body, Spirit, as well as Mind

Sense-Making in turn mandates that information-making, seeking, and using not be limited to the cognitive realm (as it usually is in information seeking and use studies) but rather to any realm of experiencing that actors define themselves as using in their sense-making. The patient who says "my body told me" is making sense, so is the problem-solver who said "God told me" or "I listened to my feelings" as well as the one who said "I looked it up on the Web" or "I asked an expert." The point here is not that Sense-Making wishes to topple the edifice of knowledge-making that is one of the finest heritages of the modernist movement. Rather the point is that Sense-Making aims to arrive at a useful understanding of human sense-making to be used in the design of information and communication systems and procedures. In method, then, Sense-Making asks actors if they bridged gaps and how. The how is not constrained: Actors are explicitly asked what emotions they felt, what feelings they had, what ideas or conclusions they came to; and actors are asked how each of these helped and/or hindered.

"Information" with Good Outcomes and Bad

In contrast to most information seeking and use studies which assume information use is always good because it allows the user access to established expertise, Sense-Making assumes that sometimes the fodder which sense-makers use is seen as leading to useful outcomes and sometimes to hurtful and non-useful outcomes. This assumption harkens back to Sense-Making's fundamental assumptions about epistemology and ontology. In method, then, every Sense-Making study asks actors the consequences, the helps and the hinders, the positive and negative outcomes, of coming to a conclusion, arriving at a fact, having a thought, feeling a feeling. In research questions, Sense-Making would mandate attention to the negative outcomes as well as positive as essential for research mandated to assist system and procedure design.

"Information" Bridging Gaps in and Between Material and Interpretive Worlds

In contrast to most traditional information seeking and use studies, Sense-Making posits information as sense-made that stands as a bridge over a gap between one time-space moment and another and simultaneously between material and interpretive worlds. Sense-Making, thus, explicitly mandates attention to the space between so-called realist, foundational conceptualizations of information and so-called constructivist, subjectivist conceptualizations. In research questions, Sense-Making attends to this by addressing, for example, the conditions leading to differing interpretations of the same material circumstances; or how people use "information" to make sense differently in the same material conditions. When comparing different material conditions (e.g., sometimes called domains, or contexts), Sense-Making always mandates attention to differences within as well as between. In method, Sense-Making implements this by attending to specific situated events or moments in actor's lives so comparisons can be made within specific kinds of situations as well as across situations and/or times. The primary means for implementing this attention is the Sense-Making metaphor which conceptualizes a human anchored in a history, a structure, and a time-space, moving across gaps, constructing bridges using different verbings for doing so, and arriving at outcomes and consequences. The metaphor is not intended as a literal description of human sense-making (e.g., information seeking and use) or meant to imply that sense-making is linear or purposive although these would be subsets of all possibilities. Rather, the metaphor is intended as a highly abstract methodological tool, a way of looking.

The Actor as "Information" Expert and Theorist

In traditional information seeking and use studies, the respondent/informant is not defined as information expert or as theorist. Hence, the actor is not conceptualized as a source of information (as a scientist would be) nor as a source of understanding regarding the nature of information seeking and use. Sense-Making makes different assumptions, first, by assuming the actor is expert in her world (e.g., of her body, her work, and/or her life). This does not mean there are not other expertises that can be useful as well but it does imply that the actor is conceptualized as a source of expertise. Secondly, Sense-Making assumes the actor as theorist of her world, with hunches, hypotheses, and generalizations about how things connect to things and how power flows. In interviewing method, Sense-Making attends to this by asking actors explicitly how they bridged gaps—what conclusions they reached and insights they arrived at as well as how they got to those conclusions. Further, Sense-Making asks actors explicitly how they see power and authority relating to their time-space moments; and it asks them how things ought to have been if they had worked well for them. In a more general way, Sense-Making aims toward achieving these ends by implementing an interviewing approach that does not name the world for the actor but rather mandates the actor to name the world for herself.

"Information" as Verb

Most information seeking and use studies assume information as a given, as isomorphic (even if tempered as in critical realism) description of a real world. Given this assumption, most studies also implicitly focus on information transmission as outcome as if the receipt of information was sufficient. This privileges outcome over process. For Sense-Making, the difficulty with this conceptualization is that it freezes time-space and person and restricts information to that produced and used by one narrow set of sense-making strategies. Sense-Making calls that narrow set "factizing" and assumes that the human species has historically used and needed a wider set of information seeking and making and using strategies. Further, this traditional approach also collapses many instances of sense-making into one final outcome. In contrast, Sense-Making mandates attention to process, not eliminating attention to outcomes but setting outcomes into process. This interrupts the usual emphasis in information seeking and use studies on "the" outcome as defined by the system and admits multiple outcomes, even contradictory ones. This mandate is best illustrated in the Sense-Making interview approaches where actors are routinely asked "how" things came to be (e.g., What led to this? How did it connect to your life? How did you get an answer?) as well as "how" they evaluated events (e.g., How did it help? How did it hinder?).

"Information" as Making and Unmaking, from Order to Chaos, Stability to Change, and Back Again

Traditional information seeking and use studies bracket information to that which consensually describes order. As a result, we know little about information seeking and use in terrains that require new connections, insightful extrapolations, and the hundreds of different strategizings humans do to bridge gaps between formal information (which is always tied to a past) and the necessities of moving into the future in their material worlds. Sense-Making assumes that the gaps between information and the actions which information might usefully guide always occur in a new here-and-now. Each new here-and-now always includes the potential for not merely grabbing an understanding already constructed but creating one that is new at least in part. Sense-Making assumes this because as a metatheoretic framework it opens up research to the most general level of framing.

Thus, Sense-Making, extrapolating from its metatheoretic assumptions, assumes information to be an in-flux creation of a power structure always subject to the forces of power both for its maintenance and its resistance and change. In framing research questions, Sense-Making mandates attention not just to the maintenance of conditions as they stand and how well users access expert information that mirrors those conditions. Rather, it also mandates attention to how and when expert information fails people in the struggles of their lives and work and how ordinary humans create counter-informational worlds that serve their purposes. In interviewing practice, Sense-Making mandates actors be asked not only about gaps bridged, but gaps created—what muddles and struggles they faced, what constrained them, what questions remained unanswered, what they would have mandated if they'd had a magic wand.

"Information" Habits and Inventions, of Two Kinds

Most information seeking and use studies focus on information seeking and use as habitual habit patterns. They ask what kinds of people seek what information extracting habit patterns that link people conceptualized as static entities to information also conceptualized in static boxes. Sometimes the studies ask what strategies different people use to seek information. Here the emphasis switches to habits in behavior assuming that a given person strategizes the same way across time. Sometimes this extends to a focus on behavior strategies in particular kinds of situations with the situations defined externally in the categories of the dominant system. Here the question is whether the seeker seeks one way in one kind of context and another in another kind. The history of all this work has typically shown low explanation and variance accounted for.

Sense-Making mandates that all these questions be opened up by anchoring information seeking and use in time-space and in movement through time-space. When time, space, and movement become mandated metatheoretic constructs, method must explicitly attend to them. Sense-Making does this by assuming that while people move across time-space their information seeking and using behaviors (both internal and external) can remain static, can change responsively, and can even change chaotically. Method must, then, allow an examination of each possibility. Underlying this is a mandated attention to both stability and change, as well as rigidity and flexibility, and caprice and invention. In specific studies, Sense-Making implements these mandates in a variety of ways. A few examples include: by looking at sense-making in one or more situations as they move across time, or different situations at different times, or in the same situation type at different times. Linking this to the idea of the actor as an expert, Sense-Making would also privilege the actor to do her own "re-evaluation" of change over time with such probes as: Do you think of this differently now? Has your approach to this changed? What led to the change? If you could wave a magic wand, what would you do ideally? What would make it possible?

Predicting "Information" Seeking and Use and the Render-Unto-Caesar Principle

In line with the above, Sense-Making mandates time-space conceptualizations as central to any attempts to predict or explain information seeking and use. Sense-Making asks: When should sense-making be more constrained, exhibit less change across time? Sense-Making answers, drawing on its use of recent philosophy: when external forces are greatest. Thus, Sense-Making expects less variation in information seeking and use in those conditions highly constrained by external authority and hegemonies. This is the "Render-unto-Caesar principle," the idea being that when the state holds sway agents have less room for invention and caprice and change. Thus, for example, it would be expected that information source-using would be more predictable based on across time-space predictors (such as demography) than would what users thought of a particular piece of expertise. Source-using being more constrained by economic forces (hence, the state) would be better indexed by attributes ascribed to persons which mirror the state (i.e., education, and income) while evaluations would be better indexed by attributes of persons-acting-in-situations (i.e., how the actor evaluates her movement options).

Even within this guidance, however, Sense-Making assumes that it is in the realm of sense-making that we find the first hints of resistance and challenge to dominant systems if we can create interviewing situations with enough trust to allow resistant voices to emerge into the light. The Sense-Making interview does this by mandating minimal intrusions and "namings of the world" by interviewers. Except for eliciting attention to a set of critical situations, the Sense-Making interview is constrained to queries based on the Sense-Making metaphor with its emphasis on time, space, movement, gap, power, history, constraint, outcomes, repetition, and change. No other noun-based questions are asked.

Transcending Idiosyncratic "Information" Seeking and Use in the World of the Personal

Information seeking and use research has had limited ability to explain or predict user behavior using traditional categories such as across time-space characteristics of people (e.g., demography or personality), domain characteristics of collections (e.g., humanities, sciences, biology, psychology, entertainment, or news), and topical categorizations of life and work situations (e.g., group collaboration, problem-solving, or leisure time needs). Sense-Making acknowledges each of these as useful attentions but also mandates a more generalizable view that incorporates the actor's world. Traditional categories of situations rarely constitute usual actor names of the world because actors, unless explicitly trained in the discourse of a particular domain, have no reason to adopt its vocabulary.

Traditionally, this kind of non-systematic behavior on the part of individual actors has been marginalized as non-systematic and relegated to error variance because it was assumed that the individual sense-makings involved were capricious and solipsistic. Sense-Making counters this with a metatheoretic mandate: We must add to our perspectives conceptualizations of the personal and that this does not imply a descent into solipsism. Instead, Sense-Making mandates the construction of attributes which capture aspects of movement in time-space bound moments, attributes which attend in some way to Sense-Making's central concepts: time, space, movement, gap. Examples include whether a person sees her movement in time-space stopped in particular ways (i.e., two or more roads ahead, one road ahead but barrier on the road, one road ahead and being dragged down it, no road ahead, etc.). Another example is looking at what the person conceptualizes as appropriate sense-making in the time-space moment (e.g., getting the big picture, finding examples, following someone else's lead, etc.). Another is how the actor defined information as helping (e.g., got an idea, found direction, got a skill, got pleasure, got motivation, got support, etc.). Sense-Making studies have generated a host of these alternative time-space bound predictors. A typical Sense-Making study compares the predictive power of across time-space characteristics of people, domain memberships, topical foci of contexts, and time-space bound movements of actors. These are conceptualized in terms of the breadth of their time-space coverage: Demography is wide, for example; topical context or domain narrower, and a specific micro-moment the narrowest. The question becomes: What accounts best under what conditions?

Even more generally, Sense-Making mandates as its central concepts: time, space, movement, gap, power, constraint, and force. These are applied in every Sense-Making study and to every specific move within a Sense-Making study. If a study focuses on a moment of information sought, Sense-Making applies the entire battery of concepts to that moment in the interview with such questions as: What question did you have? What led to the question? How did it connect to your life? How did it connect to authority/power/history? Did you get an answer? Did the answer help and/or hinder? How? Was the answer complete? What leads you to say that? In essence, then, Sense-Making assumes that a verbing conceptualization offers a way of understanding what is human about information seeking and use in a framework that is not anchored in any given noun structure (e.g., the nouns of a domain world). At the same time, the same verbing conceptualization can be applied to both individual agency and collective agency, whether that agency be based on repeatings that maintain past habits and dominant structures, or resistings and challengings that struggle with them, or inventions and caprices that by design or accident transcend them. In this way, Sense-Making mandates an organizing conceptualization that stands between structure and agency, habit and resistance, flexibility and rigidity. It incorporates them all in a verbing framework.

"Information" on the Horizon

Most traditional information seeking and use studies implicitly bracket information to the now. Sense-Making, specifically through the use of the Sense-Making metaphor, mandates that attention be focused on the phenomenological horizon of the actor's world—the past (including the historical past), the present, and the future; as well as the connections (verbings) between past-present-future. Sense-Making mandates this both for the immediate moment and for the more transcendent slice of time that provides the paradigmatic brackets for the research. If, for example, a Sense-Making study focuses on people's information needs vis-à-vis sexual harassment, each sense-making instance would be anchored in the actor's horizon and the project as a whole would be anchored as well to the discourses regarding harassment—past, present, and potential future—which both informs the work and with which the work struggles.

Barriers to "Information" Seeking and Use, of New Kinds

Traditionally, research in information seeking and use assumes that barriers to information seeking and use have been of two kinds. At the macro level, much attention has been paid to information inequity usually defined as lack of access to information either because of lack of resources or training. This concept it then typically ascribed to individuals who are labeled information poor. From here the work has slid into conjuring a host of attributes of persons which are seen as preventing or deterring them from access to or attention to factual, expert information. Various measures of poverty are so conceptualized as are various measures of human inadequacy. The better information seekers and users, it has been assumed, have been less resistant to information, more open-minded, less emotional, more internally controlled, more networked, more oriented toward facts, more coherent and orderly, as well as more economically affluent, more educated, more culturally ready, and so on.

The result is a deficit approach to examining information use, an approach that ends up blaming the victim and assuming that the information world of the expert is the requisite information world of each and every user no matter how alien or distant that world may be from everyday experience.[17] In contrast, Sense-Making mandates a research approach based on a more general and broader conceptual framework. The approach does not deny the possibility that individual human frailties may stand between a person and information, but it attempts to methodologically free the research from imposing this finding in method.

The change mandated by Sense-Making is one which essentially enlarges the concept of barrier from that which stands between a person and what a system thinks ought to be that person's goal to what stands between a person and her life-facing. Part of the change comes from redefining the nature of reality, information, and human beings. Part comes from explicitly mandating an attention to issues of power. And part comes from mandating that barriers to information seeking and use be defined by actors in situated moments and not be assumed to be of any particular kind but rather of multiple kinds. A typical research question coming from Sense-Making asks under what conditions actors faced what they defined as emotional barriers to information seeking and what led to them; whether actors had struggled with these barriers or came to accept them and how; if alternative routes were found that were more useful and what made it possible. As another example, a Sense-Making study might focus on teasing out sense-making situations in a job context where different kinds of sense-making strategies helped and hindered with an aim toward teasing out the strategies actors use to make sense of situations with variabilities in predictability and power constraints. Yet another study might focus on how actors bridge gaps in situations where massive information databases are assumed by the structure to be helpful but in lived experience are not.

It must be emphasized that Sense-Making does not assume that expert information is or is not helpful. Rather, it attempts to open up a way of not making the assumption a priori based on any traditional conception of what should and should not be helpful information. Further, it opens up to examination the ways in which information helps rather than assuming, as most studies have, that help is inherent in information.

"Information" in the Between

In traditional information seeking and use studies, information has been implicitly or explicitly cast as description of reality. Social structure was not considered. The person—as intended and potential user of information—was usually conceptualized as a de-socialized independent entity. Given the paradigmatic dialogues and contests of recent years, we see emerging a bewildering number of approaches that attempt to bring a more structural, social analysis to information seeking and use, or a more phenomenological, lived experience view. Sometimes we see efforts to do both although too often by collapsing one into the other.

Sense-Making is informed by these struggles, of course, and attempts to mandate attention in the middle by assuming that human life is usefully described both with structural descriptions and with agency descriptions and, most usefully, with intersections of the two which do not give dominance to either. In method, Sense-Making implements this in a number of ways. For example, a Sense-Making study of patient information seeking and use in cancer treatment would, if fully informed by the Sense-Making metatheoretic mandates, attend to such questions as: What information gaps did patients see? Did they see power/authority as impacting this? Where did the patients see information contests? How did they interpret and navigate these? With what outcomes? What helped? What hindered? How?

In this way, Sense-Making mandates an examination of how information seeking and use is used by actors to maintain and collaborate with systems of power as well as resist and challenge them as well as move inventively beyond or capriciously oblivious to them. None of these is valued as better than the other, rather all are conceptualized as possible. Further, by addressing the "in-between" using a verbing framework, Sense-Making privileges neither a realist-foundationalist definition of information nor a subjectivist-constructivist definition. Alternatively, Sense-Making privileges them both while humbling them to verbings.

"Information" and Hidden Depths

The traditional information seeking and use study assumes implicitly that the phenomena being studied is mined easily at shallow depths. Sense-Making, in contrast, assumes that articulation of one's lived experience, including its struggles and resistances as well as alignments with given order, is in itself a Sense-Making journey. Further, Sense-Making assumes, drawing particularly on works in critical pedagogy, that articulating one's world without limiting it to how it can be easily described by dominant discourses requires a process of bringing the unsaid and unarticulated into consciousness, that is, conscientizing. For these reasons, the Sense-Making interview constructed to study information seeking and use has a circular and repetitive character and enlists the informant/respondent as collaborator in shared control of that redundancy. The deliberate design of the interview invites the respondent to bridge gaps usually left to the experts— connections between past and present, present and future; relationships and impacts of power; the very value, or lack of it, of formal information. This invitation is typically a shock but is often warmed to enthusiastically over time. The actor might be asked to describe in detail in terms of micro-moments how she moved through and made sense of a situation with each moment triangulated using the Sense-Making metaphor. Or, a given situation might be mined for the questions, barriers, conclusions, emotions, physical feelings, and insights connected to it with each of these likewise triangulated. In a Sense-Making interview, the actor more often than not adds things remembered later, even calling interviewers to make the additions. Given this description, some might relegate the Sense-Making designed interview to the terrain of the therapeutic. Indeed, it puts onto the plate of the study of information seeking and use an array of interests traditionally seen as irrelevant—emotions, hunches, wishes, dreams. While these are traditionally marginalized by being relegated to the therapeutic, Sense-Making mandates attention to them as verbings relevant to the study of information seeking and use.

The Researcher as the Researched: A Humbled Ordinary "Information" Seeker

The traditional information seeking and use study has not typically attended to the researcher as an information seeker to whom the metatheoretic premises of the study also apply. Sense-Making's mandate makes this explicit. The researcher is involved in information seeking and use. Every premise that Sense-Making mandates for the study of the researched mandates the researcher self-reflexively attend to her role as researcher, and as researched. In studying information seeking and use, this mandates that the researcher interview herself both as she would interview her informants/respondents and also in terms of her ongoing relationship to the project—funders, collaborators, those researched, procedures, outcomes. Sense-Making mandates that this analysis be anchored in attentions to time, space, movement, gap, power, force, constraint, constancy and change and that the researcher attend to not only what is orderly and linear and articulate but to that which is disorderly, troubled, and inarticulate.

"Information" in Contest and Connection

The typical information seeking and use study searches for centrality in its findings (one pattern) or at most limited diversity around centrality (a small set of alternative patterns). Sense-Making mandates a broader attention, not eliminating this traditional emphasis but enlarging it with an eye to research as a long-term project. A Sense-Making study would use whatever tools (statistical, thematic, or so on) it finds useful for unearthing pattern but, at the same time, would explicitly look for exceptions and disruptions. If, for example, a study focused on predictors of information seeking, Sense-Making would mandate not only a search for what set of predictors accounted for the most variance in information seeking, it would also mandate a comparison between predictors, and an illumination of how users different in important other ways were alike in this way; and how users alike in this way were different in important other ways. Further, a fully elaborated Sense-Making study would invite observations of contests and commonnesses from outside the data—from respondents/interviewees, for example; from like-minded colleagues; and from colleagues working out of different traditions. Finally, a fully-elaborated Sense-Making study would mandate that the question be asked of every instance that does not fit the central patterns: Under what conditions could this have emerged? It is in the dialogic intersection of these interrogations that Sense-Making assumes that the research project will advance.

CONCLUSION

A major point is this: Paradigmatic debates have propelled us to thinking about research in new ways. What was assumed to be charted in the past is now uncharted. In particular, the ways in which metatheoretic assumptions (explicitly stated or implicitly held) impact research methods have been little mapped. Ironically, the study of information seeking and use stands at the very center of the issues which have impelled us to the postmodern condition. We are all embroiled, no matter what our position, in a challenge to traditionally accepted authority even when that authority is implemented in the name of knowledge or science or truth.

A movement is afoot in both the social sciences and the humanities which has profound consequences for the study of information seeking and use. This impact can be seen in the emerging diversity and simultaneous lack of dialogue in information seeking and use studies. It can be said the studies are getting more sophisticated and in non-dia-logic ways they draw on each other with the traditional nods of recognition for each other required in the academy. Yet, across this emerging diversity this work has such varied conceptualizations and assumptions that comparison and growth seems at best capri-cious and at worst impossible. Most difficult of all is that the metatheoretic assumptions information seeking and use researchers make are rarely carried forward in coherent ways into method.

To say this of information seeking and use research is not, however, to criticize this research genre per se. The criticism applies as well to the entire edifice of academic work that attends to human beings and the social worlds they live in. One finds, for example, cultural studies scholars inviting reader interpretations of media and then selecting one interpretation as best and explaining the deviations in a way prescribed by a non-interpretive theory of reality and message production. Or, one finds a realist pur-suing context non-contextually as if it were one more variable in a roster of variables in a realist's description of the world.

This foray into Sense-Making Methodology has not assumed that Sense-Making can or should solve these ills. Rather, the purpose has been to use Sense-Making as an exemplar of what methodology might be when it more explicitly serves as bridge between metatheory and method opening up guidance both for the methods of doing research and the methods of theorizing phenomena (i.e., unit or substantive theorizing). Sense-Making is, thus, presented as methodology which provides guidance both as the-ory of method and method for theory.

What we learn from the presentation is a reaffirmation of a point made earlier—that there is an inextricable relationship between metatheory, methodology, substantive theory, and method. They live in each other. The very potentials for theorizing and understanding information seeking and use are constrained and even defined by the metatheoretic premises that drive the research methods. The traditional work on infor-mation seeking and use has been based on a host of assumptions about information seek-ing and use which have never been tested because the assumptions were never logically carried to their sites of potential test in method. Are emotions the antithesis of informa-tion seeking and use, as has been traditionally assumed? Are information resisters more emotional, more externally controlled, less patient? Are the poor information poor? Are people inadequate observers of their worlds? Such propositions have received substan-tial support from so-called research but an examination of their methods suggest that the results are tautologically linked to implicit assumptions. One major point here is that metatheory can be used in such a way that it releases research in always partial but still significant ways from implicit assumptions and draws these assumptions out into the light of day where they can be examined, interrogated and tested.

Perhaps even more fundamental is the issue of the inherent relationship between information seeking and use research and the systems and practices it is designed to inform. If these system and practices are framed as the standards against which information seeking and use is measured, the resulting research will not only find users lacking but will never be able to address issues of potential system change. This conclusion is neither utopian nor ideological. It does involve, however, pointing toward the possibility of change for the better as a methodological direction.

A methodological framework must, then, reach for the most general net to guide research. This involves two contradictory moves. One is freeing oneself of a host of assumptions about the nature of the phenomenon. The other is building the methodological edifice on a host of assumptions that are abstractly and philosophically derived and explicitly stated. It is with the later that the researcher can release the former as empirical questions rather than biases. The margins between these are not hard and fast, but it is by bringing metatheory into method in explicit moves that the research project can reach for maximum productivity from a single study and maximum dialogue and growth across studies.

This does not involve recipe-use. It requires a deeper and more programmatic emphasis on research than has been standard academic practice. It is not quick and dirty. Perhaps most difficult of all is that it requires as a methodological move that information systems as now designed not be assumed the implied baseline for the study of information seeking and use. This is not a mandate to be radical or ideological. It is a mandate to be methodological. Given that the very essence of information seeking and use research involves that very contested thing called information, there is no escape. One's methodological framing must find a route to attend to information seeking and use outside of that contest, in a way that can allow patterns to emerge on either side.

NOTES

1. Some observers (e.g., Giddens, 1984; Slack & Allor, 1983) argue that the social sciences are distinctively different from the natural and physical sciences because the social sciences involve interpreting human beings studying interpreting human beings (what Giddens calls the "double hermeneutic"). Others argue that in fact all sciences, and indeed for some all systematic scholarships, have common interests and common struggles (e.g., Bhaskar, 1986; Blumenberg, 1983; McGuire, 1986; Murdock, 1997; Wilson, 1998).

2. In this section, I have relied heavily on: Bhaskar (1979, 1986, 1989), Bohman (1991), Fonow & Cook (1991), Gadamer (1975), Galtung (1977), Lather (1991), Morrow (1994), Murdock (1997), Outhwaite (1987), Rabinow and Sullivan (1987), Ricoeur (1981), Rosnow and Georgoudi (1986a), Sayer (1992), Seidman (1986), Slack and Allor (1983), and Turner (1989). I am grateful to Peter Shields for our useful discussions and his continuing patience.

3. Hollinger (1994) provides a critique of this treatment of the postmodern debate as being launched by free-floating radicals.

4. Morrow (1994), and Slack and Allor (1983).

5. Berger, Wagner, and Zelditch (1989) ask sociologists reaching for metatheory not to roam into philosophical stratospheres to become "our philosopher kings" (p. 11). In contrast, Mouzelis (1994) provides an example of a scholar warning against leaving philosophy too far behind.

6.   For this section, I found the following especially useful: Berger, Wagner, and Zelitch (1989), Blau (1989), Ganguly (1992), Maines and Molseed (1986), Ritzer (1992), Sarbin (1993), Scolari (1998), Slack and Allor (1983), Swain (1993), and Wagner and Berger (1986).

7.   Methodology is, of course, a branch of philosophy and, thus, inherently metatheoretical. The separation is made here to put special emphasis on methodology as metatheoretical consideration of method, an emphasis which has been marginalized for different reasons in both the scientific and humanist branches of the study of the human condition. One sees the term *analytics* emerging in place of the term *methodology*, in part it seems as a way of interrupting the dominant reduction of the term *methodology* to method in science and its disappearance into other kinds of philosophical debate in the humanities. The first use I have uncovered of the term *analytics* used in this way is in Foucault (1975) where he focused less on a theory of power and knowledge and more on analytics of subjects and subjectivities. The difficulty with the term, of course, is that it is very close to the often-used analytic and analytical used in positivist-based science to refer to the variable analytic approach and the operations of statistics. On the other hand, the plural term—*analytics*—may provide enough of an interruption of normal discourse to be useful.

8.   Substantive theory is also found referred to by a variety of other names: unit theory, empirical theory, analytical theory, propositional theory, and most frequently of all just theory, as in the famous statement by Popper (1961): "... theories are nets we cast to catch what we call the world, we endeavor to make them ever finer and finer."

9.   The following provide examples of journeys to the "in-between" from a variety of different beginning stances: Bourdieu (1984, 1989, 1996), Caws (1989), Gould (1981), Halfpenny (1987), King, Keohanne, and Verba (1994), McGuire (1986), Morrow (1994), Murdock (1997), Swain (1993), and Zaret (1987).

10.   Especially helpful have been the efforts of social psychologist William McGuire (1973, 1983, 1985, 1986), trained in quantitative science, to create a genuinely contextual approach to his work and the efforts of Morrow (1994) to merge a form of critical realism with its emphasis on structure with the interpretive with its emphasis on meaning-making. Both attend to metatheory, methodology, and method, and apply these to the terrains of their interest.

11.   The version of Sense-Making presented here is, of course, the one most properly labeled as "Dervin's version, 10 March 1999." This discussion of Sense-Making draws on the full history of its work and development as documented on: *http://communication.sbs.ohio-state.edu/sense-making/*. For the most recent discussions of Sense-Making's metatheory, see in particular: Dervin (1991a, 1993, 1994, 1997, 1998) and Dervin and Clark (1993); for the most recent overviews of the Methodology and exemplar studies and applications, see in particular: Dervin (1989a, 1992); the earliest overview paper (Dervin, 1983b) while out-of-date is available on the web-site mentioned above; one of the most recent quantitative applications of Sense-Making is in Dervin and Shields (1999); Shields, Dervin, Richter and Soller (1993); Shields and Dervin (1998); one of the most recent qualitative applications is in Huesca (1995). The most recent application to practice is Dervin (1999a).

12.   Sense-Making's earliest development is documented in a study of the information needs of urban residents funded by the then Office of Libraries and Learning Resources of the U.S. Office of Education: Dervin, Zweizig, Banister, Gabriel, Hall, and Kwan (1976).

13.   I owe a debt most of all to R. F. Carter (1990, 1991) for the impacts of his work on the development of Sense-Making, in particular his theoretic inventions which have focused on the development of communication approaches to the study of communication. Others to whom allegiance is due in particular include: Bourdieu (1996) whose critical focus on practices as habitus has informed Sense-Making's attention to social structure manifested in practice; Bruner (1990) whose writing has never stopped pushing the edge and whose move from a focus on information to a focus on meaning has informed my own journey; Foucault (1972) whose treatments of power helped free my treatment of it as tautologically linked to top-down structures; Freire (1970) whose work on critical pedagogy and the concept of conscientizing most informs the foundational premises of the Sense-Making interview; Gadamer (1975) whose treatment of philosophical hermeneutics in its relationship to method propelled my own quest; Habermas (1987b) whose focus on the development of communication-based theorizings of social structure have provided both foil and fodder; McGuire (1986) whose persistence in developing a contextualizing approach to social psychology has been inspirational; and Morrow (1994) and Murdock (1997) for their persistent callings for a more methodological critical research. See references for samplings of their works.

14. As development of Sense-Making has evolved, I have begun to talk of the methodology as Sense-Making Methodology and the phenomena to which it attends as sense-making. The term *sense-making* seemed to emerge in the early years of the phenomenological tradition although I have not yet located what I consider a first use. There are many uses of the term sense-making as phenomena in the literature (spelled myriad different ways) which have no relationship to the Sense-Making Methodology. For example Weick's (1995) *Sensemaking in Organizations* proposed looking at organizational life by examining the phenomenon—sensemaking.

15. It is important to note that as Sense-Making's primary author I am in Buber's (1965) terms in the "process of becoming." Hence, for example, in Dervin (1983b) I described Sense-Making as a constructivist approach, while now I describe it as post-constructivist, or postmodern modernist. In Dervin (1994), I termed Sense-Making as communitarian, but revised my thinking in Dervin (1998) when I termed it a verbing approach.

16. This section of the chapter is based on an understanding of research on information needs, seeking, and use drawn from Dervin and Nilan (1986), Hewins (1990), Sugar (1995), and Vakkari, Savolainen, and Dervin (1997). Additionally, the papers from the 1998 Conference on Information Seeking in Context held at Sheffield, U.K. inform this discussion.

17. For critiques of writings that specifically attend to conceptualizations of the information poor, knowledge gaps, media literacy, and related concepts by defining groups of persons as in gap based on external standards, see in particular Dervin (1980, 1989b).

Chapter 9

Communication and Democracy:
A Mandate for Procedural Invention

Brenda Dervin & Kathleen D. Clark

PURPOSE

The purpose of this chapter is to develop an argument which suggests that the current emphasis on macrolevel issues in discussions of "democratic" communication must be expanded to include emphasis on microlevel issues and, in particular, to include emphasis on the communicating procedures by which macro- and micro- are linked. We argue that most discussions of democratic communication now focus on "whos" (who gets to speak, who has power) and "whats" (what is communicated) but not "hows" (how do individuals connect to and make sense of self, other, society, culture, institutions; how do societies, cultures, institutions connect with individuals and with each other).

This chapter examines the causes and consequences of this de-emphasis of the "hows" and challenges that failure to attend to the procedural linkages between macro- and microlevels seriously hampers our efforts to study and practice democratic communication. An alternative conception of communication-as-procedure is presented.[1]

THE PROBLEM:
THE MISSING PROCEDURAL LINK

Calls for the "democratization of communication" frequently get lost in an eddy between two major streams of academic attention. Most theorists focus their attention on macrolevel structures in society, in particular, on the distribution of power and resources. In these discussions, "whos" and "whats" are emphasized: who has control of what

This work originally appeared as: Dervin, B., & Clark, K. D. (1993). Communication and democracy: A mandate for procedural invention. In S. Splichal & J. Wasko (Eds.), *Communication and democracy* (pp. 103–140). Norwood, NJ: Ablex. Reprinted by permission of Greenwood Publishing Group, Inc., Westport, CT. Contains material presented as: Dervin, B., & Clark, K. D. (1988, July). *Democritization of communication: The invention mandate.* Paper presented at the annual meeting of the International Association of Mass Communication Research, Barcelona, Spain.

media, what messages, what content. The "hows" of communicating—the procedures by which the communication is done—are de-emphasized. The emphasis is placed on inputs and outputs. This stream of attention attempts to develop generalized understandings of democratic communication but these understandings do not include actual acts of communicating at the microlevel; the step-taking which connects the macro to the micro and vice versa. For the purposes of this chapter, this stream will be labeled the macro approach.[2]

The second stream of attention seems to focus more directly on "hows" but in actuality still attends to macro issues without regard to how the macro- and microlevels link. This stream essentially sees democratic communication as participation that evolves from the bottom up in spontaneously created forms unique to specific moments in time and space. These forms are seen as arising culturally and cultural analyses are assumed to be the best frames for accounting for them. Emphasis is placed on cultural inputs and outputs. While "hows" get attention in this stream, the intent is not to arrive at understandings of individual acts of communicating at the microlevel or the step-taking done by individuals which connects cultural input to output or vice versa. For the purposes of this chapter, this stream of attention will be labeled the cultural stream.

Both the streams of attention rise from the same ideas about communication and, in fact, from ideas about communication that they actively protest. Both acknowledge the mandate for dealing with pluralistic perspectives as a reality of the modern world, yet both end up studying communication without studying communicating and, thus, end up failing to enrich our understanding of how to deal with pluralism. The macro stream does so by assuming that equitable distribution of communication access and resources will lead directly to equitable communication ends. No human acts are conceptualized as intervening between structure and result. The communicating individual is essentially ignored.

The cultural stream, on the other hand, acknowledges all sorts of human acts but opts out into a solipsistic position. This position assumes so much uniqueness in these acts that no connections of understanding are sought between structure and act, act and consequence. Explanatory emphasis is placed on cultural uniqueness. Again, while the communicating acts of an individual may be described, they are not systematically addressed. Descriptions of individual acts are used to inform discussion of culture, not discussion of communication. The result is that individual acts of communicating are essentially ignored. In this way, no lessons can be derived that might help in the doing of communicating—the *hows*.

Ironically, both perspectives, while radically different in their assumptions, end up in the same place: The "how" of communication is left without systematic examination. And, somehow the structure (the system, institution, culture) is conceptualized as having some kind of mysterious being—an existence held in place by caveat. For the macro stream, the caveat is ownership and power and access. For the cultural stream, the caveat is culturally transmitted norms, rules, and understandings. Essentially the individual is ignored—as a communicating individual and as a communicating member of institution, culture, society. Both streams of emphasis disempower and rob the individual of the very pluralistic perspective that is the mandated focus of democratic communication.

It is important to note here that what we are proposing should not be construed as a return to "individualistic" ideas about communication. Rather, we are proposing that individuals constitute society/culture/institutions and these collective entities have no existence without the energizing behaviors of individuals. Thus, a formulation of communication must account for the individual. One of the questions we address is how it is appropriate to do this communicatively.

ROOTS IN NONCOMMUNICATION IDEAS ABOUT COMMUNICATION

The caveats that drive the macro and cultural streams of attention described above are both rooted in ideas about communication that focus on transmission rather than dialogue. For one, power and ownership define the world; for the other, cultural rules and norms define it. Individual variation is de-emphasized as are the means by which individuals connect themselves to and make sense of the world. An isomorphism is assumed between structure/culture and individual: the meaning making in the middle is left out.

The purpose of this chapter is not to suggest that either the macro or cultural streams of attention are wrong. Both must be given their due: Power and ownership do define the world; so do cultural rules and norms. But these elements are not *all* that define the world and they do not have a direct isomorphic relationship to individual behavior. Virtually all discussions of democratic communication acknowledge this, yet few do so as a central feature. It seems as if the problem of individuality is dealt with by opting out—either entirely into macro foci or solipsism.

The difficulty with this conception is that it is basically a noncommunicative way of approaching the communication problematic.[3] Individual human beings exist in structures, contexts, institutions, cultures. They are constrained and informed by these but never entirely. This is so because there is no complete isomorphism between structure, context, institution, culture and the individual human mind. No individual human mind has direct access to "reality." Observation is always constrained by time, place, background, and individual perceptual limitations. While humans set up standards for judging whose observations are better, these standards are created and contested. No matter how strong a culture, structure, institution, or context, there is always a mandate for the individual alone to make sense of the self's relationship to that culture, structure, institution, context. This intersection of self with structure (sometimes resulting in contests, sometimes in acculturation) is the stuff of myth, fable, and novels.

Both the macro and cultural streams of attention acknowledge these points. Yet, both end up studying pluralism and how humans deal with it not as a process but as end product. The macro stream looks at whose perspective wins; the cultural stream assumes culture wins. And the daily acts of communicating which form the web within which individual and structure/culture interact (contest, confuse, delimit) remain unattended.

This lack of attention to communicating is in many ways understandable. In one sense, the idea of communicating as dialogue is a relatively new idea for the species. Dialogue is not an issue when absolute power can punish any behavior regardless of whether its origins are based on misunderstandings. Dealing with human heterogeneity is not an issue when it is assumed that one central power holds the correct views of reality.

Any number of examples can be found to illustrate the point. In U.S. liberal democracy, for example, the founding fathers specified the structures they considered essential for democracy. Yet, few of these specifications pertained to communication per se. Their worldview found no necessity because for them in an open market place of ideas, correct ideas would by some magical process win. And education was a path to achieving correct ideas. The possibility that there would be competing sets of "correct" ideas depending on one's time and place was not part of the framework. Also unimagined was the possibility that ideas, the products of communicating, are not properly treated as commodities if one is focused on communication.

While some have suggested that pluralism is the problem of the modern age, it cannot be said that the modern age invented pluralism. Rather, the species has arrived at a point, for a host of reasons, where traditional means of resolving conflicts do not work and where there are increasing demands for resolving conflicts as contact heterogeneity increases. At the same time, the species has arrived at a point where those subjected to authority more frequently question authority and, in particular, challenge authority's right to impose its own worldview or assume homogeneity in worldviews. Unfortunately, however, we arrive as a species at this point without a robust history of experience with communication as dialogue, either as practitioners or as scholars.

LOSS OF THE INDIVIDUAL

We are further unhelpfully constrained by our attempt to avoid repeating past mistakes. We have been trying to stay away from any semblance of a return to ideas about communication that ignore structure, context, and history. The well-intentioned aim is to avoid a return to the now disavowed "individualistic," "personality," and "blame-the-victim" theories of communication. The irony in this is that we may have thrown the baby out with the bath water.

The "administrative" approach to the study of communication attempted to arrive at instructions that would allow communicators to transmit their messages to receivers completely, accurately, and with desired effect. This approach has been cast as the prototype of a non-pluralistic view of communication. Certainly, it exemplifies the transmission idea taken to an extreme in a manifestation that is unambiguously open to ideological attack. In a pluralistic world, it is considered inappropriate to ram your ideas down the throats of others. Further, focusing on individual behavior became synonymous with the "administrative" approach, so it has been ideologically incorrect, or at least difficult, to return attention to the individual.

Nonetheless, the ideological attack, however appropriate in many respects, results in a limited understanding of what is going on. Attacking the "administrative" approach solely on the grounds that it is nonpluralistic obscures the fact that models of communication based on ideas of campaigns or transmission constitute a weak conceptualization about communicating. The transmission model did not work very well either empirically or practically. It accounted for very little variance in human behavior and served badly as a model for communication design. It rarely was able to isolate strong communication effects and was unable to point to larger and stronger social forces.

Thus, there are two different, although sometimes overlapping, reasons for retreating from or rejecting the "administrative" approach: one ideological, the other theoretic. Ideologically, nonpluralistic ramifications condemned it. Theoretically, the inability to find strong effects condemned it. The ideological condemnations have received considerable coverage in the literature, but the theoretic condemnations require more attention than they have been given to date.

The question that must be asked is: Does our current understanding of the problematic of the individual in a communication context provide any useful guidance for study or practice? Most of our understandings of individual communication behavior have been derived from research and practice that has been transmission-oriented. If we assume that the transmission idea of communication is misguided and severely limited, then we must conclude that our ideas about individuality are also misguided and severely limited.

This conclusion is easier to accept when we focus on individual behavior per se. In rejecting the transmission model with its unfortunate link to the individual, the macro and the cultural streams have essentially rejected individual behavior as being an ideologically wrong site for attention. Both streams have implicitly accepted the idea that individual behavior at a level more micro than structure or culture is too chaotic for attention.

To briefly amplify this point consider these questions: What if, in actuality, the apparent chaos of individual behavior is a result of the application of inappropriate or wrong ideas about communicating to theorizing about individuals? What if it is not individuality that is chaotic but rather the paucity of our theorizings which leads to impressions of chaos?

An examination of past use of the transmission model suggests several stumbling blocks. First, we attempted to find constant impacts from message. This was inappropriate ideologically and weak theoretically. We then looked for constant impacts from culture or structure. This worked as long as we stayed at the macro level but fell apart at the micro level. We tried to differentiate people into subgroups based on differences we thought accounted for the plurality: sex, race, class, education, and so on. Again, this worked at the macro level but not the micro. From this experience we must conclude either that individual communication behavior is solipsistic or admit the possibility that there is something that eludes us. In order to do this, however, we must acknowledge the possibility that the fundamental idea that was found unacceptable about the concept of individuality—the idea that the individual can be treated as an atomized entity—is also the very same fundamental idea that sustains our retreat from individuality.

COMMUNICATION PROCEDURES: REINTRODUCING THE INDIVIDUAL IN A DIFFERENT FORM

The question becomes: Where does one look for something systematic about communication? Our attempts to find something systematic have all focused on states (rather than processes), on causes or on outcomes. All have de-emphasized change over time. And, fundamentally, all have ignored the daily struggling step-takings—sometimes arduous, sometimes routinized, but never entirely unproblematic—by which individuals make sense of and live in their worlds and by which structures, cultures, and institutions are introduced, maintained, and changed.

Is there something systematic about individual communicating that has eluded us because we have been looking in the wrong places? At states rather than process? At the individual human entity rather than at the step-takings by which an individual connects to self, other, and society—and by which individuals attempt to connect society, culture, and institution to individual? In this chapter we suggest reintroducing the individual for consideration in communication theorizing but in a different manifestation: not as an individual per se but as an individual moment of communicating. The focus here is not on people (states) but on behavings (processes)—on acts of connecting and disconnecting, constructing and deconstructing, imagining and changing, on the communicatings which connect and disconnect individual, culture, institution, society. These moments of individual communicating are a manifestation of the structure or culture having its impact. These moments are also where we find the limits of impact.

A comparison may help. A macro or cultural perspective would expect that different people, classes, or cultures would decode messages differently. A communication procedure perspective would suggest that bringing a different sense-making procedure to bear is what makes a difference. For this second perspective it is not the state condition of being of a different culture or class that matters but rather the process condition.

The communication procedure perspective assumes that the individual giving meaning is actualized in behaviors—all manner of communicating behaviors. These behaviors include internal acts (observings, categorizings, definings, encodings, decodings, etc.) and external acts (talkings, gesturings, etc.). Each of these acts can be seen as a formal or informal routine—a step or series of steps. Some of these steps repeat the past while others break with the past. These behaviors apply to relating to self (remembering, forgetting, making up one's mind, changing one's mind, etc.), and to others (loving, hating, deciding, disagreeing, etc.). They apply to relating to individuals when seen independently as well as when constrained or limited by or enjoined by a collectivity. All these behaviors are driven by individual human consciousness (which may be operating consciously or unconsciously), the only site that directly drives individual behavior.

In this formulation, we recognize that individual behavior, constructed uniquely (at least in part) for each new moment of living, is susceptible to change as each individual constructs ways of dealing with the inherent unmanageability of reality. It is this individuality that appears chaotic. On the other hand, we assume that there is something systematic to be understood by looking at behavioral or procedural consistencies, rather than individual consistencies, by changing the focus from person to behavior, from state to process.[4]

COMMUNICATION-AS-PROCEDURE: A MANDATE FOR INVENTION

By leaving a focus on the individual as entity behind and introducing moments of behaving as carried out by individuals, we move to the idea of communication-as-procedure and the idea of procedure as the energizing linkage between the macro and the micro as well as the micro and the macro. A focus on communication procedure is not proposed as either ahistoric or acultural. Procedures are seen as themselves ideologically bound. They have social histories and purposes. They were invented (constructed) by human beings to serve needs at particular times and places. Because they are routinized and frequently ritualized, they can easily persist even after the social conditions of their origins disappear. Further, their impacts and the ways in which they have ideological force may be hidden in the same sense that it has been suggested that manifestations of power are often hidden.[5]

We have suggested above that the individual is actualized in behavior. We suggest that the structure (culture, institution, system) is actualized in behavior as well.[6] A social structure that is not reenergized regularly with acts of communicating dies; it simply does not exist. Structures are maintained, reified, rigidified, and changed through acts of communicating. Some of the acts are formalized and routinized. Examples of these include the systematic categorizations that journalists bring to reporting; the rules of parliamentary procedure used in many collectivities; the agenda-setting mandated to those who run group meetings; the ways in which professionals elicit information from their clients. Other acts are less formal but still routinized. Examples include the aspects of reality which friends bring to attention in their daily greetings to each other; the ways in which people disagree; turn-taking behaviors in conversations; wearing clothing considered appropriate to an occasion.

We propose that by focusing on communication-as-procedure we can begin to unravel the problem of the elusive "communicating individual" and at the same time begin to rise to a higher level of theoretic abstraction where we will be able to reach for the lessons to be shared between our current seemingly disparate approaches to studying communication: political economy versus cultural studies; qualitative versus quantitative; and so on.

Further, we suggest this conceptual move will allow us to unravel a host of practical communication problems faced in attempts to arrive at more democratic forms of communication. One of these is the frequently observed phenomena whereby newly designed, supposedly more democratic structures decay over time so that eventually they look like the authoritarian structures which preceded them. In a communication-as-procedure formulation, one explanation for this is that in introducing change only new ideas of structure were attended to, while the actual procedures which would energize the structure and hold it in place were not.

Another practical concern is the problem of citizen participation in the collective. Without attention to procedure, participation is energized in old authoritarian forms. Over time, the relationship between the citizen and the collective deteriorates to a for-or-against procedural strategy. Examples here can be found in almost any individual's daily life: cooperating relationships at work disintegrate over time; egalitarian marriages fail. Myriad examples are available as well at the national level: The failure of U.S. leaders to hear the citizenry's position regarding the Vietnam War and the persistence of leadership's view that their views were the correct and only views; the decay of egalitarian ideas about citizen participation in China to old feudal procedures.

One important element of what is being proposed here is the idea that a communication-as-procedure approach introduces a consistency between theory and practice that allows the former to attend to where the action is in the latter. In this context attention can be placed not only on how structure restrains but how it frees; not only on how people are victimized but how they manage to find ways to *not* be victimized despite considerable odds; not only on how structural power limits potential but also on how individuals creatively empower themselves and how structures sometimes become empowering.

More fundamentally, however, this consistency between theory and practice allows the possibility that the practice of communicating can become not merely an "art" form, but rather a practice both informed by scholarship and by the understandings of practitioners.

There are no end of important questions for which we need some understandings of the "hows" of communicating. A few examples: How does a leader facilitate pluralistic input? How can news writing be designed to help citizens inform themselves efficiently and effectively about others in a pluralistic world? How can we categorize documents in a retrieval system so they will be maximally useful to citizens mandated to participation in democratic decision making? How can we prevent old authoritarian forms from taking over even when we intend otherwise?

For purposes of this chapter what is more important than the individual questions, however, is the central idea that a communication-as-procedure approach will help us bridge a gap between polarities in communication scholarship and practice which now impede us: structure versus individual; positivism versus postmodernism; absolutism versus relativism. For each of these oppositions, the polar ends are like opposite sides of the same coin. Each essentially assumes that heterogeneity means cacophony. And, since each rests its models of communication on state rather than process conditions, logically each can only end up in providing support for the assumption.

There is one additional bit of mischief which results—the idea that to focus scholarship on the invention of new communication forms is idealistic and utopian. A state view of communication necessarily leads to this conclusion for a state view searches for transmitted order. In doing so, a state view misses the daily inventings and creatings which are a mark of the highest qualities of the human species. The communicating steps which make up individual and collective life are all human inventions—some ancient, some recent. Some rigidify; some metamorphize; some appear and disappear like lightning. It is only by looking at communication as process, however, that the inventive character of the behavior which energizes individual and collective life comes into view.

A FRAMEWORK FOR THINKING
ABOUT DEMOCRATIC COMMUNICATION INVENTION

The communication-as-procedure perspective mandates that we focus on behavior at specific moments in time-space, but at the same time extract fundamental dimensions of these behaviors that are applicable across time-space. This idea will be illustrated here with a beginning framework. When one surveys the literature on democratic communication a number of dimensions or conditions can be extracted as necessary under one definition or another. Each of these conditions implies a set of communication procedures which can be observed, experimented with, or tested. The literature, however, has not focused on these procedures in systematic ways. What we are attempting in this section is a beginning model for doing so.

The fundamental question we are trying to answer is: What are the range of possible communication mandates of democratic communication? This leads us to a second fundamental question: What do people need to do communicatively to make sense of and participate in their worlds? Drawing heavily on the work of Carter, we propose a beginning template to organize our search for answers.[7] This template, shown in Figure 9.1, proposes that we need to examine two dimensions of communicating: situation-defining strategies and communicating tactics. The essential idea is that what people do communicatively depends both on how they define their situations and on what they are attempting to do communicatively in these situations. Both situation-defining strategies and communicating tactics are defined as procedures because both involve behavings. Strategies involve cognitive behavings while tactics involve communicative behav*ings*.

The two procedural dimensions we have selected for development in this chapter are ones we propose as fundamental. We do not suggest they are the only fundamental dimensions to consider in a communication-as-procedure perspective. Rather, we suggest that they are illustrative of the kind of conceptualizing that we need to pursue.

In Figure 9.1, the vertical axis focuses on situation-defining strategies. The particular situation-defining strategy we have developed for use here focuses on how the communicating entity (individual or collective) sees itself at a specific moment relating to other communicating entities: What relationship to the world is the entity working on at that specific moment in time and space? In a world where sense is not given, every relationship involves daily acts of constructing via communicating. The individual needs to relate to self, to other individuals, to collectivities; collectivities also need to relate to self, and to individuals as well as other collectivities. For our purposes here, we will propose six different situation-defining strategies:

• *INDIVIDUAL RELATING TO SELF: Here the individual is thinking, creating, observing, arriving at personal sense and understandings of self.*

• *INDIVIDUAL RELATING TO OTHER INDIVIDUALS: Here the individual is relating to other individuals, learning about others, comparing self to other, connecting or disconnecting with others.*

• *INDIVIDUAL RELATING TO COLLECTIVITY: Here individual communicating focuses on participating in a collectivity which can move as one.*

• *COLLECTIVITY RELATING TO SELF: Here a collectivity is focusing on itself.*

• *COLLECTIVITY RELATING TO INDIVIDUAL: Here a defined collectivity is focusing on individuals.*

• *COLLECTIVITY RELATING TO OTHER COLLECTIVITY: Here one defined collectivity is relating to another defined collectivity.*

It is important that these different situational definitions be understood as procedures for defining the situation. What this means is that, theoretically at least, the actor is free to apply any one of these strategies to any given situation depending on what the

FIGURE 9.1

An example of a communication-as-procedure framework utilizing two procedural dimensions: Situation-defining strategies and communication tactics

Situation defining strategies	Communication Tactics								
	Attending	Creating ideas	Finding direction	Expressing	Finding connection	Confronting opposing	Mediating	Recalling	Undoing rigidities
Individual relating to self									
Individual relating to other individuals									
Individual relating to collectivity									
Collectivity relating to self									
Collectivity relating to individual									
Collectivity relating to other collectivity									

175

actor brings to bear cognitively when constructing a sense of the situation. This begins to allow us to focus on moments of behaving by individuals and collectivities rather than being limited to a static view of these merely as entities. Situation-defining strategies are proposed here as fundamental procedures in that sense that every collectivity that pursues democratic communication must necessarily account for each of the defining situations. The foci of communicating entities will vary depending on which of these defining strategies is adopted. The individual, for example, who is attempting to relate to self will differ communicatively than the individual who is attempting to relate to an other or collectivity. Likewise, the collectivity that is attempting to relate to self will differ communicatively from one that is attempting to relate to another collectivity.

In essence, the situation-defining strategy is a cognitive choice, sometimes individually produced, sometimes collectively produced. Other possible situation-defining strategies are, for example, assessments of situational constraint (e.g., how free the entity is to move) or situational power (e.g., how much power the entity has to define the situation). These alternatives are seen as examples of other fundamental situation-defining strategies. We are not incorporating these into our framework for the purposes of this chapter.

The importance of these defining strategies becomes clearer when we introduce the second procedural dimension, that of tactic. In order to construct and deal with their worlds humans must necessarily perform different communicative tasks. One possible set of tactics to accomplish these tasks includes:

- *ATTENDING to self, environment, each other, and collective being. This tactic involves generalized observing.*

- *CREATING IDEAS about self, reality, each other, institutions, collectiveness. We assume that since there is no isomorphic relationship between "reality" and individual, it is a human mandate to create ideas.*

- *FINDING DIRECTION. Determining possible directions in which to move, alone or together. Again, we assume that direction is not predetermined even in the most rigidly controlled collectivity. Even the implementation of societally homogenous direction requires individual and collective reenergization.*

- *EXPRESSING. Here the communicating activity is directed toward giving symbolic expression to individually or collectively created ideas.*

- *FINDING CONNECTEDNESS. Here the communicating activity is directed at getting connected to others—allies, interest groups, sympathizers, sources of ideas.*

- *CONFRONTING, OPPOSING. Here the focus is one entity contesting against other.*

- *MEDIATING. Here the focus is on compromising or resolving disagreements.*

• *RECALLING. Here the focus is on creating memory of own, other, or collective past and bringing memory to bear on the present.*

• *UNDOING RIGIDITIES. Here the focus is on a conscientizing process by which human entities come to grips with the rigidities with which they face life. We assume these rigidities have been induced in them by their experience, cultures, structures, and so on. During the conscientizing process rigidities dissolve and behavior becomes more flexible. This frees inventive potential.*

We are not suggesting that these communicating tactics are the only ones necessary to democratic communication situations. We are proposing, however, that they are one set of necessary tactics. By pitting these two sets of procedural dimensions against each other, we create the 54 cells in Figure 9.1. This chart is presented as a very fundamental illustration of a way to think about the communicating mandates of any human condition. Figure 9.1, therefore, provides a perspective for looking at how the microworld of individuals is connected to the macrolevel world of cultures, structures, and institutions, and vice versa. Thus, for example, in order of an individual to relate to his or her society and world, the individual needs to relate to self, others, and collectivities. Essential components of the individual's situation, as well, are how collectivities in that society relate to self, individuals, and each other.

Each of the cells is seen as a site for isolating communication behaviors—the communicating procedures performed at specific moments in time-space. The *situatedness* of this formulation is important and can be understood in two ways. One way involves understanding that life-facing involves daily constructings, even when some (or perhaps many or even all) of those constructings are repetitions of habitualized constructings used in the past. Since no moment in time-space has theoretically occurred before, each act of communicating is situated. The second meaning of situatedness refers to the idea that communicating behavior is situation-responsive. An inherent assumption of the framework represented in Figure 9.1 is that communicating tactics are potentially responsive to situation-defining strategies. How an individual creates ideas when relating to self potentially differs from how that individual may do so when relating to others or collectivities. As one example, the individual may use a wide-open categorizing strategy when relating to self but a highly closed and polarizing one when relating to others. Or, a collectivity may have developed formalized procedures for creating subtle variations in ideas when relating to individuals but gross differentiations when relating to other collectivities. Each of these means of creating ideas is seen as a communicating "how." Each is assumed to be an invention of past and/or present. Each is assumed to have the potential to become very rigidified so that the communicating entity never varies its tactic in a given kind of situation or, at an extreme, across all situations. At the same time each is assumed to have the potential for responsiveness; for being used or not used depending on how the communicating entity defines the demands of a current situation.

This framework is proposed as a guide to description; to examine how it is that humans now or in the past engaged in these communicatings. What are the ways in which attending is done when individuals are relating to themselves? How do these vary? What consequences seem to relate to what ways of communicating? What are the ways in which attending is done when individuals are attempting to operate in collectivities? How do these vary? Under what conditions? What consequences seem to relate to what ways of attending? The framework illustrated in Figure 9.1 is also proposed as a guide to invention: What alternative ways to communicating need to be invented in order for the species to move into the modern/postmodern age of democratic pluralism?

This latter point is important. Most of the work on democratic communication has limited itself to understandings of the ways things *are*, not the ways they *might be*. Yet clearly, humans now face communication demands for which the species is unprepared and for which humans have had little experience. Further, the traditional procedures of communicating established to handle problems of human heterogeneity in the past are less and less useful. These procedures were invented for particular time, space, and situation demands. They no longer function well because the time, space, and situation have changed. A primary change is the move from more homogenous, more stable social contexts in which authoritarian procedures seemed to work reasonably well to more heterogeneous, less stable social contexts that demand procedures that the human species has not yet invented. One of the difficulties in understanding this point is that when authoritarian procedures are the operating communication procedures in a situation, it actually looks as if there are no communication procedures operating. In essence, the *hows* of those in authority are translated into *whats*, as if they are the nature of reality and not the behavings via which reality was constructed. With the demand for democratic communication that allows a plurality of voices to speak and be heard, the species must in essence make what has been hidden and assumed—that is, the hows of communicating—obvious and flexible.

This is what is meant by the title of this chapter: the mandate to invent. The question raised is what communication inventions have humans already created and used with what consequences? What inventions are now necessary because of changing species conditions.

PROCEDURE-LESS PROCEDURES

Before attempting to illustrate the discussion above with examples of some commonly used communication procedures, we must discuss what is perhaps the most visible manifestation of the fact that most formulations about communication structures and practice are actually noncommunicatively informed. If one starts with absolutist assumptions about the nature of reality and the nature of human observing, one arrives at a conception of communication that does not involve behavior: Ideas get into heads, messages get made, reality is assumed to be obvious. There is no need to talk about alternative ways in which people make observations, construct ideas, decide on directions, and so on. These are all given.

However, they are not given. But operating under assumptions that they are, we construct communication structures without attention to procedure: They are procedureless. We will provide three examples: (a) media ownership structures; (b) agenda-setting practices in organizations; and (c) organizational member relationships to organizational leaders.

A current contest illuminated by studies of telecommunication is the structures of media ownership.[8] In the United States currently, it is assumed that privately owned media regulated via privatization and deregulation policies will allow people to hear the heterogeneity of understandings present in society. However, this structure is in one sense procedure-less because the problem of heterogeneity is resolved without explicit attention to the communication problematic. This problematic is: How can all individuals participate in the society using the media? How can they access the media and get on with attending, creating ideas, finding direction, confronting, opposing, mediating, recalling, and undoing rigidities as an active members in the collectivity of a democratic society supposed to do? The privately owned media regulated via privatization and deregulation policies basically assumes ownership and access is all that is necessary to yield heterogeneity of voice. Such a policy ignores, most obviously, the problem that only a limited number of voices can gain access and ownership. Even more important from a communication-as-behavior perspective is the fact that such a policy ignores the sense making that communicating entities must do to deal with a cacophony of diverse voices. Mere presence without procedures that allow comparison and comprehension is equivalent to nothing. So even if ownership and access patterns truly allowed diverse voices to speak, it can not be concluded that understanding of diversity would result.

Our second example involves agenda-setting which when examined from a communication-as-procedure perspective also remains essentially procedure-less.[9] This means that agenda-setting in organizations is usually accomplished in a noncommunicative or, at best, haphazardly communicative way—the leader or facilitator is given the power to set the agenda for all the others to follow. This agenda then channels attending, creating ideas, recalling, and expressing into particular conceptual frames, and so on.

Often, in an informal group, not specifically set up to accomplish a task, an agenda will play an unacknowledged role. If an informal group leader talks more, talks louder, has some tie of loyalty or influence with some other member of the group, reiterates a single point of view, interrupts others, is viewed as having more power or authority than others, denigrates other ideas or expressions, holds the floor more often, captures the attention of others, then that leader's own personal, and perhaps unacknowledged, agenda will come to have a great influence on the group. Others voices will not be acknowledged, and over time, others in the group will learn to be silent or only to venture those utterances that they have learned are acceptable.

Our third example involves how individuals in collectivities relate to their leaders and to other members of the collectivity. These relationships are also often procedure-less. The member defers constructing power to the leader even, some research suggests, when the leader wants diverse input. Such deference is understandable given the nature of most power structures. From a communication-as-procedure perspective, however, it becomes important to notice that this is an arena in which behavior has rigidified. And, in the absence of an explicitly stated procedure that would work against this rigidity, again we find that power rules the day. Instead of procedure that mandates the individual and collective constructing and communicating, we defer to the right of power or authority to do the constructing and communicating: advertising dollars direct news values; powerful news sources define reality; the leader sets the group's direction; the personality of the journalist or leader takes precedence over ideas.

This challenge is seen as applying equally to situations where diverse voices are present and to those where they are not present. The former requires a more subtle analysis, however—an understanding that the mere presence of diverse voices that are allowed to speak as if diversity did not matter can result in cacophony rather than heterogeneity. In the presence of cacophony sense cannot be made and old rigidities take hold. The energization of the system is given over to the hands of power, hidden or obvious, routinized or capricious. Whichever communicating behaviors are used by power become the energizers. But since explicit attention is not paid to these procedures, we have labeled this phenomena as procedure-less procedures. This argument will become clearer as we proceed in the sections that follow.

EXAMPLES OF COMMUNICATION PROCEDURES

Theoretically, each of the 54 cells in Figure 9.1 could be filled with a set of communicating procedures. Figure 9.1 is proposed as a framework for discovery and exploration of description and invention. It is beyond our task at this point to discuss and fill in every cell. Instead, we will discuss examples of procedures for each of the situation-defining strategies in order to illustrate the potential of this approach for examining the way in which procedures serve to define relationships between the micro and the macro and vice versa and how procedures constrain or limit potentials for democratic communication.

Individual Relating to Self

This is the situational context in which it is most difficult to develop examples because views of reality based on positivist or authoritarian ideas actually do not propose the individual relationship to self as a communication problematic. Only when society sees the individual's behavior as intrusive has attention fallen here, usually cast off to the psychiatrist's couch or to a counselor or magician. There are examples however. One useful one is the "how" of creating ideas about one's existence in time.[10] Anthropological work identifies, for example, different ways in which people locate self in time: linear versus cyclical for instance. Another useful example is the how of recalling—remembering what has occurred in the immediate or distance past. Tactics here deal with the "hows" by which people create narratives or stories about their lives and range all the way from methods of recording (e.g., the orally-told folk tale vs. the journal or diary) to those "hows" that are creating a coherency to the story narrative. One more example is the "how" of deciding—choosing what road to travel.[11] Tactics might range all the way from chance (e.g., flipping a coin), to matrix-resolving (e.g., putting all options and all characteristics comparing options in a table), to wait and see (e.g., not doing anything and seeing if circumstances point to a direction).

While typically the tactics used as examples above have been seen as defining state characteristics of one culture versus another, from a communication-as-procedure perspective they are seen as processes, which are potentially changeable across changing conditions. Indeed, if an individual's behavior is rigidified into any one of the tactics in any given kind of situation, that has enormous implications for collective life. A rigid linear conception of time, for instance, has consequences for how people are able to share ideas. It could lead, for example, to an approach to journalistic encoding behavior that permits bullet news. Or, if most individuals in a given culture define themselves in terms of cyclical time at all times, this has implications for the flexibility that culture is able to bring to bear on changing world conditions.

Individual Relating to Other Individuals

It is easier to find examples of procedures via which individuals relate to each other because the ways in which people think about and talk to each other have been important foci for the study of interpersonal communication, represented in research genres under such names as interpersonal perception or cognition, and conversational rules. In thinking about each other, for example, Rokeach isolated cognitive tactics that he labeled generally as open- and close-mindedness.[12] While he applied these to individuals as state conditions, for our purposes we will think of them as process conditions that may or may not be manifested rigidly in a given person or for a given person in given situations. Open-mindedness involves making fine gradations in distinguishing self from others while close-minded involved making gross and often polarized gradations.

The ways in which people attend to, share ideas with, make decisions, express, confront/oppose, mediate, and so on between each other are generally studied under the rubric called conversational rules. Conversational rules are informal sets of routines humans have developed in order to regulate communicating with each other. Rules govern turn-taking, how to give criticism, face-saving, who may speak when and how, who has authority, and cues about power and intimacy relationships.[13]

Two examples of conversation rules involves turn-taking (how do we share ideas) and topic setting (how do we decide what to share ideas about). Literature on communicating between U.S. men and women shows, for example, that men capture a significantly greater share of the talking time and are significantly more likely to set the topic.[14] Women, on the other hand, are more likely to interrupt, particularly with questions. Clearly such rule patterns, if rigidified, do not address a definition of democratic communication which suggests that the voices of diverse observers need to be heard.

The very concept of conversational rules suggests a repetitiveness to these behaviors, at least situationally (i.e., in a given situation, this is how one disagrees with another). Indeed, the literature on conversational rules suggests that the rules are learned out of consciousness. Virtually all children will learn the rules as they learn language and are heavily influenced by the family, community, and cultural environment in which they are raised.

Research focusing on conversational rules has in actuality given rather explicit attention to the long-term goal of improving communication by bringing rules to consciousness and modifying rules in order to achieve different communicative results. Conversational rules then are a crucial site for isolating communicating rigidities and reaching for greater communicative flexibility.

Individual Relating to Collectivity

Here the focus is on how the individual makes sense of and deals with his or her membership in a collectivity. Relatively little academic work has focused on this connection although discussions of how members of organizations deal with leadership are relevant.[15] What the literature suggests, as one example, is that many individuals in U.S. organizations focus their attending in collectivities on the leader—what the leader thinks, how the leader compares to self. Another example is how the individual attempts to make contributions to the group discussion. One tactic, a common one in U.S. group meetings, is for the individual to present his or her idea as an absolute position which does not need illumination or comparison with other ideas or clarification via example.

Both these examples focus on rigidified communicating procedures—attending which leaves the individual without ideas about members of the group other than the leader, or expressing that assumes absolute positions and leaves listeners unable to make sense of the ideas expressed on their own terms. For these examples, however, as with the examples in other sections above, theoretically the communicating tactics are responsive to changing situational conditions and communication mandates.

Collectivity Relating to Self

Parliamentary procedure is perhaps the most well-known example of a collectivity relating to self-communication procedure: a set of defined rules which set up a framework for discussion.[16] Parliamentary procedure governs what shall be talked about, when, in what order, and for what actions and is used by such diverse collective bodies as the U.S. Congress and small clubs and organizations. Parliamentary procedure was developed to allow meetings of diverse individuals with diverse opinions to argue in an orderly and productive fashion and to reduce the likelihood that decision making would revert to a shouting match or blows.

Yet, at root, parliamentary procedure is a procedure based on transmission ideas about the communication problematic—the procedure rests on an ideology which suggests that correct ideas will surface and become clear in an open marketplace. For parliamentary procedure, meaning making is not considered. The procedure ignores, for example, the need for individuals to create ideas or understand how others came to have their ideas. In effect, parliamentary procedure confounds tactics into a process where people are required to be attending, creating ideas, finding direction, recalling, expressing, deciding, mediating, and confronting all at once.

As a result of these communicating constraints, only those individuals with already formed ideas can participate and only those willing to speak up will be heard. Further, only that part of thinking that has been defined as relevant by the collective is permitted to be voiced or heard. Each of these steps reduces the likelihood that a variety of views will be heard or that participants in the process who have not arrived with already-formulated views will have the opportunity to contribute.

Another example of communicating tactics in the situational context of collectivity relating to itself is journalistic practice, the set of hows by which an institution mandated to facilitate the sharing of ideas in the collectively goes about defining the nature of collective reality.[17] Different journalists in different societies around the world all have some set of journalistic practices which they are required to follow.

Taking U.S. journalism as our example, we find a journalistic practice that conceptualizes itself as capable of accurate observation. Guided by such an ideology, this journalistic practice places high value on the idea that one well-trained journalist is an invaluable asset. From here, it is possible to create a "fact"-oriented journalism which implements the famous "5W" lead as well as a "personality" journalism which makes the journalist more important than idea sharing. Further, since it is assumed that reality has a naturally given order that can be observed equally well by one well-trained journalist or another, the idea of bullet or spot news as journalistic practice takes root. Too, in a naturally ordered reality, history also is assumed as a non-contested given, so a journalistic practice that ignores history also takes root.

Another example in this situational context is the practice of public opinion polls.[18] Here, the collectivity assesses the opinions and inputs of individual citizens and collates them presenting them as the "collective mind." There are at least two problems with this procedure. The first is that the methods of conducting polls are generally derived from authoritarian assumptions—the individual is not genuinely asked how she or he understands the world. Rather, the individual is typically asked to respond on a template which represents how those in power understand the world. The second problem is that the procedure assumes that somehow the "collective mind" is adequately represented via a statistical amalgam of individual opinions. In reality, of course, there is no collective mind. The collectivity exists, as Dewey proposed, in communicating.[19] An idea created by a collectivity as a representation of the whole is always created via struggle—not only the struggle of contesting viewpoints, but the struggle of trying to understand others.

Collectivity Relating to Individual

Here we focus on procedures by which a collectivity (structure, institution) explicitly focuses on its relationships to individuals. Common examples are the host of service professions and organizations that human beings create to serve their individual and collective needs.[20] Two examples will be presented: One focuses on the formalized procedures that collectivities use in order to learn about individuals and their needs or how well their needs have been satisfied; the other focuses on the formalized procedures by which collectivities attempt to find something within its resources that is useful to the individual.

When an organization attempts to determine an individual's needs or satisfactions, the organization is dealing with essentially opposite sides of the same coin: What does the person need? Did we give the person what was needed? Yet, the literature shows that in actuality neither of these questions are often addressed by organizations. Instead, the questions become: What of the things we do do you need? Which of the things we do did you use? What of the things we do do you like?

The procedures as described here are widespread. Two examples: A doctor questions a patient about his or her health problem by asking the patient which of a series of health problems as defined by the system the patient has—Do you have x? Have you had y? Did your mother have z? Likewise, a librarian questions a patron about his or her information need by asking the patron a series of dichotomized questions designed to zero in on which part of the library collection meets the need—Do you want this or that? One or several?

Similarly, the doctor will assess how well the health care system did on a series of system-oriented measures: Did the patient get better? Was he or she cured? How long did he or she live? Did the patient follow orders? The library will assess how well it did by also asking a series of system-oriented questions. Do you like our book collection? Do we have enough of x? How often have you used us?

These procedures can be seen as all based on an absolutist worldview. What those in power in the system see as valuable is deemed to be what is valuable. Use of these procedures has at least two consequences. One is that the way in which the system attempts to understand the individual in actuality deters understanding of the individual. The second is that the way in which the system attempts to evaluate itself using individual input reifies the system as it is now defined.

Another cut into the problematic of the collectivity relating to individuals is how the collectivity attempts to assist individuals in locating what they will find useful among the collectivity's resources. A prime example here is the category schemes in which communication systems store, retrieve, and transmit information. In journalism, for example, categories focus on local news, national news, entertainment, sports, and so on. In libraries, categories focus on hierarchically organized noun groupings as represented in Dewey Decimal or Library of Congress cataloguing systems. A third example is in database management systems where noun-oriented keywords are used as retrieval indexes.

What is interesting about all of these categorizations is that almost without exception it is assumed that the way in which the system categorizes is the correct way. No procedures allow for alternative categorizations or for users to move through a selection of alternative systems, some of which may be more relevant to particular users than others. Very little academic research has even been addressed to the question.

Collectivity Relating to Another Collectivity

Here we focus on the situation of one collectivity relating to another: organization to organization, state to state, nation to nation, alliance to alliance. Generally, such relationships are governed by law and agreement. Usually we do not think of these as communicative relationships. Rather the concerns have focused on the distribution of hard resources. In our recent history, however, we have seen instances where the problematic of the communication procedures by one collectivity is relating to another have received attention. A prime example is the call for a New World Information Communication Order by Third World and nonaligned nations.[21]

Criticisms, particularly against First World media, have focused on how Western interests control press services and use only Western input when reporting on and defining other countries. Views of other countries are described as stereotyped and based on Western myths, misunderstandings, and purposive distortions. Alternatively, concern was expressed for how much of the media space in Third World and nonaligned nations is occupied by Western media products. A fundamental complaint is that Western interests prevent self-expression both intranationally and internationally.

From one perspective, this set of concerns fits best under the discussion included earlier of procedure-less procedures. The First World nation position which argues that there ought to be no controls on freedom of the press is justified as the best way to produce a heterogeneity of voices. Clearly the justification is more myth when applied to international communication than it is when applied to intranation communication. From another perspective, however, what we see here is the implementation of non-communicatively oriented media practice tactics. In the absence of explicit procedure, the procedures of stereotyping and polarizing become a normative part of a journalistic practice. The irony is that in most cases it is probably not intended. This is a good example of the problem of well-meaning systems decaying over time into authoritarian structures. Without explicit attention to the problematic of communication, there is no alternative. Any attempt to describe the world from one vantage point must necessarily be implemented narrowly and nonpluralistically.

SOME INVENTIONS

The examples given above of commonly used communication procedures have focused on procedures which are rigidly or mindlessly applied.[22] In some cases, the procedures are seen as state descriptions—the way, for example, people in a particular culture are. In other cases, the procedures are seen as the formalized rules by which communicating gets done. In other cases, the procedures seem to be haphazard results of assuming that communication is procedure-less. In all cases, however, the procedures have been described as being applied by a given communicating entity at all times, or a given communicating entity in all situations of the same type.

But the formulation presented in this chapter assumes that communicating is necessarily the most responsive and flexible of behaviors, that humans can change how they construct and deal with their worlds depending on the mandates of the situations in which they see themselves. In fact, this formulation assumes that such flexibility and responsiveness is a requisite for democratic communication no matter what definition of democratic is brought to bear and that there are communicative tasks which theoretically are mandated: Individuals need to construct ideas in order to move; collectivities need to allow individual members some level of understanding of each other; diverse viewpoints need to be represented efficiently; people need some mental hooks on which to hang their own understandings of the diversity within which they live; institutions need to understand the people they serve and find ways to effectively and efficiently help them as they wish to be helped; communication institutions need to find ways to display the diversity of opinion in the collective without opting out in the choices of power. How each of these communicative tasks may be accomplished is theoretically varied, across time and space and in response to ever-changing conditions.

The fact that we do not see a lot of flexible communication behavior around us does not deny the possibility. Part of the problem is that we have not been looking for it, focused as we have been on trying to find consistency across time in state conditions. Part of the problem is that we haven't conceptualized communication communicatively so that neither communication scholarship nor communication practice has served the species' need for invention very well.

There are, however, a variety of examples of explicit attempts to invent alternative communication procedures. At one extreme we have a host of examples of individual efforts at changing self, for example: learning to artfully mix abstract and concrete thoughts in messages, remembering to praise before criticizing, learning to ask questions before stating one's own opinion, or expanding the ways in which one categorizes the world. At the other extreme, we have examples of explicit efforts by collectivities to develop and use more effective communication procedures. A few examples of such inventions will be presented here as a means of displaying potentials.

The conscientizing process. In this approach, developed by Freire, procedures are instituted by which every group member can and must be heard until all have had a chance to say what they have to say. This procedure insists that all must speak everything they wish; that there is no reliance on loudest voice, sqeakiest wheel, or power and authority. The conscientizing process continues, in essence, as long as necessary.

Agenda canvassing. In this approach, attributed historically to some groups of U.S. Native Americans, the chiefs brought to the meeting circle their agenda items. These were then canvassed without counterargument until all had proposed topics of discussion at which point the group's agenda was easily set by consensus.

Brainstorming. In this approach, one of the most frequent alternative procedural forms used in mainstream organizations, recognition is given to the idea that when an organization wants creative input different forms of communicating must be used than in the usual authority-run or parliamentary-procedure run meeting. In brainstorming, everyone is given a chance to speak and no one is allowed to criticize any idea. Further, ideas are recorded but without reference to who stated them thus preparing the way for a later evaluation phase which will not be met with defensive reactions.

Speak bitter, speak easy. In this approach, attributed to Mao, representatives of an "oppressed" group are given the floor to talk of their frustrations, angers, and hurts without interruption or comment by the "oppressor" group. The idea is that with these procedural controls, to speak bitter becomes easier.

Communication task assignments. In this approach, the assumption is that there are different communicative tasks to accomplish in any meeting and that this requires that some members of the group attend explicitly to the communicating process. Certain members of the group are given this assignment and given the right to interrupt the proceedings to call attention to events that need attention. Examples of such events include: a squabble when in effect the participants are arguing from different definitions; a point in time when only a few members of the group are participating; and, a point in time when participants are talking about different agenda items as if they were all the same.

Constructive criticism of the leader. In this approach, the procedure acknowledges how difficult it is for most people in most cultures to hear and act on criticism. For this reason, the procedure suggests that group members evaluate the leader by answering two questions: What has the leader done well? What could the leader do better?

Sense-Making questions. In this approach, proposed as an alternative means by which professionals conduct needs assessments of individual clients/patrons/customers/users whom they serve, the professional's questions focus on learning and understanding what it is that brought the person to the system, what gaps the person faces, and what helps the person hopes to find. The questions, derived from an elaborate theoretic orientation to the problematics of communicating in systems, are seen as to going to the heart of what it is that brings a person to a system for help.

Pluralistic journalism. This proposal for journalistic practice attempts to incorporate into procedure the sense-making needs of members of the collectivity. The proposal mandates that 3–4 maximally different observers make observations and construct independent journalistic reports. They are then asked to explicitly address why they think their report differs from that of the other journalists. This latter material pertaining to understanding why observations are different allows readers to comprehend and make sense of heterogeneous voices. This proposal has been utilized in journalistic products created for a health clinic with enormous success.

User-based helps as retrieval tools. In this proposal, the readers of books (or articles) are asked to indicate how utilizing the materials helped them. The statements of the most recent group of readers are then made available to prospective readers as an alternative means for locating what would be useful to them. In one experiment, handwritten paragraphs were posted on a bulletin board; in another, they were pasted inside the book covers; in another, they were made available via computer. In all cases, readers were more likely to utilize these entry points than traditional ones.

Good news. In this approach, it is assumed that formalized discourse in society, via media, in organizations, and interpersonally, increasingly focuses on the negative and that individuals have trouble thinking and acting flexibly when weighed down in negativity. This procedure mandates that a group meeting, for example, require each group member to share positive news about self, organization, leader, world. In media, this procedure mandates that a portion of the coverage of all issues focus on the positive— accomplishments, instances of compassion and caring, examples of beauty and peace, or whatever is valued in that context.

All of the examples above share one thing in common—an acceptance of the dialogic nature of communication, the here-and-now making of meaning that involves continuing interaction between individuals, environments, and collectivities. By explicitly acknowledging the dialogic nature of communication, these inventions attempt to prevent or forestall the decay back into authoritarian power structures that confound even the most well-intentioned democratic communication designs. By acknowledging the dialogic nature of communication, these inventions also bring out for attention the ways in which micro and macro relate to each other, rather than assuming that these worlds are in opposition.

SOME PROBLEMS WITH INVENTION

The framework above is proposed as an example of a procedurally defined template for studying democratic communication. Studying is proposed both for descriptive and historical approaches: What *have* we done procedurally with what consequences at both macro and micro levels? Studying is also proposed as inventive: What *might* be done procedurally with what consequences at both macro and micro levels?

For the context of democratic communication, however, description and invention are not enough. A problem is allowing the system (i.e., the humans whose communicating behavior energizes the system) to accept new/alternative procedures. In this regard, one difficulty is that procedures are "rigidified" into systems because they are ideologically bound. Another difficulty is that they are rigidified because they are behaviorally bound; embedded into repetitive behavioral patterns almost out-of-consciousness. Learning such patterns is easier than unlearning them.

The situationally defined strategy noticeably de-emphasized in the examples above is that of individual relating to self. The communication tactic noticeably left out is that of undoing rigidities. Both cases demonstrate that as a species we have not paid explicit attention, either through research or practice design, to the need to build in procedures to deal with the fundamental intersection of situational strategy and communication tactic. Any time individuals singly or in collectivity come to a communicative moment, they are facing a new moment. This moment has not occurred before. It may be usefully addressed with tactics or strategies used in the past, but the communicating entities involved will be unable to perform responsively to the moment if they are not flexible and able to construct appropriate tactics and strategies. If they are hampered by rigidity, and our assumption is that it is part of the human condition to carry around rigidities, then it is impossible to proceed flexibly. We therefore assume that that necessity demands procedures for undoing these rigidities.

Yet, to allow procedures to keep pace with structural changes, the communication procedures which serve to energize structures must be amenable to change. This does not mean eliminating an "old" procedure, for the "old" procedure is seen as theoretically having utility depending on situational conditions. Rather it means removing the rigidity from the old procedure to allow for an increase in the diversity and flexibility of the communicative repertoire. The point is to make available to the communicating entity alternative communicating behaviors that can be brought to bear in the situation depending on how the situation is assessed.

The situation is made complicated because of the fact that the human's ability to change procedural skills depends not only on awareness of alternatives, but on the availability of repetitive practice. The way a human truly learns a behavior so that it becomes second nature is to perform it over and over again. Any procedure performed regularly will have power over a new procedure until that new procedure has been repeated enough to make it second nature—available for spontaneously rapid use. Therefore, to modulate a new procedure into a structure requires repetitive practice. The goal is to increase communicating capability

Awareness of alternatives is not alone sufficient for the improvement of communicating capabilities. Since all structures are energized via communicatings performed by individual human beings either individually or in collectivity, what is envisioned here is a need both to increase awareness and to diversify habits. Increasing awareness is seen as the easier task since diversifying behavioral routines requires both practice and an acknowledgment of the anxiety and inefficiency that necessarily accompanies any behavior change process.

A further complication is that behavioral routines (particularly communication behavioral routines) are a site where oppressive or hurtful learning conditions are likely to show their damage.[23] As specified earlier under the tactic "undoing rigidity," if an individual is not flexible in a communication situation, that individual is unlikely to perform any of the tactics well. A crucial step that has not been given much attention (because the focuses of the macro and the cultural streams have been elsewhere) is the necessity to free current communicating habits from their rigidity. This freeing up of flexibility must be accomplished before appropriate communication tactics can even be learned, let alone practiced.

Behavioral routines, no matter what their sources, are often learned by humans while they are being systematically oppressed or hurt by the structures of their societies or systematically taught to oppress. The "essence" of psychoanalytic theory and research suggests that behaviors learned in such oppressive and hurtful circumstances are not available to change simply as a result of awareness and practice. Rather, the behavior will be habitualized in a qualitatively different way.

Behaviors that become habitualized without oppressive or hurtful circumstances surrounding their acquisition are easily observed by actors and reasonably amenable to change via practice. This is because they are in the realm of consciousness where aware-ness of them is stored both digitally and analogically. In contrast, behaviors that are learned in oppressive and hurtful circumstances are not easily observed by actors are per-formed out of consciousness, and awareness of them is stored only analogically. An important aspect of what is being proposed here is that we are challenging the assumed-to-be unconsciousness of the performance of communicating procedures (e.g., the rules and norms of cultures). We are suggesting that unconsciousness, an inability to be aware of behavior, is a special case involving learning which was in some way oppressive or hurtful. What this means is that the habitualization of the behavior is deeply enmeshed with acceptance of oppression and hurt and with the inability to think and observe that results from oppressive and hurtful circumstances.

Behaviors habitualized in this way need more than thought and practice to make them amenable to change. The actor must go through a self-controlled consciousness-raising process. The actor may artfully use others (as confidants, counselors, spiritual leaders, etc.) during this process but, as the essence of psychoanalytic theory suggests, the process is a self-controlled one, an act of individual emergence from past circumstances.

Most societies have very few existing procedures for what is regarded here as a fundamentally requisite tactic. Communication research has paid little attention to this concern since Western societies have, in essence, relegated the world of the "subjective" to the psychiatric couch and out of the system mainstream. A possible exception to this may be entertainment media programs which studies show have at times served thera-peutic and conscientizing functions.

A crucial element of the perspective on communication proposed in this chapter, then, is the idea that in establishing democratic means of communicating it will be nec-essary to assist communicating entities in this process by incorporating conscientizing tactical procedures. This undoing of rigidities is seen as a necessary part of attempts to gain greater flexibility—in essence, to become more communicatively competent. Further, the capacity for communicative competence is seen as inherent in the human species and necessary to the implementation of democratic communication designs by whatever definitional context they are proposed.

NOTES

1.   We owe a particular debt to writings by Richard Carter (1989b); John Dewey (1915); Paolo Freire (1970); Anthony Giddens (1989); Jurgen Habermas (1979, 1984, 1987b); Stuart Hall (1989); Harvey Jackins (1973); Hamid Mowlana (1986); Jan Servaes (1986); and Majid Tehranian (1979, 1982, 1988). In addition, the discussions in Dervin, Grossberg, O'Keefe, & Wartella (1989a, b) were helpful. The ideas developed in this paper received initial treatment in Dervin & Clark (1989) and Dervin (1983a; 1989a, b; 1991a).

2.   For a good overview of various positions relating to democratic communication, see, in particular, *Communication Research Trends* Vol. 9, No. 3.

3.   This conceptualization of the communication procedure perspective rests heavily on the theoretical work of Richard Carter (see Carter: 1980, 1982, 1989b; and Carter, Ruggels, Jackson, & Heffner, 1973; and Carter, Ruggels, & Simpson, 1975). Carter (1980) states that collective behavior proceeds by and in step-taking. He calls for inventive approaches to step-taking behavior in seeking the well-being of humanity, and suggests that the focuses of control are the specific place to intervene in a behavioral step in order to affect it. Carter (1982) suggests that communication produced by communicating may be connection, correspondence between two or more persons with respect to a shared condition, a focus of attention, a notion, an expression. Communicating may be focusing attention, cognizing about a focal condition, expressing oneself, or coding the expression. He notes that mass media and educational institutions can be seen as tools which respond to the need to deal with the amount of work associated with the communication among large numbers of people—the need to span space and time.

4.   E. C. White (1987) argues that ". . . instead of viewing the present occasion as continuous with a causally relation sequence of events, *kairos* [the will to invent] regards the present as unprecedented, as a moment of decision, a moment of crisis, and considers it impossible, therefore, to intervene successfully in the course of events merely on the basis of past experience. How can one make sense of a world that is eternally new simply by repeating the ready-made categories of tradition? Tradition must answer to the present, must be adapted to new circumstances that may modify or even disrupt received knowledge . . ." (p. 14).

5.   The conceptualization of power used heavily here is by Lukes (1974).

6.   Anthony Giddens (1984) discusses rules, procedures, and tactics as used by actors in the course of their everyday life to routinely negotiate the situations of social life. He argues that this routine use of rules, procedures and tactics constitutes and reconstitutes social life.

7.   See footnote 3.

8.   For examples of work which discusses this issue see Hachten (1982), Hamelink (1983), Head (1985), and Mowlana (1986).

9.   For various discussions involving agenda-setting in organizations and groups see Dutton (1985), Hirokawa (1988), Poole & Roth (1989a, b), and Stohl (1989).

10.   Anthropological literature includes many rich examples of differences in communication between culture. See, in particular: Geertz (1973), Murdock (1967), and Textor (1967). A major difference is that anthropological discussions of communication behavior are usually presented as state conditions, not process conditions—assumed to characterize members of that culture across time and space.

11.   For some discussion of decision-making, see Dutton (1985), Hirokawa (1988), Poole & Roth (1989a, b), and Stohl (1989)

12.   See Rokeach (1960).

13.   For examination of various aspects of conversation see Goodwin (1989), Kellerman & Lim (1989), Knapp, Stafford, and Daly (1986), McLaughlin (1984), O'Keefe & McCormack (1987), Tracy (1989), Tracy, Van Dusen, & Robinson (1987), and Yelsma (1986).

14. For discussion of conversation rules such as turn-taking and topic setting, see Fitzpatrick (1983), Foss & Foss (1983), Nadler & Nadler (1987), Spitzack & Carter (1987), Talley & Peck (1980).

15. A number of how-to-do-it books are available, particularly those oriented to helping individuals achieve success in organizational settings. For overviews of academic work on organizational communication, see Jablin, Putman, Roberts, & Porter (1987) and Goldhaber & Barnett (1988).

16. For a concise description of parliamentary procedure see Ryan (1985) which summarizes the main points of the classic *Robert's Rules of Order Newly Revised.*

17. See the following authors for discussions and descriptions of various journalistic practices: Altheide (1985), Bruck (1989), Ettema & Glasser (1988), Gitlin (1980), Hall, Chricter, Jefferson, Clarke, & Roberts (1978), Jensen (1987a), Katz (1987), Kress (1986), Tuchman (1978), and Van Driel & Richardson (1988).

18. For a critique of public opinion research, see Carter et al. (1975), Dervin (1989a), Edelstein (1974), and Splichal (1987).

19. See Dewey (1915), and also Rakow (1989).

20. For a review of literature pertinent to this section, see Dervin & Nilan (1986), and Dervin (1989a, b).

21. For discussions of issues relating to this debate, see Argumedo (1981), Arusha Declaration on World Telecommunications Development (1985), Jayaweera (1987), Resolution of the Administrative Council of the International Telecommunication Union (1985), Schiller (1978), Servaes (1986), and R. A. White (1987).

22. Many of the examples of inventions presented here have been developed and tested by Dervin and colleagues (see Dervin & Dewdney, 1986; Dervin & Nilan, 1986). Also utilized is the following: For inventions focusing on retrieval of information, Belkin (1978, 1982a, b); for inventions relating to conscientizing, Freire (1970); for a variety of inventions focusing on interpersonal and group interactions aimed at undoing communicating rigidities, Jackins (1973); for journalistic inventions, Matta (1986); for the invention of "speak bitter, speak easy," Mao (Dreifus, 1973).

23. The discussion of consciousness raising, conscientizing, and increasing communicative flexibility presented here rests heavily on works by: Breuer & Freud (1957), Freire (1970), Jackins (1973), and Rogers (1961).

PART II

RESEARCH, DESIGN, AND PRACTICE

Chapter 10

Mass Communicating:
Changing Conceptions of the Audience

Brenda Dervin

TRADITIONAL CONCEPTIONS

A Consensual Portrait

A designer of a public communication campaign who reaches out to mass communications researchers for advice will receive back, with only a few minor variations, a relatively stable consensual portrait of audiences.[1] Audiences, he will be told, are attentive to and motivated about only a small number of issues that have immediacy in their lives. They are unwilling to attend to or act upon most public communication campaign messages. Typically they use the media to be entertained, not informed. Campaign messages work best only when they are supportive of other activities such as interpersonal network strategies.[2] In short, a campaign designer will be told to expect only very limited effects from his campaign.

    The stability of the consensus behind this portrait rests on the large amount of evidence that generated it. As a result, a campaign designer can feel that he has not only received from the mass communication researchers a state-of-the-art portrait of audiences but also something more—a set of statements that are so firmly supported that they appear to have truth value.

    It is unlikely that the campaign designer will be cautioned that this view of audiences, while prevalent and well-supported, is merely one possible idea about audiences, an idea supported in a given research context, and that other ideas supported in other research contexts are possible. Nor would he be cautioned that other conceptions of

This work originally appeared as: Dervin, B. (1981). Mass communicating: Changing conceptions of the audience. In R. E. Rice & W. J. Paisley (Eds.), *Public communication campaigns* (pp. 71–87). Beverly Hills, CA: Sage. Reprinted by permission of Sage Publications, Inc., Thousand Oaks, CA. Contains material presented as: Dervin, B. (1980, October). *Mass communicating: Changing conceptions of the audience.* Paper presented at the Stanford University Institute for Communications Research, Public Communications Campaign Conference, Asilomar, CA.

audiences might engender entirely different portraits and, thus, different conclusions which impact the nature of public communication campaign design.

It is not, however, surprising that a campaign designer would not be cautioned in this way for, at root, the core conceptions which have guided audience research since the beginnings of communication research as formal enterprise have remained essentially unchanged. These core conceptions form a nest of interlocking assumptions. The audience is seen *as* audience. The term is, by definition, a source's construct. The source sees self as having a message to send to receivers with the hope of producing with the message some desired result. The receivers are to gain new ideas, change old ones, gain new attitudes, change old ones, gain new behaviors, change old ones. The source selects the desired outcome and frames a message to achieve that outcome. The source then transmits that message via some channel to the audience seen as a collectivity of receivers. Receivers are then studied to see if they exhibit the expected results.

A Brief History of Research Strategies

Over the past 40 years in the field of communications, this set of assumptions or conceptions about audiences have been translated in what on the surface looks like a widely variant set of research strategies. It is said, for example, that our view of audiences today, when the consensual portrait suggests we can only expect mediated or limited effects from media messages, is a radically different view from an earlier consensual portrait which expected direct and marked effects.

These differences in research strategy, however, can be looked at as symptoms of the impact of the use of the source-oriented, audience-as-receivers conceptions. As one looks at the trends in the communication field, what is most readily apparent is that it is a field marked by fads, with each succeeding fad responding to a failure of the earlier fad in its attempt to determine the ways in which sources can get impacts in receivers from media messages.

In the 1940s, for example, the field was characterized by the search for direct hypodermiclike effects. When the evidence did not agree, it was reasoned that perhaps what was operating was that some message characteristics were effective while others were not. In the 1950s, then, attention turned primarily to attempting to isolate those characteristics of messages which would impact audiences. When results showed only limited utility from this approach, it was reasoned that there must be some consistent cognitive processing mechanisms which, when understood, would allow more effective message design. Typical of this trend which dominated the late 1950s and early 1960s were the studies in the balance model tradition which attempted to force receivers to cognitively entrap themselves into change in the source's direction by pitting conflicting cognitions against each other. When this strategy showed highly inconsistent results across studies, it was reasoned that there must be some systematic differences between receivers that meant some receivers could be reached while others could not. What followed into the 1970s, then, was an attempt to isolate systematic receiver differences which could be the focal point of message design. As the 1970s ended, however, it had become apparent that the potential for this approach was also limited, with statements being made that, at the most, receiver differences could account for only 10% of the variance in the message impact.[3]

Throughout all this effort, the idea of the recalcitrant, obstinate receiver gained more and more credence. This idea manifested itself in varying forms. Sometimes flat statements were made about only limited effects being possible. Other times, it was suggested that media communication campaigns could not work directly but rather as support or complement for other approaches such as the use of interpersonal networks. At other times, it was suggested that communication campaigns could work best only if they were designed to reinforce existing norms.

For purposes of this chapter, however, more important than the findings generated by the successive research strategies is the fact that all the findings were generated essentially within the constraints of one interlocking set of assumptions about receivers. The core conceptions remained the same—that sources with purposes designed messages to send to audience-receivers to achieve those purposes. Even the introduction of the concept of feedback into the source-message-channel-receiver-effects-feedback paradigm did not alter the basic conceptions. The source still decided purpose; the receiver was still viewed in terms of his compliance (or lack of it) with that purpose.

Yet, there were some counter-voices.[4] These voices began to suggest that the entire portrait of limited, mediated, conditional impacts from media messages on receivers might, in fact, be an artifact of the ways in which researchers had been looking at audiences. It was possible, it was suggested, that messages can have a much greater impact than our evidence suggests, but that we have been unable to isolate these impacts not because they are not there but because our view of audiences-as-receivers of messages constrains our vision.

For the first time, instead of merely seeing a call for looking at receivers in a different way, one began to see a call for looking at *our* ideas *about* receivers in a different way. A first step in this process was examining the fundamental idea that seemed to engender the consensual portrait of audiences.

The Fundamental Idea Behind the Consensual Portrait[5]

The first research strategy that was brought to bear on audiences shows most directly the fundamental idea behind our conceptions of audiences. This strategy, labeled the "hypodermic" or "direct effects" model, assumed that messages should have direct impact.

When this strategy did not work, its assumption was neither rejected and cast aside nor examined and analyzed to unearth possible constraints in the ideas behind it. Rather, 30 years of research was conducted attempting to find a way to make the assumption work.

The assumption—that messages should have a direct impact—rests on a number of other implicit assumptions. It assumes, for example, that messages can have direct impact, that somehow they can get into receivers the same way they left sources, and that they produce in all receivers the same impact. It assumes that a message is seen the same way by source and receiver and by one receiver and the next receiver. It assumes that there is nothing unique about the receiver that will impact his or her use of the message. It assumes that there are no cognitive processes intervening between message and use.

At root, behind all these assumptions, is a core assumption dealing with the nature of information, that information can be dumped into people's heads as if people's heads were empty buckets. To make this assumption, it must be assumed that information is a thing rather than a construction, that it exists independently of observers and has an inherent, correct, absolute, and isomorphic relationship to the reality it describes. Within the context of these assumptions, it is reasonable to expect that a receiver exposed to information should ipso facto respond.

AN ALTERNATE CONCEPTION

An Alternative Idea[6]

One way to more fully understand how the "information-as-thing" idea has constrained us is to compare it with an alternative. This alternative—the "information-as-construction" idea—is based on a different set of assumptions about the nature of information and its relationship to man and, thus, a different set of assumptions about the nature of audience use of messages.

The core assumption in this alternative is that information is not a thing. Instead, all information is seen as a product of human observing. All human observing is assumed to be constrained by the limits of human perceptual equipment, by the control exerted on perception by unique human minds, and by the boundaries placed on perception by time and space.

In this view, then, if information is seen as a product of human observing and human observing is seen as constrained, information is itself seen as constrained. Instead of being seen as having an absolute, accurate, isomorphic relationship with reality, information is seen as being a product, a creation of human observing at specific points in time-space. Information has meaning only in the context of the constraints on the human observing that created it. It is relative to its creator and meaningful only in that context.

It cannot be lifted meaningfully out of context and treated as a thing independent of that context. In short, the information-as-construction idea requires that all information be understood as subjective and transmitted as subjective.

The Juxtaposition of Two Ideas

The information-as-thing idea says messages will have impact because the information in the message is assumed to have the kind of reality that things have, that is, physical substance. Because of this, it is assumed that the information in messages can be transferred from place to place without change and that its applicability to one place is the same as its applicability to another.

The information-as-construction idea says that information is not a thing that can be transmitted as substance but rather a creation inexorably tied to the time, place, and perspectives of its creator. Because of this, it is assumed that a message has information value to a receiver only to the extent that it can be interpreted, understood, and applied by that receiver to his or her own time, place, and perspectives.

The information-as-thing idea is so pervasive that one can see its impact in the execution of communication campaigns, the design of communication systems, and the conduct of communication research. It is useful, in understanding how the information-as-thing idea has impacted these activities, to use the information-as-construction idea as a vantage point. Several examples will serve the purpose.

First, what we have done is allowed a relatively few people, those who control our media and information systems, to transmit as if it were truthful absolute information, what is actually nothing more than their personal, subjective observations. A common message strategy, for example, is the use of the single authoritative voice. Such a strategy works for those members of the audience whose time, space, and perspectives are comparable to those of the message creators. But, in fact, this accounts for only a small share of the audience, those middle- to upper-middle-class individuals who have been inculcated into the same kind of life perspectives as the message creators. Interestingly, even these audience groups have been shown in study after study to be using information systems designed expressly for them at rates far below what is expected. A good example is the very low use by professionals of information systems made available so they could access social science research relevant to the practice of their professions.[7]

Second, application of the information-as-thing idea requires that messages present an objective face.[8] Reporters, scientists, and others in the observing professions are, in essence, required to remove themselves as much as possible from their observations and to construct messages without reference to their feelings and biases and the perspectives that led them to their observations. This, from an information-as-construction perspective, makes the resulting messages far less useful to audiences who, it is assumed, need to relate to such subjective cues in order to determine the applicability of the message to their own contexts.

Third, since it is assumed that information is a thing and has a known and given relationship to reality, it becomes possible to rely on spot or bullet presentations where observations are presented without reference to how they are connected to each other in the mind of the message creator.[9] This means the messages are less useful to the audience who, it is assumed in the context of information-as-construction view, need to understand how others see their observations as being connected in order to make use of messages.

Fourth, since the information-as-thing idea assumes a given relationship between observations and reality, it also becomes possible to de-emphasize possible ways in which observations can be used, in essence to de-emphasize how-to-do-it observations.[10] This is done, in part, because such observations are clearly more subjective in that they deal with the future, while the information-as-thing perspective requires that what is transmitted be as objective as possible. As a result, the receiver is left without possible linkages between the message and the action.

The examples above all illustrate the same point—that a major consequence of applying the information-as-thing idea to message design is to make the resulting messages less useful to audiences and, in particular, to those members of the audience who do not share time, place, and perspectives with the message creator. When one posits information as thing, it becomes possible to take the message creator's observations, call them information, and set them up as a standard against which all receivers are judged. If receivers do not share the same observations, they are called uninformed. If they do not seem to care about the same arena of concern, they are called unmotivated. If their observations disagree, they are called biased. If they do not attend, they are called selective. In such a context, it is possible to look at the entire consensual portrait of audiences as an artifact of the information-as-thing perspective.

This research, in turn, can be used to perpetuate message designs which further reify the portrait. For example, one common generalization is that larger audiences will be obtained for entertainment fare than information fare. Yet, it is possible to ask if this is a statement of the actual interests of the audience or an artifact of media designs in which entertainment fare is allowed to retain the personalness and individualness that permit members of the audience to use it while informational fare is required to put on a less usable objective face.

Another common generalization is that a certain audience segment is virtually unreachable.[11] Yet, one possibility is that researchers have created this picture by judging these groups against information standards neither useful nor relevant to their worlds in the context of a media system which has not been obliged to help audiences see the connections between observations made in one place and their possible utility in another place.

This line of thinking puts those interested in campaign design in a very difficult position. It suggests, for one thing, that we may in actuality understand very little about how people *do* use information. Further, it suggests that when we attempt to make breakthroughs in campaign and message design, we are constrained by both our assumptions and by the fact that the available evidence has been engendered by those very assumptions. Further, it suggests that the very media systems we use are themselves constrained by the same assumptions as are audiences who are conditioned to those systems.

The above discussion suggests that changing the conceptions of audiences upon which campaign and message design rest is not an easy task because of the deep-rootedness of the fundamental ideas that engender traditional conceptions. The discussion also suggests, however, that there are alternative conceptions that can guide the conduct of research and that the results of such research should offer guidance for alternative approaches to message and campaign design.

The changes in thinking about audiences referred to above are not new to this chapter or, for that matter, to the social sciences. Elements of the alternative conception of audiences have appeared in isolated, primarily nonempirical, work.[12] What is new, however, is that the empirical social sciences are beginning to cope in systematic ways with the implications of having accepted traditional conceptions.[13] And, one can identify specific researchers and theorists who have begun to develop alternative research models.[14]

For the purposes of this chapter, one example of a research application generated from the information-as-construction idea will be presented. In this application, called the Sense-Making approach, it is assumed that a useful way to determine how to design campaigns and messages is by looking at how people construct sense out of situations which are to be the foci of the campaigns and messages.

A RESEARCH APPLICATION

Baseline Assumptions

The Sense-Making approach rests on a set of baseline assumptions about the nature of audiences and their uses of information.[15] Each of the assumptions is derived from the information-as-construction idea and yields its own set of specific guidances to the research approach. For purposes of brevity, the assumptions can be summarized as answers to four questions: When do people use messages? How static is message use behavior? What do people use messages for? What will predict message use?

When Do People Use Messages?

The information-as-construction idea rests on the assumption that people must construct sense in a world where no external, absolute sense is provided. Since no observations made by one person perfectly fit the time and place of another, it is assumed that each person must construct his or her own sense. And, since time passes and things change, the sense made by one person today does not automatically fit tomorrow.

In this context, message use is seen as an active purposive behavior, part of the individual's constant, ongoing requirement of constructing cognitive order for his or her world. Further, while the observations of others (i.e., external information) have utility in that process, it is assumed that the only way the individual can use this input is if he or she is able to make connections between it and his or her own world.

This discussion leads to a basic premise of the Sense-Making approach: people seek external input (i.e., information) to help them fill the gaps they see in their understanding of their worlds. Based on this thinking, a core element of the Sense-Making approach is to ask respondents what questions they had about situations, what understandings they saw self as needing, what they needed to make sense out of, find out, learn, or unconfuse.

In the Sense-Making approach, the kinds of gaps respondents see self as having are a major element of the model. Content analytic schemes have been developed to tap the kinds of gaps respondents see, based on the assumption that while each individual sees uniquely, there are some universals about how people move through time and space which allow the researcher to look at what is in actuality controlled behavior.

Among the schemes developed to date to assess the nature of gaps respondents see is an analog to the famous 5-W approach used in journalism: who, what, when, where, why, and how. Each respondent's questions are assessed for whether the respondent is attempting to bridge gaps relating to identity and characteristics of people (who), the event (what), the location of entities in time (when), the location of entities in space (where), the reasons behind events (why), and the manner in which things can be implemented (how).

Another scheme looks at the way in which respondents see gaps in their pictures of how they are moving through time and space and categorizes each respondent question into one of these categories: Where was I? How did I move from there to here? Where am I? Where am I going? How can I move from here to there? Other templates assessing the nature of gaps seen have focused on other dimensions; the nature of the entity to which the gap is seen as applying and whether the gap is related in the respondent's mind to positive or negative consequences, for example.

How Static is Message Use Behavior?

If, as the discussion above suggests, message use is behavior that responds to gaps seen in movement through time-space, then message use cannot be characterized as a constant, unchanging set of behaviors but as changing with time and space.[16] For this reason, the Sense-Making approach is based on an interviewing technique called the "Time-Line Interview," in which respondents are asked to reconstruct, step by step, their sense-making as they moved through a series of related events. Examples in studies to date include asking respondents to describe step by step the events that occurred during: a recent exposure to a message, a recent day, a recent experience they had, a recent conversation. Each step in the time-line is considered a separate situation for which sense-making could occur if the respondent saw self as having cognitive gaps at that point in time-space. In the actual process of the in-depth version of the Time-Line Interview, respondents are asked to first describe the events step by step, then to describe in detail how they saw each event, and, finally, to describe in detail the gaps they had during each event and if and how they filled them. The average in-depth Time-Line Interview takes two hours. Shorter versions have been developed for specialized purposes.

What Do People Use Messages For?[17]

The information-as-construction assumptions suggest that what people see in messages and what they do with them are in themselves constructions. While traditional conceptions of audiences assumed that message exposure should be sufficient to produce specific uses, the Sense-Making approach assumes that there are a variety of different ways in which respondents can put messages to work for them with these ways depending on how they see themselves moving through time-space. While the choice of how to use input is up to the individual, again it is assumed that there is something universal about the nature of movement through time-space which allows systematic study of this uniquely controlled activity.

In particular, the uses people make of information are tapped in the Sense-Making approach by asking respondents how they saw input as helping them.[18] A content analysis scheme developed to assess the verbal responses focuses on how respondents saw information as helping movement. Categories include: helped me make progress, helped me to get where I wanted to go, helped me get out of bad places, helped me avoid bad places, helped me get connected to other people, got me started or motivated, helped me find directions to travel in; and, the general category, helped me get pictures (ideas) about self, others, situations, and objects.

What Predicts Information Use?

It is a basic premise of the approach that information use is predictable based not on static portraits of people (i.e., their demographic or personality characteristics, their life contexts prior to message use) but on their perceptions of the specific moments in time-space when information is used.[19] For this reason, the Sense-Making approach focuses not on the individual person as its unit of analysis but on the sense-making situation or instance. Further, it is assumed as was above that while any individual's perception of a moment in time-space is unique, there are universals that apply to movement through time-space that can guide the selection of predictors.

A series of possible predictors has been developed. Situation movement state is one: a content analytic scheme which assigns a situational moment to one of a set of categories based on how the respondent described his movement as being blocked. The categories include: decision (when a choice must be made between two or more roads); barrier (when something blocks progress to a chosen goal); problematic (when the respondent sees self as being forced down an unwanted road); and worry (when there appears to be no possible road). Other situational predictors deal with the extent to which the respondent sees the road he or she is traveling on as fogged over (perceptual embeddedness), filled with other people (social embeddedness), or intersecting with other aspects of his or her life (situational embeddedness).

Some Sample Studies

To date, a total of 15 studies have been conducted within the perspective of the Sense-Making approach. These have included studies that have looked at: how citizens in Seattle and in the state of California have made sense out of recent troublesome experiences they faced; how blood donors made sense out of recent blood-donating experience; how patients made sense out of a recent visit to the doctor; how college students made sense out of a recent classroom lecture and a recent paper writing assignment; how newspaper readers made sense out of newspaper articles; and how friends made sense of a recent interpersonal conflict in which they were involved.[20]

In each case, the results obtained offer specific guidance for message or campaign design or, more generally, for communication system design. In the study on blood donors, for example, the concern was for locating those points in the donating process when donors seemed to need specific kinds of input. In the study of patient behavior, the concern was for the kinds of message design and communication planning doctors need to be involved in to help patients cope optimally with their illnesses. In the study of newspaper readers, the data speak to the issue of how to specifically design messages so they can be optimally useful to readers.

Some Major Findings

It is not the purpose of this chapter to track any one of these studies in detail either in terms of specific methods or results. Rather, a more useful activity is looking at some major trends in the findings gleaned to date both in terms of how the findings change our conceptions of audiences and in terms of how they change our conceptions of what we are about when we design communication campaigns. A selection of major findings that change our conceptions of audiences will be presented first, followed by a discussion of implications for practice.

In terms of changing our conceptions of audiences, the studies completed to date intersect on four major classes of findings, each of which contradicts a well-established component of the consensual portrait of audiences. Again, it is useful to look at these as answers to questions: How much do people use information? What kinds of information do people need? What do people use the information for? What predicts their information use?

How Much Do People Use Information?

Traditional studies, guided by traditional conceptions of audiences, have developed a fairly pessimistic portrait of the information use potential of audiences. In contrast, studies done in the Sense-Making frame have found typically high levels of information use. The study of Seattle citizens dealing with recent troublesome situations, for example, showed that 80% of the respondents talked to someone about their situations, 76% spent time thinking, and 42% read something (Dervin, Zweizig, Banister, Gabriel, Hall, & Kwan, 1976). Preliminary results from the study of newspaper readers showed an average of five questions asked per article attempting to make connections in understanding beyond the article (Dervin & Martin, 1980). Results from the study of blood donors showed donors had an average of six questions while donating (Dervin, Nilan, & Jacobson, 1981).

What Kinds of Information Do People Use?

Traditional studies have not looked at the nature of people's information needs per se, having started with the assumption that the source's message should meet needs of audiences. As a result, traditional studies provide little guidance for message design. In contrast, the Sense-Making studies focus centrally on the kinds of gaps respondents had and how they filled them.

Across studies, for example, results have consistently shown that "why" questions constitute from 20% to 35% of the questions respondents report they had in situations. "Why" questions are also the ones least likely to have been successfully answered. Typical results from the study of patients coping with recent visits with doctors showed that 28% of the patients' questions focused on "why" and, while 65% or more of all other questions were answered, only 45% of the "why" questions were answered (Dervin et al., 1980). The same pattern was shown in the study of Seattle citizens coping with recent troublesome situations. Here, 20% of their questions focused on "why" and, while 72% or more of all other questions were successfully answered, only 52% of "why" questions were successfully answered (Dervin et al., 1976).

These findings are of particular interest as we attempt to deal with the impact of traditional conceptions on our understanding of audiences. In the context of the information-as-thing idea, "why" questions should be de-emphasized in media and message design because they are the most subjective and require personalization in answers. Yet, when an approach to audiences is utilized that looks at information use on their terms rather than the source's terms, the need to focus on such questions clearly emerges.

What Do People Use Information For?

Traditional conceptions of the audience have looked at information use as an end in itself. The Sense-Making approach, as one possible alternative, assumes that there are a variety of different uses possible from any message. In the study of Seattle citizens and their coping with recent troublesome situations, only 3% of the respondents said they were helped because they got information and only 27% said they were helped because they got some kind of general or specific clarification or understanding. Rather, the responses were most frequently tied to specific actions and plans the respondent was working on: 36% evaluated information in terms of whether it helped them make progress; 18% in terms of whether it helped them plan; 6% in terms of whether it helped them get support or encouragement; and 6% in terms of whether it helped them gain or regain control (Dervin et al., 1976).

In other studies the relative distribution of mentions across the different kinds of uses varied. In the study of patients coping with recent visits with doctors, for example, there was much greater use of getting control answers (40% of all uses named) but above the same level of use of getting understandings and clarifications (20%; Dervin et al., 1980). In the study of blood donors, on the other hand, the level of mention of the getting pictures (clarifications, understandings) category was higher (41%; Dervin et al., 1981).

More important than the specific distributions, however, is the fact that in all the studies 50% or more of the answers to how information helped were not couched in terms that looked informational but rather in terms that related to movement through time-space. And, rarely across all studies did respondents simply say they were helped simply because they got information.

The lack of emphasis by respondents on information as an end unto itself and the relative overemphasis on this idea by practitioners was confirmed in a study that compared Seattle citizen answers on how information was used to practitioner estimates of how the citizens answered. Results showed that practitioners overestimated citizen emphasis on "got information" as a criterion for evaluating information helpfulness by 32%.

What Predicts Information Use?

Traditional conceptions of audiences attempt to predict their behaviors based on their demographic or other constant characteristics (such as personality). The Sense-Making approach, in contrast, suggests that information use is predictable based on how respondents see specific moments in time-space. Several explicit tests of this proposition have been made with all tests confirming the Sense-Making expectation. In a study of the information needs of Californians during recent troublesome situations, for example, race was pitted as a predictor against respondent descriptions of how their movement was blocked at specific moments in situations and without exception the situational perceptions not only proved a better predictor but the only significant predictor (Atwood, 1980b; Atwood & Dervin, 1981). In a study of blood donor sense-making during a recent blood donation, three classes of variables, (a) demographic, (b) a priori time-space (the situational conditions of the respondent prior to entering the blood donation), and (c) time-space bound (situational conditions as seen by respondents as they moved through the blood donation), were pitted against each other as predictors of information uses. Without exception, the time-space-bound predictors proved best (Dervin et al., 1982).

Some Implications for Practice

The alternative conceptions presented here, developed in the context of the information-as-construction idea and the Sense-Making approach it led to, generate some beginning implications for practice, both the practice of research on audiences and the practice of campaign and message design.

Implications For Research

Perhaps the most obvious implication is that there are ways of researching audiences that allow them to tell us what they need if they are to make connections between our messages and their worlds. The approach suggested here is one that is unobtrusive in the sense that it does not impose content on respondents but is highly obtrusive in the sense that it does impose a structure by asking respondents to detail their Time-Lines, their situational perceptions, their cognitive gaps, and their information uses. Innovative aspects of the approach include that it looks not at people as units but as sense-making instances and thus requires fewer interviews to generate comprehensive portraits of sense-making in given contexts. The most important aspect of the approach, however, to be emphasized above all others, is that it looks at information use from the eyes of the user (audience/receiver) rather than from the eyes of the source. As such, it allows the users to speak to message creators in terms that provide the creators with specific guidance for message design.

Implications For Message and Campaign Design

It is clear from the results to date that each specific message context requires a somewhat different design approach and studies in the specific context will have to provide that guidance. It is also clear, however, that there are some general procedures for message and campaign design, which the alternative approach points to. The most important, perhaps, because it contrasts so markedly with current approaches, is the idea that receiver research should be used as the basis for the design. In a sense, what is being called for here is responsive design, design that looks first at possible message users and what information they need and then and only then sees how observations that sources have may serve those needs.

A second important implication, also in conflict with current norms, is that messages need to provide users with multiple access points—multiple cues which allow users intersecting with the message with different perspectives to grab hold of message sections relevant to their perspectives. This goal can be achieved in several ways. One is to include multiple voices in messages, increasing the chance that a given voice has meaning for a given member of the audience. A second is to require that subjectivity be included in the message allowing receivers to relate to sources on human and, thus, comprehensible terms. A third approach is to cue the message to some of the universals unearthed in the Sense-Making approach: the different ways in which people see gaps in their situations, the different perceptions of their movement through situations, the different uses to which they employ input. A fourth approach—which is, in essence, mandated by the three already suggested—is that messages need to be formatted differently than they are now, allowing different users to access that which will help them or that which relates to their gaps more quickly and, thus, allow them to see that the message has relevance for them.

CONCLUSION

The implications presented above are just a beginning. The findings presented earlier are also just a beginning. The Sense-Making approach that generated both the findings and the implications is itself just a beginning and only one example of possible alternative approaches to looking at audiences. What is more important from their presentation is neither the specific findings nor the specific approach but the possibilities they suggest for benefits to be gained from searching for alternative conceptions of audiences.

Right now, the typical campaign designer has ample reason to approach the task of campaign design with foreboding. The value of searching for alternative conceptions of audiences is that it allows the campaign designer to play "what if." Now, it is assumed that reaching most audiences on most subjects is extremely difficult, that most people just cannot be moved to care about things beyond the close confines of their own worlds. Mostly it is assumed that most people will find most campaigns irrelevant to their worlds.

Alternative conceptions of audiences suggest that one can ask "what if?" What if we can assume otherwise? What if we can assume that audiences have far-reaching interests and attention for many concerns and the problem is finding ways to show them how our messages are, indeed, relevant to their worlds?

The thing about conceptions of audiences is that no one conception is right or wrong, merely different in usefulness within stated confines. The traditional conception of audiences based on the information-as-thing idea was useful within its confines. It shows clearly, for example, that most people were not tuning in to sources on sources' terms. The utility of an alternative conception of audiences based on the information-as-construction idea is that it may suggest ways for sources to tune into receivers on receivers' terms.

NOTES

1.   This chapter is based on extensive literature reviews. When conclusions are drawn from comprehensive literature reviews conducted by the present author, only the literature review will be cited and not the entire list of supporting studies. The literature reviews most relevant to this article are Dervin and Greenberg (1972), Dervin (1976b, 1980), and Dervin et al. (1976).

2.   For the classic review of mass communications research up to 1960, see Klapper (1960). For conceptual reviews of latter periods, see Dervin (1976a, 1980), Ettema and Kline (1977), and Hornik (1980). For a comprehensive discussion of communication networks, see Rogers and Kincaid (1980).

3.   For recent discussions of the failure of the personality approach to individual differences, see Bem (1972), Bem and Allen (1974), Hewes and Haight (1979), and Mischel (1973). For a discussion of the failure of demographic variables, see Dervin (1977b, 1980).

4.   The specific counter-approach presented in this chapter is that of the present author's and its weaknesses should not be blamed on others. For other voices talking of related issues, see Carter (1973, 1974a, 1974b), Dallmayer and McCarthy (1977), Grunig (1975, 1978a, 1978b), and Stewart (1978).

5.   For more extensive treatments of these criticisms, see Dervin (1976a, 1977b, 1980).

6.   The author is grateful to Carter (1973, 1974a, 1974b), whose work has served instrumentally in preparation of the ideas presented here. Other significant contributions came from Bruner (1964, 1973), Cappella (1977), Clarke and Kline (1974), Edelstein (1974), Holzner (1968), Nordenstreng (1977), Stewart (1978), and Weimar (1978). For more extensive treatments of the information as construction idea, see Dervin (1976a, 1977b, 1980) and Dervin et al. (1980).

7.   Dervin (1980) reviews studies supporting this issue. See also Brittain (1970).

8.   Many of the criticisms reviewed here have been mentioned by Third World researchers as they have attempted to understand why U.S.-created message dissemination systems do not work in developing countries. See, in particular, Beltrán (1976), Diaz Bordenave (1976), Friere (1970), Rogers and Adhikarya (1979), and Röling, Ascroft, and Chege (1976).

9.   Nordenstreng (1977) emphasizes this point.

10.   Several researchers (Dervin & Greenberg, 1972; Lemert, Nitzman, Seither, Cook, & Hackett, 1977; Wade & Schramm, 1969) have researched what they call ways-means or mobilizing information and concluded that while the media de-emphasize it, people need it.

11.   For reviews of literature on the so-called "unreachable," and "information poor," see Childers and Post (1975), Dervin (1976b, 1980), Ettema and Kline (1977), Dervin and Greenberg (1972), and Greenberg and Dervin (1970).

12.   For an edited volume that brings together many of these thrusts, see Dallmayer and McCarthy (1977).

13.   See, in particular, the work of Carter (1973, 1974a, 1974b), Carter, Ruggels, Jackson, and Heffner (1973), Mischel (1973), and Rotter, Chance, and Phares (1972).

14.   See the work of Grunig (Grunig, 1975, 1978a, 1978b; Grunig & Disbrow, 1977; Stamm & Grunig, 1977).

15.   The Sense-Making approach is developed further in Atwood (1980b), Atwood and Dervin (1981), Dervin et al. (1976, 1980, 1981), and Dervin (1976a, 1977b, 1980). It owes a large debt to the work of Carter, cited earlier.

16.   One way of looking at this is that life, in both the long and short run, involves moving through "passages" to which one's communication behaviors (information use, in particular) are responsive.

17.   A tradition of research called "uses and gratifications" has looked at how people use information. See, in particular, Blumler (1979), Elliott (1974), Katz, Blumer, and Gurevitch (1974), and Swanson (1979). These works have enriched the Sense-Making approach. A crucial difference seems to be that the Sense-Making approach has generated a theoretically based content analytic scheme for coding information uses and has adopted a strict information-as-construction view. "Uses and gratifications" as an approach appears to fall somewhere between information as thing and information as construction.

18.   In some studies, respondents have also been asked how information hurt, with these answers still conceptualized as the uses to which respondents put informational input.

19.   This premise and related ones have been called the "situationality" assumption. For other researchers taking situational approaches, see, as examples, Grunig (in the works earlier cited) and Edelstein (1974).

20.   Citations for the studies that have been formally written up are: Seattle citizens and their recent troublesome situations, Dervin et al. (1976); California citizens and their recent troublesome situations, Atwood (1980b), Atwood and Dervin (1981), and Palmour, Rathbun, Brown, Dervin, and Dowd (1979); blood donors and their recent donations, Dervin et al. (1981); and patients and their recent visits with doctors, Dervin et al. (1980). All of the remaining studies have not yet been developed into reports. The following current or former graduate students at the University

of Washington School of Communications have played important roles in the conduct of this series of studies: Rita Atwood, Nancy Dudley, Carol Garzona, Ed Hall, Sylvia Harlock, Colleen Kwan, Tom Jacobson, Fiona Chew-Moosdeen, Michael Nilan, and David St. John. Some of the studies utilize components of the "stopping technique" developed to look at message handling in process by Carter et al. (1973).

Chapter 11

Audience as Listener and Learner, Teacher and Confidante:
The Sense-Making Approach

Brenda Dervin

The most widely accepted rationale for the idea of public communication campaigns is embedded in a social engineering philosophy. It assumes that social engineers have noble purposes: the prevention of individual and collective disasters; the protection of the citizenry, their abodes and environment; and the preservation of democracy. These purposes translate into responsibilities to the public that require that institutions designated as "protectors" use communication campaigns to educate, inform, and entice members of the public concerning the acceptance and execution of these responsibilities (see Paisley, 1989).

Working within the framework of this rationale, researchers and campaign planners can point to a number of successes. However, practitioners and academics alike acknowledge that public communication campaigns are effective only at great cost and within very definite constraints.

When all is said and done, the effectiveness of most campaigns is far less accounted for by campaign design than by the brute force of the public's experiences, direct or vicarious. Somehow, and usually quite independent of any campaign planner's efforts, members of the public become cognitively involved with the subject that a public communication campaign addresses.[1]

Sometimes these experiences are direct—six cars pile up on the way to work and only people wearing seat belts survive; a daughter comes home after her health education class and begs her father to stop smoking. Sometimes these experiences are vicarious but made real by repeated personalized involvements with media personalities—Betty Ford faces her problem with drugs; Nancy Reagan is diagnosed as having breast cancer after a routine examination. Occasionally the magnitude of a crisis is sufficient-

This work originally appeared as: Dervin, B. (1989). Audience as listener and learner, teacher and confidante: The Sense-Making approach. In R. Rice & C. Atkin (Eds.), *Public communication campaigns* (2nd ed., pp. 67–86). Newbury Park, CA: Sage. Reprinted by permission of Sage Publications, Inc., Thousand Oaks, CA.

ly large that media coverage allows more members of the audience than usual to connect in their minds with groups of strangers—the Blacks of South Africa, or the citizens of earthquaked Mexico. Through these experiences, individual members of the amorphous public potentially act in new ways: A mother insists that her children buckle up; a father tries to stop smoking.

At least two factors operate here. The first factor is that whatever the action the campaign calls for, campaign messages will be attended to only if the dangers and/or benefits associated with those actions have taken on some kind of personal reality or usefulness for the individual. The individual must choose to attend to and ascribe reality and significance to the message. The second factor is that at whatever point this happens, a connection between the individual and the campaign will be made only if campaign messages are around to be attended to or have in some way become part of the individual's stored understandings of the world.

When one examines the set of strategies that have become commonplace in the design of public communication campaigns, one finds an acknowledgment of these factors. Two universally accepted campaign strategies are these: (a) Find ways to make the campaign's prescribed actions real to the individual, and (b) buy as much redundancy as you can afford. Three corollary strategies also exist: (a) Reach the captive-audience young through the school system (so that the young, in turn, will carry the message home), (b) get the media gatekeepers on the campaign's side to get the boost of media hype, and (c) incorporate networking and community-based programs as part of a campaign.

Even when reality, actual or vicarious, is entirely cooperative, any given campaign measures its success in small degrees of change. Further, some campaign goals seem unachievable beyond a certain point. At best, it is agreed, the business of launching public communication campaigns is difficult, chancy, and costly. The question raised here is this: Is this the limit—the best we can do? The answer this chapter presents is no. But going beyond this limit requires a fundamental reconceptualization both of the *nature of audiences* and the *nature of campaigns*.

AUDIENCING AND BEING AUDIENCED

The conventional concept of public communication campaigns is based on a very stable set of assumptions about the nature of audiences and the nature of campaign messages. Campaign messages are assumed to be truths, usually discovered by scientific research, that must be diffused to the populace. Because many issues demand attention in society, campaign messages must compete in the marketplace of ideas. Audiences are conceptualized as people to whom these truths must be transmitted—audiences, like messages, are treated as commodities. Since audiences are known to be evasive at best and recalcitrant at worst, every effort is made to communicate artfully and well. While communication is conceptualized as a one-way flow, efforts are directed at targeting messages for different audience segments and promoting audience involvement wherever possible.

In this scenario, the populace is *audienced*—they are objectified by the campaign planners, who define the relationship as follows: me, source; you, audience. In the context of recent advances in communication scholarship, we can identify several related difficulties with this conceptualization. These will be examined below in terms of both the inappropriateness of the models on which the conceptualization is based and the impact of the conceptualization on our thinking about audiences, the practice of communicating, and the construction of society.

Models of Information

The model of *information* that provides the foundation for public communication campaigns assumes that information has truth value, that it is objective, and that when one acts on information the resulting actions must lead to better ends. Many theoretical and ideological arguments currently circulate in the communication field about the construct *information*.[2] The most fundamental of these arguments has to do with the nature of the reality described by information. Stated in polarized extremes, one view says the world is "out there" to be described and the problem is human inability to observe accurately; the other says no world exists outside the human act of creation.

For the purposes of this chapter, both views are accepted. First, it is assumed that a world out there exists apart from the human act of creation. For example, a geological formation that we humans have put into a class of objects we call mountains and have given a specific name—"Mt. St. Helens"—did erupt at a time we have agreed to call May 1980, spewing forth a great deal of a substance we call volcanic dust on a place we call western Washington State.

However, it is assumed that in actuality only a small portion of human existence involves this kind of "natural" event, that "natural events" are in part discontinuous, that most of human reality exists in acts of human creation, and that all "observations" of "reality" are human creations. Further, it is assumed that the observations that human beings create of "reality" are both constrained and illusive. Constrained because they are limited to a particular time and space and to whatever capacities humans have for observing generally and a particular human has for observing specifically. Illusive because, given that no direct, immutable observation exists, all "observations" are created by some unknown combination of the human ability to observe what is out there and the inherent, ever-present reality-creating powers of the species.

This means that whatever one group of individuals calls "information" or "knowledge" at any given point in time is applicable only to that time and space and to the self-interests and observing capacities of the "observers." Untangling which factors account for the "observation" is impossible, and even when observation is prescribed by a set of rules (as in scientific observation), most scholars agree that even the most "brute" of those observations—the so-called empirical facts—are subject to the same limitations.

In this context, what decides whose "observations" get preference when observations disagree? Power decides. Certain "knowledges" in society—the knowledges created by those in power—get preferential status. Other knowledges are "subjugated," reduced in availability to "alternative" outlets or diminished by lack of media space or resources.[3] History provides us with numerous examples of the difficulty that innovative views and the views of the oppressed have in finding a place. Recent emphases in social science scholarship document how knowledges are tied to power structures and how knowledges serve to reify and maintain those structures.

These points are important in understanding the need for a change in how we conceptualize audiences and campaigns. To illustrate, let us take one campaign directive— one that is so emotionally charged that it will serve our purposes well: *Women should have breast cancer check-ups*. From the perspective of the conventional Western medical system (allopathic medicine), this statement is a conclusion based on a series of assumed facts: Women get a disease that is called breast cancer, the rate of this disease goes up as women get older, early detection means early treatment, early treatment means longer life.

Yet, a number of competing perspectives exist. Some come from alternative or "countercultural" institutions, such as practitioners of naturally-oriented medical approaches who challenge the very definition of cancer as disease and the value of allopathic treatment, or environmentally and/or feminist-oriented groups who see the demand that women have breast cancer checkups as focusing the problem in the wrong place—on women instead of on corporations who pollute food and environment with harmful chemicals. The challenges also come from individuals based on their experiences, such as women who refuse to submit themselves to what they see as the emotionally demeaning and/or physically devastating medial regimes endured by their friends while undergoing allopathic diagnosis and/or treatment.[4]

The arenas of breast cancer and women's health serve as particularly good examples for looking at models of information because, despite the very factual tone of communication campaigns, there is evidence of informational "contests" on many fronts. Popular women's magazines often feature first-person stories of how women disagree with the ways in which they are objectified and defined by medicine. Well-publicized is how many nonessential surgeries are recommended for women "for the good of their health" by male doctors. Many women experience an a priori climate of mistrust between themselves and the medical establishment. Many aspects of alternative medical treatments for preventing cancer rejected as recently as 15–20 years ago now are being supported by allopathic medical research. And the way in which conventional medicine treats breast cancer has itself changed, making what was "fact" as recently as the 1970s (e.g., that women with breast cancer required radical mastectomies) no longer "fact" in the 1980s.

The above serves to portray the arena of "breast cancer treatment" as one charged with informational contests. Within this arena, those in the allopathic medical establishment have a preponderance of power to name and define the reality that gets prime attention and space. In such a contest, most people's reality is defined within the dominant frame. But some do contest, and those who do so must try to make space for their viewpoints, working against the overwhelming access to resources, time, and space given the dominant pictures.

The irony is that, from a communication standpoint, this power to create dominant pictures of reality has its limits. This power can produce the accepted definings and orderings of reality. It can try to demand that women have breast cancer checkups. It can severely restrain the individual's capacity to create or have access to alternative orderings. But such power *cannot* make women attend to messages or force them to the doctor's office. And, once women are at the doctor's office, such power cannot command compliance.[5]

While the informational arenas of some campaigns are not as contested as in the example provided above, all are in some way contested. It is because of this pervasive contesting that this chapter assumes that an *information-as-construction* model is more appropriate in communication situations than an *information-as-description* model. The information-as-description model assumes that information has truth value, has a known, testable descriptive relationship with reality, and can be separated from observers. The information-as-construction model assumes that information is created by human observers, is inherently a product of human self-interest, and can never be separated from the observers who created it.

From a communication standpoint, the information-as-description model implies a transmission model of the communicative relationship. A source, assumed to be privy to specialized observations, is charged with the responsibility of transmitting that information to people who need it. The receiver is pictured as an empty bucket into which these informational gems may be deposited.

No matter which way one looks at the difficulties of this model, the conclusion is that it is inappropriate communicatively. The inherent discontinuities of reality, the marked differences in human experience, and the variable ways humans deal with discontinuity mean that informational descriptions of reality are inherently contestable.[6] Communication cannot be conceptualized as *transmission*. Rather, it must be conceptualized in terms of both parties involved in creating meanings, by means of *dialogue*. The sense people make of the media messages is never limited to what sources intend and is always enriched by the realities people bring to bear.

Deleterious Consequences

It is important to review some of the consequences of using the information-as-description and communication-as-transmission models because they provide a context within which to place our understandings of the limitations of the current perspectives used in communication campaigns and to define the possible goals for an alternative conceptualization.

Consequences for Thinking About Audiences

The most obvious impact of these models is casting the audience as "bad guys" who are hard to reach, obstinate, and recalcitrant. Audience members get most of their information from friends and neighbors even though expert advice is available. They like entertainment more than information. They watch too much television. Some subsegments of the population are simply unreachable. These conceptions about audiences are pervasive in society. The context of communication campaigns merely crystallizes the use of these conceptions as explanation for the failure of messages to reach targeted audiences. Yet, the application of the alternative information-as-construction and communication-as-dialogue models directs us to ask if it is our systems and messages that are inaccessible and irrelevant.

Consequences for the Practice of Communicating

Our conceptions of the audience lead to our conceptions of how we involve ourselves in communicating. The impacts can be seen in every realm of communicative activity.

When *interpersonal communication* occurs in professional contexts, the interaction between professionals (e.g., librarians) and lay persons (e.g., library users) is oriented toward categorizing lay persons in system terms. Patrons are asked in the library "reference" interview to describe needs, not on their own terms, but in terms of how they fit within a series of dichotomous cuts of the collection: Do you want a or b? If a, do you want a1 or a2?[7] In *small group* and *organizational* settings, a common set of procedures applied to group processes is parliamentary procedure. By focusing discussion on the presentation of motions and arguments for and against motions, the procedures constrain discourse that focuses on getting unconfused, exploring, and brainstorming. Further, use of these procedures both inhibits contributions by those not seasoned in their use and facilitates manipulative control by those who are practiced.[8]

In *mass communication* settings, news programs rely heavily on the use of the single authoritative voice, spot news, and personality journalism. Each of these communicating strategies assumes that "information" can be "observed" by any single trained observer and moved from place to place without damage. In the context of such a view, the "personality" of the deliverer becomes one of the few remaining marketable commodities.[9] In *community participation* programs, community input is relegated to reacting rather than acting. Even when citizen participation is mandated, frequently citizens are involved only at the very end of decision-making processes.[10] In *international* arenas, non-Western journalists call for attention to communication issues such as whether Third World countries get a chance to describe themselves in the media.[11]

"Audience" research conducted in all these communication settings is both a product and a reification of the communication-as-transmission model. The typical audience research project defines as respondents all members of the "targeted audience," with little regard for how these targeted individuals define themselves. Respondents are typically asked to respond to predefined options. Does the respondent believe a or b or c?

A conception of communication-as-dialogue requires an open-endedness in the institution's approach to the audience. At a minimum, the institution and the audience should be conceptualized as equal partners. More fundamentally, the institution—particularly when mandated as an institution that serves the public—should be conceptualized as responsive to that public (see Dervin & Clark, 1987; Dervin & Nilan, 1986; Rakow, 1989). The public would then become empowered with voice, and communication strategies would constitute a repertoire.[12]

Consequences for the Nature of Society

The difficulties outlined above lead to larger negative consequences for society. Some scholars suggest that the communication-as-transmission model creates a communication context within which the rich get communicatively richer while the poor get communicatively poorer.[13] Further evidence suggests that as various new communication technologies are introduced, the gaps between the managed and the managers grows larger and those who wish to move in the communication "fast lane" have to sacrifice their uniqueness and cultural diversity to so do.

To assume that the "information poor" are only society's least educated peoples would be a mistake. One excellent instance of well-educated people remaining information poor is the case of the large database system designed to speed the process by which the findings of social science research are introduced into the practice of teaching in the nation's classrooms. In actuality, the nation's teachers rarely use the system. Filled with "information" from researchers, the database is most-used *by* researchers.[14]

The difficulty may be conceptualized generally as our communication systems reifying and legitimizing only one set of "knowledges" about the nature of reality. This robs society in several senses. Institutions mandated to serve the public often fail. The professionals who work for those institutions burn out. Society is denied the process of bringing different understandings together, comparing, deliberating, negotiating, and constructing a shared reality. Those left out of the process are isolated from the messages of our systems and, more important, do not contribute to the construction of those messages.[15]

More subtle is the impact on our collective understandings of "reality." A fuller comprehension can be realized only by the sharing and confronting of many perspectives, differing in small ways and in large, contestable, unresolvable ways. By comparing and trying to understand why and how perspectives differ, humans anchor themselves in an informed sense of their own time-place and become able to take individual and collective actions.

Without this kind of sense, a woman cannot decide to have a breast cancer screening, or choose a mode of treatment should she be diagnosed as having cancer. Nor can she accept with any degree of equanimity the consequences if a mode of treatment is imposed on her by others. From such points of non-sense, evidence emerges about how seldom patients follow doctors' orders, or how often they are angry after having done so because their actions have not arisen from an informed personal sense, but rather from submission to professional directive.

AUDIENCE RESEARCH AS DIALOGUE

The remainder of this chapter will use audience research as an exemplar of the utility of adopting a communication-as-dialogue approach.

Several points need to be made before proceeding. The problem is not only to conceptualize communication-as-dialogue, but also to practice it as dialogue.[16] One major reason that we have not developed a dialogue-based communication practice is that until very recently demands to do so were not compelling, and even when humans have attempted and achieved communication-as-dialogue, they have not built up a systematic practice. Second, adopting a communication-as-dialogue approach to audience research yields a fundamental change in the conception of the audience and the campaign. In one sense neither term is any longer applicable. The terms will be retained in this chapter with the assumption that the "audience" involved is both the public and the institution, both willingly audienced and audiencing, and that the campaign involved is one consented to and dealt with in shared and interactive consent.[17]

Finally, the findings from research based on the communication-as-dialogue perspective inherently mandate responsive system design—that is, that the perspectives of those defined as "respondents" will be not only heard but acted upon. Further, appropriate "audiences" in campaign designs based on dialogue principles will involve not only the public but the planner and other institutional actors as well.

The Purpose of Sense-Making: A New Way of Listening

Audience research, conceptualized within the framework of a communication-as-dialogue perspective, is a new way of listening to the public. In recent years, communication scholars from a wide variety of perspectives have called for new approaches to audience research.[18] While these scholars differ on important details, all agree that the new approach ought to focus on finding effective ways to hear how members of the audience make sense of their everyday lives and how their personal actions are linked to both the messages they attend to and the social structures they live in.

For the purposes of this chapter, one particular approach is used as an exemplar—the Sense-Making approach. Developed through a programmatic series of studies since 1972,[19] the approach is simultaneously *ethnographic* because it allows respondents to define and anchor themselves in their own realities, *qualitative* because it is built on open-ended interviewing and reports findings primarily in qualitative terms, *quantitative* because procedures for quantitative analysis have been developed, and *systematic* because a general theory guides the approach to listening—a theory that is applicable to all situations but allows specificity in any situation.

The term *sense-making* is used both to designate the approach (called the Sense-Making approach) and the focus of the approach (how people make sense of their worlds). Sense-Making as an approach is primarily a methodology, providing a conceptual framework within which to specify what aspects of situations ought to be attended to and how. Sense-Making attempts to provide a systematic approach to listening to the audience—how they see their situations, past, present, and future—and how they move to construct sense and make meaning of these situations.

Sense-Making rests on the discontinuity premise.[20] It assumes that, given discontinuites in natural reality and in human observations of reality, the useful research focus is how humans make sense of discontinuity. The core construct of Sense-Making is the idea of the gap—how people define and bridge gaps in their everyday lives. Discontinuities (gaps) are faced everywhere—when attending to messages, when relating to others, when attempting to pursue tasks or reach goals, even when attempting to stand still. Gaps are always cognitive (i.e., constructed in the head) and sometimes are overbearingly physical as well (i.e., coping with illness).

The Sense-Making methodology is built on the metaphor pictured in Figure 11.1. The human moves cognitively through time-space using whatever sense he or she has already constructed based on personal as well as vicarious experiences. Given that life is inherently discontinuous, sense frequently runs out. A gap is identified. The human must build a bridge across the gap. In doing so, the human will answer questions, create ideas, and/or obtain resources. The situation that leads to the gap, the gap itself, the bridge, and even what the human does after crossing the bridge, are all best understood as constructions.

In all Sense-Making methods, the listener (i.e., the researcher) is mandated to listen to the respondent tell of how he or she moved through time-space. In particular, for each step of the journey, the researcher is mandated to attend to what is called the *Sense-Making Triangle*: how the *respondent* sees the situation, what gaps the respondent sees self as facing and/or bridging, and what ways the respondent saw self as helped by the bridge he or she built.

The core method of Sense-Making is the Time-Line Interview. The researcher asks the respondent to recollect what happened in a situation as a series of steps—what happened first, second, and so on. This does not impose a linear time order on the respondent's recollection—the respondent may recollect things in whatever order is relevant to him or her at the telling. Further, the time frame may be extended to include historical moments as well as anticipated future moments. Finally, for each step in the time-line, the researcher explores with the respondent how the respondent saw and defined that situation, its gaps, its gap-bridging, its helps, and so on. Sense-Making also incorporates a number of alternative methods, all derived from the core Time-Line Interview. Some are encapsulated and abbreviated versions of the time-line. Others zero in on particular aspects of the gap or the gap-bridging.

Sense-Making has been used to address a variety of questions potentially useful to those planning public communication efforts, including the following: What ideas or images have people created about a particular topic, institution, or program? How useful have people found the efforts of a particular institution? What sense-making needs do people have that if bridged would allow them to inform themselves more usefully in a particular arena? What barriers do people see as standing between them and their efforts to make sense?

An important aspect of Sense-Making methods is that they are all situated in real moments in time-space. Sense-Making posits no hypothetical questions to respondents, nor does it present elaborate lists of options as defined by institutions to which respondents must reply. While Sense-Making occasionally uses close-ended interviewing approaches, these uses are all defined within the framework of understanding how respondents see themselves stopped in their movement through time-space with how they make sense of discontinuity.

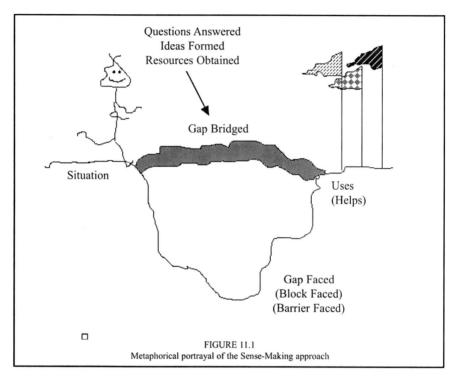

Questions Answered
Ideas Formed
Resources Obtained

Gap Bridged

Situation

Uses
(Helps)

Gap Faced
(Block Faced)
(Barrier Faced)

FIGURE 11.1
Metaphorical portrayal of the Sense-Making approach

EXAMPLE STUDIES AND THEIR IMPLICATIONS FOR ACTION

Since 1972, some 40 studies have used the Sense-Making approach.[21] They have focused on a wide variety of topics, including cancer communication, family planning, public opinion, library use, media use, blood donating, coping with a toxic waste site, and coping with university life. They have involved a wide variety of "publics": general population adults, minorities, teenagers, children, patients, students, peasant women, recent refugees. They have been conducted in a number of countries.

Many of the studies have focused on general methodological issues in the continuing attempt to develop and perfect systematic ways of listening to people on their own terms. The result has been the development of a set of listening methods for conducting audience research as well as for conducting in-person one-on-one interviews with people (e.g., patients, patrons, clients) who have come to professionals with needs.[22]

General Conclusions from Sense-Making Studies to Date

The Sense-Making studies to date have provided confirmation for many of the general assumptions that led to the creation of the Sense-Making approach. The research has shown that people inform themselves primarily at moments of need. Given needs, people rely first on their own cognitive resources. If these are not sufficient, they reach out first to sources closest to them or those contacted on their habit paths. When they find useful information, they judge it not on its expertise or credibility, but rather in terms of how it helped them. They find it useful because they can put it to use. Only when it does not help do they focus on credibility and expertise of source or message as explanations of why what was offered did not help.

People seem inherently interested in contested views. They deal with competing information claims well when these claims are anchored and explained in terms of what it is about the observers and/or time-places of the observings that make a difference. In study after study, people have indicated that they want to learn about motives and reasons and the causes of events. These "why" questions have been asked frequently, ranked as important, and judged as least addressed by information systems.

Results have also suggested that people treat the use of information (and of information and communication systems) as means to ends and not ends in themselves. Their seeking and use of information is best predicted based on how they see their situations, the constraints they face, the gaps they need to bridge, and the kind of bridges they would like to build across their gaps. Except for those information-seeking and -using behaviors such as habitual channel use, most information-seeking and -using behaviors are not predicted well based on across time-space attributes of people such as personality and demographic characteristics.

The following sections briefly describe three sense-making projects selected because they illustrate different conceptual conclusions pertaining to the use of a communication-as-dialogue approach to audience research.

Goal: A Library Wants More Hispanic Patrons

A public library with a large number of Hispanic citizens on its mandated patron roster searched for ways to entice the Hispanics into the library (see Dervin & Clark, 1987, pp. 211–230; Dervin & Nilan, 1986). Previously, a number of study approaches were tried and met with hostility. The traditional methods of publicity had failed. The Sense-Making research project focused on users of the library's audiovisual services and serendipitously provided a breakthrough for serving the Hispanic community. One study asked 30 randomly selected recent users what happened that brought them to the library, what they got while there, and how they were helped. A second study asked 64 randomly selected borrowers of library videotapes how the specific videotapes helped them.

The librarians reported that for the first time they had conducted interviews with Hispanic patrons and were not met with hostility. They learned that their videotape checkout service was providing these patrons with enormous numbers of important helps. Further, the videotapes were an important link for these patrons with other library services—literacy training, juvenile books, and how-to books, for example. One librarian summed it up: "It helped us see patrons from a different point of view, to understand them better, and to be better able to tolerate the crowds around the audio-visual desk." The library staff voted to move funds from other services to video services.

Goal: A Blood Center Wants Donors to Donate Again

A city blood center commissioned research because staff were convinced that they lost some donors because the donors left unhappy or confused about the donating experience (see Dervin, Jacobson, & Nilan, 1982; Dervin, Nilan, & Jacobson, 1981). A recent study had specifically suggested that they lost some repeat donors because the potential donors were not aware of eligibility requirements for repeat donating.

One study involved in-depth Time-Line Interviews asking "what happened during your most recent donating experience" of 80 randomly selected frequent and new donors. For each event respondents reported as happening, they were asked what gaps they faced, what questions they had, whether they got answers to their questions, and how they were helped or hindered. Results showed that while demography did not predict donor information needs and seeking, where respondents were in the process did. Each step in the donating time-line was associated with its own characteristic set of questions. Eligibility questions, for example, were more likely to be in donors' minds when they checked in to donate, whereas blood center personnel had been trying to convey eligibility information when donors were recovering and leaving.

A second study compared 105 new, dropout, and frequent female blood donors in terms of their recollections of what facilitated and what stood in the way of donating. Results showed that the primary difference between dropout and frequent female donors was the ease of access to donating.

The two studies provided directions for communication planning. They showed that a public communication campaign to convince women to repeat their donating would be ineffective. Attention was redirected to improving access. Second, a plan was established to provide a user-friendly computerized question-answering system at five different points during the donating process. Typical questions at each point were to be displayed on the screen of a terminal. Donors could simply touch the question of interest to them. Answers would be available from a variety of sources—center personnel as well as other donors.

Goal: A Cancer Clinic Staff Wants to Handle Anxious Patients Better

A cancer detection and treatment clinic staff felt that patient confusions and resentments were contributing as much to the daily stress of their jobs as the seriousness of cancer as a disease.[23] A Sense-Making study of 30 randomly selected patients asked them to detail the events of their contacts with the clinic, the ways in which they felt impeded, the types of confusions they had, and the ways in which they wanted to be helped as well as the ways in which they were actually helped.

Results showed that patients wanted more chances to explore and discuss their confusions and concerns with others who were sympathetic; they wanted acknowledgment of the contested nature of the information circulating about cancer and its treatment; they wanted help getting more information, particularly from other cancer patients; they wanted social support; and they wanted staff to see them as human beings and not walking tumors.

Clinic staff responded by designing group support sessions for patients in which concerns were openly discussed and disagreements openly admitted. They also instituted a "mass communications" wall of information sheets, each of which addressed a common patient question. "Answers" to the questions implement the idea of contested information. Answers were provided by different doctors and nurses and by patients. Each answerer was asked to interpret what he or she thought accounted for how his or her answers differed from that of the others. In addition, clinic intake personnel began using Sense-Making approaches when they talked with patients. Questions asked were those defined in the Sense-Making Metaphor (see Figure 11.1): What brings you here today? What confusions or problems are you facing? How do you hope we can help you today?

Sense-Making interviews were also conducted with clinic staff—nurses, technicians, and doctors. Results indicated that staff needed their own support groups and needed to connect with their patients outside their "cancerness." They also indicated that staff needed a more rational way of handling the inherently contestable nature of the medical services they were providing. These results led to regular staff support groups and to staff volunteering to rotate their own attendance at patient support groups in order to be able to see patients as people. In addition, staff decided to take whatever steps were needed to empower each patient or each patient's family to make their own decisions.

Results of these actions to date have been favorable. Staff report, for example, feeling more hopeful about their relationships with patients and their capacities to be genuinely helpful. They also report a significant reduction in clinic stress levels and greatly reduced time spent with upset patients.

CONCLUSION

In each of these examples the audience is no longer conceptualized as an amorphous mass. Rather than being portrayed as a sample of people of whom x% agreed with this and y% wanted that, the respondents became situated in real circumstances for which the logic of what the respondents have to say is validated by and anchored in that experience.

Each of the three example studies provides results that inform the institution about the experiential realities of the respondents. In each case, institutional representatives learned something they did not know, and even had their expectations changed. The librarians had thought that they had had few successes with Hispanic patrons; they identified an open door of acceptance. The blood center staff was planning to spend money advertising for women donors by emphasizing eligibility requirements; they learned that they had to emphasize access and provide actual means of access. The cancer clinic staff felt they had to protect patients from the uncertainties of cancer treatment information; yet most of the patients wanted the full picture no matter how uncertain.

In each case, too, results of the studies provided professionals with explicit avenues for possible negotiated interactions. The librarians, for example, transferred more funds to their video collection and at the same time planned activities to tie the video collection to the book collection and literacy services. They also found a potential hunger for public service advertisements to the community. At the same time, they gained respect for an aspect of their own service that previously they had undervalued.

The same kind of give-and-take potential is illustrated in the blood center and cancer clinic data. Blood donors indicated, for example, that there was a lot they wanted to learn about donating, but only when the learning was pertinent for them. The staff began to think about the use of a flexible computerized question-answering system. Cancer clinic staff reported that once patients understood that their questions would be taken seriously, they became remarkably more willing to consider alternative points of view.

One parsimonious way to think of these studies is to suggest that each told the institution how it could change *itself* rather than how it could change the audience. In doing so, the results laid out for the institution explicit possibilities for dialogue.

Also of importance is the fact that the results focused on what "audience" members need rather than on "campaigns" and possible "message" elements. Because of this the results lend themselves to a number of different avenues of communication design. Mass communication is not artificially separated from interpersonal communication; communication is not artificially separated from action; the "campaign" is not artificially removed from its consequences. The librarians, for example, uncovered keys for both program design and public service advertising messages; cancer clinic staff ended up creating their own mass communication messages (information sheets answering typical questions) as well as changing how they greeted patients; blood center staff planned ways to increase access for women donors and to use a computerized information system to allow donors access to information at the moment of need.

Of particular importance is the way in which these studies provide findings that directly informed communication practice. By focusing on real situations in which members of the audience are relating to real experiential circumstances, the point of focus moves from people, conceptualized as static entities, to circumstances and to actions that can be taken with people in those circumstances. While past Sense-Making studies have confirmed the greater predictive power of situational conceptions, the important utility of the situational approach is in practice. In essence, findings from these studies provide practitioners with some insights about how to be both *efficient* and *effective* in their communicating efforts.

Traditionally, communication efficiency and effectiveness have been conceptualized as opposing trade-offs. Efficiency requires members of the audience to be treated amorphously and to bend to the institution. Effectiveness requires that individuals be helped on their own terms. Traditional communication approaches have argued that the only way to communicate systematically is to ignore individuality. In contrast, these Sense-Making studies suggest that individuality has been conceptualized inappropriately. In Sense-Making, individuality based on across time-space characterizations of people is replaced with a concept of individuality based on situatedness.

A public communication campaign conceived within a communication-as-dialogue perspective is, by definition, a campaign pointing in at least two directions: one to the public, the other to the institution. The communication dilemma for the institution is that if it expects its communicative efforts to be used and useful, it must treat communication as dialogue and it must find ways to empower publics. Recent testimony from the arena of the practice of risk communication confirms the point again and again. Even in this highly technologized arena, people are willing to involve themselves, to listen, to be reasonable, and to act, but only if empowered and heard.

Institutions in our societies have a long tradition of top-down, information-as-description, and communication-as-transmission practices. Habits are hard to break, but developing new ways of listening is of prime importance. The research approaches exemplified in this chapter illustrate that alternatives are possible.

NOTES

1. Dewey emphasized the point as early as 1938. Dupuy (1980) made a recent strong restatement.
2. The conceptualization of information and communication rests heavily on Carter's (1974b, 1980) explication of the discontinuity condition, as well as on Foucault (1980), Freire (1983), and Habermas (1984).
3. The term is Foucault's (1980). See also Wallack (1989).
4. For examples of feminist versions of informational contests, see Ehrenreich and English (1979) and Ferguson (1984). The stories reported here come from interviews with women patients of naturally oriented clinics in Seattle.

5. Patient "compliance" rates may be only 50% (Dervin & Harlock, 1976; Ley, 1982).

6. Giddens (1989) emphasizes the point that something is inherently contestable about being human and that social scientists must incorporate this in both their theorizings and their observings.

7. See, for the medical context, Pendleton (1985), and for the library context, Dervin and Dewdney (1986).

8. For discussion of the constraining and defining impacts of communicating procedures in group and organizational contexts, see, Conrad (1985) and Putnam (1982).

9. Many authors discuss the potentially inhibiting and biasing impacts on society of prevalent journalist news practices (Bennett & Edelman, 1985; Gitlin, 1980; Tuchman, 1978).

10. The arena within which citizen participation is receiving its sternest test and greatest challenge is risk communication (such as the siting of toxic waste dumps) (Sandman, 1987; Sandman, Weinstein, & Klotz, 1987).

11. For a review of the controversy regarding the UNESCO mass media declaration, see *Journal of Communication, 34*(4).

12. *Repertoire* in this context means a set of alternative communicating behaviors arranged in some kind of coherent, theoretically organized pattern that allows for choice based on understanding of need and expectation.

13. See Gandy (1988) and Rice (1980); for related references, contact the author.

14. DeMartini and Whitbeck (1986) and Ward and Reed (1983) discuss the underutilization of the social science literature by public school teachers.

15. Baudrillard (1983) makes this point.

16. This chapter rests heavily on Carter's (1982) conceptualization of communicating behaviors as the tools by which members of collectivities may arrive at shared ideas, and the need to develop new tools continually.

17. In no sense does this chapter mean to suggest that communication-as-dialogue processes alone will solve the problem of the gaps between institutions and people; appropriate communication models are necessary but not sufficient (see Dervin, 1980).

18. The call for the development of approaches to studying human behavior that are dependent on contests and full of individualized meanings are not new. See, for instance, Dworkin (1987), Jensen (1987b), Liebes (1989), Murdock (1989), and Rakow (1989).

19. See the reference section of this volume for works by: Atwood, Allen, Bardgett, Proudlove, and Rich (1982), Atwood and Dervin (1981), Dervin (1976a, 1980, 1983b), Dervin et al. (1981), Dervin and Clark (1987), Dervin and Dewdney (1986), Dervin and Harlock (1976), Dervin, Harlock, Atwood, and Garzona (1980), Dervin, Jacobson, and Nilan (1982), Dervin and Nilan (1986), Dewdney (1986), Dworkin (1987), Grunig (1983), and Nilan (1985).

20. The Sense-Making use of this premise rests heavily on the work of Carter (1974b, 1980) and Carter, Ruggels, Jackson, and Heffner (1973).

21. A comprehensive overview (Dervin, 1983b) may be obtained from the author.

22. A technique for interacting with clients, patients, users, and patrons called "Neutral Questioning" is based on Sense-Making assumptions and is termed "neutral" only in the sense that it allows the "listener" to ask questions only sense-making questions (about moving and facing discontinuous situations, and not about content in the usual sense of the word). Close-ended or dichotomous queries are not permitted (see Dervin & Dewdney, 1986; Dewdney, 1986).

23. This reimbursed project is unpublished by agreement with the clinic staff. The purpose of the study was to make full use of an offered and tough setting for the application of Sense-Making principles. See, however, Dervin et al. (1980).

24. The unpublished results are available from the author.

Chapter 12

Sense-Making Methodology:
Communicating Communicatively with Campaign Audiences

Brenda Dervin & Micheline Frenette

The purpose of this chapter is to describe an approach to researching, designing, and implementing public communication campaigns based on a theoretically defined methodology called Sense-Making. We intentionally refer to members of our audiences as listeners and learners and as teachers and confidantes because the approach we describe rests on philosophic assumptions that mandate that communication (between researcher and researched, policy setter and citizen, professional expert and intended recipient) be conceptualized, designed, and practiced dialogically. Treating communication as dialogue (i.e., communicatively) requires fundamental redefinitions of the terms *audiences* and *campaigns*. In one sense, both terms are no longer applicable— audiences become peers and collaborators—and if there are "campaigns" involved, they are two-way. We continue to use the familiar terms here with the assumption that audiences include both publics and institutions, and campaigns involve shared interaction and intentions (see also Dozier, Grunig, & Grunig, 2001).

To approach the communication campaign communicatively means facing ethical and procedural challenges. It means audiences will not only be heard but also that their perspectives will be acted upon. It means approaching the campaign in a position of self-imposed reflection, being open to disagreement, even coming to understand that one's well-meaning intentions may be mistaken, may foster unintended deleterious consequences, or may simply be of no interest to another.

Calls for moving toward more dialogic campaigns have come from many quarters. We review these calls to provide context for our presentation of Sense-Making, which, as a methodology, is an example of one such call and also a systematic approach responding to it.

This work originally appeared as: Dervin, B., & Frenette, M. (2001). Sense-Making methodology: Communicating communicatively with campaign audiences. In R. E. Rice & C. K. Atkin (Eds.), *Public communication campaigns* (3rd ed., pp. 69–87). Thousand Oaks, CA: Sage. Reprinted by permission of Sage Publications, Inc., Thousand Oaks, CA.

THE CALL FOR DIALOGIC CAMPAIGN DESIGN

There is widespread agreement that most communication campaigns directed at bettering audiences have either failed or have met only modest objectives, at extraordinarily high cost and with requisite high redundancy in message transmission. This negative analysis, however, applies to the traditional one-way public communication campaign assumed to infuse audiences with the will to change because of sheer transmission of "expert" information. In actuality, there have been calls to reconceptualize campaigns in more dialogic ways since the 1960s.[1]

Four Mandates to Approach Campaign Communication Dialogically

To summarize this literature, we have extracted four mandates, arrayed on a continuum from "soft" at one end to "hard" at the other because each successive mandate requires more changes in our conceptualizations.

Go Beyond Campaign-Designated Expert Information

The softest call for designing campaigns dialogically essentially retains the idea of the campaign as a one-way transmission of expert information. What differs is the idea that information transmission does not in itself produce change. A variety of strategies are proposed for adding "something more" than expert information to campaign messages. One strategy is to provide instructions on how to use information as a means of encouraging audience efficacy. Another is to incorporate message elements that are tailored to the information-processing proclivities of the intended recipients or that in other ways trigger audience involvement. Given evidence of rising distrust of experts among laypersons, other strategies call for engendering trust, using sources who are attractive and credible, emphasizing audience life interests and entertainment preferences, and highlighting human stories. Common to these strategies is that campaign messages still focus on information as prescribed by the campaign's designated experts, but something more is provided in hopes that messages will be more acceptable.

Appeal to Audiences in Their Social Contexts

The second mandate is still based on the top-down campaign. What differs is recognition that understandings of the world change markedly from culture to culture and community to community. The primary mandate here is to redirect major portions of campaign efforts from one-way mass-mediated designs to communication approaches anchored in specific audience social networks. Implementation takes one of two forms. The first involves target audiences in campaign design, such as by asking for their recommendations for achieving campaign goals. The second incorporates a variety of communicatively involving activities (e.g., call-in talk shows, hotlines, community forums, and family conferences) as relays for message transmission. Whereas the first form mandates attempts to make campaign messages more acceptable to audiences, the second goes further by using audience networks as vehicles for framing messages in ways suitable for the socially inscribed communication contexts in which audiences live.

Absorb and Reflect Audience Perspectives

The third mandate gives status to nonexpert views, even when these differ from those of experts. Campaigns typically focus on goals (e.g., quitting smoking, stopping drug use, and eating more vegetables) that are defined as remedial actions directed at problems (e.g., lung cancer, crack babies, and obesity). Campaigns rest on networks of causal and descriptive facts supported by scientific evidence, itself based on an assumed rightness in naming and explaining the world. Most campaigns measure success by compliance with goals. What is labeled noncompliance by institutions, however, may be strength and survival outside institutions, what institutions define as causal problem-solution chains may be debated outside institutions, and what experts consider facts today may be challenged by these same experts tomorrow. What differs in this mandate is the more radical idea that the assumptions and goals of experts must, at a minimum, be tested and tempered by audience input and, in a more genuine dialogic spirit, challenged, changed, or even replaced with alternatives.

Attend to Issues Relating Social Power and Ethics

Traditionally, campaign goals have been assumed to be universally applicable and benevolent. The fourth mandate—the most challenging, and which we identified as emerging in recent campaign literature—confronts this assumption and calls for attending to issues of ethics and social philosophy. This mandate involves two aspects: (a) problematizing truth claims about reality and (b) focusing on how issues of social class and structure, politics, and economics are implicated in expert knowledge statements and the uses of these statements in social policy. There are two primary arguments supporting the importance of this mandate. First, audiences are becoming weary of being judged wanting by experts and more savvy about contradictions in an increasingly uncontrolled information marketplace. Second, campaign environments that do not foster disagreement are likely to overlook unwittingly possibly negative campaign out-comes (e.g., stigmatizing subgroups, depriving humans of pleasures, and exploiting community members).

SENSE-MAKING METHODOLOGY

Sense-Making as a methodology was developed to study and implement communication communicatively. It is based on a core assumption that dialogic communication inten-tions are not enough. Dialogue happens only if communication is designed to nurture its unfolding. Sense-Making assumes that all communication is designed but that most designs, even when well meaning, are habitual, unstated, and based on transmission assumptions. Sense-Making's intent is to provide general guidance for how to ensure as far as possible that dialogue is encouraged in every aspect of communication campaign research, design, and implementation.

Sense-Making has been under development by Dervin and colleagues since 1972. The approach is defined as a methodology for studying and facilitating the making and unmaking of sense in any communication situation, particularly where professionals are mandated to serve groups of people usually designated as audiences (e.g., patients, patrons, users, audiences, and customers). Many more formalized presentations are available (Dervin, 1992, 1999a, 1999b), so the following review focuses on major ques-tions in campaign research and design.

Sense-Making's Basic Assumptions

Sense-Making rests on an elaborate set of theoretic assumptions and guidances for meth-ods. The central idea is simple, however. Communication programs are doomed mostly to failure unless they focus on how audiences interpret their worlds and live and struggle in the complexes of social networks and everyday experiences that bind them. This focus on audiences, however, should not be merely a tool for constructing more persuasive mes-sages. The communication campaign must place primary attention on creating procedur-al conditions that promote and invite two-way sharing and negotiating of meanings.

In Sense-Making, this is accomplished by refocusing attention away from nouns of interest to the campaign (e.g., its goals and its evidence) to verbs that permit a dialogic interface to be established. In simple terms, a nouning approach implies that we have come to a fixed understanding of a problem and its solution, whereas a verbing approach implies that we pay attention to how people are making and unmaking sense in the con-texts of their lives. For example, in a nouning approach, obesity might be defined as a physical condition that must be alleviated to prevent ill health. In a verbing approach, we would learn how people make sense of obesity in their experiential contexts: One group may tell of its fat ancestors who lived long lives, another may tell of its anger at a society that promotes unhealthy eating habits but has made obesity one of its worst stigmas, and another may tell of lifelong struggles with physicians who have demanded they as patients submit themselves to a succession of new diet regimes, each one presumably more efficacious than its predecessor.

In Sense-Making, understanding the sense that audiences have made and unmade as they move through their life experiences is achieved by applying the Sense-Making verbing analytic as the central organizing tool. Sense-Making's verbing analytic is based on two intersecting requisites. The first requisite is the assumption that the only way to hear another's world is to invite and assist the other in describing that world as much as possible entirely in the context of his or her own experiences, understandings, and meanings. The second requisite is that because of the power differentials inherent in the institution-audience or researcher-researched relationship, procedures must be found to bracket or tame the power of the institution or researcher.

It is assumed that there are both value constraints and time-space limitations to understandings created with the communication practices of science and expertise, just as there are constraints and limitations for understandings created with the communication practices of lived experience. Therefore, it is assumed that expert categorizations can be entirely wrong, irrelevant, or inappropriate impositions when applied in the contexts of other lived experiences. This does not mean that the voice of the institution or researcher should be silenced. Rather, it means putting that voice into dialogue along with other relevant voices—intended message recipients, their families, community, and so on. There is a yawning gap between institutional and researcher views and the world of the everyday. Sense-Making as an approach explicitly assumes that it is possible to bridge this gap by implementing alternative procedures.

The Sense-Making Verbing Analytic: The Sense-Making Metaphor

Sense-Making incorporates a repertoire of potential procedures for accomplishing the goals discussed previously. All these are drawn from a central metaphor, shown in Figure 12.1. Here, one sees a human moving across time and space, facing a gap, building a bridge across the gap, and then constructing and evaluating the uses of the bridge. This metaphor rests on a discontinuity assumption—that gappiness is pervasive both in and between moments in time and space and in and between people. Gappiness is assumed to occur because of differences across time (e.g., self today vs. self yesterday and scientific fact today vs. scientific fact tomorrow) and across space (e.g., the experience of a particular condition in differing cultures, contexts, communities, material circumstances and the sense of an experience physically and the articulation of it verbally).[2]

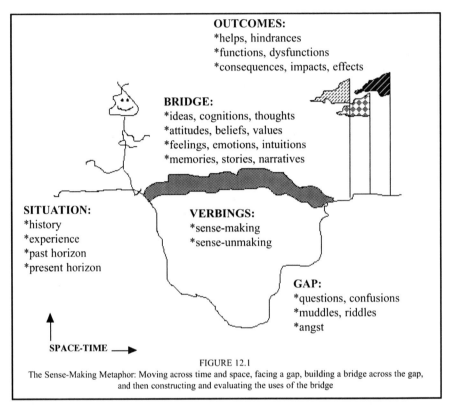

FIGURE 12.1

The Sense-Making Metaphor: Moving across time and space, facing a gap, building a bridge across the gap, and then constructing and evaluating the uses of the bridge

The facing of gaps and building of bridges is Sense-Making's central metaphor. The metaphor is not intended to imply that life facing is only linear, logical, or problem-oriented. Sense-Making assumes there are many ways to bridge gaps. Sometimes we imitate a role model, repeat what was done in the past, do what we learned in our childhood, or follow a leader; sometimes we look to authority or expertise; sometimes we follow hunches, bumble along, and do what our feelings tell us; and sometimes we let circumstances toss us about. Across the range of conditions humans face, it is assumed that every potential mode of gap bridging is useful in some context. In Sense-Making, these myriad ways are conceptualized as verbings.

The implication of this in the campaign context is that a campaign objective is designed to bridge an institutionally perceived gap arising from an institutionally perceived worldview with its institutionally accepted categories. As an objective, it applies only to the time and place of its making and is constrained by the knowledge-making tools of its creation. Across time and across space, the objective may be seen as no bridge at all or as an entirely different kind of bridge. Every aspect of the campaign—every definition, goal, mandate, and argument—is open to potential challenge or reinterpretation when seen from another vantage point. Furthermore, because gappiness applies to both ontological conditions (i.e., the nature of reality) and epistemological conditions (i.e., the nature of knowing), there is no way to fix communicatively any particular campaign objective as absolutely correct. Hence, the only alternative is dialogue. The question becomes how to procedurally nurture dialogue between care-taking institutions with good intentions and mandated audiences. In working toward this goal, Sense-Making draws on the idea of pervasive gappiness, proposing that sense-making and sense-unmaking, whether institutionalized or individual, is usefully conceptualized as building bridges across gaps and then unmaking the bridges when they no longer serve. From this central metaphor is derived the core set of assumptions that Sense-Making mandates methodologically. Every Sense-Making application to campaign research and design requires the use of at least some, and ideally all, of the following assumptions:

1. Sense-making is gap-bridging. Individual humans are conceptualized metaphorically as moving across time and space by bridging gaps inherent in the human condition—between times, spaces, people and events, self today and self yesterday, and so on. No amount of external information, prior instruction, or acculturation is sufficient to bridge a gap here and now. This is done by mind-body-heart-spirit step-takings of singular human entities, consciously or unconsciously, habitually or innovatively, and acting alone or in community.

2. There are many ways to make sense. Sense-making is accomplished by verbings that involve the making or using of ideas or both, cognitions, thoughts, and conclusions; attitudes, beliefs, and values; feelings, emotions, and intuitions; and memories, stories, and narratives. For example, sometimes sense-making involves borrowing an idea, sometimes it involves making one, sometimes it involves rejecting one.

3. Sense-making is anchored in time and space. Each moment of sense-making is anchored in its own time and space, moving to another time and space. Sense-making is most usefully conceptualized as situated communicative practices, internal (e.g., thinking and remembering) and external (e.g., asking and objecting).

4. Sense-making occurs at the intersection of three horizons: (a) past, (b) present, and (c) future. Every moment of sense-making is anchored at the intersection of horizons—past (histories, memories, and narratives), present (current conditions, material and experiential), and future (hopes, dreams, plans, and trajectories).

5. Sense-making can be either flexible or inflexible. It is assumed that there is potential for rigidity (habit, repetition, and stability) in human sense-making when compared across time and space, but also potential for flexibility (innovation, responsiveness, and caprice). Attention must be paid to both possibilities.

6. Sense-making involves energy, both propelling and constraining. Every moment of sense-making involves energy—force, power, and constraint. These energies come from within (e.g., motivation, resistance) and without (e.g., barriers, help from society, others, institutions), and from unique circumstances and enduring social conditions.

7. Every sense-maker is inherently a social theorist. Ordinary human beings are assumed to be capable of discussing the connections they see between past and present and between present and future; between self and one's own struggles; between self and others; and between self and society. These perspectives are assumed to be as essential to understanding campaign phenomena as are the perspectives of experts and researchers. The larger the power differential, the longer the time needed and the more difficult it will be to establish the necessary trust between researchers and researched.

8. Comparing sense-making across time, space, and people is more powerfully done with verbing analytics. If we focus only on the nouns of experience and phenomena, the understandings of the world of ordinary persons seem overbearingly unique and unamenable to systematic analysis. By focusing on the verbs of sense-making—how people see themselves as moving through life, the gaps they face, and the help they seek—we can compare sense-makings of one human to those of another, of one human to self across time and space, and so on without imposing nouns alien to sense-making experience.

9. Comparing sense-making across time, space, and people will yield patterns of both centrality and dispersion. Any comparison of sense-making activities will necessarily yield patterns of centrality (homogeneity and agreement) and patterns of dispersion (diversity and disagreement). Each is to be pursued by asking fundamental questions: Under what conditions would this occur? What implications result?

10. Campaign planners, researchers, and policymakers are sense-makers. The expertise of planners, researchers, and policymakers is sense-making and must be examined as such. This is a fundamental source of the self-reflexivity that is assumed to be essential for communicating communicatively.

How Sense-Making Is Applied in Campaign Research and Design

Each of the previous assumptions implies potential communicative procedures to be implemented in Sense-Making-informed campaign research and design. There are three primary applications that will be discussed later: (a) interviewing, (b) analyzing data, and (c) planning campaign designs. It is important to first emphasize two points. First, Sense-Making is a methodology for communication practice in general; thus, Sense-Making applies to both research and campaign design. Second, Sense-Making has been developed to avoid traditional polarizations between so-called systematic quantitative and contextual qualitative approaches, aiming for qualitative sensitivity amid analytic systematization.

Applying Sense-Making to Interviewing

Sense-Making has been applied in both qualitative and quantitative interviews, in-depth and brief, phone and in-person, one-on-one and focus group, interviewer-administered and self-administered. The use of Sense-Making rests on a foundational interviewing approach called the *Micro-Moment Time-Line*. In this approach, informants are asked to describe a situation relevant to the research focus—a situation important to them in some way (e.g., a time when they were concerned about AIDS or remembered hearing about it in the media and a time when they were concerned about their health or tried to take action to improve it). The situation is described in Time-Line steps—what happened first, second, and so on. For each step, Sense-Making elements are extracted: What questions arose at this step? What thoughts? What feelings? What emotions? Each of these elements is then triangulated with the Sense-Making metaphor, with its emphasis on situation, gap, bridge, and outcome. For example, in triangulating a question, the informant is asked the following: What led to this question? How does it relate to your life? Society and power? Did you get an answer? How? Any barriers in the way? Did the answer help? Hinder? How?

From this basic approach, many variations have been derived. Some, for example, involve surveying an informant's entire lifeline of experiences vis-à-vis an issue (e.g., one's history with ill health) and then selecting one or more incidents for in-depth analysis. Others involve positioning informants directly as research collaborators. An example is an interview that asks informants to talk about how and why their views differ from those of others. A policy position established by an agency might be described in detail, with the informant asked for his or her thoughts, confusions, and conclusions. In another variation, the informant is asked to read an institutional policy statement and to indicate every place in the statement the person "stopped" to ask questions, raise objections, and so on. In both variations, each informant response is pursued with Sense-Making triangulations as described previously: What leads you to say this? How does this relate to your life? and so on.[3]

Applying Sense-Making to the Analysis of Research Data

Each of the metatheoretical assumptions of Sense-Making mandates particular approaches to data analysis. The researcher is directed to look, for example, at how informant sense-making varies across time and space; for both stabilities and habits as well as flexibilities and changes; for connections between past, present, and future; and at how the informant sees self as constrained and struggling as well as moving and free. The aim of the Sense-Making-informed analysis is to provide contextually unique detail and a means of ordering unique lived experience in terms of universal categories of movement.

From many Sense-Making studies, a set of universal verbing categories have been developed that allow researchers to interpret data without imposing institutional judgment on it. This is done by intersecting a deductive set of frameworks based on Sense-Making's verbing analytic with the inductive qualities of the data. For example, in one study (Dervin, Harpring, & Foreman-Wernet, 1999), several informants described themselves as being concerned that their fetuses had been hurt by drug addiction, but each recollection of the lived experience was very different. This is a noun focus. The Sense-Making interview added a verbing focus by asking each informant how she saw this moment of concern—how it blocked her, how it related to her life, what would have helped, and what hindered. These kinds of data become the focus of a Sense-Making verbing analysis. By codifying how informants described themselves as stopped, struggling, and moving, what seems chaotic across different cases becomes more orderly.

The important idea here is that Sense-Making categories lay a verbing interface (how sense is made and unmade) over a noun interface (the goals of campaign designers). In this way, Sense-Making provides a set of universal descriptors that allow the researcher to compare audience members to campaign designers, audience members to themselves over time, and one group of audience members to another. Furthermore, quantitative Sense-Making studies have shown that in contrast to noun categories typically used in campaign research (e.g., demographic groups, personality factors, lifestyles, and interests), Sense-Making categories account for more variance in understanding audience sense-making with fewer categories. An explanation for this is that Sense-Making's verbing analytic attends to the essence of communicating—the making and unmaking of sense. In this way, Sense-Making provides a systematic means of addressing the interpretive world of target audience members without sinking into the overbearing contextual uniqueness that has for a long time seemed the outcome of interpretive analyses.

Figure 12.2 provides examples of two of Sense-Making's verbing-focused category schemes—situation movement states and utilities (helps). The former is a set of categories that focus on how the informant sees self as stopped or moving at a particular moment in time. The actual categories vary from study to study, but the nine category examples provided in Figure 12.2 are illustrative: decision (where one needs to choose between two or more roads ahead); problematic (being dragged down a road not of your own choosing); spinout, washout (not having a road, losing a road); barrier (knowing where you want to go but something blocks the way); being led (following someone down the road who has traveled it before); observing (watching without being concerned about movement); out to lunch (tuning out, escaping); waiting (waiting for something in particular); and passing time (spending time without waiting for something in particular).

Figure 12.2 also displays utilities (helps) used to evaluate outcomes in terms of how they facilitated movement through time and space. The 15 help categories displayed have been derived from many studies. Figure 12.2 also shows the typical pat-

SENSE-MAKING MOVEMENT STATES	UTILITIES (HELPS) USED TO EVALUATE OUTCOMES 1 = got pictures, ideas 2 = found direction 3 = able to plan 4 = got skills 5 = got started, motivated 6 = kept going 7 = got out of bad place 8 = got control 9 = got connected 10 = got support 11 = got pleasure 12 = took mind off things 13 = got rest 14 = reached goal 15 = went on to other things														
	1	2	3	4	5	6	7	8	9	10	11	12	13	14	15
Decision			●	●											
Problematic							●	●	●	●					
Spin-out, wash-out		●				●	●	●		●					
Barrier			●	●	●		●								
Being led			●		●				●	●					
Observing	●														
Out to lunch												●	●		
Waiting					●									●	●
Passing time										●			●		

FIGURE 12.2
Application of Sense-Making Verbing Analytic to data analysis
with a portrait of typically strong relationships gleaned from past systemic analyses

terns of significant relationships found between situation movement states and utilities in systematic analyses across Sense-Making studies. For example, it can be seen that informants in decision states have been more likely to evaluate outcomes in terms of whether they were able to plan or obtained skills. In contrast, informants in problematic situations were more likely to evaluate results in terms of whether they got out of a bad place, got control, got connected, or got support.

Applying Sense-Making to Campaign Design

There are two avenues for applying Sense-Making to campaign design: theoretically and empirically. Theoretically, the procedural mandates derived from Sense-Making must be implemented. For example, campaign interaction procedures would elicit the different situational conditions, paths of situation facing, and outcomes valued by different audience subsets. Major controversies would be acknowledged and made a topic of focus. Campaign messages would attend to both centralities and agreements across

TABLE 12.1
A model applying Sense-Making's Metatheory to the potential construction of campaign messages

Sense-Making Metaphor	Aspects of Life-facing Situations	Potential Audience Member Goal	How a Campaign Message Might Help
Where one is coming from	Experiences preceding the current situation	To acknowledge	To reflect
	Situation currently experienced	To identify	To reflect To clarify
	Needs served by the situation	To recognize	To reflect To identify
What one is struggling with	Problems seen as requiring a solution	To clarify	To reflect To identify
	Questions and confusions faced	To express	To reflect To raise
	Obstacles, constraints standing in the way	To overcome	To reflect To identify
	Gaps preventing movement forward	To bridge	To reflect To bridge
Where one is going	Resources (helps, answers, and information)	To identify To obtain	To suggest
	Solutions (ways to move forward)	To apply	To suggest To demonstrate
	Uses (helps, hindrances from solutions)	To evaluate	To confirm

informants and to dispersion and contests, and would also elicit a variety of explanations for these differences.

Empirical applications of Sense-Making to campaign design involve using results of Sense-Making-informed research. For example, each of the intersections of movement states and helps pictured in Figure 12.2 implies a different set of sense-making needs that could guide message development. Alternatively, systematic analyses informed by the Sense-Making metaphor focusing on where informants are coming from, what they are struggling with, and where they are going, could be used as a basis for evaluating proposed campaign messages and designing new ones. This alternative is shown in Table 12.1, resulting from Frenette's (1998, 1999) explorations of the potentials of Sense-Making specifically for media campaigns. Table 12.1 is intended to be suggestive rather than exhaustive. The specific ways in which Sense-Making might apply to campaign message evaluation and design would vary across subject areas, population, and media. The important point is that Table 12.1 illustrates the use of Sense-Making in designing the campaign as dialogue.

SENSE-MAKING APPLICATIONS TO CAMPAIGN FOCI

In this section, we describe four actual applications of Sense-Making and then draw the strands together by focusing on how these examples implement the mandate to communicate communicatively in the campaign context.

Sense-Making has been applied in a wide variety of public education and communication contexts (e.g., utility restructuring, interracial dialogue, and everyday problem solving). It has been used to evaluate existing or proposed campaigns and conduct formative research as a basis for campaign design. In all cases, research has culminated in recommendations for campaign practice, some of which have been implemented. The following four examples from the health communication context span some 20 years of applications, representing some of the earliest efforts and some of the most recent, and they exemplify different ways in which Sense-Making has been used as a tool to address communication communicatively.[4]

Goal: Seeing Antismoking Messages Through Adolescent Eyes

In a series of qualitative studies, Frenette (1998, 1999) analyzed focus group interviews conducted with approximately 100 French-speaking adolescents in Quebec, Canada, about their experiences with cigarettes and their perceptions of different antismoking campaign messages. Although there was a wide range of individual circumstances that guided the sense-makings of her informants, Frenette extracted three categories of patterns revealing the conditions under which adolescents found antismoking messages to be supportive of their sense-making, neutral, or hindering. On the positive side, her results showed that antismoking messages were sometimes used by adolescents as stepping-stones. This happened, for example, when adolescents saw messages relating to personal experiences and current life situations and had no restraining conditions that led them to be defensive about themselves or their peers. Likewise, when adolescent smokers viewed messages as acknowledging needs satisfied by smoking, they felt respected and were more inclined to listen to suggestions of alternative ways to meet these needs.

On the negative side, Frenette's (1998, 1999) results showed numerous instances in which antismoking messages were neutral with regard to teenager sense-makings. This happened when the lived context of smoking was ignored and when obstacles encountered by those attempting to quit were not acknowledged nor gaps attended to. Finally, there were circumstances in which teenager sense-makings about smoking seemed to actually be hindered by antismoking messages. Examples include the following: (a) when young smokers were unfairly portrayed as dependent or uncaring of others, (b) when messages seemed oblivious to the social dynamics surrounding smoking, and (c) when message ambiguity was such that it drew teenager attention away from thinking about their lives and absorbed them instead in trying to figure out what the message meant. Frenette's primary conclusion was that media messages (i.e., public service announcements, which often provide the foundation of a communication campaign) can play a more vital role in campaigns if we understand more fully how potential audience members use them in their sense-makings.

Goal: Understanding How General Population Adults Theorize AIDS

Brendlinger, Dervin, and Foreman-Wernet (1999) compared general population responses to a traditional health department survey of knowledge, attitudes, and behaviors to an exploratory Sense-Making survey. The traditional survey consisted of a series of close-ended knowledge, attitude, and behavioral report items; the Sense-Making survey consisted of a series of open-ended items appropriate to Sense-Making's verbing analytic. Each informant was asked to describe three situations—a time when he or she had heard or learned something about AIDS; when he or she or someone he or she knew was exposed to AIDS; and when he or she read, heard, or saw something about AIDS in the mass media. For each situation, informants were asked to (a) describe the situation; (b) indicate any new ideas they derived during the situation and what effect these ideas had on them; (c) indicate any questions they had in the situation; and (d) for their most important question, report how important the question was, how easy or difficult it was to answer, if they tried to get an answer and if not, why not, whether they ever got an answer, how they tried, what barriers they encountered, and how the answer impacted them.

Results showed that the map of categories regarding AIDS imposed by the traditional survey was a weak fit when applied deductively to narratives provided by Sense-Making informants. Only 31.7% of 63 Sense-Making informants mentioned one or more of the specific issues implied by the traditional survey's 10 knowledge items, only 17.5% mentioned any of the specific attitudinal items, and only 25.4% mentioned one or more of the risky or protective behaviors named by the health department. The authors concluded that their informants were neither apathetic nor passive in their relationship to AIDS. On average, their informants named five cognitions (new ideas or questions) each, but their cognitions rarely coincided with health department framings. The difference was that Sense-Making informants did not focus on technical details that interested a health department intent on transmitting expert information but rather on issues pertaining directly to their lives.

Goal: A Blood Center Wants Donors to Donate Again

A city blood center commissioned two studies because staff were convinced, based on prior evidence, that the center was losing some potential donors because of ignorance regarding eligibility requirements. Two Sense-Making studies were conducted (Dervin, Jacobson, & Nilan, 1982; Dervin, Nilan, & Jacobson, 1981). One did in-depth Time-Line interviews asking the 80 randomly selected frequent and new donors, "What happened during your most recent donating experience?" For each Time-Line step, informants were asked what gaps they faced, what questions they had, whether they got answers to their questions, and how they were helped or hindered each step of the way. Results showed that although demography did not predict donor information needs and seeking, where informants were in the process did predict information needs. Each step in the donating Time-Line was associated with its own complex of questions. For example, eligibility questions were more likely to be in donor minds when they checked in to donate. Instead, blood center personnel had been trying to convey eligibility information when donors were recovering and leaving.

The second study compared 105 new, drop-out, and frequent female blood donors in terms of their recollections of their donating experience—what facilitated and what stood in the way. Results showed that the primary difference between drop-out and frequent female donors was access to donation sites. The frequent donors were more likely to report that signing up and participating in donating was available to them through their workplace or near their homes or because of their association with someone who donated and provided transportation.

The two studies provided directions for communication planning. They showed that a campaign to convince women to repeatedly donate would be ineffective and that attention should be redirected to improving access. Second, a plan was established to provide a user-friendly question-answering system at five different times during the donating process. Typical questions at each time were to be displayed on a computer screen that donors could activate to obtain answers. Answers were to be provided on screen from a variety of sources implementing the Sense-Making assumption that a given question rarely leads to only one answer.

Goal: A Cancer Clinic Staff Wants to Reduce Stress from Anxious Patients

A cancer clinic staff felt that patient confusion and resentment were contributing as much to the daily stress of their jobs as the seriousness of cancer.[5] A Sense-Making study of 30 randomly selected patients asked them to detail the events of their contacts with the clinic, the ways in which they felt impeded, the confusions they had, and the ways in which they wanted to be helped or were actually helped or both. Results showed that patients wanted more chances to explore and discuss their confusion and concern with others who were sympathetic; acknowledgment of the contested nature of the information circulating about cancer and its treatment; help getting more information, particularly from other cancer patients; social support; and staff to see them as human beings and not walking tumors. Clinic staff responded by designing group support sessions for patients in which questions and concerns would be openly discussed and disagreements openly admitted. They also instituted a wall of "info sheets," each of which addressed a common patient question (e.g., Can you get well without any treatment at all?).

"Answers" to the questions were provided by different doctors and nurses as well as by patients, thus implementing the Sense-Making mandate to attend both to centrality and to dispersion. Each answerer was asked to provide his or her own explanations for why answers differed across sources. In addition, clinic intake personnel were trained to use Sense-Making questioning when they talked with patients as they approached the desk: "What brings you here today?" "What confusions or problems are you facing?" and "How do you hope we can help you today?" Sense-Making interviews were also conducted with clinic staff—nurses, technicians, and doctors. Results indicated that staff needed their own support groups to handle the daily sadness of their jobs, and they needed to connect with their patients outside the reality of their "cancerness." They also indicated that they needed a more rational way of handling the inherently contestable nature of the medical services they were providing. These results led to regular required attendance at staff support groups and to staff volunteering to rotate their own attendance at patient support groups to keep in touch with the dialogic spirit they represented. In addition, staff decided to do whatever was needed to make it possible for each patient or patient's family to make their own decisions.

COMMUNICATING COMMUNICATIVELY

Our primary intent in this chapter has been to use Sense-Making as a exemplar of what it means to address communication communicatively. In each of the previous examples, the audience was no longer conceptualized as an amorphous mass. Rather, informants become situated in real circumstances for which the logic of what was said was validated and anchored in that experience. In each case, institutions learned something they did not know and even had their expectations changed. Teenage smokers, for example, listened to campaign messages if the realities of their lives and conditions were respected. General population adults paid much attention to AIDS, even if close-ended surveys judged them otherwise. The problem for women donors was not ignorance about eligibility requirements but ease of access. Many cancer clinic patients wanted exposure to the very contradictory kinds of information from which cancer clinic staff were trying to protect them. They too, however, became willing to listen when their questions and points of view were acknowledged.

It could be said that the potential directions for campaign design derived from what informants said. They became our teachers and our confidantes and trusted that we had listened; they also became our listeners and our learners. This is the essence of what it means to design communication communicatively to be dialogic. Being dialogic is not simply a matter of packaging messages to match audience information-processing styles or finding ways to transmit messages via trusted, credible, or intimate others. It is a matter of acknowledging in the core of the campaign the everyday sense-makings of audiences. All communication is ultimately dialogic. The dialogue will either be driven underground by institutions that cannot hear and therefore will not be heard, or be nurtured into the open.

Traditionally, communication efficiency and effectiveness have been conceptualized as opposing trade-offs (see Salmon & Murray-Johnson, 2001). In contrast, Sense-Making addresses both simultaneously by reconceptualizing what attention to individuality means. Sense-Making does not focus on static characterizations of individual people who are assumed to behave the same in varying circumstances. Rather, it focuses on the idea that communicating is responsive to situational conditions—a moment of sense-making replaces the person as primary focus. These situational moments are addressed in interviewing, analysis, and design with Sense-Making's verbing analytic, which focuses on aspects of audience needs that were formerly construed as chaotic and elusive. It is this reconceptualization that is the foundation of Sense-Making's claim that it is possible for institutions to implement dialogic communication systematically—in essence, to communicate communicatively with audiences.

NOTES

1. This section is based on an extensive review of the public communication campaign and audience survey research literature. Because of space limitations, we list only a few especially helpful recent works: Baer (1996), Check (1999), Clatts (1994), Guttman (1997), Krosnick (1999), Proctor (1999), Tardy and Hayle (1998), and Yankelovich (1996). For a copy of our full bibliography, contact: *dervin.1@osu.edu* or *frenettm@com.umontreal.ca*. Our bibliography for this chapter also builds on that used in the chapter on Sense-Making in the second edition of this book (Dervin, 1989a).

2. Sense-Making owes a debt to many philosopher-theorists. See Dervin (1999a) for a recent list, and see Carter (1990, 1991) for his work focusing on the development of theory for the study of communicating. For bibliographies and exemplars relating to the uses of Sense-Making in theory, research, and practice, see *http://communication.sbs.ohio-state.edu/sense-making/*.

3. The use of Sense-Making triangulations in conjunction with message stops builds on Carter's "signaled stopping technique" (Carter, Ruggels, Jackson, & Heffner, 1973).

4. See *http://communication.sbs.ohio-state/sense-making/* for up-to-date listings of Sense-Making studies. Volume 9 (issues 2–4) of the *Electronic Journal of Communication* (1999; *http://www.cios.org/www/ejcrec2.htm*) reports 18 empirical Sense-Making studies, including 5 focusing directly on public communication campaigns. Two are described briefly in this section. The other three are Dervin et al. (1999), Madden (1999), and Murphy (1999).

5. The cancer clinic permitted access on the proviso that the data would not be published except in brief abstract.

Chapter 13

A Theoretic Perspective and Research Approach for Generating Research Helpful to Communication Practice[1]

Brenda Dervin

THE GAP BETWEEN RESEARCH AND PRACTICE

Even though it seems difficult to talk about or even describe, most scholars and practitioners in the field of communications agree that there is some kind of wide chasm in the field between research and practice, researcher and practitioner. This seems true regardless of whether the arena is journalism, broadcasting, public communications, or public relations. It seems true when the focus is on mass communication as well as interpersonal. It seems true when the context is national, international; First World or Third.

The irony of the chasm should not be missed. *Communication* is a term used to refer elusively to events that involve some kind of communicating. Communicating, when systematized as it is in public relations, journalism, education, or development, is practice. Many explanations are given for the chasm. Most usual is the relativistic explanation—we live in separate worlds, we go our separate ways, this is the nature of things. And, it appears true. Mostly we do go our separate ways despite the fact that the lifeblood of the researcher and the lifeblood of the practitioner involve the same phenomena.

An alternative explanation for the chasm is proposed here not as the "correct" explanation but rather for the utility it offers in understanding the state of communication research generally. This explanation is that communication practitioner and researcher are divided by a model of communication, currently used both in practice and in research, which prevents both useful diagnosis of communication practice as it cur-

This work originally appeared as: Dervin, B. (1984). A theoretic perspective and research approach for generating research helpful to communication practice. *Public Relations Research and Education, 1* (1), 30–45. Reprinted by permission of the Association for Education in Journalism and Mass Communication, Columbia, SC. Contains material presented as: Dervin, B. (1983, August). *A theoretical perspective and research approach for generating research helpful to communication practice.* Paper presented at the annual meeting of the American Association for Education in Journalism and Mass Communication, Corvallis, OR.

rently exists as well as the invention of alternative means of practice. The model does not work well, and thus drives practitioner and researcher apart.

A POSSIBLE EXPLANATION FOR THE GAP

Understanding this possibility requires us to take an encapsulated look at the normative approach to current communication research, first in terms of core assumptions made by the normative approach and then in terms of results it has produced.[2] For purposes of this chapter, the term "normative" refers to the most frequently used approach.

Core Assumptions

For purposes of this chapter, it is helpful to designate the following features of the normative approach:

> • *The approach typically starts with the source and the source's message and then goes looking for impacts from the message on receivers.*

> • *The approach typically looks for impacts wanted by sources—usually some kind of attitude or behavior change is most desired. Since research has suggested that these rarely result from message use, the approach now looks for knowledge gains and understandings which it is hoped will combine with other factors to lead to attitude or behavior change.*

> • *It is usually assumed that the source's message should lead to the impacts the source wants to see.*

> • *The characteristics and life contexts of receivers are looked at primarily as barriers to and mediators of message effects.*

> • *Both message-using and message-making have been looked at as input-output activities in which the researchers can measure what goes in and what comes out. Few studies have been done that look at message-using and message-making per se or allowed variations in these other than those expected in input-output analysis.*

> • *Messages have been assumed to contain "information." Information, in turn, has been assumed to be a thing that can be transferred via messages.*

> • *Attempts to predict audience use of messages have sought stable portraits across time and space. One example is the heavy emphasis on market segmentation using demographic or lifestyle characteristics that assume messages can be predicted by stable personal characteristics.*

While clearly there have been some exceptions to this normative approach, there is common agreement that these characteristics describe most communication research intended to assist communication practitioners.

Results

After almost 50 years of such research, the results of the work have been disappointing both for the researcher and the practitioner:

- *It is universally agreed that effects have been hard to find and hard to achieve.*

- *The ability of the researcher to predict the conditions that lead to effects is very limited. Further, most of the conditions that do predict effects appear to be entirely outside the control of the practitioner.*

- *The most predictable aspects of communicating behaviors are the least useful to practitioners. Researchers can predict habit patterns in general media use, for example, but rarely what someone thinks about or will do about some issue.*

- *A portrait emerges of the audience that is alternatively pessimistic and resigned. When pessimistic, it pictures the audience as passive, lazy, unconcerned, uninvolved. When resigned, it acknowledges that the audience is busy, involved elsewhere, walking different roads.*

Given this record, it is not surprising that both researcher and practitioner have been disappointed. Further, the conclusions generated by research based on the model have led to actions by researchers that could only widen the gap between researcher and practitioner. For example, the research led to the conclusion that effects are hard to find. Thus it was assumed that only complex conceptualizations and multivariate statistics could possibly unearth them. With each new complexity, the languages and worldviews of researcher and practitioner grew further and further apart. The process of doing research in practitioner settings became in many contexts a necessary ritual—not expected to enrich practice but required by supervisors, board, or funders. The chasm between research and practice grew.

SENSE-MAKING: AN ALTERNATIVE RESEARCH APPROACH

Within the communications field, there is growing recognition that the normative approach has been restricting.[3] Much of the discussion has been merely rhetoric. But fortunately one also finds rare but isolated cases of work on alternative approaches to research that have the promise of providing immediate and direct assistance to communication practice.[4] This chapter describes one such approach developed over the past ten years in a program of research and application.

The alternative—called Sense-Making—was developed in part to provide data useful to both interpersonal and mass communication practitioners who work with laypersons or design programs for change agents and experts. The approach looks specifically at how people construct and fill information needs and use the new sense that results.

Sense-Making differs widely from research approaches typically used in these contexts. In every respect, the core assumptions of Sense-Making differ from those typical of the normative research approach:

- *Sense-Making starts with the receiver and looks at message use only in terms of how it intersects with the receiver's present, past, and expected future.*

- *Sense-Making does not presuppose impacts of messages but rather lets receivers define how messages impacted them.*

- *Sense-Making sees the characteristics and life contexts of receivers not as barriers to and mediators of messages but rather as the contexts within which receivers use messages to make sense of their worlds.*

- *Message-using as well as message-making is looked at not as an input-output system but rather as a "constructing" activity. In this context, different users can create different sense from the "same" message.*

- *Information is defined as that which informs from the receiver's point of view. It is seen as the sense the receiver makes to bridge the gaps in his or her world.*

- *Attempts to predict audience responses to messages do not seek to create across time-space portraits but rather focus on situational contingencies—predicting the different kinds of sense people seek in different kinds of situations.*

Merely stating the differences, however, addresses only surface issues, focusing on the easily visible differences between Sense-Making and traditional approaches. Sense-Making departs radically in its assumptions about the nature of reality, the human relationship to that reality, the nature of information, the nature of human information seeking, the nature of communicating, and the most useful ways to research communicating behavior. This set of assumptions has been presented in detail before.[5] For this chapter, therefore, the following brief statements will suffice.

- *Sense-Making assumes that reality is neither complete nor constant but rather filled with fundamental and pervasive gaps. Resting heavily at this point on Carter's discontinuity theory, Sense-Making assumes that this gap condition is generalizeable both because all things in reality are not connected and because things are changing.[6]*

• *Sense-Making assumes that information is not a thing that exists independent of and external to human beings but rather is a product of human observing. It assumes that all information is subjective, even information agreed upon and called fact. It assumes that all observing is relevant to both the physical time-space at which the observations were made as well as the psychological time-space of the observer.*

• *Because of the gap between the observer and the observed, Sense-Making assumes that information seeking and use is not transmission-receiving activity but rather constructing activity—the personal creating of sense. Sense-Making looks at how individuals use their own observations as well as the observations of others (that which is usually called information or messages) to construct their pictures of reality and use these pictures to guide their behavior.*

• *Sense-Making assumes that the mandate to construct sense of the world arises from the gap condition—that the changing nature of time-space reduces gaps in a person's understanding that require the making of new sense. Because of this, Sense-Making assumes that sense-making behavior is responsive to and mandated by changing situational conditions. Sense-Making also assumes that the model used to predict information seeking and using behaviors must use situational conditions as predictors rather than such traditional measures as demography and personality.*

• *Sense-Making assumes that there is a situational logic to how people construct sense of their worlds and that because of this there are universals of sense-making that will allow successful prediction and explanation. Drawing heavily on Carter, Sense-Making assumes that the key to identifying these universals lies in focusing on the human mandate to move through time-space. This then draws attention to the ways in which movement can be stopped (as a perspective for looking at situational conditions), the kinds of gaps humans need to bridge in order to keep moving (as a perspective for looking at sense-making or information needs), and the different ways in which people assess success in gap-bridging (as a perspective for looking at information use or actor-created effects of information-sharing and communicating).*

• *Sense-Making assumes that studying communicating behaviors in the context of current communication systems leads to distorted views of communication potential. This is so because it is assumed that our communication institutions and practices are primarily all descendents of historical prototypes invented in the context of more traditional and authoritarian assumptions about communicating. Because of this, it is assumed that useful communication research in order to inform the practice of communicating requires that the researcher involve him or herself actively in communication invention. Alternatively, Sense-Making assumes that the researcher must look at receivers as much as possible on their own terms rather than only within the constraints of their interactions with specific institutions.*

The premises above are highly abstract. They can be brought to earth for research purposes in three ways. One is the Sense-Making model, which specifies what the researcher should measure when studying sense-making. The second is in a series of data collection methods developed specifically to implement interviewing within the context of the Sense-Making premises. The third is in the ways in which variables have been conceptualized and operationalized in Sense-Making studies. Each of these will be described in turn below.

CURRENT SENSE-MAKING MODEL

The set of premises listed above have embedded in them the core elements of a model. They suggest:

> • *That sense-making is situational and will be predicted by situational conditions.*
>
> • *That the gaps seen at a specific moment by an observer will depend on where that observer is in time-space and how he or she sees that time-space. Thus, different observers will see different gaps.*
>
> • *That even supposing two people see the same gap, the ways in which they bridge that gap will be different depending on where they are in time-space, where they have been, and where they are going.*

These three elements—situations-gaps-uses—have become the core elements in the Sense-Making model. Situations consist of the time-space contexts in which sense is constructed. Gaps are where the individual sees something missing in his or her sense. New sense is created when the individual sees a gap as bridged. Uses are the ways in which the individual puts the newly created sense to work in guiding his or her behavior.

In Sense-Making, the three dimensions of situations-gaps-uses identify categories of variables that a researcher measures. The three dimensions are examples of the kind of "universals" specified in the conceptual premises. Thus, Sense-Making assumes that people have gaps in situations, that they bridged these gaps, and that they put their new sense to work in guiding their behavior.

METHODS OF DATA COLLECTING

To date, we have devoted a major portion of the effort in developing the Sense-Making approach to the invention of alternative means for interviewing respondents. Several techniques have been developed. For purposes of this chapter only one will be described in detail—the Micro-Moment Time-Line Interview.

The Micro-Moment Time-Line Interview is the core technique of the Sense-Making approach. It allows respondents to define, in their own terms, their situations, gaps, how they bridged their gaps, and the ways in which they put new sense to use. It allows them to create their own context and to fully inform the interviewer about their worlds. At the same time, however, it does so within a tight theoretic structure that guides the interview. The structure is as "neutral" as possible in that it provides no specific content but instead asks respondents to talk about their worlds in the context of the situations-gaps-uses assumptions of Sense-Making.

Specifically, the respondent in a Time-Line Interview is asked to detail what happened in a situation step-by-step. The specific situation selected depends on the research purpose. In one study, it was the most recent intersection with an organization. In another, it was the most recent interpersonal conflict. In another, it was the most important, recent troublesome situation.

After the situation has been described step-by-step, the respondent is asked, for each step (called a Time-Line Step), what gaps he or she had and/or what gaps he or she bridged. In a study attempting to determine information needs, for example, respondents would be asked what gaps they faced—what questions they had, what things they needed to find out, come to understand, make sense of, unconfuse. In a study attempting to determine images of a large company, on the other hand, respondents would be asked what ideas they created in the situation.

The Time-Line Interview then concludes with in-depth analyses of one or more gaps. These in-depth analyses focus on the situational conditions that the respondent saw as leading to the gap, the nature of the gap, how the respondent hoped the gap-bridging would help, the ways in which the gap was bridged, and the ways in which the respondent saw the new sense created by bridging of the gap as guiding behavior.

To date, the Micro-Moment Time-Line Interview and its variations have been used successfully with cancer patients, blood donors, internal medicine patients, college students, disabled adults, children, low-income and general population adults, and Asian refugees. It has been applied to intersections with many organizational contexts as well as communication contexts. Most respondents and interviewers report high interest and involvement. An example of an excerpt from a Micro-Moment Time-Line Interview is included in Table 13.1.

The description above is of the most complete and most used Time-Line Interview. Around this model, a variety of adjustments have been made depending on both the funder's and the researcher's purposes. In one study, for example, only the most important question (i.e., gap) was analyzed in detail. In another, respondents were asked to choose only a crucial moment in a situation. Table 13.2 provides examples of a recent data collection in which respondents were asked to think of a time when they were more helped by a media message than they were by messages from the people around them. Excerpts from seven randomly selected respondents are listed in Table 13.2 with the respondents' descriptions of the "essence" of the situation and the ways in which they were helped.[7]

TABLE 13.1
Excerpt from a Micro-Moment Time-Line Interview

SAMPLE: 80 blood donors residing in the city of Seattle, selected from the donor rosters of the Puget Sound Blood Center in a disproportionate stratified random sample defined by three strata (i.e., two levels of age, sex, and new vs. repeat donor). In-person interviews to an average of 93 minutes, with a range of 50–130 minutes.

METHOD: Each respondent was asked to describe his or her recent blood donation. For this administration, Time-Line steps were elicited first; then questions were elicited for each Time-Line step. Finally, in-depth analyses were elicited on all questions.

CITATIONS: Dervin, Nilan, and Jacobson (1981); and Dervin, Jacobson, and Nilan (1982).

EXCERPT: What is presented below is an excerpt from the Time-Line (consisting of Time-Line steps and accompanying questions). This is followed by a complete example of an in-depth Time-Line step analysis. This, in turn, is followed by a complete example of an in-depth question analysis. Respondent is a 16-year-old male new donor.

THE TIME-LINE
STEP 1: We were told we would get extra credit in health class for donating.
        Q1: *How much did I have to give?*
        Q2: *What are the procedures?*

STEP 2: A friend who had donated told me about it so a friend and I decided to donate.
        Q1: *How long would it take?*
        Q2: *Would it hurt?*
        Q3: *How big is the needle?*
        Q4: *How much blood do I have to give?*

STEP 3: I got my parents' permission.
        No suggestions

(SKIPPING DOWN TO STEP 7)
STEP 7: She called me in and I didn't know what was going on.
        Q1: *What are they going to do?*
        Q2: *What is all this equipment for if they are just going to take my blood?*

(SKIPPING DOWN TO LAST STEP)
STEP 11: After eight minutes I went to the canteen for cookies and juice.
        No suggestions

IN-DEPTH ANALYSIS OF STEP 7
How clear was the event? (Scale of 1 = very unclear to 10 = very clear)
        3

How many people were involved?
        Only me

Did you see event as just happening or was it seen as a result of something that happened earlier?
        Just happened

Did you see event as having possible good consequences?
        No

(Continued)

TABLE 13.1 (Continued)
Excerpt from a Micro-Moment Time-Line Interview

IN-DEPTH ANALYSIS OF STEP 7 (Continued)
Did you see event as having possible bad consequences?
>*No*

Which of the situation movement state pictures fit the event best? (R chose from: decision, barrier, problematic, and worry)
>*Problematic*

How important was the event? (Scale of 1 = very unimportant to 10 = very important)
>*10*

Did event help in any way?
>*No*

Did event hurt in any way?
>*No*

IN-DEPTH ANALYSIS OF Q2, STEP 7
Q2: What is all this equipment for if they are just going to take my blood?
How easy was it to get an answer to this question? (Scale of 1 = impossible to 10 = very easy)
>*1*

How many people would ask this same question in this same situation? (none, a few, about half, a lot, or all of them)
>*About half*

Did you ever get an answer to this question?
>*No*

Why didn't you get an answer?
>*Because they didn't tell me anything. They just did it. They thought I knew what was going on.*

Did you expect the answer to help? If so, how?
>*I wouldn't have been scared or in suspense wondering what they were going to do.*

Did you expect the answer to hurt? If so, how?
>*No*

VARIABLE CONCEPTUALIZATION AND OPERATIONALIZATION

The Sense-Making model focuses on three classes of measures: situations-gaps-uses. The specific aspect of these to be measured has varied from study to study. In all cases, however, conceptual and operational definitions of variables relate to the core conceptual premises.

Of all the premises stated earlier, one stands out as most central in guiding conceptualization. This is the idea that sense-making is mandated by one's own movement through a changing time-space. An examination of the situations-gaps-uses measures most used to date shows how this idea has been implemented.

TABLE 13.2	
Excerpts from a Modified Time-Line Interview	
SITUATION	**HELPS**
About a year ago, my car began to give me problems right after the warranty expired. I wanted to sell the car but my parents and friends said keep it. I saw an article in the *Wall Street Journal* on the model of car.	The article showed me that the best action was to sell my car. I did this and saved money in the long run.
I was planning a trip to Eastern Washington and my friends all told me the passes were clear and that I would not need chains. I turned on the radio which reported one pass was closed with snow slides.	I took a different route and saved time and frustration. I got to my appointment on time and the people there didn't get upset. Things went well at the meeting.
I had a bad cold and was eating lots of chicken noodle soup. Everyone I lived with told me it was just superstition that chicken noodle soup helped colds. Then I saw an episode of *FYI* on TV.	I learned that there is evidence supporting my view. I felt good because I was doing something to help myself.
Before I turned 21, I had wanted to try alcohol but my parents were always giving me lectures on how bad alcohol is. Since I could not drink at home, some friends and I decided to go out and give alcohol a try. But before I left, I was watching the TV news and saw a news brief on how four minors died in a car crash after drinking.	The show gave me a clear picture of what might happen to me. I didn't go.
I was having trouble breathing and thought I might have a lung infection but my friends and coworkers said it was probably stress related and caused by the nervous tension. So I didn't go to the doctor. Then I saw a program on the health channel in which a doctor discussed pleurisy.	I went to the doctor and my suspicions were confirmed. I got medicine and got better.
I was really depressed about my job because everyone seemed so paranoid, always blaming others for things that go wrong and never trying to really communicate with others so things would go better. It was about this time that I read a biography of Gandhi.	It helped me regain my optimism and confirmed my belief that we must work first on changing ourselves. It also gave me a great sense of not being alone.
I was planning to run a race and being a beginner I needed advice. My friends were giving me lots of advice but they couldn't back up their advice with reasons. A magazine article I saw helped.	The article gave me information and this helped me gain confidence so I could run a good race.

The Measurement of Situations

This core idea suggests that it is appropriate to measure how individuals see themselves moving or stopped from moving in situations. Most central of all the situation measures has been one labeled *Situation Movement State*. This measure taps the different qualitative ways in which the respondent sees his or her movement through time-space blocked. The different Situation Movement States are all different ways of being stopped. For example, being stopped at a decision point means (a) having two or more roads ahead and being unable to move because one cannot travel two roads at one time; (b) seeing self as being dragged down a road not of one's own choosing; or (c) knowing where you want to go but having someone or something standing in the way. Table 13.3 includes an overview of this measure.

The Measurement of Gaps

Several methods have been developed to assess the nature of gaps seen and bridged. Each of these is a different way of describing the different kinds of ideas people create as they move through time-space. Five of the different content analysis templates used to date have coded gaps in terms of whether they involved:

1. *Identifying a who, what, when, where, why, or how.*

2. *A focus on the past, present, or future.*

3. *The determination of whether a road was (or is/will be) a good one or a bad one.*

4. *A focus on self, another, an object, or a process.*

5. *A focus on where one was, how one got to the present, where one is, how one can get to the future, or where one will be.*

In addition to these theoretic templates, most of the applied studies have also developed detailed descriptions of gaps in terms useful to practitioners. Examples include a list of several hundred different "images" for a large company and several hundred different questions asked by people giving blood at a blood donation center.

The Measurement of Uses

For the final class of measures—uses—we have developed a theoretically guided scheme to tap the ways in which people see the new senses they create as helping them (i.e., guiding their movements). Operationally, this has most frequently been measured with a scheme tapping the ways in which people have believed the answers to questions or new ideas helped or hurt them. In some studies, we have asked people how a new idea or answer to a question affected them—how it led them to behave.

The most comprehensive content analysis scheme developed to assess uses (or impacts, effects) has been based on theoretic assumptions about what the human needs to move through time-space. A category of uses called "got pictures," for example,

TABLE 13.3
The Situation Movement States

Different studies have treated these states in different ways, sometimes eliminating some, sometimes combining some. The description below is the most expanded version.

DECISION	Being at a point where you need to choose between two or more roads that lie ahead
PROBLEMATIC	Being dragged down a road not of your own choosing
SPIN-OUT	Not having a road
WASH-OUT	Being on a road and suddenly having it disappear
BARRIER	Knowing where you want to go but someone or something is blocking the way
BEING LED	Following another on a road because he or she knows more and can show you the way
WAITING	Spending time waiting for something in particular
PASSING TIME	Spending time without waiting for something in particular
OUT TO LUNCH	Tuning out
OBSERVING	Watching without being concerned with movement
MOVING	Seeing self as proceeding unblocked in any way and without need to observe

acknowledges that the mind guides behavior and that without ideas no movement can be made. A category called "able to plan" acknowledges that in order to move one needs direction. A category called "got started, got motivated" acknowledged that sometimes humans find it hard to get going. Other major categories include: got skills, kept going, got control, things got easier, got out of a bad situation, reached a goal, went on to other things, avoided a bad situation, took mind off things, relaxed, got pleasure, got reassurance, and got connected to others.

Other Measurements

Through the Sense-Making studies, other measures have been included in addition to those noted above. In the situations category, other measures have included the importance, clarity, and complexity of situations. In the gaps category, other measures have included the importance, clarity, and complexity of situations. In the gaps category, other measures have included ease of bridging, success in bridging, barriers to bridging, completeness of answer, and adequacy of answer. In the uses categories, other measures have included a differentiation of expected versus actual uses.

WORK TO DATE

In order to begin to bring all of this down to the reality of communication practice, three of the Sense-Making studies completed to date will be used as illustrations.

Study of Blood Donors

In 1980-81, Micro-Moment Time-Line Interviews were conducted with 80 donors drawn randomly from the rosters of the Puget Sound Blood Center. Respondents named 480 gaps that they faced (an average of 6 per respondent) during their most recent donations. One published report on this study focused on the power of different kinds of predictors to predict information uses (i.e., how donors actually used or expected to use answers to questions to guide their behavior). The study compared several demographic predictors (defined as tapping across time-space); six a priori situational predictors (defined as tapping time-space at the point of entry into the communication situation); and time-space bound, situational measures, including six measures of situation perceptions and six measures of the nature of the gaps seen. It was hypothesized and found that the time-space bound measures accounted for more variance in information uses than either across time-space or a priori time-space measures. The time-space bound measures accounted for 17.4% of variance in information use on the average, compared to 1.7% and 1.6%, respectively, for across time-space and a priori time-space measures.

A typical finding was that respondents who asked questions about the future focusing on possible pain and the donating process were more likely than those asking other questions to report that answers helped them to avoid bad situations. In contrast, those who asked questions focusing on their own self-control in the future were more likely to report that answers helped them to get started or keep going on the road toward donating and its completion.

A second published report of this study described the different kinds of gaps people faced during donating—how frequently the gaps were faced, how much they were emphasized, how hard they were bridged, and how successfully they were bridged. Results showed that 20 out of 24 statistical tests completed were statistically significant using qualitative differences in gaps as predictors of the frequency, emphasis, ease, and success in gap-bridging. Typical findings showed that most frequently asked questions focused on the future; most-emphasized questions involved self; questions seen as hardest to answer involved the future and understanding the connections between different time-space points and the evaluations of events; least-answered questions were why questions; and most completely answered involved exclusively personal assessments by the question-asker.

Other unpublished data showed what kinds of questions donors asked at different points in the donating process, the barriers seen to getting answers, and question-answering success at these time-space points.[8]

Study of Adult Information Needs of Californians

In 1979, a random sample of 646 adult Californians aged 14 or older was interviewed using a modified Micro-Moment Time-Line Interview. The one published report of this study to date pitted race against Situation Movement State as a predictor of the nature of question-asking in troublesome situations. It was hypothesized and found that: (a) Situation Movement State significantly predicted nature of questions asked; and (b) Situation Movement State and race in interaction significantly predicted sources used to get answers. Reasoning behind the hypothesis was that race taps the structural or system constraints within a society and, thus, should play more of a role in predicting behaviors that are constrained by society (i.e., source use) than in predicting behaviors that are more in the individual's control (i.e., gap-defining, question-asking).

The large body of as-yet-unpublished data from this study includes a list of the different kinds of questions respondents reported having as they faced their everyday situations, the sources they used to get answers, and the success they had in getting answers.[9]

Study of Adult Images of a Large Company

In 1981-82, 1,030 adults randomly sampled from a metropolitan city population were interviewed with a modified Time-Line Interview approach about their contacts with a major company whose home office is located in the area. They were asked to describe the nature of their contact situations, the ideas (images) that resulted from these situations, and the ways in which the ideas impacted their behaviors involving the company.

Among the many findings were results showing that: Respondents relied on their closest contact situations (e.g., knowing someone who works for the company, visiting company headquarters) to create their images even when they had more distant contact situations (e.g., exposure to media ads); virtually all contacts led to having images and 50% led to specific impacts on behavior; impacts on buying behavior resulted from all kinds of images, even those not involving the company product per se but involving instead the company's role as employer and community member.

The database, as-yet-unpublished, also includes a detailed list of the different ideas respondents got about the company in different situations, an analysis of what kinds of situations were more likely to lead to negative images, and an analysis of what kinds of images were more likely to affect buying.[10]

APPLICATIONS

There is much that is relevant to discuss about the three research examples above and the Sense-Making approach generally. For purposes of this chapter, attention will be focused on the potential of the findings and approach to assist communication practice.

Perhaps the most obvious potential can be seen from the fact that the results to date have contradicted prior work. They show, for example, a great deal of information seeking and use, while most traditional studies have shown very little. They show many impacts from messages and contacts, while prior research has typically shown few. Sense-Making assumes that these results have occurred because in Sense-Making studies receivers are allowed to talk about what they call information and what they call effects rather than being forced to respond only in terms of what researchers or institutions call information or effects.

A second obvious potential for practitioners can be seen from the fact that the work to date has increased the ability of research to predict the specific kinds of information needs people have and the specific kinds of ideas they create. Since all planning requires an ability to predict, this result is encouraging as well as instructive. It suggests that practitioners can profitably turn their attention from the across time-space approaches to communicating that they were taught to approaches rooted in situational theory.

A third potential comes from the fact that the data have yielded actuarial findings that are immediately useful to practitioners. For example, the findings detailing the different kinds of questions asked at different points in the blood donation process provided blood center planners with data immediately useful in designing information-sharing activities and locating the most useful points for these activities. The findings in the California study on information needs not met (i.e., gaps not bridged in troublesome situations) suggested areas for system development. The findings from the company images study on which kinds of situations were more likely to lead to negative images provided specific direction for the improvement of practice.

A fourth potential, although not described in this chapter in full detail, is the utility of the data collection methods for allowing organizations and systems to assess what happens when people intersect with them. The data collection methods, tested and used successfully already in many situations, can be generalized widely because they are not structured in terms of specific content issues but rather in terms of the generalizeable time-space and gap-bridging premises posited by Sense-Making.

A fifth potential results from both the generalizeability of the approach and the success of its applications to date. These suggest that the approach can provide general theoretic guidance in inventing communications procedures directed at improving practice. One example resulted from the California information needs study. The Sense-Making idea which says that situations-gaps-uses are universals and therefore useful to address in all gap-bridging situations, led to the development of an interpersonal communicating tactic called Neutral-Questioning.

Neutral-Questioning directs the communicator to ask others three classes of questions that are content free except in their allegiance to time-space premises. Each class of questions taps one of the three elements in the Sense-Making model. To tap situations, practitioners ask such questions as "What happened?" or "What led up to this point?" To tap gaps, practitioners ask "What questions do you have?" or "What confuses you?" To tap uses, practitioners ask "What help would you like?" or "What would you like to see happen?"

Instruction in the use of Neutral-Questioning has been systematically given to several professionals, including doctors and librarians. An explicit comparison of the tactic with the traditional approach to the library reference interview is now being conducted.[11] Informal reports to date from a variety of professionals suggest that after the initial shock of the change, the tactic allows professionals to determine more effectively and efficiently what users of systems want. One power of this result is that it suggests that one of the standard caveats of communication practice—that effective communication always takes more time—may itself be the result of the normative model of communication that has been applied to practice.

A second example of how Sense-Making has provided general theoretic guidance for invention in practice comes from the use of the category schemes for coding situations, gaps, and uses as possible information storage and retrieval categories. One library, for example, has successfully had patrons report on how books helped them and has tabulated these for use by other patrons, providing patrons with an alternative to the traditional Dewey Decimal or Library of Congress access categories.

CONCLUSION

As an alternative approach to research, Sense-Making is relatively young, best seen as having had a modest beginning. Sense-Making is important because it provides an example of a highly theoretic approach to research that has already shown useful applications to communication practice. It provides, thus, a rare example of research and practice moving together.

There has long been a saying that there is nothing as powerful as a good theory. For the practitioner of communication these words must seem hollow. The field of communication is beset with a plethora of things called "theory." Yet, for the practitioner most seem useless, unnecessarily complex, too far removed from practice, too unrelated to human activity, too pessimistic. One major point of this chapter is that these and other reactions of practitioners to communications research are rooted in more than lack of understanding.

Anyone who has been a thoughtful communications practitioner knows that practice frequently runs on hunch, insight, and talent. And, anyone who has been a thoughtful communications practitioner knows that these attributes, while commendable, are not enough. Something more would help. There hasn't been much clarity about what the something more should be. Research, of course, is an obvious place to look.

The issue of improving practice is more complex than simply blaming researchers, however. Both research and practice are based on the same normative assumptions about communication. Our communication structures are as confined as our research. Many practitioners will, at least in confidence, tell how in the practice of their art they feel as unaided by the communication structures within which they work as by research. Individual practitioners sometimes attempt, at the expense of possible burnout, to rise above constraining systems and communicate differently, more responsively to system users. Unfortunately, without system support, they cannot do so. In addition, practitioners are hampered by lack of systematic understanding of how to communicate responsively without being involved in the seeming chaos of the uniquenesses of all the individual people with whom they or their messages intersect.

The problem of generating research useful for communication practice, then, has at least two parts. Clearly, researchers must generate and use approaches that can produce useful data. Equally clear, however, is the need for both researchers and practitioners to enlarge their view of what is involved when people intersect with and communicate with systems.

The approach to research described in this chapter is not intended to be merely an approach to research. If it were, its relevance to practice would be limited. Rather, it is intended to be a perspective for looking at the practice of communicating both by those doing the practicing and those observing it.

NOTES

1.   This paper reports on a 10-year programmatic series of studies using an approach to research called Sense-Making. For reports on this research, see all citations for Dervin and co-authors listed in references. See also the Sense-Making website at: *http://communication.sbs.ohio-state.edu/sense-making*. The author owes a debt to the many people who have contributed to Sense-Making studies since the beginning. Rita Atwood (at the University of Texas-Austin) and Michael Nilan (at Rutgers University) deserve mention in particular. Others have included: Sylvia Harlock, Carol Garzona, Tom Jacobson, Colleen Kwan, Payson Hall (now at the University of Delaware), Michael Banister, Benson Fraser, Michael Gabriel, Claudia Krenz, Scott Wittet, and Douglas Zweizig (at the University of Wisconsin-Madison). In addition, input from colleagues doing related work has been very helpful: John Bowes, Dick Carter, Alex Edelstein, Keith Stamm, Ken Jackson at the University of Washington, James Grunig at the University of Maryland, Patricia Dewdeny at the University of Western Ontario. Richard Carter, in particular, needs mention. His theoretic work has been crucial to the development of Sense-Making. Financial and moral support from several institutions has been vital as well: The U.S. Office of Education Bureau of Libraries and Learning Resources, the Puget Sound Blood Center; the Graduate School Research Fund of the University of Washington, the California State Library, the National Cancer

Institute, the *Seattle Times*, and the Safeco Insurance Companies. While each of these institutions has provided support, the ideas and opinions expressed in this chapter are solely those of the author and are not to be construed as official positions of any of the named organizations.

    2.   For extensive reviews of the normative approach, see, in particular: Dervin (1976a, 1977b, 1980, 1981).

    3.   In coming to grips with these constraints, the current author has relied heavily on: Beltrán (1976), Bernstein (1976), Bronowski (1956, 1969, 1973), Bruner (1973), Carter (1972, 1974a, 1974b, 1975), Delia (1977a), Freire (1970), Habermas (1971, 1973), Jackins (1973, 1981), Kuhn (1970, 1977), Piaget (1962), Röling, Ascroft, and Chege (1976).

    4.   See, in particular, the citations for Carter (1972, 1973, 1974a, 1974b, 1975), Edelstein (1974), Grunig (1978a, 1978b), Grunig and Disbrow (1977), and Stamm and Grunig (1977) in the list of references.

    5.   See, in particular, Dervin (1981), Dervin, Nilan, and Jacobson (1981), Dervin, Jacobson, and Nilan (1982).

    6.   See the citations for Carter (1972, 1973, 1974a, 1974b, 1975) in references.

    7.   This paragraph was omitted from the original published article.

    8.   Dervin et al. (1981, 1982).

    9.   Atwood and Dervin (1981); Palmour, Rathbun, Brown, Dervin, and Dowd (1979).

    10.   Dervin, unpublished data.

    11.   Patricia Dewdeny, personal communication, 1983.

Chapter 14

From the Mind's Eye of the User:
The Sense-Making Qualitative-Quantitative Methodology

Brenda Dervin

INTRODUCTION

The purpose of this chapter is to set forth the Sense-Making methodological approach which has been developed since 1972 in a programmatic research effort specifically focused on developing alternative approaches to the study of human use of information and information systems. In terms of research genres as identified in the current literature, Sense-Making has been used to study the needs, images, and satisfactions of users and potential users of information/communication systems—in short, what users want from systems, what they get, and what they think about them.[1]

In the first section of this chapter, the underlying assumptions and theoretic foundations of the methodology are set forth. This is followed by a description of the methodology and its derivative methods. A third section presents exemplars of how the approach has been used in several different studies of users and potential users of information/communication systems. In a final section, the approach is positioned in the context of the current debates in the social sciences generally and specifically in terms of the qualitative-versus-quantitative research distinction.

Since the focus of this book is on qualitative research, it is important at this point to note that the approach being described in this chapter is a qualitative approach. However, it is also a quantitative approach. It can in some senses be said to stand between methodological divisions, in that it cannot be placed at either one end or another of the many polarities that form the current contests in the social sciences: for example, qualitative versus quantitative, administrative versus critical, theoretic versus

This work originally appeared as: Dervin, B. (1992). From the mind's eye of the user: The Sense-Making qualitative-quantitative methodology. In J. D. Glazier & R. R. Powell (Eds.), *Qualitative research in information management* (pp. 61–84). Englewood, CO: Libraries Unlimited. Reprinted by permission of Jack D. Glazier.

applied, structuralist versus individualist. These matters are discussed in greater detail in the final section of this chapter.

UNDERLYING ASSUMPTIONS AND THEORETIC FOUNDATIONS

The term *Sense-Making* has come to be used to refer to a theoretic net, a set of assumptions and propositions, and a set of methods which have been developed to study the making of sense that people do in their everyday experiences. Some people call Sense-Making a theory, others a set of methods, others a methodology, others a body of findings. In the most general sense, it is all of these.

It is, first and foremost, a set of metatheoretic assumptions and propositions about the nature of information, the nature of human use of information, and the nature of human communicating. Some of the assumptions of Sense-Making are properly seen as axiomatic, in that they are taken as given. Others are derived deductively. Others are propositions that have received empirical support.

The assumptions and propositions of Sense-Making, taken together, provide methodological guidance for framing research questions, for collecting data, and for charting analyses. Derived from these assumptions are a set of methods, particularly methods for interviewing humans about their experiences. Sometimes, therefore, one sees Sense-Making referred to as a theory of conducting interviews about sense-making. It is that as well.

In essence, then, the term *Sense-Making* refers to a coherent set of theoretically derived methods for studying human sense-making. The coherence is of the kind where it may be said that method is a residual of theoretic effort: it falls out from, or is a result of, the conceptual frame which defines it. This is an important point because, in fact, all method is residual of theoretic effort. The difficulty is that for most use of methods for studying human behavior, particularly human information-using behavior, the coherence among assumption, proposition, and method is hidden. Certain things are assumed to be true and entire enterprises for studying human use of information systems are derived as if no other approaches were possible. The best way to develop this point is to extract at a very high level of abstraction the assumptions and propositions which guide most research on human use of information and information systems and to contrast these with the assumptions and propositions which guide Sense-Making.

It is useful to start by delineating the core assumption on which Sense-Making rests—the assumption of discontinuity.[2] This assumption proposes that discontinuity is a fundamental aspect of reality. It is assumed that there are discontinuities in all existence—between entities (living and otherwise), between times, and between spaces. It is assumed that this discontinuity condition exists between reality and human sensors, between human sensors and the mind, between mind and tongue, between tongue and message created, between message created and channel, between human at time one and human at time two, between human one at time one and human two at time one, between human and culture, between human and institution, between institution and institution, between nation and nation, and so on. Discontinuity is an assumed constant of nature generally and the human condition specifically.

Arguments can be offered for the utility of invoking the discontinuity assumption for many realms of study, but our concern here is its utility for the study of human use of information and information systems. Sense-Making assumes that the discontinuity assumption is an important one to invoke in the study of human information use for those occasions when one wants to know about behavior that is internally controlled. One can propose many research questions that do not require the discontinuity assumption, for they pertain to questions relating to information when conceptualized as something that exists apart from human considerations. For example, if one sets standards of accuracy for answering questions at the reference desk, then one can examine how many questions are answered accurately by comparing question-in and answer-out to some externally defined standard. Or, if one wants to know what elements of a current information system's database (collection, etc.) are used, one can examine the number of times each element is somehow activated (checked out, examined).

However, many, perhaps most, of the questions that concern us in information management, design, and practice do involve human actors. How can we design databases so they will be maximally used? What services should we offer? How satisfied are our users? Why don't some potential users use us? How can we capitalize on the flexibilities that new technologies allow rather than merely using them, as we are, to do what we now do in greater quantities, from further distances, and at faster speeds?

What follows below is a series of contrasts between the assumptions of traditional research approaches and the assumptions of Sense-Making, all of which are derived from the core discontinuity premise. These contrasts lay out a logic that explains why the discontinuity assumption is seen as a required assumption for much information research.

It is also important to point out at this juncture that the assumptions reviewed in this chapter pertain not just to research but also to information management, design, and practice. What Sense-Making has tried to do in its development over the past seventeen years is break with the undergirding assumptions that guide our current system designs which, in turn, mandate our research.

Information Use as Transmission Versus Construction

Fundamental to the specific application of Sense-Making to the study of human use of information and information systems is the way in which information is conceptualized. Drawing from the discontinuity assumption, information is conceptualized as that sense created at a specific moment in time-space by one or more humans. Information is not seen as something that exists apart from human behavioral activity. Because there is no direct observation of reality, all observations result from an application of energy from humans in one or more forms.

This is not to say that Sense-Making takes a radical constructivist (sometimes called postmodern) position, assuming that there is no order out there or that there are no tools humans can use to arrive at more comprehensive and more stable pictures of that reality. Rather, it assumes, first, that whatever order is out there is itself potentially discontinuous from time to time and space to space. It also assumes that whatever order is out there is not directly accessible by human observers whose observations are constrained by time, space, and species as well as personal capabilities. Further, it assumes that humans do not have available to them an external standard to which they can turn for an assessment of their truth, either in an absolute or even a relative sense.

The standards humans use for personal as well as collective conduct are themselves constructed and created in interaction. From a Sense-Making perspective, the use of a standard is itself a constructing. One human may wish to judge a moment of information use by a standard he or she calls accuracy while another may wish to judge by expediency or familiarity or comfort. Further, the order that humans live within cannot be seen as given. It is made. Humans by continuing dialogue and sharing of personal observations do arrive at always limited but more stable observations.

What is important about this is what one proposes to study based on one or another set of assumptions about information. If one assumes that information has an existence apart from human construction, one focuses exclusively on transmission questions (e.g., How much information did someone get? Was the information they got accurate? What can we do to be sure people get more accurate information?) rather than on construction questions (e.g., What strategy did that individual apply that led him or her to call that information accurate? What strategy did he or she apply that led to rejecting information another might call accurate? How can we design systems that allow people to apply the criteria they want to their information searches?)

The point here is not to propose that there are no situations under which accuracy questions are ever relevant. Rather, it is to propose that if one assumes that information has existence apart from human observations and has the capacity to provide complete instruction (that is, continuity), then one studies human information use only in that subset of human conditions to which continuity applies.

Information Use as Seen by the Observer Versus the Actor

Directly derived from the preceding discussion is another Sense-Making assumption: that human use of information and information systems needs to be studied from the perspective of the actor, not from the perspective of the observer. Almost all our current research applies an observer perspective. We ask users questions which start from our worlds, not theirs: What of the things we can do would you like us to do? What of the things we now offer do you use? Do you like us? Which of the things we do do you like? Are we convenient for you? How much of what we have is good for you? Would you use this service if we provided it? Are your skills sufficient to use us? And so on.

While some of these questions are more user-oriented than others, all start with a system microscope. They are predicated on the idea that the system is the essential order and the person/user bends to it rather than the other way around. When one presents users with a long list of services and has them check off which ones they want, one has constructed a world for users. The extrapolation from data to practice appears straight-forward, but the examples of the failures of information systems based on such input are legion. The difficulty is that the data tell us nothing about humans and what is real to them and do not show us how people manage to get utility out of systems which systems do not even predict, or how what looks like a failure from the system's perspective is actually a success when seen from the human's eye. The data do not help us understand why a service people said they wanted goes unused, or why as communication tech-nologies spread we appear to be creating a more demarcated world of communication haves and have-nots. The data do not tell us where we might move our system if we are to really serve people on their terms.

Information Use as State Condition Versus Process Condition

Sense-Making focuses on behavior. As such, it assumes that the important things that can be learned about human use of information and information systems must be conceptu-alized as behaviors: the step-takings that human beings undertake to construct sense of their worlds. These step-takings, or communicatings, involve both internal behaviors (comparings, categorizings, likings, dislikings, polarizings, stereotypings, etc.) and exter-nal behaviors (shoutings, ignorings, agreeings, disagreeings, attendings, listenings, etc.).

While almost all social science-guided research now professes a belief in the power of process views of human behavior, in fact little research implements such a view. Usually, the focus is on states and entities rather than process and behavioral strategies and tactics. For example, the typical study will ask who uses an information system and formulate an answer in terms of who the user is, what the user has access to, how con-nected the user is to other users, what skills the user has, and so on. The typical study does not ask what constructed views lead a person to reach out to an information system. In fact, the constructed view is assumed as a constant—a state of information need. The qualities of this state of need are not explored because they are actually not assumed to exist. In a monolithic view of information use as transmission, the state of need is necessarily assumed also to exist monolithically.

The use of state assumptions has numerous consequences for the conduct of research. Typically, for example, information research attempts to predict and explain human use of information and systems based on across-time-space formulations rather than time-space-bound formulations. We focus, for example, on levels of analysis (e.g., interpersonal information exchanges vs. mass media information exchanges) as if they ought to explain differences in behavior. Or, we assume topical contexts as we define them ought to explain the difference (e.g., health information vs. political information vs. science information). Or, we focus on across-time-space characteristics of the person (e.g., demography, personality, skills, resources) as if they ought to explain behavior. In fact, all of these explain very little.

The use of state assumptions has had enormous consequences even for what we think is possible in understanding human information use. It has frequently been charged, for example, that individual behavior vis-à-vis information is too chaotic to expect much from systematic study. Proof here is the frequently low variances accounted for in attempts to predict anything more complicated than habitual patterns of channel use. A result of this assumed chaos is that we find voices calling for two radically different kinds of retreat: one is the retreat to qualitative and highly contextualized understandings of individuals; the other is the retreat from individual to structural understandings.

It is not the purpose of this chapter to suggest that qualitative approaches or structural understandings are not useful. Rather, what is being suggested is that these responses, when framed as ways of handling the chaos of individuality, are consequences of the application of state assumptions. If human information use can best be understood using process assumptions, then attempts to do so using state or entity assumptions will yield limited results. These limited results will suggest that individual behavior is at worst chaotic and at best capricious and recalcitrant. In fact, though, it may be quite systematic if studied from a process perspective.

The difficulty we have is lack of examples that allow us to envision the possibility. Sense-Making assumes there is something systematic about individual behavior when the individual is reconceptualized not as an entity but as an entity behaving at a moment in time-space. It is assumed that the individual constructs ideas of these moments, that these constructings are themselves strategies, that these constructings are sometimes repetitions of ideas used in the past and sometimes newly created because of how the individual defines the new situation. It is further assumed that the individual will implement his or her pictures using behavioral tactics which are responsive to the individual's ideas of the situation. Some of these tactics will again be repetitions of past behaviors, given the rule-based characteristics of much of human behavior. What tactic is used has consequences for the kind of idea created; the kind of idea created has implications for which tactic is used.

This formulation leads to a proposition which states that individual use of information and information systems is responsive to situational conditions as defined by that individual. In essence, the individual defines and attempts to bridge discontinuities or gaps. It is this focus on gap-defining and gap-bridging which is seen as offering a way of introducing order to conceptualizations of individual behavior. It is not the individual entity that is seen as ordered but rather the gap-defining and gap-bridging that is ordered.

What is proposed here is the idea that the essence of the communicating moment is best addressed by focusing on how the actor in the moment defined that moment and attempted to bridge that moment when conceptualized in gap terms. It is assumed that the "gap" idea gets to the essence of the communicating moment both in terms of describing and explaining that moment as seen by the actor and in terms of predicting the behavior of that actor in that moment.

At a specific moment in time-space, therefore, an individual who defines self as facing a gap of a particular kind may use communicating tactics of a particular kind. In a different moment, facing a different gap, he or she may use a different tactic. He or she may, in fact, be very rigid, but the rigidity may be of the kind which says "given this gap, then this tactic." Or, the individual may be very flexible—or perhaps entirely capricious. The point, though, is that by focusing on the gap-defining and gap-bridging we allow to emerge for examination human flexibilities and rigidities and allow the possibility that both are amenable to systematic analysis.

Sense-Making, thus, sets forth the gap idea as a theoretic assumption and as a guiding frame for method: methods of framing questions, methods of interviewing, and methods of analysis. It is proposed that focusing on the gap idea moves research toward a new kind of generalizability, at a more abstract, more fundamental, and more powerful level applicable across situations but at the same time more pertinent and more relevant to specific moments in time-space.

In proposing that by assuming across-time-space constancy we have missed time-space-bound constancy, it is not suggested that there are no across-time-space rigidities or patterns in human use of information and systems. Sense-Making assumes that humans are to varying extents under varying conditions responsive to external constraints on their behavior. Given the law of least effort, for example, we would expect humans to repeat applications of past strategies and tactics to new moments in time-space if these new moments are themselves seen as repetitions of the past. However, since much of human life is inherently unpredictable, much of human behavior involves creating new responses. However, external conditions such as economic class, income, and education are illustrative of the kind of structural constraints which delimit the creating of new responses. To the extent that these external conditions are perceived as operating, we would expect to find constancies across time-space in human behavior. It would be expected, therefore, to find constancies in use of channels (e.g., how much a person uses a library or even reads a particular class of book) more than constancies in use of information (e.g., what a person does with what he or she reads).

An important aspect of this formulation is the idea that communicating behaviors are the link between individuals and structures, institutions, and cultures. While current contests in the social sciences seem to pit individual against structure and conceptualize the structure as an across-time-space entity that persists despite individuals, in fact they are part of a whole. It is a whole we have often missed, in part because just as we have assumed that information-sharing could be conceptualized as transmission or transfer, we have assumed that the relationship between structure and person could be conceptualized as transmission or transfer. Anthropological terms such as "acculturation" arise from such a formulation.

Sense-Making does assume that the individual is situated at cultural/historical moments in time-space and that culture, history, and institutions define much of the world within which the individual lives. Nevertheless, Sense-Making also assumes that the individual's relationship to these moments and the structures that define them is always a matter of self-construction, no matter how nonindividualistic the person or the time-space may seem. Structure is energized by, maintained, reified, changed, and created by individual acts of communicating. Because we have sought only across-time-space understandings, we have missed much of the whole range of human existence that involves struggling with, breaking with, coming to terms with, and changing whatever structure humans find themselves in.

In essence, we have done better at developing understandings of human rigidities than of human creativities. One reason for proposing the use of discontinuity assumptions in the study of human use of information and information systems is that it is in the realm of information behavior that we ought to find humans at their most creative, least constrained by external forces, because so much of individual information use is private.

THE METHODOLOGY AND ITS METHODS

In the most general sense, the methodological approach that is called Sense-Making is an approach to studying the constructing that humans do to make sense of their experiences. For our purposes in this chapter, the experiences we want to study are experiences relevant to information and communication system design, management, and practice.

There is no direct way we can point to standard genres in the literature and say that this is the focus of Sense-Making. It is true that the approach has been used to construct studies of aspects of experience which systems (and the researchers hired by these systems) call information need, satisfaction, or image studies. What this means is that Sense-Making has been used to study human sense-making in situations where humans reached out for something they called information, used something they saw as a potential source and judged whether it helped or not, or created an idea about an institution based on experience with the institution.

Sense-Making is seen, thus, as a generalizable methodology developed for the study of all situations that involve communicating. It is implemented in all studies with a simple operational metaphor, derived directly from the discontinuity or gap idea pictured in Figure 14.1. While it can be applied to entities other than individual human entities (e.g., collectivities), it will for purposes here be applied to individual behavior.

Assume a human being taking steps through experiences: each moment, a new step. The step may be a repetition of past behavior, but it is always theoretically a new step because it occurs in a new moment in time-space. Assume a moment of discontinuity in which step-taking turns from free-flowing journey to stop. Focus on the individual at this moment of discontinuity, this stop which does not permit the individual, in his or her own perception, to move forward without constructing a new or changed sense. Determine how the individual interprets and bridges this moment: what strategy he or she used to define the situation which was the gap; how he or she conceptualized the discontinuity as gap and the bridge across it; how he or she moved tactically to bridge the gap; how he or she proceeded with the journey after crossing the bridge.

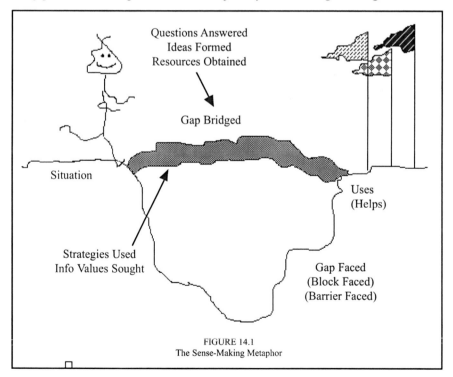

FIGURE 14.1
The Sense-Making Metaphor

This metaphor constructs the Sense-Making Triangle of situation-gap-help/use, pictured in Figure 14.2. As an individual moves through an experience, each moment is potentially a sense-making moment. The essence of that sense-making moment is assumed to be addressed by focusing on how the actor defined and dealt with the situation, the gap, the bridge, and the continuation of the journey after crossing the bridge.

The metaphor is a highly abstract one seen as applying at all levels (intrapersonal, interpersonal, small group, organizational, mass, telecommunication, database, societal) of information use and information-seeking and in all contexts (health, political, scientific, instructional, etc.). It directs attention to the steps the actor takes as defined on the actor's own terms to address the gaps he or she faces as defined on his or her own terms. It is not intended to suggest that all situation-facing is linear or purposive. When seen from the actor's perspective, time can be constructed in a variety of ways, linear, cyclically, and otherwise. Also, situation-facing may or not be goal-oriented in the usual sense. Sense-Making assumes that there is always a mandate to cope with self even if

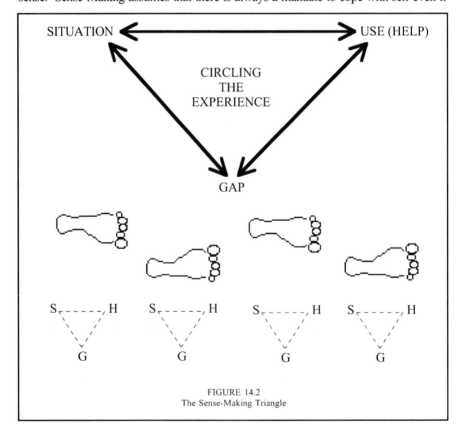

FIGURE 14.2
The Sense-Making Triangle

the purpose in the situation is defined by the individual as forgetting self or losing control of self. Nor does the method enforce any idea of correct divisions of situations into moments. Given the discontinuity assumption, the moments are seen as vehicles for examining gap-defining and gap-bridging, not representations of reality as it is.

As was noted previously, the Sense-Making approach is applied throughout the research process in framing questions, in collecting data, and in analyzing data. All of these are part and parcel of the same holistic process. Sense-Making methods show most clearly in collecting data, so this will be the focus of this section. The approach's impact on the framing of research questions, as was illustrated in this chapter's first section; the impact on the analysis of data will be illustrated in the third section.

Sense-Making provides a theory of how to conduct interviews with respondents. It is seen as applicable both to formalized and extended interviews in research studies as well as the less formalized and often briefer interviews during which the institution intersects with its users or potential users to provide service. Both of these interview situations are seen as requiring implementation based on gap assumptions. Our focus in this section is on research interviews.

Showing the variety of Sense-Making interviewing methods requires that we start with the core method, the one which is most clearly theoretically derived and most isomorphic with the Sense-Making assumptions. This is called the Micro-Moment Time-Line Interview. An example of such an interview is presented in Figure 14.3. In the Micro-Moment Interview, the respondent is asked to reconstruct a situation in terms of what happened in the situation (the time-line steps). The respondent is then asked to describe each step in detail. The core focus of the description is directed to the Sense-Making Triangle, circling the micro-moment in terms of how the actor saw the situation, the gap, and the help he or she wanted—that is, where he/she wanted to land after crossing the bridge. What additional elements are examined and what elements are stressed depend on research purposes.

In studies of *information needs*, emphasis has been placed on understanding how the individual saw self as stopped, what questions or confusions he or she defined, what strategies he or she preferred for arriving at answers, what success he or she had in arriving at answers, how he or she was helped by answers (i.e., how he or she put the answers to use), and what barriers he or she saw standing in the way to arriving at answers. The situations or experiences which have been the foci of interviews directed at needs assessment have been ones pertinent to the service mandate of the institution. In a study for a public library, for example, the situations involved all everyday-need experiences, situations in which the actor needed an answer to one or more questions, for example. In a study for a blood center, the situations involved each donor's last experience with donating. In a study of cancer patients, the situations involved each patient's most difficult treatment session. In a study of users of television programming guides, the situations involved each viewer's last use of such a guide.[3]

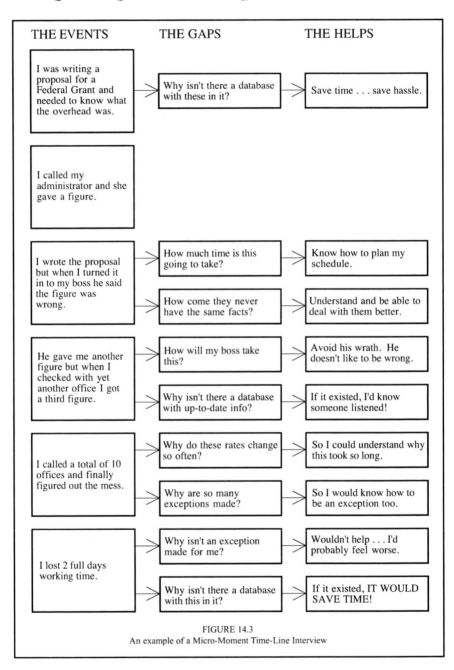

FIGURE 14.3
An example of a Micro-Moment Time-Line Interview

In contrast, studies of *satisfactions* with an institution have focused on descriptions of the actor's last (in other studies, worst, best, most memorable, and so on) use of the institution from the time when the possibility of use came to mind. Again, time-line interviews focus at each step on the Sense-Making Triangle. A satisfaction study focuses more emphasis, however, on what helps actors sought and what ones they found, what barriers they saw standing in the way, what they saw as causing barriers, what barriers they got around, and the ways the institution or its representatives helped in this process. Again, situations which are the focus of the interview are selected to fit research purposes. In studies for public libraries, for example, situations have focused on the user's last use, worst use, or most remembered use. In a study for an archdiocese, respondents were asked to recollect situations in which they were helped by the church, and situations in which they were hindered by the church.[4]

As a third example, studies of *images* of institutions have examined the most recent situation in which the institution was in the actor's consciousness via contact, conversation, media, or simply memory. Again, the Sense-Making Triangle is used to focus attention, with special emphasis placed on what ideas the actor saw self as having as a result of this most recent situation of consciousness and what impacts these ideas had on his or her behavior (that is, how she or he made the ideas useful).[5]

In each of these research genres, Sense-Making is focused on different elements, depending on the research purpose. For each of them, the respondent is asked to reconstruct different situations, again depending on the purpose. What is common to all, however, is that the respondent is focused on real experiences. While these experiences can be infinitely variable across respondents, they are given systematic order because recollections are guided in terms of the Sense-Making Metaphor and focused on gap-defining and gap-bridging.

A number of derivative interviewing methods have been developed to suit different purposes. One of these is the Abbreviated Time-Line Interview, in which respondents are asked to focus on only one (e.g., the worst, the best, the most important, the most troublesome) step, or question, help, or barrier. This interviewing method is useful particularly in research situations involving routine or habitual behavior, where the depth and detail of the Micro-Moment Interview would be unwarranted.

Another approach, called the *Helps Chaining Interview*, focuses on how the respondent constructs the connection between information, system, or structure and self. Here the respondent is asked to chain his or her answers to the query: How did (the library, book, database, article, etc.) help you? The chaining involves repeated queries to the respondent of the type "And, how did that help you?" until the respondent feels the statement of help has been made in the most personal and life-relevant terms.

Another approach is *Message Q/uing* in which the intent is to utilize respondent sense-making to understand and/or improve specific messages, such as software manuals. Here the respondent is asked to focus on elements of a message which involved gap-defining and/or gap-bridging in some way. The element may have led the respondent to have an idea, or face a confusion, and so on.

These four examples of interviewing approaches do not constitute all the approaches developed to date. They do provide the major examples, however. An important element in all of them is that the respondent is conceptualized as a colleague. No element of the study purpose is hidden in any way. Frequently, respondents are involved in a quite lengthy process during which they are taught many aspects of the interviewing approach so they can control the pace of the interview itself. At first, some respondents and some interviewers balk at the approach. Interviewers balk because they want to be more directive and need assistance in learning how to redirect the respondent to the Sense-Making Metaphor and how to assist the respondent in reconstructing their sense-makings. Respondents, on the other hand, need assistance in learning how to present all the personally important details that they wish while at the same time utilizing the interview structure. The relationship is presented as a quid pro quo and results to date suggest that the large majority of respondents accept it as such. Using the approach, studies have successfully utilized phone interviews which lasted well beyond the accepted fifteen-to-twenty minute average which survey researchers say is the maximum tolerated time. In many studies, respondents have volunteered to be interviewed again. Results suggest that there is, when Sense-Making interviews are at their best, a consciousness-raising and therapeutic value in the process for respondents.

EXEMPLARS

Exemplar studies were selected for presentation here to illustrate important elements in the preceding discussions. Exemplars are used to illustrate the genres of research to which Sense-Making has been applied, namely studies of information needs, images, and satisfactions. Exemplars are also used to demonstrate the use of Sense-Making in descriptive work, in system design, and in hypothesis-testing work. In addition, these exemplars show the use of the approach to yield data that are dealt with primarily in what has been traditionally called qualitative terms (e.g., as case studies) as well as to yield data which were then further analyzed via content analytic and other tools to yield systematic results. Further, although it is a rare application, the exemplars present studies which have been primarily close-ended, asking respondents to describe which of a series of gap-bridging and gap-defining categories describes their situations best.

Any given study can serve more than one exemplar function, of course, so the selected studies follow one after the other, with each described in terms of the different ways in which it illuminates the points previously listed. Six studies in all are described from the set of forty or more studies done to date.

Exemplar One

In a study for the California State Library, the research purpose was to identify the "information needs" of Californians and to elaborate ways libraries could usefully help with these needs.[6] Black, Asian, Hispanic, and Anglo individuals were asked to describe step-by-step what happened to them in the most important recent troublesome situation they faced. For each step, they were then asked to indicate what questions they had. They were further asked to select the most important question they had and, for this question, to indicate whether they got an answer and how the answer helped. Each of these elements was seen as the implementing of communicatings by the individual—definings of gaps and actings to face "gappiness." Here are excerpts from a sample interview of an eighteen-year-old female:

The time-line

Step 1:	*I quit school because I got pregnant.*
Step 2:	*I had the baby one month ago.*
Step 3:	*I didn't know whether to go back to school or not.*
Step 4:	*I am only 18 and my folks thought it was important.*
Step 5:	*I live at home so I have no expenses and my mother babysits for me.*
Step 6:	*So I am going back to school.*

Questions asked

At step 3:	*How important is returning to school?*
At step 4:	*How much do I really want to go back?*

Analysis of most important question (question at step 3)
How got answer: *My own thinking and parents' advice.*
How did answer help: *Made me feel better about me. Got me started toward going back to school.*

The study classified, using content analysis, ways in which individuals conceptualized themselves as stopped or hindered in these situations and hypothesized that these conceptualizations would be a better predictor of information-seeking (question asking) and using (how the individual applied answers to gaps, that is, how they were helped) than race. Thus, for example, it was assumed that two individuals, one White, one Black, both of whom saw themselves as being dragged down roads not of their own choosing, would be like each other communicatively at that moment. They contrasted with two individuals, both Black, one of whom saw self as being dragged down a road not of his or her own choosing and the other of whom saw self as faced with a host of alternative roads from which to choose. The hypothesis was confirmed.

Some kinds of communicating are highly constrained by the kind of socio-economic forces for which race is constructed as a descriptor of human entities. It was found that while race did not predict information-seeking in terms of questions asked, it did predict, in interaction with gap-definings, what channels or sources individuals used to get answers.

In addition to the data used for hypothesis testing, results of this study provided a large amount of descriptive data regarding the nature of need situations, the kind of questions people had, the barriers they saw to question-answering, the strategies they used to get answers, the success they had with different strategies, the helps they wanted from answers, the barriers they saw as standing between them and getting help. Essentially the same approach to information needs assessment has been applied in a wide variety of contexts, for example, with Hmong refugees regarding their health information needs, with cancer patients regarding their information needs while undergoing treatment, and with blood donors regarding their information needs pertaining to donating blood.

When researchers are interested in quantification of their qualitative results, each specific study context can involve its own detailed set of content analytic categories. Blood donors often ask, "Will I faint?" Cancer patients ask, "Will I die?" Citizens facing everyday situations ask, "How long will it take me to handle this?" Much of the quantitative work of Sense-Making studies, to date, has also focused on developing generic categories to describe needs, barriers, and helps wanted—categories which are universal in the sense that they pertain to gap-bridging and gap-defining across situations while at the same time capturing important aspects of particular situations.

Across studies, these category schemes have stabilized. Several examples will be given here. To capture the ways in which humans see their journeys blocked, a set of categories has been developed under the label *situation stops*. Among the categories in this schema are these stops: the decision stop, where the human sees two or more roads ahead; the barrier stop, where the human sees one road ahead but something or someone stands on the road blocking the way; the spin-out stop, where the human sees self as having no road; the wash-out stop, where the human sees self as on a road that suddenly disappears; the problematic stop, where the human sees self as being dragged down a road not of his or her own choosing.

To capture the questions people ask in situations in terms of universal gap-definings, these categories have been developed to capture human attempts to bridge gaps relating to characteristics of self, characteristics of others, characteristics of objects or events, the reasons or causes of events, the consequences of actions or events, the connections between things. The foci of these questions change depending on whether the individuals are defining gaps they see in the past, present, or future.

To capture the ways in which people put answers to questions to use, these *help* categories have been developed: creating ideas, finding directions or ways to move, acquiring skills, getting support or confirmation, getting motivated, getting connected to others, calming down or relaxing, getting pleasure or happiness, and reaching goals.

These three examples illustrate content analysis schemes that have been developed across a series of studies to capture the gap-defining and gap-bridging aspects of situation-facing. Sense-Making theory leads to predictions, for example, that the ways in which people see their gaps will be related to the ways in which they try to bridge them and not to characteristics of persons independent of the gaps. Results to date confirm this prediction. Such findings are seen as potentially applicable to system design not only in terms of how practitioners interact with users to determine their needs but also in terms of actual elements of the design of information storage and retrieval systems. For example, a portrait of how a book was seen as helpful to the past ten readers may be a more useful retrieval device for the next reader than traditional categories. An information agency should have better success in educating its mandated public if it gives the public control of the entry point to the information exchange. This becomes possible if the users can enter the system in terms of the questions they have.

Exemplar Two

In a study of information-seeking by blood donors, donors were asked to describe their donating situations in terms of what happened, what questions they had during the process, and how they hoped answers to their questions would help them.[7] Again, responses from the donors were conceptualized as strategies of gap-defining and tactics of gap-facing. Excerpts from a sample interview follow:

The time-line and questions at each step

Step 1:   *We were told we could get extra credit in health class for donating.*
        Q1:   *How much did I have to give?*
        Q2:   *What are the procedures?*

Step 2:   *A friend who had donated told me about it so a friend and I decided to donate.*
        Q1:   *How long would it take?*
        Q2:   *Would it hurt?*
        Q3:   *How big is the needle?*
        Q4:   *How much blood do I have to give?* (Skipping to step 7)

Step 7:   *The nurse called me in and I didn't know what was going on.*
        Q1:   *What are they going to do?*
        Q2:   *What is all this equipment for if they are just going to take my blood?* (Skipping down to last step, 11)

Step 11:   *After eight minutes I went to the canteen for cookies and juice.*

In-depth analysis of Q2, step 7
How easy was it to get an answer to this question? *1* (on a 1–10 scale)
Did you ever get an answer to this question? *No*
Why? *Because they didn't tell me anything. They just did it.*
How would the answer have helped? *I wouldn't have been scared or in suspense wondering what they were going to do?*

A battery of different predictors were compared in terms of their power to predict how donors wanted to be helped by information: across-time-space measures (e.g., demography), a priori time-space measures (e.g., interests and focus of attention at the moment of entering the donating situation), and time-space-bound measures (e.g., how the donors defined their gaps and how they acted to face them). Results showed that across-time-space and a priori time-space measures accounted for an average of only 3% of the variance in several criterion measures tapping how donors wanted information to help. In contrast, time-space-bound measures accounted for an average of 17%.

Detailed qualitative analysis of the primary statistical patterns showed that each step in the donating process had its own characteristic pattern of information-seeking and using. Based on these results, a design was constructed to provide a user-friendly computerized question-answering system at five different points during the donating process. Typical questions at each point were to be displayed on the screen of a terminal. Donors would simply touch the question of interest to them and they could then choose from a variety of question-answering strategies. For example, two donors, each asking the same question—"Will I faint?"—could choose to select answers from doctors, or other donors, or statistical counts, or any combination.

Exemplar Three

A public library with a large number of Hispanic citizens on its mandated patron roster searched for ways to entice the Hispanics into the library.[8] Previously, a number of study approaches were tested and met with hostility. The traditional methods of publicity had failed. The Sense-Making project focused on users of the library's audiovisual services and serendipitously provided a breakthrough for serving the Hispanic community. One study asked thirty randomly selected recent users what happened that brought them to the library, what they got while there, and how they were helped. A second study asked sixty-four randomly selected borrowers of library videotapes how the specific videotapes they used helped them. Here are excerpts from two examples from the second study:

Example #1
What was the title of the video taped borrowed? *Ghandi.*

How did the video help? *It helped me set some positive goals and not give up until we succeed.*

Example #2
What was the title of the video tape borrowed? *Rumpelstiltskin.*
How did the video help? *This move let me sit down and watch television with my children. It was a movie they picked. They decided on the movie and the time for themselves. The movie makes my children ask questions about what is real.*

Librarians reported that for the first time they had conducted interviews with Hispanic patrons and not been met with hostility. They learned that their videotape checkout service was providing these patrons with important helps. Further, the videotapes pointed to a link for these patrons with other library services—literacy training, for example, and how-to-do-it books. One librarian summed it up: "It helped us see patrons from a different point of view, to understand them better, and to be better able to tolerate the crowds around the audio-visual desk." The library staff decided to move funds from other services to video services.

Exemplar Four

In a study of images of an institution, a random sample of 1,006 residents of a city were asked about their last contact with that institution and what that contact involved.[9] They were asked what ideas that contact led them to have and what impact they saw each idea as having on their thinking about, talking about, and relating to the institution. The study was an attempt to understand public images regarding the institution and the effects interactions with and/or awareness of the institution had. All elements—situation definitions, images, and effects—were conceptualized in consonance with the Sense-Making formulation as *hows*, the hows of the situation-defining and gap-facing. Two sample interviews follow:

Example #1
Nature of last contact: *I passed the building when I was downtown.*
Idea that resulted from this contact: *How come they get to have such a big building?*
Impact from this idea: *I think of them as not being good members of the community. I wouldn't be lenient with them in a pinch.*

Example #2
Nature of last contact: *I talked to someone who worked there.*
Idea that result from this contact: *They treat the people who work there badly.*
Impact from this idea: *I don't want to use their service or have any contact with them.*

A comparison of what best predicted images and effects showed that situation was far more powerful as a predictor than demography. Thus, for example, two citizens, one old and one young, both of whom had contact involving interpersonal interactions with employees who worked at the institution, were likely to share the same ideas about the institution and to see themselves as affected by these ideas in the same way.

For this particular institution, results showed that citizens whose last consciousness of the institution involved coming to the idea that the institution treated its employees badly were significantly more likely to report that they were explicitly avoiding use of the institution as a result. The results pointed, therefore, to specific changes the institution had to make in itself if it were to change its image.

Exemplar Five

College students' information-seeking and use in a series of twelve different situations was compared.[10] The situations were created by pitting three situational dimensions against each other. One dimension focused on how the individual defined his or her status in the situation (low or high). A second focused on how the individual defined the openness of communication in the situation (open or closed). A third focused on how the individual saw self as stopped: as having to choose between two or more roads seen ahead, as having to cope with being dragged down a road not of his or her own choosing, or as having to follow another more experienced person down the road.

Each person was asked to recall a time when he or she was in a situation of each type: for example, where he or she had low status, was making a decision, and communication was open; or a time when he or she had low status, was making a decision, but communication was closed. In this way, all individuals were asked to report on twelve situations and, for each, were asked to indicate what questions they had in the situations and what ways they wanted to be helped.

Again, all elements were conceptualized as communicating strategies and tactics. A predictive analysis showed that situational measures predicted information-seeking and use. The important finding was that neither demography nor the individual as state entity did so. No statistically significant consistency was found in information-seeking and use in terms of individual behavior across the twelve situations. Rather, how the individual defined the situation predicted how the individual faced it, thus supporting a hypothesis derived from Sense-Making theory.

Exemplar Six

In a study of southeast Asian refugee health information needs, intact groups of southeast Asians were interviewed in bilingual settings using the Sense-Making format.[11] Respondents were allowed to talk in their native language or in English, as they wished. The group facilitator translated. The refugees were asked to recall their recent visits to a hospital or clinic, to describe the events, and for each event describe the questions they had, whether they got answers, and how. Here are the results of the interview with one respondent, a thirty-five-year-old female whose first visit to a United States hospital was to have a baby:

> **Situation 1:** *The last time I went to the hospital is I have my baby and then after I have my baby the doctor and nurse bring me cold water. So that in my culture that's different and I keep asking them about the question: Why the people that has new baby they keep drinking very cold water?*

> **Situation 2:** *After I have my baby, I am very new, my body is changing and they let me take a walk every two hours or three hours. I keeping thinking that my body is new and that I'm so tired so that they're doing these things and it's so hard for me to understand. And also I think that many things in my body is not wrong and there is no illness but I just have a bay and I am thinking that in a few days I'll get better. I'll get strong but the doctor say you have to walk and I was thinking: Why he say this?*

Case-study results of the project were useful in helping medical practitioners serving the new refugees answer their patients' questions about medical services. Alternatively, they were useful in tempering and changing medical practitioner demands on the new patients.

CONCLUSIONS

The six exemplars just presented are only a few of the more than forty different Sense-Making studies conducted to date. Studies have been conducted with a wide variety of populations (e.g., preschool children, teenagers, doctoral students, developmentaly disabled adults) pertaining to their information needs in a variety of situations (e.g., health, environment, politics, science, childcare, education, finances, leisure time, everyday life) and their interactions with a wide variety of communication systems (e.g., libraries, databases, media, books, newspapers, software manuals) for a wide variety of institutions (e.g., California State Library, National Cancer Institute, Ohio Department of Health).

    The intent here has been to present a representative sampling of a methodological approach which has been widely applied to research questions relating to human use of information and information systems but which is itself conceptualized as a generalized methodological approach for the study of any situation in which one wishes to focus on how people construct sense of their experiences.

Having presented the preceding discussion and exemplars, it is now possible to address the aspect of Sense-Making which brings it into this volume—the qualitative nature of the approach. The issue of quantitative versus qualitative approaches to the study of human behavior is one of a set of interrelated issues which have come to be known as the ferment in the social sciences, or the paradigm crisis.[12] These include, among others, the issues of theoretic versus applied research, individualistic versus structural research, and administrative (serving established institutions) versus critical (criticizing institutions) research, as well as qualitative versus quantitative.

The presence of "versus" in these ferment descriptions generally implies that the researcher must choose between one or the other: theoretic *or* applied, individualistic *or* structural, administrative *or* critical. Although the arguments cannot be fully developed in this chapter, Sense-Making as an approach has explicitly cast itself in the middle as all of the above. It is theoretic because it sets out to test hypothetical propositions and is itself based on a coherent set of theoretic premises and assumptions. It is applied because the work is directly applicable to information system management, design, and practice. In fact, in its focus on communicating behaviors, Sense-Making sets out explicitly to develop theoretic understanding directly useful to practice; to be, in effect, a theory of practice. Sense-Making is individualistic in its focus because it acknowledges that individual humans are the carriers of communicative action, the acts by which meaning is made and systems are energized. But it is also structural, because it acknowledges that individuals live in and embody structures and have varying degrees of consciousness of this. The approach is administrative, in that it sets out to improve systems, and critical because it serves as a vehicle for the users of those systems to speak to those systems on their own terms. In essence, the approach attempts to provide a vehicle for giving voices to users and potential users of systems so that the systems can be responsive to them.

In the argument between qualitative and quantitative approaches to research, Sense-Making likewise refuses to choose a side. It is explicitly both qualitative and quantitative. Even more important, Sense-Making does not see any of these choices (e.g., qualitative vs. quantitative, administrative vs. critical) as legitimate or binding choices, but rather as polarizations that have at least in part resulted from specious understandings of the nature of research growing out of the application of weak and limiting assumptions of the nature of human information behaviors.

To illustrate this argument, return to the idea that the behavior of individuals can look chaotic if one keeps looking for constancy in the wrong place, as carried by entity rather than by process. Given an assumed chaotic individuality, it becomes rather easy to frame qualitative research approaches, particularly those forms of qualitative research which are proposed as having to be systematically unsystematic, as the necessary response. Sense-Making, on the other hand, assumes there is something systematic about individual behavior to be found by pursuing process orientations. In this way, then, Sense-Making casts itself as systematic qualitative research, an approach with qualitative sensitivity which is amenable to the systematic power of quantitative analysis.

To understand this more fully, it is necessary to examine the several meanings of the word *qualitative* which apply to Sense-Making. One of these is fundamental to the theory of Sense-Making: the assumption that human use of information and information systems *is* qualitative, not monolithic. This implements the discontinuity assumption. Information is not seen as something that describes a given reality in an absolute and potentially accurate way, which can't be transmitted from source to receiver through channels, which can be counted by external standards and pigeon-holed for all time. Rather, information is constructed. The act of constructing and the act of using that which is constructed is a qualitative act. It varies in kinds.

Sense-Making assumes that the essential aspects of information use can be captured by looking at qualities of gap-defining and gap-bridging. A person in a moment defines that moment as a particular kind of gap, constructs a particular strategy for facing the moment, and implements that strategy with a particular tactic. Gap-defining and gap-bridging become, therefore, the essential qualitative aspects to be examined.

A second way in which Sense-Making is qualitative is that its implementation in method is at least in part what we usually term *qualitative*. This is a given based on the assumption, set forth earlier, that method is residual of theoretic assumption. Sense-Making methods, therefore, yield data which are identifiable as qualitative. It consists of open-ended responses to questions, for example, and can be constructed as case studies, records, or interactions with messages, and so on. In the few studies which have been entirely close-ended, the close-endedness has involved respondent assessments of qualities of gap-defining and gap-bridging.

What is different about Sense-Making, however, is that the qualitative data-collection and analysis methods are all guided by the same general theory of what is appropriate to capture in these qualitative analyses. This theory introduces, therefore, a means of systematization across qualitative analyses.

NOTES

1.   References to Sense-Making studies are incorporated throughout this chapter. For the most recent published pieces, see: Dervin (1989a, 1989b), Dervin and Nilan (1986). The most comprehensive description to date is available from the author as: Dervin (1983b).

2.   Sense-Making as an approach rests heavily on the work of Richard Carter. See, in particular: Carter (1973, 1974b, 1980, 1989b); Carter, Ruggels, Jackson, and Heffner (1973). Sense-Making owes a debt, as well, to the works

of: Bruner (1973), Delia (1977a), Freire (1970), Geertz (1973), Giddens (1984), Habermas (1984, 1987b), Jackins (1973), and Krippendorff (1989).

3. For information needs assessments directed to public libraries, see, in particular: Atwood and Dervin (1981), Dervin and Clark (1987). For information needs assessments of blood donors, see, in particular: Dervin, Jacobson, and Nilan (1982); Dervin, Nilan, and Jacobson (1981). Those interested in the study of users of TV programming guides are referred to Dias (1990).

4. For Sense-Making designed accountability studies of public libraries, see, in particular: Dervin and Clark (1987), and Dervin and Fraser (1985).

5. Brief reports on image studies are included in references listed in note 1.

6. Atwood and Dervin (1981).

7. Dervin et al. (1981, 1982).

8. Dervin and Clark (1987), pp. 211–230.

9. Dervin (1989a).

10. Nilan (1985).

11. Wittet (1983).

12. Particularly helpful to the author in developing this section have been: Carter (1989a); Ferment in the Field [Special Issue], *Journal of Communication, 33*(3) (Summer 1983); Giddens (1989); and Hall (1989).

Chapter 15

Information as Non-Sense;
Information as Sense:
The Communication Technology Connection

Brenda Dervin

> *This . . . is a tale of a stately ship adrift in . . . [an] unforgiving sea . . . . We're awash in a sea of information. (Brown, 1991)*

> *There once was a monkey and a fish who were best friends. A terrible storm came and churned the river and the fish was tossed about violently. The monkey was beside himself with worry for his friend. He saw a low branch that spanned across the river and jumped on it. Reaching down, he pulled his friend from the water. "There, there, my friend, now you are safe." (Old West-African fable)*

> *We have to cure ourselves of the itch for absolute knowledge and power. We have to close the distance between the push-button order and the human act. We have to touch people. (Bronowski, 1973)*

The tragedy of the new information/communication technologies is this. The enormous capacities that these technologies offer for assisting humans in the flexible handling of information/communication processes remain virtually untapped. Instead, we use these technologies to do what we have always done in the past, only in far greater quantities, faster, and at greater distances. And, of course, we are necessarily multiplying with consonant geometry any errors of the past.[1]

On the one hand, these technologies have been heralded as offering the species an exponential leap in the quality of information processing and, by implication, the quality of the human condition assumed to be consequentially improved. Yet, on the other, as the evidence begins to come in, we are faced with unfulfilled expectations. Automation

This work originally appeared as: Dervin, B. (1991). Information as non-sense; information as sense: The communication technology connection. In H. Bouwman, P. Nelissen, & M. Voojis (Eds.), *Tussen vraag en aanbod: Optimalisering van de informatievoorziening* (pp. 44–59). Amsterdam, Holland: Otto Cramwinckel Uitgever. Reprinted by permission of Otto Cramwinckel Uitgever, Amsterdam, Holland. Contains material presented as: Dervin, B. (1991, March). *Information as sense; information as non-sense: The communication connection.* Keynote address presented at Sommatie '91: Netherlands Communication Association annual meeting, Veldhoven, Netherlands.

has not made the workplace more efficient and effective; computerization in the schools has not produced a more educated citizenry; speeding news across the globe has not yielded a journalism more cognizant of human needs; being able to access larger quantities of research has not resulted in a cure of cancer or AIDS; providing easy access to academic literature has not improved educational practice. While we now move money, conceptualized as information, with alarming speed; while we wage more efficient, speedier war; while the privileged connect via computer networks daily; indicators suggest that the technologies are reifying and exasperating social inequities worldwide. The contributions of the new technologies to this state of affairs is double-barreled: They serve the massive movement of monetary resources with the attendant impact of this speed on those whose money is moved; and, they serve as well the bifurcation of peoples into those who are and those who are not traveling in the new technology fast lane.

As serious as the contribution of the new technologies to exasperating inequities is, at a higher level of abstraction the more serious problem, the theoretic problem, is the illusion that these technologies provide that they allow us to be better informed simply because they move something we call information about in ways that we think are more powerful. Power here is defined as more of the same, at faster speeds, and from more remote locations. It is this illusion, for example, that leads to the idea that merely providing computer hardware will bring a ghetto school into the technology fast lane. It is this illusion that dooms most such well-intentioned efforts to failure.

The purpose of this chapter is to examine this illusion—to focus on conceptualizations of the concept "information." Most often this concept is invoked as one might invoke a deity. A kinder challenge, perhaps, would be that the concept is invoked as one would a primitive term in the scientific enterprise—a term which has such consensual meaning that definition is considered unnecessary.[2] In brief overview, the argument put forth in this chapter is that traditional conceptualizations of information focus on information as a thing which is either transmitted, manufactured, or processed. The position presented in this chapter is that in order to make the term more useful in the arena of human affairs, the term must be reconceptualized in communication terms.

TRADITIONAL CONCEPTUALIZATIONS OF INFORMATION

Most approaches to the concept of *information* are based on a single central idea—that information describes something real about reality and, therefore, reduces the uncertainty of reality. Starting with this central idea[3] most treatments of the concept of information have been built on two complimentary derivative ideas.[4]

One is statistical in which information is measured as uncertainty or error reduction in much the same way that one measures the reduction in random error offered by the statistical relationship between two variables. Here, instead of variables we focus on a source and receiver and the extent to which transmission reduces noise between them. The second derivative idea is metaphorical. It conceptualizes information as a thing, a commodity which has value, which can be moved from place to place, which can be manufactured, and which can be processed. These core ideas form the foundation on which most efforts to use the new technologies to improve information processing rest. One useful—and often used—example of such an application is the decision matrix. Here, information on present conditions, alternative actions, and possible outcomes are specified and technology is used to search out optimum paths.

What is common to these standard approaches to information is that human beings are incidental to the conceptualization. They are present only as empty vessels or buckets into which information can be dropped. Sometimes the metaphor extends to conceptualizing the human as a machine that processes the commodity. In this case, the metaphor incorporates both ideas relating to transportation as well as ideas relating to manufacturing.

There are a substantial number of criticisms available of these standard treatments of information. These criticisms are complex and variable but a diagonal cut through them shows that they all challenge that the standard treatments ignore the communicative aspects of human information sharing. It is challenged, for example, that standard conceptualizations ignore such commonly understood phenomena as: There is no information sharing between humans without the use of language; all the processes by which humans construct sense of their world and attempt to share it with others are constrained by human pre-suppositions and acculturation; while decision matrices may optimize decisions, humans in experiential practice do not.

In essence, these criticisms suggest that since humans are less than perfect information processors, we must give up models which assume otherwise. It is important to note that even getting to this understanding has involved an enormous step forward. This chapter concurs: We need to re-examine and diversify our models of information. This chapter diverges, however, by suggesting that we replace the less-than-perfect-information-processor model of the human being with a model which sees differences in human observing as strength rather than weakness. The remainder of this chapter attempts to accomplish three goals. One is to trace a logic that leads to this conclusion. The second is to suggest that such a reorientation could be actualized in practice because of the enormous flexibilities that the new information technologies offer. The third is to set forth a vision of potentialities offered by such a reconceptualization.

Before embarking on this journey, it is important to emphasize that it is not the purpose here to suggest that conceptualization of information-as-thing is an entirely unuseful framing. It is such a framing, for example, that allows us to observe that inequities are being exasperated. Such a statement cannot be made unless one posits a standard for comparison. However, it is a major point of this chapter that while the information-as-thing idea allows us to diagnose the problem, its application in research prevents us from identifying and applying alternative solutions.

COMMUNICATION IDEAS ABOUT INFORMATION

In order to set forth communication ideas about information, we need to address the issue of the human capacity to make statements which say something real about reality. This is, of course, a topic which has been and remains a subject of intense philosophical debate. It is beyond the purpose of this chapter to trace the various positions. Rather, this chapter will set forth one position as an example of what a *communication* position might look like.

Embedded in the presentation above are three framings:

1. *humans can make statements of what is real about reality (and call this information);*

2. *humans can make such statements but they are always constrained and limited by the imperfections of human observing and human use of language; and*

3. *humans can make such statements but these statements will show variabilities linked to differences in time, place, and discourse.*[5]

Each of these positions implies a different set of theories about the nature of reality and the nature of human observing. The first of the framings—humans can make statements of what is real about reality—assumes that reality has a fixedness and that humans have the capacity for isomorphic observation. What is most interesting about this framing is that while few ascribe to the position, even among the most hardcore of scientists, the position is embodied everywhere in daily experiential practice. Even scientists who operate within the legacy of logical positivism take great pains to speak about the language with which they describe reality rather than reality itself. Yet, the procedural canons of the communication of bench science do not incorporate even this small recognition of the difference between isomorphic observation and communicative observation. In terms that will become clearer later in this chapter, journals mandate authors to use primarily one strategy for sense-making reality—a factizing strategy. While practice may not align with common understanding, suffice it to say that a long legacy of philosophical discussion has arrived at the now virtually consensual position that humans do not observe reality directly and that the linguistic statements made by human beings are not isomorphic with reality.

This moves us to the second framing—that humans can make statements about what they see as real in reality but these statements are always constrained and limited by the imperfections of human observing and human use of language. This position has traditionally been anchored from a tradition within psychology which posits human perception in terms of selectivity processes. The fundamental idea is that humans are less than perfect observers—they selectively attend, perceive, retain, and recall.

Some of the limitations on human observing are seen as attributable to the species. Humans, for example, have physiological limitations to their observing capabilities. And, constrained as each human is to observing at a specific moment in time-space, humans do not have the capacity attributable to an all-powerful god of observing without the constraints of perspective. Further, it is assumed that the situation is made even more complicated because humans can transmit their observations only through the limiting tool of language. Some of the limitations are ascribed with variability across members of the species. Humans differ in their physiological capacities. They differ in their cognitive capacities. They differ in their observing skills. They differ in their language using capacities. For the limitations ascribed to the species, humans quest the development of more powerful observing technologies. For the limitations ascribed to individual variability, humans call for wider distribution of technologies (both soft as in education and training, and hard as in computer hardware) in order to equalize abilities. The entire group of assumptions which accompany the human-as-imperfect-observer framing form an interesting intersection. They appear on the surface to acknowledge a communication perspective. Yet, they still imply a fixed reality which somehow given the proper technologies humans could fix isomorphically in their linguistic statements about that reality. It is this intersection which leads so artfully to the enterprise of cognitive science, for example, and to the continued use of both the transportation and manufacturing metaphors in conceptualizations of information.

This brings us to the third framing used for purposes of this chapter—humans can make statements that they consider to be about what is real in reality but these statements will show enormous variabilities across different observers and these variabilities can be conceptualized as linked to differences in the times, places, and discourses which made the speaking possible. In essence, the human-as-imperfect-observer perspective while acknowledging some fundamentals assumed in any communication perspective ends up making these acknowledgments outside any kind of coherent theory of communication. Selectivity processes are acknowledged, but constructing or constituting processes are not. Observing is acknowledged but reflexive situated embeddedness is not. Reality is seen as being processed and during the processing some of it falls by the wayside. Humans even add things that are not really there. The idea of a standard against which one can measure bias or selectivity remains, even though often hidden. In order to make a strong demarcation between the human-as-imperfect-observer framing and the human-uniquenesses framing it is useful to apply the discontinuity idea. This idea has independently emerged in the works of a variety of social scientific theorists.[6] For purposes here, Carter's formulation will be used.

There are two important applications of the discontinuity idea for our purposes here. One of them addresses the nature of human observing, recasting limitations into the strengths. The second addresses the nature of reality. Both applications are posited here as axiomatic. The discontinuity idea when applied to human observing leads one to conceptualize the gaps that exist between human observers across time and across space. Since observing is seen as experientially anchored to given moments in time-space, there are necessarily gaps in observing attributable to differences in time-space regardless of whatever limitations may exist in human observing capacities. The observations made by human 1 at time 1 and space 1 are necessarily not the same as those made by human 1 at time 2 and space 1 or time 2 and space 2. Further, the observations made by human 1 at time 1 and space 1 are not necessarily the same as those made by human 2 at time 1 and space 1. Further, human 1 and human 2 come from different time-space pasts and are moving through different time-space presents into different time-space futures.

Thus far we have accounted for different perspectives in observation. But we still have to account for differences in observing even when individuals seem to be anchored in the same past, present, and future time-space. And, we need a way of accounting for these differences that does not set one individual or the other up as standard. The discontinuity idea can serve this purpose. It allows us to posit multiple gaps in the observing process—between reality and senses, between senses and mind, between mind and tongue, between words spoken and words heard. Each of these gaps is axiomatically seen as bridged by behavior—attending in different ways, constructing messages in different ways, speaking in different ways, hearing in different ways. Each of these behavings can be conceptualized as procedural strategy. This does not mean that humans necessarily chose their behaving strategies purposefully nor that they have freedom to choose from theoretically infinite possibilities. Rather, it means that framing these gap bridgings as procedural strategies expands their import. The use of a strategy to make a bridge (i.e., a sense, a picture, something we call information) implies that the bridge is a noun manifestation while the strategy is a verb manifestation. Each noun has verb implications and each verb has noun implications. This idea will be introduced again later in this chapter.

What is most important about the application of the discontinuity idea thus far is that the gaps pointed to cannot be bridged with any externally imposed instructions. Human 1 cannot be at time 1 and time 2 nor space 1 and space 2 all at the same time. Human 1 and 2 can, via communication, attempt to gain understandings of what the other saw at the respective time-spaces.[7] In the presence of disagreement, however, there is no external standard which can be turned to for instruction. And, even if one could turn to a human with observing capabilities that transcended the time-space perspective, there would remain those troublesome gaps between reality and senses, senses and mind,

mind and tongue, tongue and ear, and so on. Only by positing a human who can make the observations of a god in the language of a god can we escape the pervasive gappiness implied in this formulation.

Up to this point, one could suggest that the journey from the second framing of human-as-imperfect-observer to this third framing of human-difference-in-observing-as-strength may seem short, hinged primarily on whether one can or cannot posit an external standard. Philosophically, of course, this distinction is not a small one. But we have not yet arrived at the full application of the discontinuity premise. The second application applies to assumptions about the nature of reality.

It is acknowledged that the assumption of pervasive gappiness in human observing makes any discussion of the nature of reality particularly troublesome. Moving ahead, however, in an axiomizing strategy, it becomes useful to accept the idea that the pervasive gappiness applies not only to human observing but to reality as well. The assumption here is that reality is not the fixed thing out there with a given order which humans try to address. Rather, it is assumed that reality is itself at least in part not entirely ordered. What this means is that not only in the realm of human affairs but in the realm of the concrete, it is assumed that the present, past, and future are not fully determined by any natural order.

One could argue that in order to move from a transmission/manufacturing conceptualization of information to a communicating conceptualization of information one does not really need to posit this second application of discontinuity. Thus, the problematics inherent in the assumption of the pervasive gappiness of human observing sufficiently imply potential utilities for a communication perspective.[8] Yet, the application of the discontinuity idea to the nature of reality not only fits the most advanced interpretations offered us by modern day physicists, it also paves the way more fully for conceptualizing human-difference-in-observing-as-strength.

Posit it this way. Not only are we assuming pervasive gappiness in human observing that can in no way be resolved or bridged by external standard, we are also positing inherent gappiness in physical reality than can also in no way be absolutely and irrevocably bridged. This brings us to a derivative axiom—the idea that it is a mandate of the human condition to bridge gaps. To set forth this mandate as axiom does not imply that individual human beings conceptualize their sense-making of the world in this way. Rather, the axiom serves as a pointing device for our own thinking. It says we assume there is pervasive gappiness: in observing, in reality. Existing and being requires that humans move forth through time-space. While a given human being may conceptualize a gapless world, across human beings there is assumed mandated gap-bridging. Given the assumption of gappiness, gap-bridging is assumed as necessary for moving. Moving, or in Carter's terms *step-taking*, is itself conceptualized axiomatically. To axiomize in this way does not imply that all humans move purposively or linearly.

Rather, all of the bridges humans make to take steps across gaps can be reconceptualized strategically as verb-nouns.

What this means is this. Given lack of complete instructions, humans build pictures of reality. Pictures of reality are necessary to direct movement because movement is instructed by mind and an empty mind provides no instruction. While these pictures of reality have been conceptualized in past formulations as either authoritative statements about what is real or authoritative but constrained and limited statements about what is real, in the discontinuity formulation these pictures become strategies for gap-bridging.[9] Each different kind of picture can be restated as a verb/noun: factizing (imputing fact to a construction), axiomizing (constructing an idea as untestable assumption), cognizing (making idea pictures), evaluating (constructing approach-avoidance pictures), entity-izing (positing entities as existing), relating (positing relationships as existing between entities), causalizing (seeing one thing as causing another), detailing (making pictures of fine points), illustrating (finding an example).

As strange as these verb words may seem, the point they imply is important. We are positing a world that is itself discontinuous at least in part and an observer who is necessarily bound in time-space and who makes observations of reality from that time-space via a set of processes which are inherently gap-filled. All bridges made across these gaps are constructions. Information in this formulation becomes that which informs. That which informs is that which bridges gaps. That which bridges gaps is necessarily that behaving, that constructing, that sense-making that built the bridge.

These behavings—internal (e.g., making pictures, finding words) and external (e.g., attending to reality, trying to share ideas with others) may all be conceptualized strategically and stated in verb/noun form. We no longer talk of processing information but rather of information as informing and informing as process. Noun becomes verb becomes noun becomes verb.

The idea of human-difference-in-observing-as-strength then follows. While it is fashionable now in the social sciences to address the problem of human difference from the perspective of the emerging vocality of pluralities which have so marked this century, applying the discontinuity formulation provides a more direct route. Figure 15.1 provides some assistance. A phenomenon—an aspect of reality—is represented by the black centers of the circles. The segments of each circle represent the perspectives of different observers at different spaces. The successive circles represent the passing of time—the perspectives of different observers at different time-spaces.

Observers at each time-space construct a sense of the phenomena from their unique vantage points. While any given observer may assume, as phenomenologists generally suggest all humans do, that the world is real in an absolute factual sense, from a perspective that compares humans we cannot posit which set of observations is the most accurate.[10] However, a communication perspective based in the discontinuity idea leads

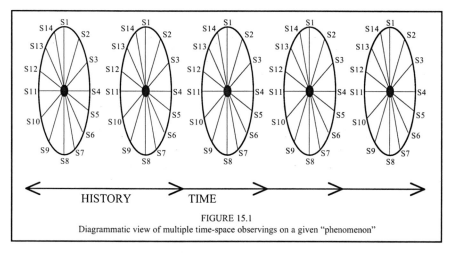

FIGURE 15.1
Diagrammatic view of multiple time-space observings on a given "phenomenon"

us to conclude that circling the phenomena from different perspectives and different times allows us to arrive at a more comprehensive, more fully informed, and potentially more useful set of pictures of the phenomena. If one adds to this formulation some of the notions of systems theory as applied to living systems, one becomes mandated to open up the observational system to observations at all the borders.[11] This necessarily means reaching for contest and for difference—asking whose observations will add a different perspective, a new nuance, another point of view, another vantage point. In one sense, the idea is as simple as the surveillance idea introduced in early models of communication.[12] But in another sense it is as complex as finding a way to walk a tightrope between the current contest in the social sciences between those who call for a return to factizing science versus those who suggest that only contextualizing interpretation is possible.[13]

Also necessarily implied by this formulation is the idea that the observing cannot be meaningfully ripped out of the time-space of its making. The perspective on information which is called Sense-Making which I have been working on since 1972 sets as one of its tasks the development of a methodology for studying informing in situated context without resorting to solipsistic contextualism or radical constructivism. It is not the purpose of this brief chapter to set forth that approach here. Suffice it to say that Sense-Making as a methodology rests on a core gap metaphor which posits humans facing stops (that moment where a gap is seen ahead) and constructing bridges in order to keep moving through internal and/or external time-space.[14]

Some of the basic assumptions of the methodology are that information seeking and use (i.e., the seeking and use of sense) cannot be understood outside the situated context but that it is possible to draw on the discontinuity metaphor to construct ways of studying these phenomena systematically across time and space in a way pertinent to specific moments in time-space. In essence, by positing the human taking steps across gaps, one arrives at an analytic pertinent to all humans but interpretable in given situational contexts. It, thus, provides a standard without relying on a standard which is derived from any given subgroup of humans. As a result one can begin to construct systematic pictures of human information seeking that more powerfully take account of human difference. This is exemplified best in a series of Sense-Making studies which have compared the power of demographic, personality, and across-time-space descriptions of human begins with actor-defined situational assessments framed in gap terms as predictors of human information seeking and use. In all such studies to date, the gap-framed situational accounts were the most powerful predictors. Further, when situational accounts were less powerful one could identify in the situation actor attention to strong structural factors which were seen as restraining individual movement.

Thus, it can be seen that an important aspect of this formulation is that informing or sense-making is seen as time-space bound and as always having the potential for flexibility across-time-space. This does not mean that a given human being sense-makes in this way. The formulation points to potential. In facing a gap, a human may apply a sense acquired during acculturation, or one newly created, or one acquired vicariously through media. The human could potentially behave almost robotically in rigid repetition of past behavior. Such a strategic approach would suggest another related set of strategies: for example, the constructing of an external controlling hegemony; or the constructing of internal demons fixing behavior. The human, in the psychoanalytic sense, may seem to be involved in no conscious sense-making activities. Or, the human may be aware but not discursively so. The individual may or may not see his or her behavings as strategic possibilities belonging to the larger set of all possible strategies.

The important point is that the gap metaphor points us as researchers and as practitioners to the idea that there is always potential for flexibility and potential for rigidity. By focusing on step-taking, on verbs, and on situated conditions, by focusing on process rather than entities, on informing rather than information, one can account for both flexibility and rigidity. In contrast, when a formulation focuses on humans as state entities independent of the time-space perspective and independent of the gap-bridging idea, one can account for only rigidity. All other movement necessarily becomes construed as random error, as chaos.

In this formulation, difference becomes potential strength in at least three senses. The first is unitizing potential. Currently, a variety of attempts to study human use of information/communication systems in essence demark as separate turf different strategies which any human might potentially use in gap-bridging through time-space. Some of us study attitudes (translated in verb terms as the making of evaluation pictures), ethics (the making of should pictures), media use (using media as input for picture making), psychoanalysis (rigidifying of picture making based on personally hurtful experiences), hegemony (rigidifying of picture making based on systematic applications of power), cognition (the construction of idea pictures), and so on. From a verb perspective, however, we have a template which allows us to compare not only individually different humans but our theorizings which attempt to account for differences in humans.

The second strength of the discontinuity formulation is that it leads to the idea that any human attempt to arrive at more consensual observations of reality (which has historically been called factual information) must necessarily be based on a circling of the sense-making that different observers at different time-spaces do of that phenomena. Since no human can observe from all time-spaces nor utilize every procedural strategy for making sense at that time-space, human diversity both in situatedness and in sense-making strategies becomes conceptualized as strength. Implied too is a strategy for maximizing this strength—by reaching, for example, for maximum diversity along such dimensions as experience, power, location. It is a basic premise of systems theory that the living system must exchange information with the environment. This formulation offers an application of this principal without resorting to the idea of information-as-thing.

There is a third way in which this perspective focusing on human difference offers potential strength. This strength results from positing that the results of research derived from use of this perspective will apply more directly to practice.[15] Here we hark back to a statement made at the beginning of this chapter that suggested that the information-as-thing idea could identify the problem of information inequities but not point to any potential resolutions. It is only in the context of the use of an analytic which transcends any one approach to human sense-making of the world that one can yield research results useful in the design of systems intended for any but the most homogeneous of users. Even systems designed for theoretically homogeneous users based on state entity perspectives and information-as-thing ideas have failed because these framings point reliably only to human rigidities while human information seeking and using involves both rigidities and flexibilities. The question then becomes how to find pattern in that which under other formulations of information is defined as chaos—the differences in how humans seek and make sense. Human flexibility in sense-making strategies and human diversity in sense-making outcomes (the verb/noun manifestations) become reconceptualized as a result of the use of the discontinuity assumptions. The application of a communication theory suggests that because it is assumed that the human condition mandates gap bridging we can look for pattern in the bridging, in the making of pictures that allow movement through time-space. To the extent that pattern emerges the communication/information system can now design itself to be systematically responsive to such patterns. To ignore this potential human flexibility and diversity is, in essence, to posit that the users of systems are clonelike replicas of the designers and operators of those systems. Worse, however, is that the result is to close the system down at its perimeters. The system will necessarily become less and less responsive to environmental conditions and more and more aberrant of human need.

COMMUNICATION THEORY
AND THE FLEXIBILITIES OF THE NEW TECHNOLOGIES

The irony of this situation in which we find ourselves is that for the first time we have a set of technologies which are capable of addressing human differences in sense-making. But we are hampered by a design legacy which, in effect, designs information/communication systems for clones. And, unfortunately, communication theory and research has both served and reified this inflexibility.

In essence, in the arduous movement of our conceptions of human beings and of reality away from ideas of a fixed reality observed by the perfect observer (if only we could make it so), we have remained caught between a conception of human beings as clones versus a conception of human beings as chaotic. On the one hand, the information-as-thing idea requires that human beings be conceptualized as clones. Positing a fixed order with perfect observing necessarily means that any deviation must be assigned to the observer. In response to this appearance of difference, as theorists and practitioners we can ignore the fluctuation. This has been the typical response in most system design. Alternatively, we can try to account for the fluctuation with a variety of sociological and psychological theories which explain human selectivity processes. In any case, we end up positing an empty bucket theory of humans (humans are there to dump information into), or a leaky bucket theory (humans can only get part of what is there), or a recalcitrant bucket theory (humans obstinately choose only what they want).

The mischief that results from these theories in system design is complex indeed. First, positing selectivity processes necessarily leads to research that measures people against external standards which are assumed to have truth value. But the standards used are necessarily those of the individuals who design and run the system; those in power. Results then identify those who can use the system and those who cannot. Those who cannot are seen as lacking—objects to be trained or resourced so they no longer lack. Those who can are individuals more like those who run the system or individuals who have acquired that chameleonlike skill of human beings to behave as if they are like those who run the system. The result is a reification of the system as it is coupled with an inability of the system to acquire the intelligence which would allow it to change itself to be responsive to not only differing needs but changing conditions as well. Over time the necessary result is the homogenization of the services the system offers to human informing activities. This, in turn, reduces the variety of sense-makings which can be brought to bear which leads to both inequities as well as enforced homogenization of users.

A second impact of information-as-thing ideas on system design is that the systems are designed as transmission rather than communication systems. Ultimately, communicating has very little to do with a process that focuses on the movement of information-as-thing. Communicating is studied, but it becomes conceptualized as impediment and the human is conceptualized as not having agency. The human is vessel and information is examined as it is moved from place to place. This is quite different from looking at what Bruner (1990) has termed *meaning-making* in his call for a turn away from cognitive science to a focus on how meanings are constituted by a constitute culture. While Bruner's (1990) call is more general than our call here, it points in the same direction. If we conceptualize information processing—seeking and use—as transmission processes we will necessarily miss constructing activity. Our systems will as a result be designed for a very limited set of strategic possibilities.

A third impact is this: positing an across-time-space framing of information means that we ignore in our research all the situated links which might allow one individual at one point in time-space to understand the informing of another at another point in time-space. The results of informing activities—what we call information—get ripped out of context and moved about without this embeddedness in the experiential conditions of their constructing. As a result, while our systems get bigger they get less and less useful. In essence, sense created at one time-space in the context of a particular time-space history, a particular situation, and a particular set of sense-making strategies becomes ripped out of this context and treated as independent thing which can be transmitted as thing to another person. It is here that it becomes non-sense.

The literature is filled with case studies of information/communication systems that have failed to serve their intended users. The argument presented above suggests that by reconceptualizing information we can conduct research more useful to system practice; that we can in effect obtain research results useful in designing systems that can respond flexibly to the differing behavioral conditions which humans bring to these systems. To provide some vision of the possibilities, consider the examples below. The examples have been selected because every case is one where the new technologies provide the flexible capacities which would make each vision possible.[16]

> • *Most retrieval systems are based on keywords, usually nouns, which locate a book along a limited number of dimensions. Envision a body of research work which has examined how it is that humans make judgments of whether to retrieve and then attend in some way to a book. Envision a retrieval system which then builds in options, such as, retrieval by title, author, table of contents, preface, last page, first page. Envision too the possibility of codifying and making available to the reader with technologies the judgments of a book by the last N readers—judgments such as how the book helped them.*

> • *Journalism as practice is currently built on conceptions of the journalistic story as a coherent narrative addressing reality as real. Envision a journalism which acknowledges that vantage point makes a great deal of difference in observation and collects from across the globe stories from maximally different perspectives and procedurally mandates coverage to encompass these differences and to attend to their experiential roots.*

• *Scholarly writing, as well as journalism, pretends to rip the person out of the text. While this is never wholly possible the canons of scholarly writing explicitly mandate against personal motivational statements. Envision retrieval statements which acknowledge that the constructor is an important part of the construction and requires that author(s) present personal statements explaining such aspects of their situation as: their own intellectual history, or how the piece of scholarship helped them handle a contest or barrier, or what the project permitted them to do. Envision a retrieval system which allows users to access these statements.*

• *Software programs for text constructing (word processing) and for text using (video-text) offer a very limited array of movement options: go to the beginning, go to the end, go to each subhead, and so on. Envision a body of research work which empowers users to create a "magic machine" that will allow them to do what they want to do and which then builds this array into software design.*

• *Manuals for the use of software programs are notoriously difficult for users, most often written from the vantage point of the computer programmer. Envision a body of research work which allows users to talk about their sense-making and the gaps they face along the way. Envision manuals which are written attending to user paths, user vocabularies, and user questions.*

• *Medical research data privilege information that focuses on diseases, symptoms, cures. Neither the practical understandings of physicians nor the experiential under-standings of patients are admitted. Yet, an examination of the progress of medical science points to the value of attending to these informational inputs as well. Envision a body of research that addresses the question of how to do this and a retrieval system which implements the results.*

• *The interactions between professionals (e.g., doctors, librarians, etc.) and their users (e.g., patients, clients, patrons) are confined within a set of assumptions which define the professional as having access to information and the user as having a need which information will resolve. Begging for the moment the idea that the users have arrived themselves at sense-makings which contribute expertise to these situations, even within the traditional definition there is little acknowledgment made of the idea that whatever expertise the professional may offer must be graspable by the user. Most attempts to diagnose the user need are based on system-defined matching schema. Users are asked which of a set of the following categories as defined by the system they fit into. For doctors, this is usually a list of symptoms; for librarians, a set of retrieval categories. Envision instead professional systems which routinely require that users and practitioners describe their experiential understandings. Envision a body of research which allows this to happen systematically. Envision the possibility of interactive technologies which speed-up the process. Envision retrieval systems which codify the results.*

• *Most information systems delimit their purview of their users to the intersections of their users with the systems. Yet, users approach systems in a wide variety of anom-*

alous states of knowledge, bringing with them cognitively the experiential conditions which lead them to the system-using detour.[17] Envision a body of research which has acquired an understanding of the variety of sense-making paths users bring to and take through systems. Envision an interactive system which allows individual users to seek assistance based on their identification of the point and path where they are traveling.

• *Most complex organizations and institutions are hierarchically organized. Given power and human constraints, obtaining a diversity of perspectives on potential dangers (i.e., surveillance) or potential actions (i.e., decisions) or even good news becomes difficult for even the most well-intentioned of leaders. Envision an electronic network that regularly queries participants and then uses some form of computerized analytic technique to group inputs for easier browsing.*

This is but a small set of examples. While research results are not presented here, over the past 20 years the Sense-Making project has conducted studies which suggest that every one of the approaches above would be useful to human beings trying to inform themselves and that every one of the approaches is a practical possibility given reconceptualizations of information in research programs and in resulting technological system designs. Results also suggest that more than utility and practicality, the approaches would have other potentially positive consequences: better decisions, fewer crises, less misunderstanding leading to charges of malpractice, more time saved.

CONCLUSION

The argument presented above has suggested that if we are to make maximum use of the enormous powers of flexibility offered by the new communication technologies we must diversify our conceptualizations of information. While the information-as-thing idea has utility under some circumstances, the information-as-construction idea offers a broad range of potential advantages, the primary one of which is giving us direct guidance on how we might design systems to use the enormous capacities of the new technologies for more than doing merely what we do now in greater quantities, faster, and from further distances.

The argument suggests that by conceptualizing information as informing and looking at informing as a kind of meaning-making, as sense-making, we can yield research more directly helpful to practice. It is suggested that this is a communication approach to the concept of information. As such it is suggested that it is more useful to design because design is actualized in communication—in the uses made of systems by human beings.

One final caveat. The statement above is necessarily idealistic. It assumes well-meaning systems which would like different world-views to flow freely. It assumes that those who run those systems and those who use them are likewise inclined. And, it assumes that at least those who run the system accept either pragmatically and/or philo-sophically the idea of human-difference-in-observing-as-strength. Self-interest could stand in the way. Elusive but nevertheless constraining hegemonies could stand in the way. Barriers usefully termed here as psychoanalytic could stand in the way. So could inertia. But these are all stories for another time, another chapter.

NOTES

1. For comprehensive literature reviews relating specifically to issues of communication/information inequities and the role of systems in alleviating or exasperating, see in particular Dervin (1980, 1989b) and Gandy (1988).

2. We shall beg off the question here of whether in social science or, for that matter any science, the use of prim-itive terms is justified given what we understand about the nature of language and the nature of human use of language.

3. This idea is most often traced back to a single theoretic formulation developed by Shannon and Weaver (1949). It is, however, very pervasive.

4. The author acknowledges the helpful thinking of Taylor (1993) which informed this section.

5. In developing this framework, the author has found the following useful: Bronowski (1973), Bruner (1973, 1990), Foucault (1972), Geertz (1975), Giddens (1984, 1989), Habermas (1971), Hall (1989), Leiter (1980), Rorty (1991).

6. For example: Carter (1974b, 1980, 1989a, 1989b), Foucault (1972), Giddens (1984), Habermas (1971).

7. This is not meant to imply that I accept a definition of communication as the "sharing" of internal pictures. For an interesting commentary on this point, see Krippendorff (1989).

8. The term "problematics" used here is not meant to imply that communication is a "problem" to be solved. Rather, the intent is to convey a picture of the unrelenting iterativeness of communicating.

9. Discussions of communicatings as behavings owe much to Carter's formulations. See, in particular, Carter (1973), and Carter, Ruggels, Jackson, and Heffner (1973).

10. See, in particular, Leiter (1980).

11. See, in particular, Miller (1965).

12. See, in particular, Lasswell (1949).

13. In addition to citations in footnotes 6 and 7, see Dervin (1991a), Krippendorff (1991), Tehranian (1991) for discussion relating to the issue of whether comparative communication theory is possible.

14. Sense-Making Methodology, developed in a series of programmatic projects since 1972, is a methodolo-gy purposefully positioned "between methodological cracks" (e.g., administrative vs. critical, quantitative vs. qualita-tive). It rests on the uses of discontinuity premises as applied in this chapter. For recent presentations, see: Dervin (1989a, 1991a, 1992), and Dervin and Nilan (1986).

15. Craig (1989) provides an interesting discussion of communication as practical discipline.

16. For other discussions of invention potentials see Carter (1982), Dervin (1989a), and Dervin and Clark (1993).

17. The term comes from Belkin (1980).

Chapter 16

Practicing Journalism Communicatively: Moving from Journalism Practiced as Ideology to Journalism Practiced as Theorized Practice

Brenda Dervin & Robert Huesca

> *He who loves practice without theory is like a sailor who boards ship without rudder and compass and never knows where he may be cast. (Leonardo DaVinci)*
>
> *Life is inherently unmanageable. (Sheldon Kopp)*

PURPOSE

The most general purpose of this chapter is to honor the work of Dr. K.E. Eapen.[1] To this end, this chapter attempts to emulate the "Socratic spirit of questioning" that has characterized Eapen's intellectual project in the very context that has been the focus of much of Eapen's work—the practices of modern journalism and the exciting potentials for those practices in an ever-expanding communicatively-interconnected world.[2]

In this spirit, this chapter spins out an argument which calls for re-theorizing journalistic practice. In order to develop this argument, this chapter starts with these four assumptions:[3]

> *1. The species is moving toward acceptance of pluralism. For myriad reasons both idealistic and pragmatic, at varying speeds, and with varying symptomatic problems, the species continues to move toward the development of structures which can handle difference. This pertains to differences found in not just obviously heterogeneous societies, but also to differences found in any society at any time—differences in how individuals see and make sense of their worlds, differences in the very character of their "facts."*

This work originally appeared as: Dervin, B., & Huesca, R. (2001). Practicing journalism communicatively: Moving from journalism practiced as ideology to journalism practiced as theorized procedure. In S. Rao & S. R. Melkote (Eds.), *Critical issues in communication, looking inward for answers: Essays in honor of K. E. Eapen* (pp. 321–344). New Delhi, India: Sage. Reprinted by permission of Sage Publications, New Delhi, India.

2. Journalism is part of that project. While definitions and roots of journalism vary from place to place, wherever we observe journalistic practice we see signs of forces acting on journalism asking that journalistic practice serve the mandates of a world that acknowledges and may eventually learn to relish and find useful its differences.

3. To the detriment of the species, most of the procedures used for communicating, including journalistic procedures, are derived from non-communication theories of communication. What this means is that most theories of communication focus on transmission ideas about communication—the making of messages which are to be transmitted—and not on dialogic ideas about communication. Dialogic ideas about communication position communication as dialogue, as a dynamic and complex process through which people create, change, and re-create sense, meaning, and understanding in their interactions with others, media, events, and experiences. A dialogic or communication theory of communication focuses not on homogenizing difference but on putting difference into dialogue and, thus, using it to assist human sense-making. Such a communication theory of communication assumes that when difference is not treated dialogically it appears both capricious and chaotic as if needing homogenization.

When non-communication or non-dialogic theories are used implicitly or explicitly to generate communication practices, the solutions offered are in effect not communication solutions. They necessarily become power solutions. Because they not the most useful kind of solutions, they cannot make a dent in the problem. In fact, they exasperate conditions. An important point here is that journalistic practice is not alone in this dilemma. Rather, it shares in effect an epistemic umbrella which constrains most thinking about formalized communication practices no matter what the context (e.g., education, health care delivery, or library practice).

4. For the species to genuinely handle pluralism it will require communication invention. Having to deal with pluralism with something other than the sheer force of overt power is a relatively new condition for the species—one which will require the invention of communication alternatives, in the form of both deductive and inductive inventions. For the former, work will involve both the invention of new procedures drawn from theories of dialogic practice; for the latter, work will involve deriving off theory from inventive but as yet unarticulated practice.

WHOS VERSUS *HOWS* IN JOURNALISTIC PRACTICE

The focus of this chapter is procedure: the *hows* of journalism practice, not the *whats* or the *whos*. It is argued that focusing on *hows*—how journalism is done in journalistic practices—is essential in the context of the basic assumptions set forth above. It is argued that it is only by focusing on *hows* and not exclusively on *whos* and *whats* that we can focus on difference and, thus, dialogically apply a communication theory of communication.

Virtually every communication-based practice (e.g., journalism, social work, teaching, or librarianship) represents in its literature a concern for the seemingly unbearable uniqueness and chaos of human sense-making. Each practice handles the "difficulty" differently. But, all basically assume that difference is troublesome, a problem in some way to be surmounted.

One finds in the literatures of all these practices essentially three different ways of ameliorating difference, each anchored in similar versions of underlying assumptions about the nature of reality and the nature of human beings. Each of these approaches is presented briefly below with examples extracted from journalistic practice.

One approach—perhaps the most prevalent—is to blame difference, to see it as caused by lazy, uneducated, recalcitrant individuals who refuse to learn the proper and right way to attend to reality. Examples of the use of this assumption are widespread in journalistic practice, ranging all the way from the often-repeated evidence showing that most users are inattentive to journalistic products and unable to attend to them unless they are reduced in quality to appeal to the so-called lowest common denominator.

A second approach still posits difference as troublesome but accepts it as a politically and economically necessary obstacle to proper practice. This is the approach to difference which mandates that difference be given a voice but then ignored in the formalized conduct of professional practice. Examples include various person-on-the-street columns asking lay persons for their opinions or popular talk shows in which difference is typically reduced to cacophony, a Tower of Babel.

A third approach to handling difference still posits difference as troublesome to the conduct of formalized practice but acknowledges that it exists because people experience reality from different places. This is the approach that typically calls for alternative media (or space within mainstream media) to be reserved for the voices of difference.

The important point to note here is that difference is not put into systematic dialogue in any of these approaches. It is our position that one primary reason for this is that the professional practices are still anchored in reality-transmission assumptions— that what journalistic communicating is about is collecting and transmitting accurate pictures of reality. At this abstract level, the actions taken by communication institutions are all the same—an attempt to systematize people so they fit in an orderly manner within systems. This is as true for journalistic practice as it is for group leadership or library service or teaching or the delivery of health care. The primary solution to difference offered in all of these systems, journalistic or otherwise, is the *whos* solution to system design—the substitution of a journalist or leader or librarian or teacher or health care provider who is more like readers/patrons/followers/clients/patients. We propose that the *whos* solution only superficially ameliorates but does not address the problematic of difference directly. Rather it addresses difference without a theory that handles difference at its heart, without putting difference into dialogue and, thus, does nothing to make difference useful. It positions difference in a way that difference ultimately becomes merely noise and inconvenience.

In the practice of journalism (as well as in other communication-based systems), the *whos* solution to difference dominates. For journalism practice, in particular, critiques of so-called authoritarian and elitist practice have focused primarily on who gets to speak journalistically and who gets to own journalistic institutions. Some attention is placed on *whats*—what gets attended to. But even this attention to *whats* is generally couched in terms of a concern for whether sufficient attention is paid to the different interests of the different *whos*. Likewise, when practices are examined they are examined primarily in terms of how they misrepresent the voices of some *whos* and thus distort the coverage of *whats*.

While attending to *whos* appears on the surface to handle the challenge of difference, we propose that as journalistic practice it fails to do so in a fundamental way. It is a non-communication solution to a communication problematic. One purpose of this chapter is to develop and clarify this argument. The difficulty is that a focus on *whos* assumes that difference is sufficiently handled by embodying the relevant differences in human beings in sets of externally-observed characteristics—age, class, ethnic origin, and so forth. A focus on *whos* also implies that if one sufficiently represents *whos* in journalism practice that the problem of difference is handled across time. Examples of these strategies include training and hiring journalists from different ethnic backgrounds, or providing alternative routes for the voices of difference to be heard.

Both of these conceptions—the conceptualization of difference in terms of externally observed characteristics of human beings, and the assumption that difference thus represented is represented over time—are non-communication or non-dialogic conceptions of the communication problematic. They derive from a non-communication theory of communication which, at root, conceptualizes humans ideally as accurate observers of reality. In this theory, the need for different *whos*, both as journalists and as owners of journalism institutions, merely acknowledges that different observers stand at different places in reality.

A communication theory of communication, on the other hand, assumes not only that different *whos* observe differently because they experience reality from different places, but rather more fundamentally, that observation is always incomplete. This incompleteness is assumed as arising both from the incompleteness of reality itself across time and space, and from the changing nature of human experiencing as it moves across time and space. Further, observation is assumed to be inextricably bound to internal worlds, and always understandable only in a dialogic framework that takes into account both personal observations and the ways in which history, culture, and hegemony both constrain and facilitate these.

Thus, in a communication theory of communication, journalism practice must account not only for people from very different worlds but for individuals from the same world who have very different views of that world. In a world assumed to be without complete order, even without considering the observing limitations of the human species, it becomes apparent that different observers will necessarily construct different pictures of reality. Further, journalistic practice must account for the inherently internal nature of observing and sense-making and, at the same time, the inherent connections and tensions between these internal acts and the historical, cultural, political, and economic contexts from which they arise. Journalistic acts are ultimately intra-personal acts, acts of individuals creating messages and other individuals making sense of those messages. At the same time the nature of these acts are acculturated, constrained, and/or facilitated by the contexts and the time-spaces in which they occur. There is chaos/change as well as order/stability and movement in between as humans move across time-space in the complex interconnections between individual and structure. Both chaos/change and order/stability are inherent to human making of sense.

The point from this foray is this—the *whos* solution to difference in practice is not a communication solution. It does not put difference into dialogue. Rather it adds more voices without implementing a communication theory for understanding the voices. The result makes difference look capricious and chaotic, sometimes foolish, rather than allowing difference to inform human struggles to make sense across an ever-changing, elusive, and complex reality. In this framework, the practices of every journalist and every communicator will of necessity decay to authoritarianism over time unless communication is dealt with as dialogue rather than as mere transmission. The question is how can this be done given what appears to be unbearable and unrelenting differences in human observations. Are we necessarily bound to a choice between the apparent chaos of individuality on the one hand and the tyranny of authoritarian systems on the other? The answer that this chapter proposes is to be found by focusing on a communication theory of procedures—a theory of the *hows* of communication practice. Such a focus suggests that if indeed we continue to attempt to deal with pluralism in communication institutions with *who* solutions we will in effect make the problem of pluralism seem less penetrable. If the fundamental problem is one of finding a way for human institutions to deal with difference in whatever form it takes then dealing with difference with a superficial solution can only in the long run only make a fundamental solution seem unachievable. It is as if the medicine applied makes the disease worse rather than better.

This can be illustrated with some hypothetical examples. A newspaper hires minority reporters and upon finding that minority readers are still unhappy reacts with the attitude of "we've done everything possible to communicate with them." Meanwhile minority readers expecting that they would be better represented react more negatively, while the minority reporters experience burnout in the face of impossible expectations. But this is not a problem of journalism alone as is illustrated by this common organizational example. A company hires a female supervisor and upon finding that female employees are still unrestful concludes that only tight discipline is the answer. The women in the meantime feel betrayed. A group of the disenfranchised join together to create their own support group and then accuse their leader of authoritarian practices. The leader, in turn, feels betrayed and burns out in the face of impossible expectations.

In all of these cases, "who" solutions have not worked because they have been implemented in terms of practices (i.e., *hows*) derived from non-communication theories of communication. Most of the formalized procedures of journalism and, in fact, communication practice generally are derived from such non-communication theories—they treat communication as objective transmission rather than situated sense-making. This chapter assumes that if as a species we can implement in practice a theory of communication that is process oriented we can, in effect, refocus our attention from persistent efforts to reduce and control difference to attempts to make difference not only more manageable but informative and useful.

Current practices of journalism—and most formalized communication activities—are not theoretically derived in any explicit way. It is useful, however, to conjecture what theoretic premises are implied by some dominant journalistic practices in order to provide a contrast for the development of our argument as it continues. For purposes here, examples are derived from studies of journalism as practiced in the U.S. but, in fact, the procedures illustrated are quite pervasive in other places too.

How does journalism practice select who gets to speak? Journalism practice typically privileges the voices of those in power. Given the assumed goal of dominant journalistic practice to represent reality accurately, it is possible to conjecture that those in power are assumed to be more expert observers of reality and, thus, more useful sources for the journalism practitioner.

How does journalism practice bring different versions of the same story into comparison? Typically, different versions of the same story are isolated from each other proliferating what are called special interest approaches to journalism. Alternatively, they are compared not in terms of understanding how different observations might legitimately arise but in terms of debate and conflict and the assumption that somehow in the midst of such debate truth will emerge.

How does journalistic practice appeal to difference? Typically and ever more increasingly, attempts to appeal to diverse audiences (readers, users) are based on personality and star appeal. It is possible to conjecture that in the absence of any theory of how to attend to difference procedurally the reduction of difference to surface appearances becomes a necessary outcome. It is also possible to conjecture that the decay to the lowest common denominator approach in journalistic practice is another symptom of not attending to difference communicatively.

How does journalism practice select what gets paid attention to? The very definition of news implies something new or recent. Above this is another rule—journalism as *surveiller* of danger, a watch dog. Thus, bad news, catastrophes, and crises get primary attention. It is possible to conjecture that the theoretic basis for this practice is the assumption that reality is ideally and inherently orderly and bad news represents a break with the natural order and, thus, a mandated focus for journalistic attention.

How does journalism practice decide what to print when and where? Newness and danger are values and so the most dangerous and most new gets the most attention. A whole set of rules regarding lead stories rest on these assumptions. The new is important so bullet news items are heavily used. Distinctions in the placement of news are made based on accepted categories—local news, national news, sports new, women's news, and so on. News is separated from entertainment, the former defined as describing reality, the latter as providing escape. The journalist is assumed to be pursuing accurate versions of reality and those aspects which are most "factual" are most important. This directs the journalist to use the 5W lead—who, what, when, where, why. Taken together, these practices can be seen as implementing a correspondence theory of journalistic observation— what the journalist observes is ideally a description of an orderly reality. Each observation has a inherent relationship with every other because that relationship is mandated by the orderly nature of reality itself to which each observation is seen as corresponding.

How does journalism practice put the pieces of a story together? The bricks of a journalistic story—the individual observations, quotes, items of history, and so on— must be fit together into a coherent narrative whole. It is this mandate to produce a coherent narrative that perhaps more than any other defines what aspirants find compelling about being a journalist—the right to construct a coherent (and assumed to be accurate) picture of the world in an artful narrative. The narrative by definition closes gaps. It becomes possible as a focal guiding practice for journalism only when it is assumed that the narrative corresponds to external reality and needs no justification outside itself and outside the assumption that journalism education trains journalists to be accurate observers of that reality.

HOW JOURNALISM PRACTICE BECOMES IDEOLOGY

The set of examples given earlier will suffice for purposes of this chapter. Much has been written relating to the impact of economic structures on journalistic practice. There is little doubt that in the context of competition most of the procedures given earlier get pushed to absurdity resulting in such consequences as: television reporters being replaced without warning because their "personality" ratings are down; one crisis being cast aside because of another; two contradictory crises receiving attention at the same time without interconnection; or, today's bullet solution to a crisis being contradicted by tomorrow's.

But, this chapter assumes that even without the force of uncontrolled pursuit of profit, the communicative procedures of journalism would still represent a difficulty for the human species. The set of procedures described above produce a portrait of reality that is necessarily limited because they implement a non-communication theory of communication. One writer's view of what is going on is transmitted. That writer is reward-ed for closing whatever gaps he or she observes in reality. The entire set of procedures, by definition, privileges the gap-bridging preferences and styles of that one journalistic observer. Further, over time, whatever differences that journalists brought to the jour-nalistic system are necessarily homogenized as the journalist is acculturated by that sys-tem. In turn, the procedures privilege whatever sources of power to which the system owes allegiance because of economic and/or political necessity.

For purposes of this chapter, the *hows* of journalistic practice are redefined as a subset of all possible strategies for observing reality, constructing bridges across the gaps seen in that reality, and then constructing messages from those observations. When looked at in this way, it can be argued that both intentionally and unintentionally the *hows* dominantly employed in journalistic practice end up reifying existing power struc-tures and implementing an authoritarian worldview based on assumptions of a stable external reality. No other consequence is possible in the context of the argument pre-sented here because current journalistic practices by definition allow one set of homo-geneous observers to construct the available pictures of reality.

The term *authoritarian* in this context has several layers of meanings. Most of the criticisms of journalism have focused on authority in the context of power and hegemo-ny, accusing journalism of serving those in power. Indeed, there is ample evidence of the problem. Unfortunately, though, when our focus on the problem of power stops here we miss the more fundamental problem of the authoritarian approach—the problem of our communication procedures empowering and privileging the observations of a select-ed few over the many. The species persists in believing in the face of contradictory evi-dence that a well-educated journalist (or, a well-chosen leader) will somehow magically represent the one reality as it assumed to be or multiple perspectives on that reality that arise from differing stances. Indeed, we can point to individuals who have shown remarkable capacities in these ways.

The point, here, however, is theoretic. To empower the observations of the few as if they can provide accurate maps of an ever-changing elusive reality ends up being a power solution to a species problematic which would be best served by a communica-tion solution. For this reason, any practice of journalism which proceeds without imple-menting a dialogic or communicative understanding of pluralism, in essence without implementing a communication theory of communication, will end up ultimately chal-lenged as authoritarian. This is as true for journalistic practices that are explicitly anchored in principles of objectivity or for those that are implicitly anchored by inatten-tion to the communication problematic.

In short, we are assuming that any formalized attempts to make observations of reality on behalf of the species (journalistic, scientific, or otherwise) must proceed by explicitly and systematically taking into account the unrelenting diversity of human observations and the origins of this diversity in both ontological and epistemological incompleteness. To do otherwise, necessarily invites the resulting observings to decay to authoritarian modes, and opens the door to journalism serving as ideological tools. The authoritarianism of journalistic practice in this sense is more often than not unintentional. Yet, unintentional though it may be it can still yield a journalism that serves power rather than people, rigidity rather than responsiveness.

To fully understand the above, it is useful to pursue the problem of the *hows* of journalism further by contrasting the sample set of procedures listed above with an alternative hypothetical set which implements a different theory of communication—a communication theory of communication.

A COMMUNICATION THEORY OF COMMUNICATION

Such a communication theory of communication rests on a recently derived (in terms of the history of the species) set of assumptions about the nature of observing, information, human beings, and reality. Fundamental to this theory is the notion of the inherent discontinuity of existence—the idea that reality is itself inherently gap-filled with gaps between entities, between times, and between spaces so that even an all-powerful observer could not make observations that would fully instruct, that is, close all gaps. Add to this the assumption that human observing is constrained not only by the inherent gaps in reality but by the limitations of species and individual physiology, technological capacities, and time-space constraints. The mischief, however, does not stop here. Add the assumption that for humans as well there are a host of non-cognitive states of being which enrich and/or constrain observings—emotions, physical feelings, unconscious moments. Finally, add the assumption that humans, by virtue of the brute force of daily experience, have quite sophisticated understandings, if not intellectually as least pragmatically, of the ways in which gap-bridging is not well-served by mere correspondence theories of observing. Studies show, for example, that people, no matter how well educated, most often turn to trusted friends first for information and find it impossible to use "facts" communicated objectively without context, history, and motive. Making sense, studies shows, is in good part based on finding ways to anchor observations of self, others, and situations in the so-called subjective. But even this term subjective arises out of correspondence theories of observing assuming that some observations are real (i.e., objective) and others unreal (i.e., subjective). Yet, studies on information-seeking clearly suggest that humans have an understanding of observing results from sense-making and it is internally driven and informed by time, place, culture, history, and struggle.

Central to this approach to communication is the idea that human beings are mandated to take steps through a discontinuous reality. Thus, reality is such that the gaps can never be completely bridged but human existence mandates bridge-building and bridge-crossing. Further, any attempt to reach out to another for complete instruction as a means of building a complete bridge is in itself destined to fail—the other is different, from a different time-space; with observing constrained and locked into mind; and facing a discontinuous reality that is by definition at least slightly different. It is this jumble which provides a better account of the chaos of individuality than either the blame-the-victim or rampant diversity theories that are widely available in professional circles. A crucial point here is that what may be ordered about human information processing is not the observations but the ways in which humans cope with pervasive "gappiness." A communication theory of communication starts with this premise.

Permeating the above is a focus on gaps: gap-defining and gap-bridging. This focus has provided the central theoretic focus for a 25-year programmatic series of studies on human sense-making. While it is beyond the purpose of this chapter to review research on human sense-making in detail, it is useful to provide a brief overview. The studies have shown, for example, that people cannot make sense of "facts" that are communicated objectively. Rather, they need to anchor these "facts" in an understanding of the past, present, and future and in an understanding of the motives and historical and situational conditions of those who produced the facts. Sense-makers are also helped by understanding how and why their own views of these "facts" differ from those of others. And, they are helped by input from others who see the situation as they do. But they are also helped by input from those who see the situation very differently. They want to know how other people put the pieces of "reality" together—how others bridge gaps—and why. It is in such a context that they can develop a personal understanding which is linked to their experiential realities—in short, to make sense in such a way that permits "information" to be used in everyday life. Information in this context is sense which informs, which helps human step-taking. The sense-making studies have gone far enough to begin to develop sets of alternative categories for designing communication systems. These will not be reported in detail here. They are implied, however, in the discussion that follows.

PRACTICING JOURNALISM COMMUNICATIVELY

What does this set of assumptions imply for the practice of journalism? The ideas presented in this section attempt to develop a beginning answer to this question. It is important to note before starting that there are many examples of alternative journalistic practice which incorporate some of the ideas below. It is not assumed that journalism has been entirely transmission oriented or that individual journalists have not attempted or succeeded in developing a host of journalistic inventions outside the transmission assumptions of normative journalistic practice. It is, however, assumed that we cannot point to a formalized communication-based journalism, one that is driven by a theory of what such a journalism might be like and/or one that is systematically practiced. What follows next is a beginning list of theoretically-derived meta-level practices which we posit as illustrative of the potentials of a formalized, communication-based journalism. These practices illustrate how difference might be conceptualized as fundamental to the purposes of journalism and how the quest for examining difference and putting difference into dialogue leads necessarily to emphasis on *hows* and not merely *whos* and *whats*.

Circling Reality

Fundamental to a communication-based journalism would be the practice of planning coverage that would circle reality. This does not mean that all possible viewpoints would be represented but rather that the coverage rule would be to maximize viewpoints by, for example, sending out three maximally different reporters, or seeking five maximally different observations or opinions. The word "different" here is intended to mean maximally different along whatever categories seem relevant to the situation at hand. One of the calls for inventing a journalism practice based on communication theory would be to conceptualize categories of difference that are more useful than the surface demographic boxes into which we usually divide people. Even with better categories for attending to difference, however, if we left journalism practice here, we would have nothing more than a more systematic variation on the *who* solution to pluralism. Implementation of this practice demands attention to the other practices listed next.

Focusing on Power and Contests

A communication theory of communication assumes that humans must construct their movements through life through an inherently elusive and changeable reality. Because of this, self-interest is assumed to be inherent to human sense-making even though its form and character change from time to time and place to place. Individuals are assumed to be self-interested both in terms of guiding their own movements as well as coordinating these movements with others, institutions, and society. Likewise, it is assumed that collectivities pursue interests and that society mindfully or mindlessly privileges the interests of some individuals and collectivities over others. Thus, a communication theory of communication assumes that communicating in the pursuit of interests is fundamental to the species. Therefore a communication-based journalism would be mandated to adopt practices which inherently focus on power, contested views of reality, and differences in interests—both those apparent in societal discourse and those hidden from (and perhaps suppressed by) societal discourse. It is assumed that it is at these sites of contest—between the individual and society, the apparent and the hidden, the personal and the political, the orderly and the muddled, the raw and the cooked—that important aspects of difference are made manifest.

Focus on Connectings

Given the fundamental assumptions of a communication theory of communication that "gappiness" is pervasive and never entirely bridged, and at the same time human step-taking requires that bridges be built, we arrive at another guidance for practice. What these assumptions imply is that one person's bridge is necessarily different from another's bridge because the bridges are constructions and even in their most empirically factual form can never provide a perfect fit with reality. The argument suggests the need for journalistic practice that would systematically attend to these bridges as constructions, that would determine from the perspective of observers what accounts for the differences in their observations of an event. This would, in essence, allow the individual observer the right of defining and accounting for self and self's place in the social order. It would also allow the reader/viewer to understand something about where a set of observations came from.

Focus on Disconnectings

It also follows from the view of reality presented here that an important struggle for human beings is not only the making of bridges, but the unmaking of bridges. Both the social order and past experiences lead humans to construct bridges which turn out to be not useful across space and time. This struggling into and out of orderliness is assumed to be an inherent aspect of human existence and, thus, becomes mandated for attention in journalistic practice.

Focus on the Subjective

Interrelated with the suggestion given here is a mandate to focus on those aspects of sense-making which are now marginalized as subjective. What this would mean journalistically would be to act on the assumption that human motives and reasons, human emotions and feelings, and human judgments of causes and consequences are essential to human sense-making and, thus, essential aspects of observing. It is in understanding how people differ in the reasons for their views of the world that each person fleshes out his or her own view. It is in connecting with others who have views useful to self (although not necessarily only views in agreement with one's own) that one develops a personal sense useful for directing one's own step-taking. Also inherent to a focus on subjectivity is the idea that humans are complex creatures who at different times and spaces have physical and emotional feelings, unconscious as well as conscious desires, states of being muddled and confused as well as states of being that are certain. All of these relate to the observings human do and are part of the context within which one human comes to understand another human's observations.

Anchoring in Time-Space

Related to the above is the mandate to focus journalistic practice with deliberate emphasis on concerns for differences in time-space. Instead of asking "who" should be allowed to speak, communication-based journalism would ask "where and when" does this phenomena manifest itself differently and "who" can give voice to these differences. History and context become systematic foci for all journalistic practice given this mandate.

Rejecting Rigid Categorizations of Form and Content

While any journalistic product will, of course, demand structure—placement, timing, categorization—a communication theory of journalistic practice requires that we re-evaluate the utility of system-imposed categories. The news versus entertainment distinction, for example, is not only questionable because modern media practices are blurring old distinctions but because it is not fundamentally a functional distinction for human sense-makers. Likewise, arbitrary distinctions such as local versus national versus international news blur the connectings that people are attempting to make that allow them to create as much of a wholeness out of their lives as reality and life permit. Research on how people make sense has shown, for example, that there are alternative sense-making-focused categorizations which can be systematically used in media products. One example is with what kind of "muddle" or "confusion" people come to a journalistic story. Because all humans must take steps in a discontinuous reality, the constructing of bridges in the absence of complete information can be seen as a universal human mandate. Given this assumption, one can look for pattern in the ways people define their muddles or gaps, the ways they attempt to build cognitive bridges, and the ways they put new ideas to use once they construct them. Each of these becomes a locus of potential categorizations for an alternative journalism.

Positioning Users/Audience/Readers at the Center

A communication-driven journalistic practice would implement an understanding of practice in which audience sense-making is central. Such a practice would use audience inputs not only to react to journalistic practice but to define it as well, determining what it is that audience members are attempting to make sense of and what inputs they would find helpful. This does not imply a silencing or de-privileging of the journalistic voice. Rather, it implies a privileging of multiple voices and a search for a viable dialogic inter-face to display difference.

Utilizing Multiple Entry Points

All of the points discussed suggest that even the physical construction of journalistic products can be reinvented in order to allow for the inclusion of multiple entry points into coverage. While journalists have been trained to revere the traditionally accepted coherent narrative, in actuality audiences may be better informed by coverage that con-sists of a series of module-like components which audience members can put together in whatever form is most useful to them. Spacings, indentations, charts, and visuals are all devices which might be used to this end. The important point here though is the idea of a journalistic practice which systematically accounts for and attends to the differing sense-making needs which audience members bring to the media.

Privileging Both Difference and Accuracy

It is important to emphasize that the argument here is not a call for a solipsistic partici-patory journalism. It is a call for developing journalistic practices that present differ-ences coherently and compare them communicatively anchored in the time-spaces from which they arise. If the guidelines presented above were fully applied they would lead to fundamental changes in conceptions of what journalism practice is about. Accuracy as a standard for practice would not be eliminated but it would be humbled by being placed into a dialogic or communicative relationship with difference. Both statements of agreement regarding reality (e.g., what it is, what is it like, or what caused it) as well as statements of disagreement would be anchored in the conditions of their making, in the contexts in which they became sense-makings for their makers. Journalistic practice would be mandated to facilitate voices of difference searching for and using commu-nicative processes to address continuities as well as discontinuities between and within.

CONCLUSION

If one compares the practice mandates immediately above with the set of examples of current journalistic practice listed earlier, the contrast is clear. A journalism based on per-sonalities and "stars," driven by rigid news values and rules for story selection, focused on the development of coherent closed narratives which reduce uncertainty in one and only one way is unintentionally, but from a communication perspective, inherently an authoritarian journalism. A non-authoritarian journalism, based on modern understandings of human sense-making, will indeed look radically different.

Can such a journalism be systematic? The position taken in this chapter is: yes. What is being proposed here is that human concerns, formerly thought of as subjective, can be dealt with systematically when one refocuses one's attention from content to process. If what is being proposed is a new journalism, then it is a new journalism focused on dialogue—mandating both that practice attend to the sense-making needs of different people and that practice attend to these needs with coverage that utilizes diversity in viewpoint to help people inform themselves. This becomes an approach in which instead of homogenizing difference as in traditional journalism practice, difference becomes a tool for communication. What prevents the attention in this practice to difference from descending into chaos is that this new journalism is guided by a theory of the universals of human sense-making: the facing, defining, and making and unmaking of bridges. This theory guides both the practice of understanding the audience, as well as the practice of designing coverage and structuring the media product.

In some senses, it is accurate to say that journalists have not been trained to attend to communicating. Rather, they have been trained to attend to the construction of messages without concern for audience. These messages are then transmitted and the sheer fact of transmission is called *communication*. The audience is then checked from time to time on whether they are receiving the transmission.

In contrast, a communication theory of journalistic practice makes craft secondary to and derivative of the communication purpose. There is little doubt that this attacks what many consider to be what is most precious about being a journalist—the honing and using of specialized observing and message-constructing skills. Such suggested changes in practice do not fall easily on most journalistic ears. The reasons are multiple, having to do not only with threats to self-definition but also with threats to routine. Humans are necessarily creatures of habit. We cannot create anew the *hows* of doing at each moment. And most of the *hows* by which we do—certainly in any professional context—have been hard won. Changing a routine is even more difficult than acquiring a new one. Set that routine in an elaborate institutional structure with its own interconnections with the forces and hegemony of the larger society and we face an understandable panorama of resistance.

Such a formidable barrier becomes less formidable, however, when we set our mission in a larger frame. Part of that frame involves remembering that humans have the capacity for change. This allows us not to disregard these proposals as mere utopian fantasy but rather to redefine them as a utopian methodology—guidelines for addressing the unrealized potentials of journalistic practice; guidelines serving the will to invent which is so characteristic of the species.

Another part of enlarging our vision beyond the seeming immutabilities of current journalistic practice is remembering that the stakes are high. Both journalism practitioners and the academics who train them and pursue research intended to inform and guide them are mandated to invent new practices that are dialogic at their core. We are concerned here with how journalistic practice serves the species. Ultimately, however, this concern becomes the survival of the species.

NOTES

1. Some portions of this chapter in an earlier version were presented by senior author Dervin under the title "Journalism Procedure as Ideology" at a seminar on Models of Journalism—West, East, and South, held in Budapest (Gödöllö), Hungary, 21–23 August 1990 and sponsored by the International Journalism Institute (Prague, Czechoslovakia). Thanks are owed to Kaarle Nordenstreng (University of Tampere, Tampere, Finland) who organized the seminar for encouraging these kinds of ruminations.

2. Harish Khanna, Executive Director of the Population Foundation of India, used the phrase "Socratic spirit of questioning" in referring to Eapen in a circular calling attention to Eapen's recent book, *Communication: A discipline in distress.*

3. We have chosen the occasion of this chapter for breaking free from the usual constraints of academic writing to spin a web of argument at several abstraction levels above the various literatures that inform this chapter. For this reason, we are not citing specific sources in text but want to call readers' attentions to the debts we owe to some authors in particular:

(a) Our understanding of dominant journalistic procedures as implied in journalistic structures and evidenced in practice have been usefully informed by: Althiede (1985), Argumedo (1981), Bruck (1989), Gitlin (1980), Hachten (1982), Hamelink (1983), Jensen (1987a), Katz (1987), Poster (1995), and Tuchman (1978).

(b) Our focus on journalistic procedures is anchored in a wider framework of understanding mass communication structures and procedures. Our thinking here has been usefully informed by these recent compendiums: Avery and Eason (1995), Berger (1995), Crowley and Mitchel (1994), and Ettema and Whitney (1994).

(c) Our understanding of the potentials for alternative journalistic practice have been informed, in particular, by: Beltrán (1980), Reyes Matta (1986), Shah (1996), and Tehranian (1982)

(d) Our critiques of journalistic practice in this chapter are based primarily in meta-theoretic or philosophic analyses—that is, the ways in which practices exemplify particular philosophic assumptions. Our thinking in this regard has been much helped by: Bourdieu (1989), Dewey (1960b), Freire (1970), Giddens (1984), Goodman and Fisher (1995), Habermas (1984, 1987b), Hall (1989), Lukes (1974), Mouffe (1992), Rorty (1979), Smith (1990), and E.C. White (1987).

(e) The underlying framework used in this chapter is derived from the Sense-Making approach to communication research—its critique, design, implementation, and application. This approach and its applications are not reviewed in detail here. Readers are directed to Dervin (1989a, 1989b, 1994), Dervin and Clark (1993), and Huesca and Dervin (1996). Dervin's work is richly informed by the work of Richard Carter (1989c, 1991) which focuses on increasing the productivity of communication theorizing.

Chapter 17

Chaos, Order, and Sense-Making:
A Proposed Theory for Information Design

Brenda Dervin

The term *information design* is being used as a designator for a new arena of activity. Their underlying assumption is that as a species we face altered circumstances that demand a new practice. They further assume that prior to the advance of the new communication technologies there was no pressing need for information design; without these increasingly unnatural channels, people effectively distributed information through existing channels in natural ways.

INFORMATION DESIGN:
SOMETHING NEW, SOMETHING OLD

While granting that others have drawn many strong arguments from these assumptions, I want in this chapter to challenge the central idea that information design is a new idea. Reducing the issues briefly to a polarity, it is useful to start by considering two ways to conceptualize information. One way, implicit in the above assumptions, is that information is something that describes an ordered reality and has some knowable, or at least idealized, isomorphic relationship to that reality (i.e., it represents in an identical way the form and content of reality). In short, information instructs us, this assumption says, about the nature of the world we live in: its history, its future, its functioning, our place in it, our possible actions, and the potential consequences of these actions. Information, conceptualized in this way, can be seen as inherently beneficial, for it offers enormous survival value. Clearly, such a set of assumptions makes the economic and effective distribution of information an uncontested mandate.[1]

Intrinsic to this way of conceptualizing information is the implication that the "something" labeled *information* can be readily distributed, like concrete objects, from time to time, place to place, and person to person.[2] To follow this metaphor to its con-

This work originally appeared as: Dervin, B. (1999). Chaos, order, and Sense-Making: A proposed theory for information design. In R. Jacobson (Ed.), *Information design* (pp. 35–57). Cambridge, MA: MIT Press. Reprinted by permission of MIT Press, Cambridge, MA.

clusion, we must put aside temporarily any misgivings we may have about the capacities of human beings to act as observers. Aside, then, from needed improvements in human powers of observation, in this metaphor we see information as a natural thing potentially movable from place to place by natural means. In our current circumstances, therefore, only the fact that unnatural forces are at work demands that we create a new practice: information design.

A second, alternative view of information contests this scenario. Evidence is accumulating that we are using the enormous capacities of the new technologies to do what we have already done in the past—though on far larger scales, much faster, at greater distances, and with much greater frequency. Further, taking a hard look at fundamentals and setting aside issues of scale, I argue in this chapter that the information design thus far offered by the new technologies is not that much different from that made possible by the old technologies or, since early history, by nontechnological human practices.

In order to consider these fundamentals in detail, however, we must start with an alternative assumption about information itself: that there is nothing natural about information. Information, no matter what it is called—data, knowledge, or fact, song, story, or metaphor—has *always* been designed. This alternative assumption about information is what drives this chapter. In it, I argue that assuming information design to be a new practice can only deter us from facing head-on some alternative conceptualizations of what that activity could be about.

In the succeeding sections of this chapter, I develop this argument by first presenting a brief history of our treatments of the concept *information* and discussing the implications of these treatments for a practice called *information design*. I then extract from this discussion guiding principles important for theorizing about the practice of information design. Next, I present an exemplar theory, methodology, and practice called Sense-Making, which embodies these principles. I conclude with several illustrations of how Sense-Making can be applied to practical situations.

CONCEPTS OF INFORMATION: A BRIEF HISTORY

It is beyond the purpose of this chapter to dig deeply into the historical roots of our treatments of the concept *information*. Rather, my goal here is to provide briefly a context for the alternative I am presenting. A complex history may be simplified by tracing the treatments of information in Western thought through seven chronological narratives:

1. Information describes an ordered reality.

2. Information describes an ordered reality but can be "found" only by those with the proper observing skills and technologies.

3. *Information describes an ordered reality that varies across time and space.*

4. *Information describes an ordered reality that varies from culture to culture.*

5. *Information describes an ordered reality that varies from person to person.*

6. *Information is an instrument of power imposed in discourse on those without it.*

7. *Information imposes order on a chaotic reality.*

While I present these narratives in the rough chronological order of their appearance in the philosophical literature, the chronology is really cumulative, in the sense that all narratives are present in our time in various combinations and in both commensurate and highly contested arrangements. We could describe the narratives extensively in terms of their philosophic underpinnings. For present purposes, however, we need provide only just enough of the basic ideas behind them to give foundation to my argument. Essentially, the argument is this: Historically, information was conceptualized as a natural description of natural reality. This way of seeing information remains the dominant conceptualization assumed in the design of information systems—and it is heavy baggage. Most of our ideas about information design attempt to achieve narrative No. 1 while struggling with narratives Nos. 2 through 7.

There are three themes that run through the chronology of narratives. One focuses on the nature of reality, one on the nature of human observing, and one on the involvement of power. Briefly, the chronology suggests that over time conceptualizations of information's capacity to describe reality (i.e., its ontological assumptions) have first been tempered and then directly contested. The tempering came first with a growing understanding of the limits of human observation (as in No. 2); then with a growing understanding of the impacts of time and space (as in No. 3). Ultimately, the very foundational assumptions of reality were shaken (as in Nos. 6 and 7). At one extreme we have an ordered and universal reality; at the other, a chaotic and inaccessible reality.

The second theme focuses on human observing, which, the chronology suggests, was historically assumed to create "informations" that were isomorphic with reality (as in No. 1). Over time, this conceptualization evolved: first to incorporate the idea that information needed a way to correct and control the potential biases and errors of human observing (as in No. 2); and then, in chronological steps, to accept the relativistic notion that observing differs according to contextual, cultural, and personal perspectives (as in Nos. 3, 4, and 5). Finally, most recently, it integrated the belief that human observing is a product of discourses of power (as in No. 6). At one extreme, therefore, we have an epistemology assuming a universally applicable ability to observe an ordered reality and at the other an entirely relativistic, solipsistic (i.e., unique to each person), or tyrannical view of observation.

The third theme focuses on the involvement of power in information. This theme is more subtle, because it does not permeate the movement across narratives but rather bursts forth suddenly in No. 6. In earlier assumptions, power was irrelevant; information was assumed to have a universal character based on an assumed capacity to precisely mirror reality. Moving through the narratives, however, we can see the impact of historical struggles with power: Cultural relativity, for example, applied to ideas about information argues for the right of peoples' observings to differ, not only across time and space (as in No. 3), but also across cultures (as in No. 4). But people within cultures differ as well, and when individual voices demand to be heard we see the emergence of personal relativity (as in No. 5) and, ultimately, the concept that all attempts to formalize information are bounded within discourses of power (as in No. 6).

We have drastically abbreviated a great deal of philosophical history in the above paragraphs. The important point for our purposes here is this: We can think of narratives Nos. 2 through 7 as resulting, in part, from struggles to maintain narrative No. 1. Nested within the narratives are a host of polarities that plague the design and implementation of information systems—not to mention the very construction of our societies. Alternatively, however, we can reconceptualize the narratives as subordinate parts of a larger picture. Sometimes, this view assumes, information describes an orderly reality; sometimes it requires specialized observing skills and technologies; sometimes it varies across time and space, and from culture to culture and person to person. Sometimes it represents the imposition of power; sometimes it imposes order on chaotic reality. If one accepts all the narratives as useful, the difficulty becomes how to transcend the seemingly inherent contradictions among them. For these purposes, therefore, I propose an eighth narrative:

> 8. *Information is a human tool designed by human beings to make sense of a reality assumed to be both chaotic and orderly.*

THE ALTERNATIVE NARRATIVE AND ITS IMPLICATIONS

It is possible to look at narratives Nos. 2 through 7 as a struggle with two ideas inherent in narrative No. 1—the notions of a fixed and orderly reality and of *a human power to observe that can accurately perceive that reality.* As the historical narrative unfolds, increasing complexities are introduced into the assumptions underlying the nature of observing, while assumptions about reality are reduced to an impossibly simple choice—either reality is orderly or it is inaccessible and chaotic.

Narrative No. 8 builds on the earlier narratives most clearly in its position on observing while at the same time as it attempts to transcend the impossible choice by accepting both the ordered realities of narratives Nos. 1 through 5 and the imposed/chaotic realities of narratives Nos. 6 and 7. Thus narrative No. 8 posits that humans live in a reality that sometimes manifests itself in orderly ways and sometimes manifests itself in chaotic ways.

The importance of this ontological position lies in its implications for how systems handle human differences in information-making. Narratives Nos. 1 through 5, after presenting all the reasons why people see the world differently, cannot resolve the differences or find a way to ameliorate them except with a tautology: People see the world differently because they differ. Thus there is no mandate (nor any possibility) for one person to learn from another. At this point, therefore, the solipsism becomes unbearable, and we retreat for resolution to narrative Nos. 1 and 2. But each chronological advance in our theories of information makes this retreat more and more difficult, and it becomes ultimately impossible, as narrative No. 7 demonstrates.

In contrast, narrative No. 8 forces us to a different resolution, one with profound implications for information design. The resolution is that in the face of differences we must look not for differences in how humans, individually and collectively, see their worlds but how they "make" their worlds (i.e., construct a sense of the world and how it works). This view is more than just a mandate to understand how others see the world; it makes that understanding an ontological necessity. For if we conceptualize the human condition as a struggle through an incomplete reality, then the similar struggles of others may well be informative for our own efforts.

Notice here how much traditional baggage we must jettison—the idea, for example, that there is a given amount or kind of information that can fully instruct us about a given reality. Instead, this narrative assumes that movement through a given time-space (as well as gaps in physical, natural, and/or social reality) introduces an inherent inability to be completely instructed (i.e., to attain complete information). By assuming ontological chaos as well as order, we force ourselves to realize that it may be more useful to conceptualize human beings as information designers rather than information seekers and finders.

Sometimes the information designing seems suggestive of a reality that is ordered; when, for example, a consensus regarding observing—process, product, and consequences—yields an informative outcome we call *fact* because its application to material conditions produces reliable and useful outcomes. But the only way we can account for the overbearing evidence that today's fact is tomorrow's folly, or worse the cause of tomorrow's rebellion, is to reconceptualize what is involved in facts. *Fact*, as a word, has traditionally had an essentialist meaning: A fact describes a reality that is. On the other hand, *factizing*, as a verb, suggests that among the many ways in which people make their worlds is a proceduring, a designing called *making facts*. There are many other words that can be used as verbs. A suggestive list might include, besides factizing: *emoting, comparing, concluding, predicting, consequenting, avoiding, communing, creating, opinioning, socializing, imposing, terrorizing, inculcating, challenging, resisting,* and *destroying*.

With this simple idea—that whatever it is that humans make informationally of their worlds, they are always involved in acts of design—we can pull together the threads offered by the discussion above. The result is a view of humans who are themselves ordered and chaotic moving through a reality that is ordered and chaotic. Humans make sense individually and collectively as they move: from order to disorder, from disorder to order.

This narrative refocuses our attention away from information as such to the constant design and redesign of the sense by which humans make and unmake their worlds. Because of its emphasis on information as designed and redesigned—as made, confirmed, supported, challenged, resisted, and destroyed—this approach positions power as a primary consideration rather than as afterthought. Borrowing from narrative No. 6, this narrative requires that the power inscribed in information be subject to continuing deconstruction (i.e., constant analysis and reanalysis). One possible consequence of doing so would be a capacity in information-system design to avoid the ways in which systems now build-in inequities. In essence, our current design situation is one in which information is assumed to be natural but is in fact designed. And, because it is designed without attention to design, it fits the needs, struggles, and resources of the designers. This puts all others at a disadvantage.

Theories that explain why the others don't make use of these valuable design systems can take a variety of forms. Nonetheless, they can be summarized in the argument that humans are too chaotic and overwhelmingly various to make responsive system designs possible. Yet, if in fact we have developed theories of information and system designs based on narratives Nos. 1 to 5, then we know that, ultimately, difference can always be measured against a standard. The system is X; people who cannot or will not use it are not-X. Research efforts to understand these recalcitrant non-users seem to show that they lack both understanding of and interest in what is deemed by the designers to be appropriate use of the system. This finding, in turn, leads some to conclude that information design must be reduced to the lowest common denominator and, in turn, to theories of madness or badness that locate the source of problems in users' defects. Such theories persist despite ample evidence to the contrary.

SOME PRINCIPLES FOR A THEORY OF INFORMATION DESIGN

Each of the earlier narratives about information moves us away from the idea that seeking and finding information does not involve design. What emerges in narrative No. 8 is a conceptualization of information that, although informed by the complexities of narratives Nos. 6 and 7, does not abandon the human potential for observing implied by the earlier narratives.

For purposes of our discussion, I label narrative No. 8 a *communication perspective on information*. The central idea here is that information is made and unmade in communication—intrapersonal, interpersonal, social, organizational, national, and global. With this view of information, information design cannot treat information as a mere thing to be economically and effectively packaged for distribution. Rather, it insists that information design is, in effect, metadesign: design about design, design to assist people to make and unmake their own informations, their own sense. Some of these metadesigns may pertain to human activities amenable to fact transmission, though studies suggest that relatively few human uses of information can be addressed solely in a factizing mode. The theory behind narrative No. 8 also contends that metadesign must deal with the entire complex range of what humans do when they make sense, when they construct their movements through what is assumed to be an ever-changing, sometimes chaotic, sometimes orderly, sometimes impenetrable time-space.

Narrative No. 8, then, mandates a particular kind of theory, one that focuses on information as made and unmade in communication; as designed by all humans, individually and collectively, in struggle and mediation; as relevant to both making and unmaking order and chaos; as theoretically incomplete and always open to potential challenge; as relevant not only to the centered human but also the decentered human; as pertinent to the human heart, body, and spirit as well as the human mind.

Further, this theory of information design decrees that we create an information system to assist people in designing their own information and, in particular, in sharing with each other the ways in which they have struggled individually and collectively to both create order out of chaos and create chaos out of order when order restricts or constrains them. Such a theory would demand that we redefine the standards by which we judge something as informative: in essence, redefine what we mean by success and failure. The system would allow not only the factizing that permits regimentation as a sometimes useful way of making sense but also the myths and storytelling that permit us to tolerate and muddle through diversities and seeming incompletenesses.

SENSE-MAKING:
AN EXEMPLAR THEORY, METHODOLOGY, AND PRACTICE

The Sense-Making approach, which has been twenty-two years in development, is in actuality a set of assumptions, a theoretic perspective, a methodological approach, a set of research methods, and a set of communication practices. The approach was originally developed to assess how patients/audiences/users/clients/citizens make sense of their intersections with institutions, media, messages, and situations and to apply the results in designing responsive communication/information systems. Since its early development, the approach has been applied in a variety of contexts (e.g., political communications, everyday information seeking, health communications, organizational images, mass media, and telecommunications). It has been used at various levels of analysis (e.g., individual, group, organization, community, and culture) in both quantitative studies with sample sizes as large as a thousand and in qualitative studies with as few as twenty participants. Work resting on the approach has been published and cited, primarily, in the various communications, information, and library science fields, with some secondary usage in other fields.[3]

The phenomena of interest for Sense-Making is *sense-making*, which we define broadly in terms of the set of assumptions about reality, observing, and power suggested by narrative No. 8. Sense-Making starts with the fundamental assumption of the philosophical approach of *phenomenology*—that the actor is inherently involved in her observations, which must be understood from her perspectives and horizons. What differs in the Sense-Making formulation is the explicit acceptance of a reality assumed to be both orderly and chaotic. Sense-Making, then, brings these assumptions together by asserting that—given an incomplete understanding of reality (ontology) and an incomplete understanding of what it is to know something (epistemology)—we arrive at an uncompromising problematic for the species: how to bridge persistent gaps in existence (gaps between self at time 1 and time 2, between person 1 and person 2, between person and society, organization and organization, and so on).

From this reasoning, Sense-Making extracts two assumed mandates for the species: one is to make sense without complete instruction in a reality, which is itself in flux and requires continued sense-making; the second is to reach out to the sense made by others, in order to understand what insights it may provide into our continuing human dilemma. Sense-Making emphasizes the importance of the latter requirement in particular, for it is not rooted (as most calls for understanding difference are) only in a relativistic epistemology but rather in the assumption that humans *must* muddle through together and that their usual tools assuming a wholly ordered reality are inadequate for making sense of all their experiences in a world that is both ordered and chaotic.

Setting this understanding within the common polarities of social theorizing today, Sense-Making explicitly enters the research situation in the "in-between" spaces between order and chaos, structure and individual, culture and person, self 1 and self 2, and so on. Sense-Making focuses on how humans make and unmake, develop, maintain, resist, destroy, and change order, structure, culture, organization, relationships, and the self.

The Sense-Making theoretic assumptions are implemented through a core methodological metaphor that pictures the person as moving through time-space, bridging gaps, and moving on. Sense-Making thus requires theorizing based on concepts relating to *time, space, movement,* and *gap*. It also rests on a theory of the subject that is consonant with its ontological and epistemological assumptions: The human is conceptualized as centered and decentered; ordered and chaotic; cognitive, physical, spiritual, and emotional; and potentially differing in all these dimensions across time and across space. Sense-Making assumes that the rigidities in information use implicitly hypothesized by demographic, personality, and many constructivist theories pertain only to a subset of human possibilities. As humans move across time-space, both rigidities and flexibilities are possible. Sense-Making assumes that one of the reasons why our theories of information use and their potential applications to design have been so weak is that they have focused primarily on predicting patterns in rigidities, rather than patterns in flexibilities.

One way in which Sense-Making differs markedly from other approaches is that it explicitly, and necessarily, privileges the ordinary person as a theorist involved in developing ideas to guide an understanding of not only her personal world but also collective, historical, and social worlds. Sense-Making must theorize about the individual human in this way because of narrative No. 8's acceptance of ontological incompleteness. If reality is incomplete, then movement through it must be guided by theory, not merely by fact. Further, in its attention to movement, Sense-Making requires us to focus on power by attending to forces that facilitate movement and forces that inhibit and constrain movement.

While Sense-Making relies heavily on concepts of time, space, movement, and gap, we must emphasize that these are not set forth as if sense-making were merely a purposive, linear, problem-solving activity. Instead, they are posited as merely a subset of human possibilities. The Sense-Making metaphor must be understood as a highly abstract framework. Similarly, while Sense-Making focuses on the human individual, it does not rest on an individualistic theory of human action. Rather, it assumes that structure, culture, community, organization are created, maintained, reified, challenged, changed, resisted, and destroyed in communication and can only be understood by focusing on the individual-in-context, including the social context. Note, however, that this is not the same as saying that the only way to look at the individual is through the lens of social context; this kind of theorizing would imply that the individual is entirely constrained or defined by that social context, which would admit no room for resisting, changing, inventing, or muddling through.

In the context of both research and applications, Sense-Making is implemented within the Sense-Making Triangle, which encapsulates the Sense-Making metaphor in a picture of the human (individually or collectively) moving from a situation (time-space) across a gap by making a bridge, and then moving onto the other side of the bridge. The three points of this triangle, therefore, are situation, gap/bridge, and outcome.

In the research context, for example, the Sense-Making metaphor may be implemented in interviews in several ways, ranging from brief interviews of twenty to thirty minutes to in-depth interviews lasting from one or two hours and up to six hours. The foundational interviewing approach, the one most aligned with Sense-Making's theory, is called the Micro-Moment Time-Line Interview. In this approach the interviewer asks the respondent to describe one or more critical situations in detail: first in terms of what happened first, second, third, and so on; then, for each Time-Line event, in terms of the situations (e.g., barriers, constraints, history, memory, experience), gaps (e.g., confusions, worries, questions, muddles), bridges (e.g., ideas, conclusions, feelings, opinions, hypotheses, hunches, stories, values, strategies, sources), and outcomes (e.g., helps, facilitations, hurts, hindrances, outcomes, effects, impacts). Since Sense-Making provides only a theory of the interview and not a script, actual implementation may take myriad forms, depending on the purpose of the study (e.g., needs assessment, evaluation, audience reception, etc.). In an alternative approach, the respondent is examined in detail about the basic Time-Line and then asked to choose the most important event, or question, or contact, and so on. Some interviews begin with the situation, others with the gap, the bridge, or the outcome.

It is important to note that Sense-Making conceptualizes the research situation as itself an applied communication situation involving attempts to understand how others have designed their senses of their worlds. In this situation, the researcher is involved in a metadesign focusing on design. Similarly, in application to what is commonly called *practice*, Sense-Making posits theory of practice, a metadesign for design. In this way, there is no discontinuity between Sense-Making as a research approach and Sense-Making as an approach to the design of practice. In the following sections of this chapter I present some illustrations of applications to practice and draw some conclusions from those applications.

SOME APPLICATIONS

To date, as Sense-Making has been applied primarily in research contexts, most of the applications to practice have been hypothetical. There have been, however, a number of practice applications. We can use these applications, along with several hypothetical cases, to show how the theoretic guidance offered by narrative No. 8 translates into a theory of the practice of information design and, ultimately, to metadesign. These illustrations are presented in no particular order; their selection has been guided only by a wish to present variety.[4] While only a few of the examples described are highly technologized, it is a fundamental assumption of Sense-Making that the flexibilities the new technologies offer make implementation of Sense-Making in practice potentially powerful.

In implementing such systems, fundamental questions would need to be answered, such as: How much diversity is sufficient to trigger user sense-making? How can we serve factizing needs without cutting-off challenges to factizing and without retreating to a conceptualization of information as a thing to be transferred? How do we handle vested interests? Can a profession serve the sense-making needs of users without being subject to the powerful influences of other professionals who have vested interests in particular kinds of sense? Given the enormity of these questions, some might contend that the illustrations presented are exercises in impractical idealism. One alternative point of view, however, suggests that there is a large space in society for professional facilitators of sense-making. Yet another suggests that the myriad challenges we see to nation-states, organizational systems, and all kinds of experts are manifestations of the failure of these structures and experts to be informationally useful to people.

Sense-Making the Reference Interview

The most extensive application of Sense-Making to date has been at the library reference desk. An estimated five hundred professional librarians at several locales have been trained to use the Sense-Making approach in the reference interview. Some reference librarians report that they have changed entirely to this approach, while others say they combine Sense-Making with other techniques. Librarians using this approach as a dialogic interface between librarian and patron focus on developing a picture of the user's Sense-Making Triangle. To do so, they ask such questions as: What led you to ask this question? How do you hope to be helped? If you could get the best possible answer, what would it be like? What are you trying to do?

Journal Authors as Sense-Makers

In a small test application, abstracts of ten journal articles were prepared for students in two classes. Traditional abstracts and keywords were presented to one class. In the second class, in addition to these traditional elements, students were given authors' answers to such Sense-Making questions as: What was it that you hoped to accomplish with this article? What led you to write it? How did writing it help you? How do you think it will help others? What was your major struggle with the article? What remains unresolved? Students were asked to rank the articles in terms of their potential usefulness and were then given copies of the actual articles to use in writing term papers. Three months later they were asked to rate the articles' actual usefulness. The actual and potential usefulness rankings of the students who received the Sense-Making abstracts were significantly closer than those who received the traditional abstracts. The implication is that author abstracts guided by Sense-Making provided more potential bridges of connection to readers.

Sacrificing the Coherent Journalism Narrative

In this small-scale test application, journalism students were taught to sacrifice the coherent narrative that is the foundation stone of journalistic practice and, instead, to surround their phenomena of interest within the kind of circling of reality mandated by Sense-Making. The students were taught to ask questions of themselves, questions such as: What leads me to care about this? Who else cares? What leads them to care? What different groups of people care? Within groups, what disagreements might there be? What would be alternative views of the reasons for the disputes? Is there consensus across groups/people on any points? What explains this? The student journalists were also taught how to select for observation and interview people at five or six maximally different sites, taking into account issues of power and difference, and, within sites, to seek out both conflict and consensus and people with and without power. In writing up the results of their efforts, the students were to display the results as a number of incomplete, sometimes overlapping, sometimes disparate narratives rather than as one coherent narrative. To assess the results, a group of student readers talked with the student journalists, focusing the discussion on such questions as: Given that a journalist cannot present all viewpoints in an article, what degree of difference among interviewees—and within the minds of individual interviewees—would be sufficient to trigger the reader's own sense-making processes? How could technologies be used to implement this kind of journalism?

Transforming A Professional Stereotype

Interested in the level of activity around its video desk, a public library asked users to explain how the videos they watched helped them. The results transformed how the librarians thought about their video collections. Users reported a range of life-enhancing and survival outcomes that ran counter to the stereotype of video as an entertainment medium. As a result, the library both increased its video budget and developed programmatic connections between the video collection and literacy training.

How Books Help

At another library, readers were invited to post their answers to the following questions on a bulletin board: How did the book you are returning today help you? What leads you to say this? Librarians observed that patrons stood at the board for long periods reading other readers' responses. They also noticed an increase in demand for several books that ordinarily had low circulations.

Student Sense-Making

A trial Sense-Making system was developed for a college class. First, researchers interviewed students who had taken the class in the past. Using Sense-Making, they asked the former students to describe the sense-making they had applied to writing their term papers. After analyzing the situations, gaps, bridges, and helps each student reported, researchers structured them into an interactive computer program so that new students could plot their own paths through the input on an as-needed basis. A large number of paths were possible; students could enter through situations, gaps, bridges, or helps. For example, a student might start by choosing a situation description ("I hate this class"), a bridge ("What's the best resource on this topic?"), a gap ("How can I choose a topic when I'm so confused"), or an outcome ("What's the easiest way to do this?"). Once through the gate of each entry, additional gates were offered, again developed inductively based on the actual sense-making needs of those who had gone through the experience in the past. Students could, for example, ask a question and then select the kind of answer they would like—for example, what a librarian said, what the teacher said, what a good student or a selection of different students said. Users could also add their own comments if they found that their own sense-making needs were not well enough represented.

Information Presentation at A Blood Donating Center

At a blood center, donors' needs for information usually arise within the context of a sequenced movement of intake, testing, preparation, donating, and recovering. Most attempts to inform donors about the process, however, occur before they come to the center. A Sense-Making study showed that there are reasonably well-demarcated sequences of sense-making that can address donors' information needs and questions at particular points in the process. Results also suggested that donors often had information needs they could not easily articulate publicly; these could be handled with a donor-controlled, interactive, path-flexible sense-making system. The research results also indicated that donors were well aware of disagreements and differences of opinion among health professionals that sometimes produced different answers to their questions, and they wanted the information system to address these varying perspectives.

Information Sheets for Patients

In a small-scale application at a cancer clinic, patient information sheets concentrated on the major questions raised during Sense-Making interviews. Each sheet focused on one question. Since patients' interviews showed they were very concerned about conflicts in information, the sheets placed major emphasis on those issues. The typical question was followed by answers from three or four doctors, one or two nurses, and several patients. The answers were followed with comments that circled around the conflicts, each source explaining her or his understanding of what accounted for the differences.

Surveilling an Organization

In an organizational context, a leader used Sense-Making to begin every staff meeting by asking each staff member to talk briefly about the preceding week's work. What successes did you have last week? What successes did we collectively have last week? What made these successes possible? What barriers or struggles did you face last week? What barriers or struggles did we collectively face last week? What do you see as leading to these barriers/struggles? What do you think would help to overcome them? The leader reported that participants resisted the process at first but that over time it become a meeting highlight. In addition, the leader noted that consensus-building became much easier and that staff members become more and more tolerant of and cooperative with each other. Further, critical needs for information collecting became more clearly apparent, and people's efforts to answer questions less wasteful and better focused.

Constructing A Research Community

Much the same approach was used in a research community where each participant presented his or her work for group discussion. Presentations were kept brief—no more than thirty minutes—and no interruptions were allowed. At the end of the presentation, each listener was asked to speak for three or four minutes in answer to these questions: What was helpful to you about this presentation? How did it help? What connections do you see between your work and this presentation? What leads you to say that? What confused you about this presentation? What would have helped you handle that confusion? What would you have liked to see in this presentation that was not there? How would that have helped you? After this round, the subject was opened up for general discussion. Evaluations by both leader and participants suggested that the process helped everyone enter more easily into constructive dialogue and find ways to connect with and assist each others' work.

Self Sense-Making

In this application, people used the detailed Micro-Moment Time-Line Interview to ask themselves about a situation of struggle or confusion or threat. Following the usual approaches to the interview, the self-interviewers described what happened in detail and then examined each Time-Line step in terms of what conclusions or ideas or thoughts had arisen, what emotions or feelings they felt, and what confusions or worries they faced. Each conclusion, idea, thought, emotion, feeling, confusion, worry was then probed. What led to it? How does it connect to the rest of my life? Did it help me or facilitate my efforts? Did it hurt or hinder me? How? What constraints or barriers or forces are at play? What explains these? Over the past twenty years more than a thousand people have conducted these self-interviews. Many have observed increases in their understanding of not only themselves but also others and the conditions and events that affect them. Further, they have reported improvements in understanding how and what information from others could be helpful in similar situations.

CONCLUSIONS

In this chapter I have traced briefly a history of theories of information design and have proposed that we must change our theory if we are to pursue a practice that is maximally helpful to the human condition. I have also presented an exemplar approach called Sense-Making, whose theory and methodology calls for a looking at information design as a dialogic circling of reality, a reality that can be reached for but never touched, described in gossamer but never sculpted. This practice focuses on metadesign—design about design—and explicitly acknowledges that its work involves not merely transferring information from here to there but assisting human beings in their information design.

If we are to pursue this challenge, we will have to examine our use of terms traditionally held to be fundamental to information processes—*fact, knowledge, data*—and, even, the concept *information* itself. Our views of information are challenged by what many observers call the most important philosophic rupture of our time, with order on one side and chaos on the other. Traditional views of information define it as serving the former and threatened by the latter. What I propose in this chapter is a reconceptualization that chooses both order and chaos and that focuses on the ways humans individually and collectively design the sense (i.e., create the information) that permits them to move from one to the other. Some may see this reconceptualization as diminishing the role of information design, but an alternative view suggests that it may enrich that role to one of far-reaching consequences for the human species.

NOTES

1. Since the mandate for this volume is to write for a diverse audience, I present the arguments in this chapter in as accessible language as possible without arduously tracing of the roots of ideas and supplying detailed footnotes. Citations are reduced to the bare essentials and to only the most recent work by scholars whose ideas I have relied on. Readers who wish more detailed and extensive presentations—albeit developed for different purposes—are directed to Dervin (1989a, 1989b, 1992, 1993, 1994). I owe particular gratitude to Richard F. Carter (1989c, 1991), whose work has informed the my own thinking more than any other.

2. In this chapter, the terms *information, knowledge, knowing, data,* and *truth* are used purposely without any attempt to distinguish precisely among them. The intent is to point out the ways we uses these terms without definition in everyday discourse, even everyday scholarship. It is a major premise of this chapter that most of the conceptual edi-

fices constructed to distinguish one term from another in fact posit *truth*—defined as statements isomorphic to reality—as the criterion for knowledge and information.

    3.   In this presentation, Sense-Making the approach is distinguished from sense-making the phenomena by the use of the two capital letters.

    4.   More complete descriptions of most of these examples can be found in Dervin (1989a, 1992), and Dervin and Dewdney (1986). More information can also be obtained from the author.

Chapter 18

Peopling the Public Sphere

Brenda Dervin & David Schaefer

There are two thrusts in current debates regarding the nature of communication for the human species. These two thrusts permeate virtually every discourse whether applied to the expanding Internet, communication technologies, journalism practice, communicating in the community, or the creation of public spheres. One of these thrusts is the structural thrust. In its most extreme form, human beings and their communication worlds are enslaved and the public sphere is nothing but a pawn of that enslavement. Whereas once the enslavement was seen as being controlled by feudal lords in kingdoms or tyrants in nation-states, now the enslavement is seen as increasingly controlled by capital, and in particular transnational corporations which, while decreasing in number, control more and more communication channels. Typically, for those writing in this thrust, the hopes for the future are few. The alternative, usually set up in opposition, is often called the postmodern thrust. This perspective points toward human freedom, resistance, and the capacity to transcend even the most enslaving of conditions, to create rapture, bliss, and pleasure in virtually all situations. For those writing in this thrust, nothing is ever totally inscribed, there are always spaces in whatever structures may attempt to enslave us. For this thrust, the new communication technologies, and in particular the World Wide Web, are seen as sites of great hope, of emerging natural communities where like-minded people find each other in order to create these moments of community and pleasure and cooperation.[1]

Obviously if one is standing outside of these two perspectives, there are potential compatabilities between them. Unfortunately, our discourses are not arranged that way. The question "how does the postmodern focus on freedoms address the structural focus on constraint and vice versa?" is rarely asked. While there are key moments when authors attempt to bridge these gaps, these moments are not the center of these discourses.

The state of our discourses is such that the in-between question is considered to be an unredemptively modernist question because the in-between, whatever it is, must be

This work originally appeared as: Dervin, B., & Schaefer, D. (1999). Peopling the public sphere. *Peace Review, 11* (1), 17–23. Reprinted by permission of Taylor & Francis, Ltd., Oxfordshire, UK (*http://www.tandf.co.uk/journals*).

made. For the postmodernists, who perceive that anything that is planned or made is by definition potentially tyrannical, this harkens back to the time of utopian hopes associated with the modernist project. In the modernist vision it was assumed that technological advances would allow an end to want and that, with an end to want, truly just societies would be created. Unfortunately, history has taught us these dreams were illusory at best.

Postmodernists typically do not focus on planning or utopias, but on an assumed natural propensity for human beings to create, in struggle, approximations of cooperative, loving, and peaceful communities, despite the many powers that attempt to enslave them. In an ironic way, then, the postmodern thrust that denies most certainties, posits a kind of certainty—a natural propensity—in human beings. But, of course, what is natural to human beings is historically the subject of long debate.

We seem, then, to be at a rather paradoxical moment. The finer qualities of the human species are relegated in our discourses to be the result of so-called "natural" community makings, which are increasingly said to exist only in cyberspace. On the other hand, we see an overwhelming body of evidence that the octopine hold of capital is becoming increasingly strong and that these natural community makings are no match for the powerful intrusions of capital in our lives.

Not only that, but attributing the finer qualities of community makings to cyberspace is in itself problematic. What naturally happens in cyberspace is well documented. When left to spontaneous activity, the communicating that results, for the most part, replicates and, in some situations, intensifies the power structures of society. For example, there is ample evidence that in cyberspace women are more silent than men and more likely to be responded to negatively than are men. At the same time, it is estimated that only 5% of the world's people have access to these technologies. Further, even within the 5%, it is estimated that 95% of cyberspace activity is still related to the hold of capital on the human condition. Perhaps as a consequence of these factors, there is clear evidence that the kinds of communities being made in cyberspace are primarily of like-minded people: neo-nazis find each other as do anti-nazis; radical feminists find each other as do anti-feminists. It is rarely evidenced, however, that communicating in cyberspace occurs naturally across these polarities or the host of other polarities that stand between the human species and their dreams of peace.

In our discourses, scholarly and lay, we are impossibly stuck between a belief that any kind of discipline is somehow naturally tyrannical and that any kind of freedom is somehow naturally not. Our discourses are replete with numerous examples of this polarity. A recent example in the communication field is the use of a framing perspective. Scholars from very different approaches nest their work under this rubric but, in fact, they profess allegiances to quite different conceptions of framing. From one humanistic perspective, framing consists of resources and tools that communicators use to maximize desired interpretations. Yet, when spoken of from a structuralist perspective, framing is a hegemonic strategy used to obscure or hide forces of power.

This polarity is frequently referred to as "structure versus agency," and is most often attributed to Giddens, even though his intent was not to propose a polarity. Indeed it is symptomatic of our difficulties that those who interpret Giddens from a structuralist perspective see him as too individualistic, and those who interpret him from an individualistic perspective see him as too structural.

Both theoretically and practically we seem to be caught between a disappearing public sphere erased by big business and capital, and natural community spheres implemented in a new kind of feudalism, a feudalism of like-minded souls who have no reason or interest in communing with others who are not like-minded.

We submit that the road out of this paradox requires invention. The invention we have in mind is the building of procedural bridges between structure and freedom, bridges that can serve people in their efforts to make peace. The highest achievements of the human species have hardly ever been natural—not the development of tools and technologies nor forms of community making. All of these were designed through intelligence, vision, commitment, and hope.

The idea of building bridges between these disparate discourses is a utopian idea, but we propose it as a direction for guiding movement rather than an absolute end. We propose that somewhere between the not natural and the natural, between modernist structures and natural communities, between normative traditional journalism and civic/public journalism, between polarized chaos and the human capacity for peace, there are procedures that can be designed to bridge these gaps, at least in part

While it may be natural (and we assume it is) for the human species to desire peace, we assume that it is not natural for the species to know how to make peace across diversity, particularly when that diversity is often imposed and inscribed by oppression. Communication practice is embodied, and it requires skill. A certain number of the skills that we have for communicating are taught to us within our cultural enclaves and by the myriad mediated and direct messages that we get as we grow up and experience reality. These skills become practices and become embodied in practice. Changing them requires the same.

We speak of the six 'H's—head, heart, hand, habit, hegemony, and *habitus* (borrowing here from Bourdieu and many others). The improvement of communication practice requires attention of the head (for the conceptual knowing that is involved), the heart (without the heart there is no will), the hand (without the body there is no action), habit (without practice new behavioral, cognitive, and emotional skills do not get into the repertoire), hegemony (mandating specific attention to the ways in which power inscribes oppressions into the communication system which surrounds the actors), and *habitus* (referring to the ways in which daily practices—i.e., our communicating habits—are themselves inscribed by hegemony).

We call this perspective on communicating for peace a "proceduring" perspective. It suggests that, if we are to know how to use communication to make peace, we need to attend to the ways in which power relationships interfere with our efforts so that they can be bracketed or controlled. We need information about, and practice using, a host of peace-making procedures. We need to attend to these, not as after-the-fact remedies, but as daily practice. For there to be just and fair public spheres in any arena, no matter how micro or how macro, these public spheres must be designed not only structurally but procedurally, for it is in procedures that structures are energized.

The discourses that define freedom-as-bliss and discipline-as-tyranny have reified, in both academic and popular discourse, a portrait of human beings that is shallow and incorrect; a portrait that assumes human beings are insular, greedy, uncooperative, and self-absorbed. Yet, there is ample evidence that many human beings can and do behave quite differently, not just those few whom the media hype as saints. Ordinary people participate cooperatively, usefully, and well in public spheres if those spheres are fair and useful and serve their interests. Note that "fair and useful" and to "serve one's interests" do not imply unfair to others, not useful to others, and not serving the interests of others.

Various literatures, for example in anthropology and communication, have documented a host of procedures invented by humans for the fair and just sharing of time in public discussion. There is, for example, the talking stick, a well-documented tool used by some native peoples in their cultural enclaves. The talking stick passes from hand to hand and gives the holder the right to speak without interruption by others and the right to hold that stick for a fair and reasonably equal amount of time. Other examples include some of the procedures used in the town meetings of colonial America.

While many theorists have conceptualized these procedures as spontaneous developments within specific cultural enclaves, we argue here that these procedures were designed and made. Given the systematic use of new communication procedures involves the interruption of embodied behavioral practice, these procedures had to have been designed.

As a species we must invent many more designs for peacemaking in everyday life and practice. Because of the ways our communication is now mediated by technologies, we need new inventions for communicating peacefully. A primary example of how our older models no longer apply can be found in the U.S. stakeholder model of democratic participation. This model is premised on the idea of high involvement by all participants and on serious dialogue between the representatives of any particular group and the stakeholders in that group. Because of the technological mediation of communication and control by vested interests of capital, the stakeholder approach no longer suffices. Communication between representatives and stakeholders has now degenerated to the point where stakeholders have become the targets of segmentation and strategic marketing communications. But segmentation as an approach to handling diversity in the human species only breeds conflict and contempt.

This is not only a hardware issue. Nor is it only an issue of access or information availability. It is a communication mandate. It is an issue of proceduring for dialogue. It is an issue of acknowledging that the human species needs to do more than simply transmit information from one place to another because transmission is not dialogue. What is involved is individual and collective sense-making, and sense-making demands not only observings, but thinkings, feelings, rememberings, self-understandings, musings, comparings, illustratings, abstractings, disagreeings, contestings. What is involved is a matter of developing new ways, in the globalized electronic context, of helping people hear themselves and each other and express themselves in ways that make hearing possible.

It is not only the intrusions by capital into the public sphere that are deleterious to human peacemaking, but also the assumptions that we make about the nature of communication and human beings which allow capital to do its dirty work. It is easy to assume that the segmentation approach is an appropriate model for human communication when communication is understood as the transmission of information, or information is defined as a commodity with an isomorphic and essentialist relationship to an assumed-to-be fully knowable reality, or when human beings are defined as buckets into which the information can be dropped. Given the apparent success of the marketing project, it is easy to assume that marketing has wisdoms to offer.

But all of this makes an emphasis on facts, what we call "factizing," the only strategy for sense-making in the human species—a clearly erroneous position. If you plan to send us to Mars in a spaceship, we do indeed want your facts, but we will want more than that—we will want your hunches, your irritations, even your misgivings. Taking one well-publicized disaster as an example—the explosion of the *Challenger*—research has pointed to a host of possible causes for the explosion, none of which involved a need to transmit more facts. Rather, in that disaster, we can see the consequences of a non-dialogic organizational community, a hesitancy to speak, and an inability to bridge discourse differences.

The invention mandate we propose is beyond information literacy. It has to do with establishing procedures and inventing new ones that help the species to enrich itself through its diversities, to use its diversities, not simply to name the different ways in which human beings look at a so-called factual reality, but rather to identify the different ways in which human beings make sense of and navigate a reality that is never fully closed, that is always moving across time and across space, and which by the estimates of the best physicists is itself, in part, gap filled.

To assume that reality is gap filled is not the same thing as assuming there is nothing but chaos. Rather, the assumption is that reality is in part chaotic, but because of epistemological differences between human beings we can never be sure whether differences between us are due to essential differences in us or our lives, or due to how we have made different bridges across a reality that is only in partly complete.

This way of looking at communication mandates a different conceptualization of the role of facts and objectivity, making factizing (the making of facts) only one of a number of sense-making strategies that must play a role in dialogue. In contrast, in an objectivity-based paradigm, differences ultimately have to be blamed on somebody, or seen as the result of the madness or badness of all those not agreeing with the "facts." When facts are treated as dogma the result is to diminish one of the highest achievements of the species. As a result, objectivity-based communication structures (which include virtually all of our structures) descend readily into cacophony.

The alternative approach to communication that we propose aims to go beyond cacophony. Right now, the primary method of the species for dealing with its diversity is to allow it to speak, sometimes even loudly and long. But for the most part, the methods of allowing diversity to speak are chaotic, capricious, and without design. They have a spontaneous and natural character. But in the end they marginalize diversity, turning it into a Tower of Babel.

We assume that there are universals to the human condition that transcend our important and materially anchored differences. We assume that there are ways for human beings to talk to each other so that their differences are more than babble. We assume, given the extraordinary evidence of the capacity of human beings to understand and be enriched by poetry, art and literature from times and spaces so radically different than their own, that there is something universal about the human condition that can be addressed in communication procedure.

We assume that we must learn to address humanity systematically instead of marginalizing what is human about human beings, then demanding that human beings be reflected in a mythological edifice of certainty and then building systems to maintain that edifice. What appears in that edifice builds upon the worst characteristics of human beings, their inflexibilities, their rigidities, the boxes that society and external impositions have put them into.

Those who work in communication practice and academia have investigated how to create dialogue. There are trainers, counselors, and mediators who assist the human species in peacemaking through communicating. They do so reliably. As individual human beings, we also do so reliably when we need to keep our families together. Not all of us, not all of the time; it's true that we make bad mistakes, but we intuitively know that there are ways to make peace through communication. Our assumption is that this is an everyday job and that we need to invent a host of procedures for doing so.

We assume that these approaches to communicating for peace cannot be built on the nouns and the substances of existence because this is precisely where diversity anchors itself in the experiential material conditions of life. We assume that the universals of human communicating and thus human peacemaking must be built on what we call the verbings, verbings such as factizing, contesting, comparing, illustrating, abstracting, feeling, struggling, resisting, raging, rejoicing, transcending, loving, and friending. There are many verbs of communicating that occur in our heads, in our hearts, in our bodies; some of them occur within us, some between us, and some between us and the tools we use to reach each other in mediated communicating.

We see the mandate to invent procedures for peacemaking as a project that demands the understandings produced by both sides of the polarity with which we started this chapter. We need the modernist understanding of using utopian visions as directions for movement. And we need the postmodern understanding of the perennial human project of interrupting tyranny and structure with resistance and invention and shared muddlings. In essence, we call for the creation of a postmodernist modern praxis, a theory and practice of communicating for peace.

NOTES

1. This article was published without footnotes or citations and ended with a list of recommended readings: Bourdieu (1989), Dervin (1994, 1998), Dervin and Clark (1993), Giddens (1984), and Habermas (1984, 1987b, 1989).

References

Abbagnano, N. (1967). Positivism. In P. Edwards (Ed.), *The encyclopedia of philosophy* (Vol. 6, pp. 414–419). New York: Macmillan.

Adams, J. B., Mullen, J. J., & Wilson, H. M. (1969). Diffusion of a minor foreign affairs news event. *Journalism Quarterly, 46,* 545–551.

Adams, K. L. (1997). Context and pragmatism: A matter of pattern. In J. Owen (Ed.), *Context and communication behavior* (pp. ?). Reno, NV: Context Press.

Agger, B. (1991). The dialectic of dialogue. In B. Agger (Ed.), *A critical theory of public life: Knowledge, discourse, and politics in an age of decline* (pp. 151–173). London: Falmer Press.

Allen, I. L., & Colfax, J. D. (1968). The diffusion of news of LBJ's March 31 decision. *Journalism Quarterly, 45,* 321–324.

Allport, G. W. (1960). *Personality and social encounter.* Boston: Beacon Press.

Altheide, D. (1985). *Media power.* Beverly Hills, CA: Sage.

Altman, I. (1986). Contextualism and environmental psychology. In R. L. Rosnow & M. Georgoudi (Eds.), *Contextualism and understanding in behavioral science: Implications for research and theory* (pp. 25–45). New York: Praeger.

Altman, I., & Rogoff, B. (1987). Worldviews in psychology: Trait, interactional, organismic, and transactional. In D. Stokols & I. Altman (Eds.), *Handbook of environmental psychology* (pp. 7–40). New York: Wiley.

Ang, I. (1996). Ethnography and radical contextualism in audience studies. In J. Hay, L. Grossberg, & E. Wartella (Eds.), *The audience and its landscape* (pp. 247–264). Boulder, CO: Westview Press.

Arbib, M. A. (1985). *In search of the person: Philosophical explorations in cognitive science.* Amherst: University of Massachusetts Press.

Argumedo, A. (1981). The new world information order and international power. *Journal of International Affairs,* (Summer), 179–188.

Arusha Declaration on World Telecommunications Development. (1985, May). At the First World Telecommunications Development Conference, Arusha, Tanzania (pp. 1–15).

Atkin, C. K., Bowen, L., Nayman, O., & Sheinkopf, K. (1973). Quantity versus quality in televised political advertising: Patterns of reception and response in two gubernatorial campaigns. *Public Opinion Quarterly, 37,* 209–224.

Atwood, R. (1980a, May). *Communication research in Latin America: Cultural and conceptual dilemmas.* Paper presented at the annual meeting of the International Communication Association, Acapulco, Mexico.

Atwood, R. (1980b). *A test of race versus situational movement state in predicting information seeking and use.* (Doctoral dissertation, University of Washington, 1980). *Dissertation Abstracts International, 41,* 4530.

Atwood, R., Allen, R., Bardgett, R., Proudlove, S., & Rich, R. (1982). Children's realities in television viewing: Exploring situational information seeking. In M. Burgoon (Ed.), *Communication yearbook* (Vol. 6, pp. 605–628). Beverly Hills, CA: Sage.

Atwood, R., & Dervin, B. (1981). Challenges to sociocultural predictors of information seeking: A test of race versus situation movement state. In M. Burgoon (Ed.), *Communication yearbook* (Vol. 5, pp. 549–569). New Brunswick, NJ: Transaction Books.

Avery, R. K., & Eason, D. (Eds.). (1995). *Critical perspectives on media and society.* New York: Guilford Press.

Baer, R. D. (1996). Health and mental illness among Mexican American migrants: Implications for survey research. *Human Organization, 55* (1), 58–66.

Barthes, R. (1985). *The responsibility of forms: Critical essays on music, art, and representation* (pp. 245–260; R. Howard, Trans.). New York: Hill and Wang. (Originally published 1982.)

Bateson, G. (1978). The pattern which connects. *Co-Evolution Quarterly, 18,* 4–15.

Bateson, G. (1979). *Mind and nature: A necessary unity.* Toronto, Canada: Bantam.

Baudrillard, J. (1983). *In the shadow of the silent majorities . . . Or the end of the social and other essays.* New York: Semiotext(e).

Bauer, R. A. (1964). The obstinate audience. *American Psychologist, 19,* 319–328.

Belkin, N. J. (1978). Information concepts for information science. *Journal of Documentation, 34* (1), 55–85.

Belkin, N. J. (1980). Anomalous states of knowledge as a basis for information retrieval. *Canadian Journal of Information Science, 5,* 133–143.

Belkin, N. J., Oddy, R. N., & Brooks, H. M. (1982a). ASK for information-retrieval: Part 1. Background and theory. *Journal of Documentation, 38* (2), 61–71.

Belkin, N. J., Oddy, R. N., & Brooks, H. M. (1982b). ASK for information-retrieval: Part 2. Results of a design study. *Journal of Documentation, 38* (3), 145–164.

Belkin, N. J., Seeger, T., & Wersig, G. (1983). Distributed expert problem treatment as a model for information system analysis and design. *Journal of Information Science, 5* (5), 153–167.

Bell, D. (1973). *The coming of post-industrial society.* New York: Basic Books.

Beltrán S., L. R. (1976). Alien premises, objects, and methods in Latin American communication research. *Communication Research, 3* (2), 107–134.

Beltrán S., L. R. (1980). A farewell to Aristotle: "Horizontal" communication. *Communication, 5,* 5–41.

Bem, D. (1972). Constructing cross-situational consistencies in behavior. *Journal of Personality, 40,* 17–26.

Bem, D., & Allen, A. (1974). On predicting some of the people some of the time: The search for cross-situational consistencies in behavior. *Psychological Review, 81,* 506–520.

Beninger, J. (1990). Who are the most important theorists of communication? *Communication Research, 14* (5), 698–715.

Bennett, W. L., & Edelman, M. (1985). Toward a new political narrative. *Journal of Communication, 35,* 156–171.

Berger, A. A. (1995). *Essentials of mass communication theory.* Thousand Oaks, CA: Sage.

Berger, J., Wagner, D., & Zelditch, M. (1989). Theory growth, social processes and metatheory. In J. H. Turner (Ed.), *Theory building in sociology: Assessing theoretical cumulation* (pp. 19–42). Newbury Park, CA: Sage.

Berger, P. L., & Luckmann, T. (1966). *The social construction of reality.* New York: Doubleday.

Berlo, D. K. (1977). Communication as process: Review and commentary. In B. D. Ruben (Ed.), *Communication yearbook* (Vol. 1, pp. 11–27). New Brunswick, NJ: Transaction Books.

Bernstein, B. (1961). Some sociological determinants of perception. *British Journal of Sociology, 12,* 159–175.

Bernstein, R. (1976). *The restructuring of social and political theory.* New York: Harcourt Brace Jovanovich.

Best, S., & Kellner, D. (1991). *Postmodern theory: Critical interrogations.* New York: Guilford Press.

Bhaskar, R. (1979). *The possibility of naturalism: A philosophical critique of the contemporary human sciences.* Brighton, UK: Harvester.

Bhaskar, R. (1986). *Scientific realism and human emancipation.* London: Verso.

Bhaskar, R. (1989). *Reclaiming reality: A critical introduction to contemporary philosophy.* London: Verso.

Bishop, M. (1973). Media use and democratic political orientation in Lima, Peru. *Journalism Quarterly, 50,* 60–67.

Blau, P. M. (1989). Structures of social positions and structures of social relations. In J. H. Turner (Ed.), *Theory building in sociology* (pp. 43–59). Newbury Park, CA: Sage.

Block, C. E. (1970). Communicating with the urban poor: An exploratory inquiry. *Journalism Quarterly, 47,* 3–11.

Blumenberg, H. (1983). *The legitimacy of the modern age.* Cambridge, MA: MIT Press.

Blumler, J. G. (1979). The role of theory in uses and gratification studies. *Communication Research, 6,* 9–36.

Bogatz, G., & Ball, S. (1971). *The second year of Sesame Street: A continuing evaluation.* Princeton, NJ: Educational Testing Center.

Bohman, J. (1991). *New philosophy of social science.* Cambridge, MA: MIT Press.

Bottomore, T. (Ed.). (1983). *A dictionary of Marxist thought.* Cambridge, MA: Harvard University Press.

Bourdieu, P. (1984). *Distinction: A social critique of the judgment to taste.* London: Routledge.

Bourdieu, P. (1989). *The logic of practice* (R. Nice, Trans.). Cambridge, UK: Polity Press.

Bourdieu, P. (1996). Understanding. *Theory, Culture, and Society, 13* (2), 17–36.

Bowes, J. (1971). *Information control behaviors and the political effectiveness of low-income urban adults.* Unpublished doctoral dissertation, Michigan State University, East Lansing.

Branham, R. J., & Pearce, W. (1985). Between text and context: Toward a rhetoric of contextual reconstruction. *Quarterly Journal of Speech, 71* (1), 19–36.

Branscomb, L. M. (1979). Information: The ultimate frontier. *Science, 203* (4376), 143–147.

Brendlinger, N., Dervin, B., & Foreman-Wernet, L. (1999). When informants are theorists: An exemplar study in the HIV/AIDS context of the use of sense-making as an approach to public communication campaign research. *Electronic Journal of Communication, 9* (2–4). [On-line serial]. Available at: http://www.cios.org/www/ejcrec2.htm.

Breuer, J., & Freud, S. (1957). *Studies in hysteria* (J. Strachley, Ed. & Trans.). New York: Basic Books.

Brittain, J. M. (1970). *Information and its users: A review with special reference to the social sciences.* Bath, UK: Bath University Press.

Bronowski, J. (1956). *Science and human values.* New York: Harper and Row.

Bronowski, J. (1969). *Nature of knowledge: The philosophy of contemporary science.* New York: Science Books.

Bronowski, J. (1973). *The ascent of man.* Boston: Little, Brown, and Co.

Brown, A. W. (1991). *The big picture.* New York: Harper Perennial.

Brown, S. R. (1979). Perspective, transfiguration, and equivalence in communication theory: Review and commentary. In D. Nimmo (Ed.), *Communication yearbook* (Vol. 3, pp. 51–65). New Brunswick, NJ: Transaction Books.

Bruck, P. A. (1989). Strategies for peace, strategies for news research. *Journal of Communication, 39* (1), 109–129.

Bruner, J. S. (1964). Going beyond the information given. In J. Bruner, E. Brunswik, L. Festinger, F. Heider, K. F. Muenzinger, C. E. Osgood, & D. Rapaport (Eds.), *Contemporary approaches to cognition: A symposium held at the University of Colorado* (pp. 41–70). Cambridge, MA: Harvard University Press.

Bruner, J. S. (1973). *Beyond the information given: Studies in the psychology of knowing*. New York: W. W. Norton.

Bruner, J. S. (1990). *Acts of meaning*. Cambridge, MA: Harvard University Press.

Brookes, B. C. (1980). The foundations of information science: Part 1: Philosophical elements. *Journal of Information Science, 2* (3), 125–133.

Buber, M. (1965). *The knowledge of man* (M. Friedman & R. G. Smith, Trans.). New York: Harper Torchbooks.

Buber, M. (1970). *I and thou* (J. Kaufmann, Trans.). New York: Charles Scribner. (Original work published 1923)

Bureau of the Census, U.S. Department of Commerce. (1987). *Statistical abstract of the United States* (Sudoc No. C 3.134). Washington, DC: U.S. Government Printing Office.

Calinescu, M. (1991). From the one to the many: Pluralism in today's thought. In I. Hoesterey (Ed.), *Zeitgeist in Babel: The postmodern controversy* (pp. 156–174). Bloomington: Indiana University Press.

Caplovitz, D. (1963). *The poor pay more*. New York: Free Press.

Cappella, J. N. (1977). Research methodology in communication: Review and commentary. In B. D. Rubin (Ed.), *Communication yearbook* (Vol. 1, pp. 37–51). New Brunswick, NJ: Transaction Books.

Carter, R. F. (1972, August). *A journalistic view of communication*. Paper presented at the annual meeting of the Association for Education in Journalism, Carbondale, IL.

Carter, R. F. (1973, August). *Communication as behavior*. Paper presented at the annual convention of the Association for Education in Journalism, Fort Collins, CO.

Carter, R. F. (1974a, October). *A journalistic cybernetic*. Paper presented at the Communication and Control in Social Processes Conference, University of Pennsylvania, Philadelphia.

Carter, R. F. (1974b). *Toward more unity in science*. Unpublished manuscript, University of Washington, Seattle.

Carter, R. F. (1975, October). *Elementary ideas of systems applied to problem-solving strategies*. Paper presented at the Far West Region of the Society for General Systems Research, San Jose, CA.

Carter, R. F. (1980, May). *Discontinuity and communication*. Paper presented at the East-West Center Conference on Communication Theory East and West, Honolulu, HI.

Carter, R. F. (1982). *Button, button . . . .* Unpublished manuscript.

Carter, R. F. (1989a, May). *Comparative analysis and theory in communication*. Paper presented at the annual convention of the International Communication Association, San Francisco.

Carter, R. F. (1989b, May). *What does a gap imply?* Paper presented at the annual convention of the International Communication Association, San Francisco.

Carter, R. F. (1989c). Reinventing communication, scientifically. In *World community in post-industrial society: Continuity and change in communications in post-industrial society* (Vol. 2, English ed., pp. 55–65). Seoul, Korea: Wooseok.

Carter, R. F. (1990). Our future research agenda—confronting challenges—or our dying grasp. *Journalism Quarterly, 67* (2), 282–285.

Carter, R. F. (1991). Comparative analysis, theory, and cross-cultural communication. *Communication Theory, 1* (2), 151–158.

Carter, R. F., Ruggels, W. L., Jackson, K. M., & Heffner, M. B. (1973). Application of signaled stopping technique to communication research. In P. Clarke (Ed.), *New models for mass communication research* (pp. 15–43). Beverly Hills, CA: Sage.

Carter, R. F., Ruggels, W. L., & Simpson, R. A. (1975, August). *Minding society.* Paper presented to the Association for Education in Journalism meeting, Ottawa, Canada.

Caws, P. (1989). The law of quality and quantity, or what numbers can and can't describe. In B. Glassner & J. D. Moreno (Eds.), *Boston studies in the philosophy of science: The qualitative-quantitative distinction in the social sciences* (Vol. 112, pp. 13–28). Boston, MA: Kluwer Academic.

Chandler, M. J. (1993). Contextualism and the post-modern condition: Learning from Las Vegas. In S. C. Hayes, L. J. Hayes, H. W. Reese, & T. R. Sarbin (Eds.), *Varieties of scientific contextualism* (pp. 227–247). Reno, NV: Context Press.

Chaffee, S. H. (1970, August). *Parent-child similarities in television use.* Paper presented at the annual meeting of the Association for Education in Journalism, Washington, DC.

Chaffee, S. H. (1972). The interpersonal context of mass communication. In F. G. Kline & P. J. Tichenor (Eds.), *Current perspectives in mass communication research* (pp. 95–120). Beverly Hills, CA: Sage.

Chaffee, S. H., & Atkin, C. K. (1971). Parental influences on adolescent media use. *American Behavioral Science, 14*, 323–340.

Chaffee, S. H., & Choe, S. (1978, August). *Time of decision and media use during the Ford-Carter campaign.* Paper presented at the annual meeting of the Association for Education in Journalism, Seattle, WA.

Chaffee, S. H., & McLeod, J. M. (1973). Individual versus social predictors of information seeking. *Journalism Quarterly, 50*, 237–245.

Cheek, J. (1999). Influencing practice or simply esoteric? Researching health care using postmodern approaches. *Qualitative Health Research, 9* (3), 383–392.

Childers, T., & Post, J. (1975). *The information poor in America.* Metuchen, NJ: Scarecrow Press.

Christians, C. G. (1988). Dialogic communication theory and cultural studies. *Studies in Symbolic Interaction, 9*, 3–31.

Clarke, P. (1965). Parental socialization values and children's newspaper reading. *Journalism Quarterly, 42*, 539–546.

Clarke, P., & Kline, F. G. (1974). Media effects reconsidered: Some new strategies for communication research. *Communication Research, 1* (2), 224–239.

Clatts, M. C. (1994). All the king's horses and all the king's men: Some personal reflections on ten years of AIDS ethnography. *Human Organization, 53* (1), 93–95.

Clifford, J. (1986). Introduction: Partial truths. In J. Clifford & G. E. Marcus (Eds.), *Writing culture: The poetics and politics of ethnography* (pp. 1–26). Berkeley: University of California Press.

Colapietro, V. M. (1988). From "individual" to "subject": Marx and Dewey on the person. In W. J. Gavin (Ed.), *Context over foundation: Dewey and Marx* (pp. 11–36). Dordrecht, Holland: D. Reidel Publishing.

Colton, K. W. (1979). The impact and use of computer technology by the police. *Communications of the ACM, 22* (1), 10–19.

Computer and Business Equipment Manufacturers Association. (1985). *Computer and business equipment marketing and forecast data book.* Hasbrouck Heights, NJ: Hayden.

Conant, R. C. (1979). A vector theory of information. In D. Nimmo (Ed.), *Communication yearbook* (Vol. 3, pp. 177–194). New Brunswick, NJ: Transaction Books.

Conrad, C. (1985). *Strategic organizational communication: Cultures, situations, and adaptation.* New York: Holt, Rinehart and Winston.

Cooke, T. D., Appleton, H., Conner, R. F., Shaffer, A., Tamkin, G., & Weber, S. J. (1975). *"Sesame Street" revisited.* New York: Russell Sage Foundation.

Corradi, C. (1991). Text, context, and individual meaning: Rethinking life stories in a hermeneutic framework. *Discourse and Society, 2* (1), 105–118.

Corradi Fiumara, G. (1990). *The other side of language: A philosophy of listening* (C. Lambert, Trans.). London: Routledge.

Craig, R. T. (1989). Communication as a practical discipline. In B. Dervin, L. Grossberg, B. J. O'Keefe, & E. Wartella (Eds.), *Rethinking communication: Paradigm issues* (Vol. 1, pp. 97–124). Newbury Park, CA: Sage.

Crowley, D., & Mitchel, D. (Eds.). (1994). *Communication theory today.* Stanford, CA: Stanford University Press.

Dahlgren, P., & Sparks, C. (1991). *Communication and citizenship: Journalism and the public sphere in the new media age.* London: Routledge.

Dallmayr, F. R., & McCarthy, T. A. (1977). *Understanding and social inquiry.* South Bend, IN: University of Notre Dame Press.

Damico, A. J. (1988). The politics after deconstruction: Rorty, Dewey, and Marx. In W. J. Gavin (Ed.), *Context over foundation: Dewey and Marx* (pp. 177–207). Dordrecht, Holland: D. Reidel Publishing.

Dascal, M. (1989). Hermeneutic interpretation and pragmatic interpretation. *Philosophy and Rhetoric, 22* (4), 239–259.

Davis, D. K. (1977). Assessing the role of mass communication in social processes. *Communication Research, 4* (1), 23–34.

Deleuze, G., & Guattari, F. (1987). *A thousand plateaus.* Minneapolis: University of Minnesota Press.

Delia, J. G. (1977a). Alternative perspectives for the study of human communication. *Communication Quarterly, 25,* 46–62.

Delia, J. G. (1977b). Constructivism and the study of human communication. *Quarterly Journal of Speech, 63,* 66–83.

Delia, J.G. (1987). Communication research: A history. In C. R. Berger & S. H. Chaffee (Eds.), *Handbook of communication science* (pp. 20–97). Beverly Hills, CA: Sage.

deMan, P. (1979). *Allegories of reading: Figural language in Rousseau, Nietzsche, Rilke, and Proust.* New Haven, CT: Yale University Press.

DeMartini, J. R., & Whitbeck, L. B. (1986). Knowledge use as knowledge creation: Reexamining the contribution of the social sciences to decision making. *Knowledge: Creation, Diffusion, Utilization, 7,* 383–396.

Derrida, J. (1988). Signature event context. In J. Derrida (Ed.), *Limited Inc.* Evanston, IL: Northwestern University Press.

Dervin, B. (1975). *Communicating ideas: A guide to picture.* Unpublished manuscript.

Dervin, B. (1976a). Strategies for dealing with human information needs: Information or communication? *Journal of Broadcasting, 20*, 324–333.

Dervin, B. (1976b). The everyday information needs of the average citizen: A taxonomy for analysis. In M. Kochen & J. C. Donohue (Eds.), *Information for the community* (pp. 19–38). Chicago: American Library Association.

Dervin, B. (1977a). *Communicating with, not to, the urban poor.* ERIC/CUE Urban Diversity Series, No. 50. Washington, DC: National Institute of Education. (ERIC Document Reproduction Service No. UD 017 930)

Dervin, B. (1977b). Useful theory for librarianship: Communication, not information. *Drexel Library Quarterly, 13* (3), 16–32.

Dervin, B. (1978, November). The human side of communication. *Theory and Methodology Division Newsletter*, 5–14.

Dervin, B. (1979a, April). *Meeting individual information needs in the midst of the information explosion of the 1980s.* Paper presented at the Colloquium-Visiting Lecture Series, All University Gerontology Program, Syracuse University, Syracuse, NY.

Dervin, B. (1979b, November). *A pre-requisite for information equity: Individual sense-making.* Paper presented at the Conference on Indicators of Equity in Information Dissemination Programs in Education, National Institute of Education, Washington, DC.

Dervin, B. (1979c, November). *Sense-Making as a prerequisite for information equality.* Paper presented at the 7th Annual Telecommunication Policy Research Conference, Skytop, PA.

Dervin, B. (1980). Communication gaps and inequities: Moving toward a reconceptualization. In B. Dervin & M. Voigt (Eds.), *Progress in communication sciences* (Vol. 2, pp. 73–112). Norwood, NJ: Ablex.

Dervin, B. (1981). Mass communicating: Changing conceptions of the audience. In R. E. Rice & W. J. Paisley (Eds.), *Public communication campaigns* (pp. 71–87). Beverly Hills, CA: Sage.

Dervin, B. (1983a). Information as a user construct: The relevance of perceived information needs to synthesis and interpretation. In S. A. Ward & L. J. Reed (Eds.), *Knowledge structure and use* (pp. 153–183). Philadelphia: Temple University Press.

Dervin, B. (1983b, May). *An overview of sense-making research: Concepts, methods, and results to date.* Paper presented at the annual convention of the International Communication Association, Dallas, TX.

Dervin, B. (1989a). Audience as listener and learner, teacher and confidante: The sense-making approach. In R. Rice & C. K. Atkin (Eds.), *Public communication campaigns* (2nd ed., pp. 67–86). Newbury Park, CA: Sage.

Dervin, B. (1989b). Users as research inventions: How research categories perpetuate myths. *Journal of Communication, 39* (3), 216–232.

Dervin, B. (1991a). Comparative theory reconceptualized: From entities and states to processes and dynamics. *Communication Theory, 1* (1), 59–69.

Dervin, B. (1991b). Information as sense, information as non-sense: The communications technology connection. In H. Bouwman, P. Nelissen, & M. Voojis (Eds.), *Tussen vraag en aanbod: Optimalisering van de informatievoorziening* [Between demand and supply: Optimization of information provision]. (pp. 44–59). Amsterdam: Otto Cramwinckel Uitgever.

Dervin, B. (1992). From the mind's eye of the user: The Sense-Making qualitative-quantitative methodology. In J. D. Glazier & R. R. Powell (Eds.), *Qualitative research in information management* (pp. 61–84). Englewood, CO: Libraries Unlimited.

Dervin, B. (1993). Verbing communication: Mandate for disciplinary invention. *Journal of Communication, 43*, 45–54.

Dervin, B. (1994). Information ↔ democracy: An examination of underlying assumptions. *Journal of the American Society for Information Science, 45* (6), 369–385.

Dervin, B. (1997). Given a context by any other name: Methodological tools for taming the unruly beast. In P. Vakkari, R. Savolainen, & B. Dervin (Eds.), *Information seeking in context* (pp. 13–38). London: Taylor Graham.

Dervin, B. (1998). Sense-Making theory and practice: An overview of user interests in knowledge seeking and use. *Journal of Knowledge Management, 2* (2), 36–46.

Dervin, B. (1999a). Chaos, order, and Sense-Making: A proposed theory for information design. In R. Jacobson (Ed.), *Information design* (pp.35–57). Cambridge, MA: MIT Press.

Dervin, B. (1999b). On studying information seeking methodologically: The implications of connecting metatheory to method. *Information Processing and Management, 35*, 727–750.

Dervin, B., & Chaffee, S. (with Foreman-Wernet, L.). (in press). *Communication: A different kind of horserace: Essays honoring Richard F. Carter.* Cresskill, NJ: Hampton Press.

Dervin, B., & Clark, K. D. (1987). *ASQ: Asking significant questions: Alternative tools for information needs and accountability assessments by librarians.* Sacramento, CA: California State Libraries. (ERIC Document Reproduction Service No. ED 286 519)

Dervin, B., & Clark, K. D. (1989). Communication as cultural identity: The invention mandate. *Media Development, 36* (2), 5–8.

Dervin, B., & Clark, K. D. (1993). Communication and democracy: Mandate for procedural invention. In S. Splichal & J. Wasko (Eds.), *Communication and democracy* (pp. 103–140). Norwood, NJ: Ablex.

Dervin, B., & Dewdney, P. (1986). Neutral questioning: A new approach to the reference interview. *RQ, 25* (4), 506–513.

Dervin, B., & Fraser, B. (1985). *How libraries help.* Sacramento: California State Libraries. (ERIC Document Reproduction Service No. ED 264 857)

Dervin, B., & Greenberg, B. (1972). The communication environment of the urban poor. In F. G. Kline & P. J. Tichenor (Eds.), *Current perspectives in mass communication research* (pp. 195–233). Beverly Hills, CA: Sage.

Dervin, B., Grossberg, L., O'Keefe, B. J., & Wartella, E. (Eds.). (1989a). *Rethinking communication: Paradigm issues* (Vol. 1). Newbury Park, CA: Sage.

Dervin, B., Grossberg, L., O'Keefe, B. J., & Wartella, E. (Eds.). (1989b). *Rethinking communication: Paradigm exemplars* (Vol. 2). Newbury, CA: Sage.

Dervin, B., & Harlock, S. (1976, May). *Health communication research: The state of the art.* Paper presented at the annual meeting of the International Communication Association, Portland, OR.

Dervin, B., Harlock, S., Atwood, R., & Garzona, C. (1980). The human side of information: An exploration in a health communication context. In D. Nimmo (Ed.), *Communication yearbook* (Vol. 4, pp. 591–608). New Brunswick, NJ: Transaction Books.

Dervin, B., Harpring, J., & Foreman-Wernet, L. (1999). In moments of concern: A sense-making study of pregnant drug-addicted women and their information needs. *Electronic Journal of Communication, 9* (2–4). [On-line serial]. Available at: http://www.cios.org/www/ejcrec2.htm.

Dervin, B., Jacobson, T., & Nilan, M. (1982). Measuring aspects of information seeking: A test of a quantitative/qualitative methodology. In M. Burgoon (Ed.), *Communication yearbook* (Vol. 6, pp. 419–444). New Brunswick, NJ: Transaction Books.

Dervin, B., & Martin, M. (1980). [Sense-making profiles of message Q/ing on *Seattle Times* leisure time coverage]. Unpublished raw data, Seattle, WA.

Dervin, B., & Nilan, M. (1986). Information needs and uses. In M. E. Williams (Ed.), *Annual review of information science and technology* (Vol. 21,pp. 3–33). White Plains, NY: Knowledge Industry Publications.

Dervin, B., Nilan, M., & Jacobson, T. (1981). Improving predictions of information use: A comparison of predictor types in a health communication setting. In M. Burgoon (Ed.), *Communication yearbook* (Vol. 5, pp. 807–830). New Brunswick, NJ: Transaction Books.

Dervin, B., Osborne, T., Jaikumar-Mahey, P., Huesca, R., & Higgins, J. (1993). Toward a communication theory of dialogue. *Media Development, XL*, 54–61.

Dervin, B., & Shields, P. (1999). Adding the missing user to policy discourse: Understanding U.S. user telephone privacy concerns. *Telecommunications Policy, 23* (5), 403–435.

Dervin, B., Zweizig, D., Banister, M., Gabriel, M., Hall, E., & Kwan, C. (with Bowes, J., & Stamm, K.). (1976). *The development of strategies for dealing with the information needs of urban residents, Phase I: Citizen study, final report* (Report No. L0035JA). Washington, DC: U.S. Department of Health, Education and Welfare, Office of Education. (ERIC Document Reproduction Service No. ED 125 640)

Dervin, B., Zweizig, D., Hall, E. P., Kwan, C., & Lalley, K. (with Banister, M., Gabriel, M., Gray, V. A., Schnelle, R., & Yung, J.). (1977). *The development of strategies for dealing with the information needs of urban residents, Phase II: Information practitioner study, final report* (Report No. 475AH50014). Washington, DC: U.S. Department of Health, Education and Welfare, Office of Education. (ERIC Document Reproduction Service No. ED 136 791)

Deutsch, M. (1965). The role of social class in language development and cognition. *American Journal of Orthopsychiatry, 25*, 78–88.

Dewdney, P. (1986). *The effects of training reference librarians in interview skills: A field experiment.* (Doctoral dissertation, University of Western Ontario [Canada]). *Dissertation Abstracts International, 47*, 3598.

Dewey, J. (1915). *Democracy and education.* New York: Macmillan Press.

Dewey, J. (1933). *How we think.* Lexington, ME: C. C. Heath. (Original work published 1910)

Dewey, J. (1960a). Context and thought. In J. Dewey (Ed.), *On experience, nature, and freedom* (pp. 88–110). New York: The Liberal Arts Press.

Dewey, J. (Ed.). (1960b). *On experience, nature, and freedom.* New York: The Liberal Arts Press.

Dewey, J., & Bentley, A. F. (1949). *Knowing and the known.* Boston: Beacon.

Dias, J. A. (1990). *Information seeking with television guides: An exploratory Sense-Making study in the home information environment.* Unpublished master's thesis, The Ohio State University, Columbus.

Diaz Bordenave, J. (1976). Communication of agricultural innovations in Latin America: The need for new models. *Communication Research, 3* (2), 135–154.

Donohew, L., Tipton, L., & Haney, R. (1978). Analysis of information-seeking strategies. *Journalism Quarterly, 55*, 25–31.

Donohue, G. A., Tichenor, P. J., & Olien, C. N. (1975). Mass media and the knowledge gap: A hypothesis reconsidered. *Communication Research, 2* (1), 3–23.

Douglas, M. (1986). *How institutions think.* Syracuse, NY: Syracuse University Press.

Dozier, D. M., Grunig, L. A., & Grunig, J. E. (2001). Public relations as communication campaign. In R. E. Rice & C. K. Atkin (Eds.), *Public communication campaigns* (3rd ed., pp 231–248). Thousand Oaks, CA: Sage.

Dreifus, C. (1973). *Women's fate: Raps from a feminist consciousness-raising group.* New York: Bantam.

Dupuy, J. P. (1980). Myths of the information society. In K. Woodward (Ed.), *The myths of information: Technology and post-industrial culture* (pp. 3–17). Madison, WI: Coda Press.

Dutton, W. H. (1985). Decision-making in the information age: Computer models and public policy. In R. Finnegan, G. Salaman, & K. Thompson (Eds.), *Information technology: Social issues, a reader* (pp. 181–190). Sevenoaks, UK: Hodden and Stoughton.

Dworkin, M. (1987). *Making sense with television news: Situation, context, and psychology of the audience experience.* (Doctoral dissertation, University of Washington). *Dissertation Abstracts International, 48*, 500.

Edelstein, A. S. (1974). *The uses of communication in decision-making: A comparative study of Yugoslavia and the United States.* New York: Praeger.

Ehrenreich, B., & English, D. (1979). *For her own good: 150 years of the experts' advice to women.* Garden City, NY: Anchor.

Elliott, P. (1974). Uses and gratifications research: A critique and a sociological alternative. In J. G. Blumler & E. Katz (Eds.), *The uses of mass communications* (pp. 249–268). Beverly Hills, CA: Sage.

Ellis, D. G. (1981). The epistemology of form. In C. Wilder-Mott & J. H. Weakland (Eds.), *Rigor and imagination: Essays from the legacy of George Bateson* (pp. 215–230). New York: Praeger.

Endler, N. S., & Hunt, J. M. (1969). Generalizability of contributions from sources of variance in the S-R inventories of anxiousness. *Journal of Personality, 37*, 1–24.

Ettema, J. S., & Glasser, T. L. (1988). Narrative form and moral force: The realization of innocence and guilt through investigative journalism. *Journal of Communication, 38* (3), 8–26.

Ettema, J. S., & Kline, F. G. (1977). Deficits, differences, and ceilings: Contingent conditions for understanding of the knowledge gap. *Communication Research, 4* (2), 179–202.

Ettema, J. S., & Whitney, D. C. (Eds.). (1994). *Audience making: How the media create the audience.* Thousand Oaks, CA: Sage.

Fells, N. W., Davis, A., Havighurst, R., Herrick, V., & Tyler, R. (1951). *Intelligence and cultural differences.* Chicago: University of Illinois Press.

Ferguson, K. E. (1984). *The feminist case against bureaucracy.* Philadelphia: Temple University Press.

Fisher, B. A., & Adams, K. L. (1994). *Interpersonal communication: Pragmatics of human relationships* (2nd ed.). New York: McGraw Hill.

Fishkin, J. S. (1993). *The dialogue of justice: Toward a self-reflective society.* New Haven, CT: Yale University Press.

Fitzpatrick, M. A. (1983). Effective interpersonal communication for women in the corporations: Think like a man, talk like a lady. In J. Pilotta (Ed.), *Women in organizations: Barriers and breakthroughs* (pp. 73–84). Prospect Heights, IL: Waveland Press.

Fitzsimmons, S., & Osburn, H. A. (1969). The impact of social issues and public affairs television documentaries. *Public Opinion Quarterly, 32*, 379–397.

Fonow, M. M., & Cook, J. A. (1991). Back to the future: A look at the second wave of feminist epistemology and methodology. In M. M. Fonow & J. A. Cook (Eds.), *Beyond methodology: Feminist scholarship as lived experience* (pp. 1–15). Bloomington, IN: Indiana University Press.

Foss, K. A., & Foss, S. K. (1983). The status of research on women and communication. *Communication Quarterly, 31* (3), 195–204.

Foucault, M. (1965). *Madness and civilization: A history of insanity in the age of reason* (R. Howard, Trans.). New York: Random House.

Foucault, M. (1972). *The archaeology of knowledge* (A. M. Sheridan Smith, Trans.). New York: Pantheon. (Original work published 1969)

Foucault, M. (1975). *I, Pierre Riviére, having slaughtered my mother, my sister, and my brother . . . A case of parricide in the 19th century* (F. Jellinek, Trans.). Lincoln: University of Nebraska Press.

Foucault, M. (1979). *Discipline and punish: The birth of the prison* (A. M. Sheridan Smith, Trans.). New York: Vintage Books. (Original work published 1975)

Foucault, M. (1980). *Power/knowledge: Selected interviews and other writings, 1972–1977* (C. Gordon, Ed. & Trans.). New York: Pantheon.

Freire, P. (1970). *Pedagogy of the oppressed* (M. Bergman Ramos, Trans.). New York: Seabury Press.

Freire, P. (1983). *Education for critical consciousness.* New York: Continuum.

Frenette, M. (1998). Une perspective constructiviste sur les messages destines aux jeunes [A constructivistic perspective on anti-smoking messages aimed at youth]. *Revue Québécoise de Psychologie, 19* (1), 109–134.

Frenette, M. (1999). Explorations in adolescents' sense-making of anti-smoking messages. *Electronic Journal of Communication, 9* (2–4). [On-line serial]. Available at: http://www.cios.org/.

Fugh-Berman, A. (1993). The case for "natural" medicine. *Nation, 257,* 240–244.

Furman, S. S., Sweat, L., & Crocetti, G. (1965). Social class factors in the flow of children to outpatient psychiatric clinics. *American Journal of Public Health, 55* (3), 12–18.

Gadamer, H. (1975). *Truth and method* (G. Barden & J. Cumming, Trans.). New York: Seabury Press.

Gadamer, H. (1976). *Philosophic hermeneutics* (D. E. Linge, Trans.). Berkeley: University of California Press.

Gadamer, H. (1981). *Reason in the age of science* (F. G. Lawrence, Trans.). Cambridge, MA: MIT Press.

Galgan, G. J. (1988). Marx and Dewey on the unity of theory and practice. In W. J. Gavin (Ed.), *Context over foundation: Dewey and Marx* (pp. 209–228). Dordrecht, Holland: D. Reidel Publishing.

Gallop, J. (1985). *Reading Lacan.* Ithaca, NY: Cornell University Press.

Galloway, J. J. (1974). *Subcultural rates of change and adoption and knowledge gaps in the diffusion of innovations.* Unpublished doctoral dissertation, Michigan State University, East Lansing.

Galloway, J. J. (1977). The analysis and significance of communication effect gaps. *Communication Research, 4,* 363–386.

Galtung, J. (1977). *Methodology and ideology: Essays in methodology* (Vol. 1). Copenhagen, Denmark: Christian Ejlers.

Gandy, O. H., Jr. (1988). The political economy of communications competence. In V. Mosco & J. Wasko (Eds.), *The political economy of information* (pp. 108–124). Madison: University of Wisconsin Press.

Gandy, O. H., Jr. (1993). *The panoptic sort: A political economy of personal information.* Boulder, CO: Westview Press.

Ganguly, K. (1992). Accounting for others: Feminism and representation. In L. Rakow (Ed.), *Women making meaning: New feminist directions in communication* (pp. 60–82). New York: Routledge.

Garfinkel, H. (1967). *Studies in ethnomethodology.* Englewood Cliffs, NJ: Prentice-Hall.

Gavin, W. J. (1988a). Introduction. In W. J. Gavin (Ed.), *Context over foundation: Dewey and Marx* (pp. 1–10). Dordrecht, Holland: D. Reidel Publishing.

Gavin, W. J. (1988b). Text, context, and the existential limit: A Jamesian strain in Marx and Dewey. In W. J. Gavin (Ed.), *Context over foundation: Dewey and Marx* (pp. 49–57). Dordrecht, Holland: D. Reidel Publishing.

Geertz, C. (1973). *The interpretation of culture*. New York: Basic Books.

Geertz, C. (1975). On the nature of anthropological understanding. *American Scientist, Jan.-Feb.*, 8–14.

Geertz, C. (1983). *Local knowledge: Further essays in interpretive anthropology*. New York: Basic Books.

Genova, B. K. L., & Greenberg, B. S. (1979). Interest in news and the knowledge gap. *Public Opinion Quarterly, 43*, 79–91.

Georgoudi, M., & Rosnow, R. L. (1985). The emergence of contextualism. *Journal of Communication, 35* (1), 76–88.

Gerbner, G., Mowlana, H., & Nordenstreng, K. (1993). *Global media debate: Its rise, fall, and renewal*. Norwood, NJ: Ablex.

Gergen, K. J. (1985). The social constructionist movement in modern psychology. *American Psychology, 40*, 266–275.

Giddens, A. (1979). *Central problems in social theory*. Berkeley: University of California Press.

Giddens, A. (1984). *The constitution of society: Outline of the theory of structuration*. Cambridge, UK: Polity Press.

Giddens, A. (1989). The orthodox consensus and the emerging synthesis. In B. Dervin, L. Grossberg, B. J. O'Keefe, & E. Wartella (Eds.), *Rethinking communication: Paradigm issues* (Vol. 1, pp. 53–65). Newbury Park, CA: Sage.

Giddens, A. (1991). *Modernity and self-identity*. Stanford, CA: Stanford University Press.

Giddens, A. (1993, June). *Keynote address*. International Association of Mass Communication Research, Dublin, Ireland.

Gitlin, T. (1980). *The whole world is watching: Mass media in the making and unmaking of the New Left*. Berkeley: University of California Press.

Goldhaber, G. M., & Barnett, G. A. (1988). *Handbook of organizational communication*. Norwood, NJ: Ablex.

Gonzales, A., & Peterson, T. R. (1993). Enlarging conceptual boundaries: A critique of research in intercultural communication. In S. P. Bowen & N. Wyatt (Eds.), *Transforming visions: Feminist critiques in communication studies* (pp. 249–278). Cresskill, NJ: Hampton Press.

Goodman, R. F., & Fisher, W. R. (Eds.). (1995). *Rethinking knowledge: Reflections across the disciplines*. Albany: State University of New York Press.

Goodwin, C. (1989). Turn construction and conversational organization. In B. Dervin, L. Grossberg, B. J. O'Keefe, & E. Wartella (Eds.), *Rethinking communication: Paradigm exemplars* (Vol. 2, pp. 88–102). Newbury Park, CA: Sage.

Gorney, R. (1972). *The human agenda*. New York: Simon and Schuster.

Gould, S. J. (1981). *The mismeasure of man*. New York: Norton & Co.

Gramsci, A. (1988). In D. Forgacs (Ed.), *A Gramsci reader: Selected writings, 1916–1935*. London: Lawrence and Wishart.

Greenberg, B. S. (1964). Person-to-person communication in the diffusion of news events. *Journalism Quarterly, 41*, 489–494.

Greenberg, B. S., & Dervin, B. (1970). *The use of the mass media by the urban poor.* New York: Praeger.

Grunig, J. E. (1972). Communication in community decisions on problems of the poor. *Journal of Communication, 22,* 5–25.

Grunig, J. E. (1973a, May). *Information seeking in organizational communication: A case study of applied theory.* Paper presented at the annual meeting of the International Communication Association, Montreal, Canada.

Grunig, J. E. (1973b, May). *New directions for research in communications and international development: From the study of individuals to the study of formal organizations.* Paper presented at the annual meeting of the International Communication Association, Montreal, Canada.

Grunig, J. E. (1975). A multi-systems theory of organization communication. *Communication Research, 2,* 99–136.

Grunig, J. E. (1978a). Accuracy of communication from an external public to employees in a formal organization. *Human Communication Research, 5,* 40–53.

Grunig, J. E. (1978b). Defining publics in public relations: The case of a suburban hospital. *Journalism Quarterly, 55,* 109–118.

Grunig, J. E. (1983). Communication behaviors and attitudes of environmental publics: Two studies. *Journalism Monographs, 81,* 1–47.

Grunig, J. E., & Disbrow, J. (1977). Developing a probabilistic model for communications and decision-making. *Communication Research, 4* (2), 145–168.

Guttman, A. (1980). *Liberal equality.* Cambridge, UK: Cambridge University Press.

Guttman, N. (1997). Ethical dilemmas in health campaigns. *Health Communication, 9* (2), 155–190.

Habermas, J. (1971). *Knowledge and human interests* (J. Shapiro, Trans.). Boston: Beacon Press. (Original work published 1968)

Habermas, J. (1973). A postscript to knowledge and human interests. *Philosophy of the Social Sciences, 3,* 157–185.

Habermas, J. (1979). *Communication and the evolution of society* (T. McCarthy, Trans.). Boston: Beacon Press. (Original work published 1976)

Habermas, J. (1984). *Theory of communicative action 1: Reason and the rationalization of society.* (T. McCarthy, Trans.). Boston: Beacon Press. (Original work published 1981)

Habermas, J. (1985). Questions and couterquestions. In R. J. Bernstein (Ed.), *Habermas and modernity* (pp. 192–216). Cambridge, MA: MIT Press.

Habermas, J. (1987a). An alternative way out of the philosophy of the subject: Communicative versus subject-centered reason. In J. Habermas (Ed.), & F. Lawrence (Trans.), *The philosophical discourse of modernity: Twelve lectures* (pp. 294–326). Cambridge, MA: MIT Press. (Original work published 1985)

Habermas, J. (1987b). *Theory of communicative action 2: Lifeworld and system.* (T. McCarthy, Trans.). Boston: Beacon Press.

Habermas, J. (1989). *The structural transformation of the public sphere: An inquiry into a category of Bourgeois society* (T. Burger & F. Lawrence, Trans.). Cambridge, MA: MIT Press.

Hachten, W. A. (1982). *The world news prism: Changing media, clashing ideologies.* Ames: The Iowa State University.

Halfpenny, P. (1987). Laws, causality, and statistics: Positivism, interpretivism, and realism. *Sociological Theory, 5* (1), 33–36.

Hall, H. J. (1981). Patterns in the use of information: The right to be different. *Journal of the American Society for Information Science, 32* (2), 103–112.

Hall, S. (1989). Ideology and communication theory. In B. Dervin, L. Grossberg, B. J. O'Keefe, & E. Wartella (Eds.), *Rethinking communication: Paradigm issues* (Vol. 1, pp. 40–52). Newbury Park, CA: Sage.

Hall, S., Chrichter, C., Jefferson, T., Clarke, J., & Roberts, B. (1978). *Policing the crisis: Mugging, the state, and law and order*. London: Macmillan Press, Ltd.

Hamelink, C. J. (1983). *Cultural autonomy in global communications*. New York: Longman.

Hamlyn, D. W. (1967). Empiricism. In P. Edwards (Ed.), *The encyclopedia of philosophy* (Vol. 2, pp. 499–505). New York: Macmillan.

Hanneman, G. J., & Greenberg, B. S. (1973). Relevance and diffusion of news on major and minor events. *Journalism Quarterly, 40,* 433–437.

Havelock, R. G. (with Guskin, A., Frohman, M., Havelock, M., Hill, M., & Huber, J.). (1969). *Planning for innovation through dissemination and utilization of knowledge*. Ann Arbor, MI: University of Michigan, Center for Research on Utilization of Scientific Knowledge.

Hayes, L. J. (1993). Reality and truth. In S. C. Hayes, L. J. Hayes, H. W. Reese, & T. R. Sarbin (Eds.), *Varieties of scientific contextualism* (pp. 35–44). Reno, NV: Context Press.

Hayes, S. C. (1993). Analytic goals and the varieties of scientific contextualism. In S. C. Hayes, L. J. Hayes, H. W. Reese, & T. R. Sarbin (Eds.), *Varieties of scientific contextualism* (pp. 11–27). Reno, NV: Context Press.

Hayes, S. C., Hayes, L. J., & Reese, H. W. (1988). Finding the philosophical core: A review of Stephen C. Pepper's "world hypothesis." *Journal of the Experimental Analysis of Behavior, 50,* 97–111.

Hayles, K. N. (1990). *Chaos bound: Orderly disorder in contemporary literature and science*. Ithaca, NY: Cornell University Press.

Head, S. W. (1985). *World broadcasting systems: A comparative analysis*. Belmont, CA: Wadsworth.

Heller, A. (1974). *The theory of need in Marx*. London: Allison & Busby.

Hess, R. D. (1970). Social class and ethnic influences on socialization. In P. H. Mussen (Ed.), *Carmichael's manual of child psychology* (Vol. 2, pp. 457–558). New York: John Wiley.

Hewes, D., & Haight, L. (1979). The cross-situational consistency of measures of communicative behaviors. *Communication Research, 6* (2), 243–270.

Hewins, E. T. (1990). Information need and use studies. In M. E. Williams (Ed.), *Annual review of science and technology* (Vol. 25, pp.145–174). White Plains, NY: Knowledge Industry Publications.

Hiltz, S. R. (1971). Black and white in the consumer financial system. *American Journal of Sociology, 76,* 987–998.

Hirokawa, R. Y. (1988). Group communication and decision-making performance: A continued test of the functional perspective. *Human Communication Research, 14* (4), 487–515.

Holland, E. (1988). The ideology of lack in Lackanianism. In R. Merrill (Ed.), *Ethics/aesthetics: Postmodern positions* (pp. 59–69). Washington, DC: Maisonneuve Press.

Hollinger. (1994). *Postmodernism and the social sciences*. Thousand Oaks, CA: Sage.

Hollis, J. W., & Hollis, L. U. (1969). *Personalizing information processes*. New York: MacMillan.

Holzner, B. (1968). *Reality construction in society*. Cambridge, MA: Schenkman Publishing.

Hornik, R. (1980). Communication as compliment in development. *Journal of Communication, 30* (2), 10–24.

Hsia, H. J. (1973, August). *A preliminary report on motivation and communication patterns of the black, Chicano, white and affluent white in a typical southwestern US city.* Paper presented at the annual meeting of the Association for Education in Journalism, Fort Collins, CO.

Huesca, R. (1995). A procedural view of participatory communication—Lessons from Bolivian Tin Miners' radio. *Media, Culture, and Society, 17* (1), 101–119.

Huesca, R., & Dervin, B. (1996, August). *Rethinking the journalistic interview: Empowering sources to name the world.* Paper presented at the annual meeting of the Association for Education in Journalism and Mass Communication, Washington, DC.

Hunter, C. S. J., & Harman, D. (1979). *Adult illiteracy in the United States: A report to the Ford Foundation.* New York: McGraw Hill.

Hurwitz, N. H. (1975). *Communication networks of the urban poor.* ERIC Clearinghouse on Urban Education, Columbia University, New York. (ERIC Document Reproduction Service No. 109 292)

Hyde, M. J. (Ed.). (1982). *Communication philosophy and the technological age.* Birmingham: University of Alabama Press.

Hyman, H., & Sheatsley, P. (1947). Some reasons why information campaigns fail. *Public Opinion Quarterly, 11*, 412–423.

Ireton, H., Thriving, E., & Graven, H. (1970). Infant mental development and neurological status, family socioeconomic status and intelligence at age four. *Child Development, 41*, 937–945.

Jablin, F. M., Putnam, L. L., Roberts, K. H., & Porter, L. W. (1987). *Handbook of organizational communication.* Newbury Park, CA: Sage.

Jackins, H. (1973). *The human situation.* Seattle, WA: Rational Island Publishing.

Jackins, H. (1981). *The benign reality.* Seattle, WA: Rational Island Publishing.

James, W. (1927). The will to believe. In W. James (Ed.), *The will to believe and other essays in popular philosophy.* New York: Longman, Green, & Co.

Janiger, O., & Goldberg, P. (1993). *A different kind of healing.* Los Angeles: Jeremy P. Tarcher.

Jayaweera, N. (1987). Rethinking development communication: A holistic view. In N. Jayaweera & S. Amunugama (Eds.), *Rethinking development communication* (pp. 76–94). Newbury Park, CA: Sage.

Jensen, K. B. (1987a). News as ideology: Economic statistics and political ritual in television network news. *Journal of Communication, 37* (1), 8–27.

Jensen, K. B. (1987b). Qualitative audience research: Toward an integrative approach to reception. *Critical Studies in Mass Communication, 4*, 21–36.

Johannsen, R. L. (1971). The emerging concept of communication as a dialogue. *Quarterly Journal of Speech, 57*, 373–382.

Johnson, N. (1973). Television and politicization: A test of competing models. *Journalism Quarterly, 50*, 447–455.

Katz, E., Blumler, J. G., & Gurevitch, M. (1974). Utilization of mass communication by the individual. In J. G. Blumler & E. Katz (Eds.), *The uses of mass communications* (pp. 19–32). Beverly Hills, CA: Sage.

Katz, J. (1987). What makes crime "news"? *Media, Culture, and Society, 9*, 47–75.

Katzman, N. (1974). The impact of communication technology: Promises and prospects. *Journal of Communication, 24*, 47–58.

Kellerman, K., & Lim, T. S. (1989). Conversational acquaintance: The flexibility of routinized behavior. In B. Dervin, L. Grossberg, B. J. O'Keefe, & E. Wartella (Eds.), *Rethinking communication: Paradigm exemplars* (Vol. 2, pp. 172–187). Newbury Park, CA: Sage.

Key, V. (1961). *Public opinion and American democracy.* New York: Knopf.

Kimbrell, A. (1993). *The human body shop: The engineering and marketing of life.* San Francisco: Harper.

King, G., Keohanne, R., & Verba, S. (1994). *Designing social inquiry.* Princeton, NJ: Princeton University Press.

Klapper, J.T. (1960). *The effects of mass communication.* New York: Free Press.

Kline, F. G., Miller, P. V., & Morrison, A. J. (1974). Adolescents and family planning information: An exploration of audience needs and media effects. In J. G. Blumler & E. Katz (Eds.), *The uses of mass communication* (pp. 113–136). Beverly Hills, CA: Sage.

Knapp, M. L., Stafford, L., & Daly, J. A. (1986). Regrettable messages: Things people wish they hadn't said. *Journal of Communication, 36* (4), 40–58.

Kozol, J. (1985). *Illiterate America.* Garden City, NY: Doubleday.

Kress, G. (1986). Language in the media: The construction of the domain of public and private. *Media, Culture, and Society, 8,* 395–419.

Krippendorff, K. (1989). On the ethics of constructing communication. In B. Dervin, L. Grossberg, B. J. O'Keefe, & E. Wartella (Eds.), *Rethinking communication: Paradigm issues* (Vol. 1, pp. 66–96). Newbury Park, CA: Sage.

Krippendorff, K. (1991). *Conversation or intellectual imperialism in comparing communication (theories).* Unpublished manuscript, Annenberg School of Communication, University of Pennsylvania, Philadelphia.

Krosnick, J. A. (1999). Survey research. *Annual review of psychology* (Vol. 50, pp. 337–367). Stanford, CA: Annual Reviews.

Kuhn, T. S. (1970). The structure of scientific revolutions. In the *International encyclopedia of unified science* (Vol. 2, No. 2, entire issue).

Kuhn, T. S. (1977). *The essential tension.* Chicago: The University of Chicago Press.

Kurtz, N. R. (1968). Gatekeepers: Agents in acculturation. *Rural Sociology, 33,* 63–70.

Lacan, J. (1977). *Ecrits.* New York: Norton.

Laclau, E., & Mouffe, C. (1985). *Hegemony and socialist strategy: Towards a radical democratic politics* (M. Moore & P. Commack, Trans.). London: Verso.

Lana, R. E. (1986). Descartes, Vico, contextualism, and social psychology. In R. L. Rosnow & M. Georgoudi (Eds.), *Contextualism and understanding in behavioral science: Implications for research and theory* (pp. 67–85). New York: Praeger.

Lannamann, J. (1991). Interpersonal research as ideological practice. *Communication Theory, 1,* 179–203.

Lasswell, H. D. (1949). The structure and function of communication in society. In W. Schramm (Ed.), *Mass communications* (pp. 117–130). Urbana: University of Illinois Press.

Lather, P. (1991). *Getting smart: Feminist research and pedagogy with/in the postmodern.* New York: Routledge.

Leiter, K. (1980). *Primer on ethnomethodology.* New York: Oxford University Press.

Lemert, J. B., Nitzman, B. N., Seither, M. A., Cook, R. H., & Hackett, R. (1977). Journalists and mobilizing information. *Journalism Quarterly, 55,* 721–726.

Levitan, K. (1980). Applying a holistic framework to synthesize information science research. In B. Dervin & M. Voigt (Eds.), *Progress in communication sciences* (Vol. 2, pp. 241–273). Norwood, NJ: Ablex.

Levin, J., & Taube, G. (1970). Bureaucracy and the socially handicapped: A study of lower-class tenants in public housing. *Sociology and Social Research, 54*, 209–219.

Levine, F. J., & Preston, E. (1970). Community resource orientation among low-income groups. *Wisconsin Law Review, 80*, 80–113.

Levine, S. L., White, P. E., & Paul, B. D. (1963). Community interorganization problems in providing medical care and social services. *American Journal of Public Health, 53*, 1184–1195.

Levy, S. (1969). How population subgroups differed in their knowledge of six assassinations. *Journalism Quarterly, 46*, 685–698.

Ley, P. (1982). Satisfaction, compliance, and communication. *British Journal of Clinical Psychology, 21*, 241–254.

Liebes, T. (1989). On the convergence of theories of mass communication and literature regarding the role of the "reader." In B. Dervin & M. Voigt (Eds.), *Progress in communication sciences* (Vol. 9, pp. 123–143). Norwood, NJ: Ablex.

Lievrouw, L. (1988, May) *Identifying the common dimensions of communication: The communication systems model.* Paper presented at the annual convention of the International Communication Association, New Orleans, LA.

Luckmann, T. (1983). *Life-world and social realities.* London: Heinemann.

Lukes, S. (1974). *Power: A radical view.* London: Macmillan.

Lyotard, J. F. (1984). *The postmodern condition: A report on knowledge* (G. Bennington & B. Massumi, Trans.). Minneapolis: University of Minnesota Press.

MacMullin, S. E., & Taylor, R. S. (1984). Problem dimensions and information traits. *The Information Society, 3* (1), 91–111.

Madden, K. M. (1999). Making sense of environmental messages: An exploration of households' information needs and uses. *Electronic Journal of Communication, 9* (2–4). [On-line serial]. Available at: http://www.cios.org/www/ejcrec2.htm.

Maines, D. R., & Molseed, M. J. (1986). The obsessive discoverer's complex and the "discovery" of growth in sociological theory. *American Journal of Sociology, 92* (1), 158–163.

Mann, D. (1973). *Shared control in urban neighborhood schools* (Rep. No. ED 083 355). New York: Teachers College, Columbia University.

Marvin, C. (1989). Experts, black boxes, and artifacts: New allegories for the history of the electric media. In B. Dervin, L. Grossberg, B. J. O'Keefe, & E. Wartella (Eds.), *Rethinking communication: Paradigm exemplars* (Vol. 2, pp. 188–198). Newbury Park, CA: Sage.

Mathiason, J. R. (1970, August). *Communication patterns and powerlessness among urban poor: Toward the use of mass communications for rapid social change.* Paper presented at the annual meeting of the Association for Education in Journalism, Washington, DC.

Matta, F. R. (1986). Alternative communication: Solidarity and development in the face of transnational expansion. In R. Atwood & E. G. McAnany (Eds.), *Communication and Latin American society: Trends in critical research, 1960–1985* (pp. 190–214). Madison: The University of Wisconsin Press.

McAnany, E. G. (1978). The role of information in communication with the rural poor: Some reflections. In E. G. McAnany (Ed.), *Communication with the rural poor in the Third World: Does information make a difference?* Stanford, CA: Institute for Communication Research, Stanford University.

McCurry, S. M. (1993). Metaphor and method in the narratory principle. In S. C. Hayes, L. J. Hayes, H. W. Reese, & T. R. Sarbin (Eds.), *Varieties of scientific contextualism* (pp. 66–69). Reno, NV: Context Press.

McDermott, R. P., Godpodinoff, K., & Aron, J. (1978). Criteria for an ethnographically adequate description of concerted activities and their contexts. *Semiotica, 24* (3/4), 245–275.

McGee, M. C. (1990). Text, context, and the fragmentation of contemporary culture. *Western Journal of Speech Communication, 54,* 274–289.

McGuire, W. J. (1973). The yin and yang of progress in social psychology: Seven koan. *Journal of Personality and Social Psychology, 26,* 446–456.

McGuire, W. J. (1983). A contextual theory of knowledge: Its implications for innovation and reform in psychological research. In L. Berkowitz (Ed.), *Advances in experimental social psychology* (pp. 1–47). New York: Academic Press.

McGuire, W. J. (1985). Toward social psychology's second century. In S. Koch & D. E. Leary (Eds.), *A century of psychology as a science* (pp. 558–590). New York: McGraw Hill.

McGuire, W. J. (1986). A perspectivist looks at contextualism and the future of behavioral science. In R. L. Rosnow & M. Georgoudi (Eds.), *Contextualism and understanding in behavioral science: Implications for research and theory* (pp. 271–301). New York: Praeger.

McLaughlin, M. (1984). What conversationalists know: Rules, maxims, and other lore. In M. McLaughlin (Ed.), *Conversation: How talk is organized* (pp. 16–34). Beverly Hills, CA: Sage.

McLeod, J. M., Rush, R. R., & Friederich, K. H. (1969). The mass media and political information in Quito, Ecuador. *Public Opinion Quarterly, 32,* 575–587.

McLeod, J. M., & Wackman, D. B. (1967, August). *Family communication: An updated report.* Paper presented at the annual meeting of the Association for Education in Journalism, Boulder, CO.

McQuail, D., Blumler, J. G., & Brown, J. R. (1972). The television audience: A revised perspective. In D. McQuail (Ed.), *Sociology of mass communications* (pp. 135–165). Harmondsworth, UK: Penguin Books.

Mendelsohn, H. (1968). *Operation gap-stop: A study of the application of communication techniques in reaching the unreachable poor.* Denver, CO: Communication Arts Center, University of Denver.

Milbrath, L. W. (1965). *Political participation: How and why do people get involved in politics.* Chicago: Rand McNally.

Miller, D. (1963). The study of social relationships: Situation, identity, and social interaction. In S. Koch (Ed.), *Psychology: A study of science* (pp. 639–737). New York: McGraw Hill.

Miller, J. G. (1965). Living systems: Basic concepts. *Behavioral Science, 10* (3), 193–237.

Mischel, W. (1968). *Personality and assessment.* New York: Wiley.

Mischel, W. (1969). Continuity and change in personality. *American Psychologist, 24,* 1012–1018.

Mischel, W. (1971). *Introduction to personality.* New York: Holt, Rinehart, and Winston.

Mischel, W. (1973). Toward a cognitive social learning reconceptualization of personality. *Psychological Review, 80,* 252–283.

Mishler, E. G. (1986). *Research interviewing: Context and narrative.* Cambridge, MA: Harvard University Press.

Moore, J., & Newell, A. (1974). How Merlin can understand. In G. Lee (Ed.), *Knowledge and cognition* (pp. 201–252). Potomac, MD: Erlbaum.

Moores, S. (1990). Texts, readers and contexts of reading: Developments in the study of media audiences. *Media, Culture and Society, 12,* 9–29.

Morawski, J. G. (1986). Contextual discipline: The unmaking and remaking of sociality. In R. L. Rosnow & M. Georgoudi (Eds.), *Contextualism and understanding in behavioral science: Implications for research and theory* (pp. 47–66). New York: Praeger.

Morris, R. (1993). Modernity's Prometheus. *Western Journal of Communication, 57,* 139–146.

Morrow, R. A. (1994). *Critical theory and methodology.* Thousand Oaks, CA: Sage.

Mosco, V. (1982). *Pushbutton fantasies: Critical perspectives on videotex and information technology.* Norwood, NJ: Ablex.

Mouffe, C. (Ed.). (1992). *Dimensions of radical democracy: Pluralism, citizenship, and community.* London: Verso.

Mouzelis, N. P. (1994). *Back to sociological theory: The construction of social orders.* New York: St. Martin's Press.

Mowlana, H. (1986). *Global information and world communication: New frontiers in international relations.* New York: Longman.

Mukerji, C., & Schudson, M. (1991). *Rethinking popular culture: Contemporary perspectives in cultural studies.* Berkeley: University of California Press.

Murdock, G. (1967). *Ethnographic atlas: A summary.* Pittsburgh, PA: University of Pittsburgh Press.

Murdock, G. (1989). Critical inquiry and audience activity. In B. Dervin, L. Grossberg, B. J. O'Keefe, & E. Wartella (Eds.), *Rethinking communication: Paradigm issues* (Vol.1, pp. 226–249). Beverly Hills, CA: Sage.

Murdock, G. (1997). Thin descriptions: Questions of method in cultural analysis. In J. McGuigan (Ed.), *Cultural methodologies* (pp. 178–192). London: Sage.

Murphy, T. (1999). The human experience of wilderness. *Electronic Journal of Communication, 9* (2–4). [On-line serial]. Available at: http://www.cios.org/www/ejcrec2.htm.

Nadler, M. K., & Nadler, L. B. (1987). Communication, gender and intraorganizational negotiation ability. In L. D. Stewart & S. Ting (Eds.), *Communication, gender & sex roles in diverse interaction contexts* (pp. 119–134). Norwood, NJ: Ablex.

National Advisory Council on Adult Education. (1986). *Illiteracy in America: Extent, causes, and suggested solutions* (Sudoc No. Y 3.Ed 8/4:2 Il 6). Washington, DC: U.S. Government Printing Office.

Nilan, M. (1985). *Structural constraints and situational information seeking: A test of two predictors in a sense-making context.* (Doctoral dissertation, University of Washington). *Dissertation Abstracts International, 46,* 1765.

Nofsinger, R.E. (1996, February). *Context and conversational processes.* Paper presented at the annual Conference of Western States Communication Association, Pasadena, CA.

Nordenstreng, K. (1977). European communications theory: Review and commentary. In B. D. Ruben (Ed.), *Communication yearbook* (Vol.1, pp. 73–78). New Brunswick, NJ: Transaction Books.

Nordenstreng, K., & Schiller, H. (1993). *Beyond national sovereignty: International communication in the 1990s.* Norwood, NJ: Ablex

O'Keefe, B. J., & McCormack, S. A. (1987). Message design logic and message goal structure: Effects on perceptions of message quality in regulative communication situations. *Human Communication Research, 14* (1), 68–92.

Olson, R. G. (1967). Deontological ethics. In P. Edwards (Ed.), *The encyclopedia of philosophy* (Vol. 2, p. 343). New York: Macmillan.

Outhwaite, W. (1987). *New philosophies of social science: Realism, hermeneutics, and critical theory.* New York: Macmillan.

Owen, H. P. (1967). Dogma. In P. Edwards (Ed.), *The encyclopedia of philosophy* (Vol. 2, pp. 410–411). New York: Macmillan.

Owen, J. L. (1996, February). *Context theory and consequated interaction.* Paper presented at the annual Conference of Western States Communication Association, Pasadena, CA.

Paisley, W. (1989). Public communication campaigns: The American experience. In R. E. Rice & C. K. Atkin (Eds.), *Public communication campaigns* (2nd ed., pp. 15–38). Newbury Park, CA: Sage.

Palmour, V., Rathbun, C., Brown, W., Dervin, B., & Dowd, P. (1979). *The information needs of Californians.* Sacramento, CA: California State Library. (ERIC Document Reproduction Service No. ED 185 967)

Parker, E. B. (1978). An information-based hypothesis. *Journal of Communication, 28* (1), 81–83.

Parker, E. B., & Paisley, W. J. (1966). *Patterns of adult information seeking.* Stanford, CA: Institute of Communication Research, Stanford University.

Parsons, C. (1967). Foundations of mathematics. In P. Edwards (Ed.), *The encyclopedia of philosophy* (Vol. 2, pp. 188–213). New York: Macmillan.

Pearce, W. B., & Cronen, V. (1980). *Communication, action, and meaning: The creation of social realities.* New York: Praeger.

Pendleton, D. (1985). Towards more effective medical practice. *Journal of Applied Communication Research, 13,* 96–102.

Pepper, S. C. (1942). *World hypotheses: A study in evidence.* Berkeley: University of California Press.

Peters, J. D. (1989). Democracy and American mass communication theory: Dewey, Lippman, and Lazarsfeld. *Communication, 11,* 199–220.

Pettegrew, L. S. (1988). The importance of context in applied communication research. *The Southern Speech Communication Journal, 53,* 331–338.

Piaget, J. (1962). *Play, dreams, and imitation in childhood.* New York: W. W. Norton.

Poole, M. S., & Roth, J. (1989a). Decision development in small groups IV: A typology of group decisions paths. *Human Communication Research, 15* (3), 323–356.

Poole, M. S., & Roth, J. (1989b). Decision development in small groups V: Test of a contingency model. *Human Communication Research, 15* (4), 549–589.

Popper, K. (1961). *The logic of scientific discovery.* New York: Science Editions.

Poster, M. (1995). *The second media age.* Cambridge, UK: Polity Press.

Postman, N. (1974). Media ecology: Communication as context. In R. Jeffrey & W. Work (Eds.), *Proceedings of the Annual Summer Conference of the Speech Communication Association, Chicago, Illinois, July 12, 1973* (pp. 1–10). New York: Speech Communication Association.

Pratt, L. (1969). Level of sociological knowledge among health and social workers. *Journal of Health and Social Behavior, 10,* 59–65.

Proctor, R. N. (1999). *The Nazi war on cancer.* Princeton, NJ: Princeton University Press.

Putnam, L. (1982). Procedural messages and small group work climates: A lag sequential analysis. In M. Burgoon (Ed.), *Communication yearbook* (Vol. 5, pp. 331–350). New Brunswick, NJ: Transaction Books.

Quay, L. D. (1974). Language, dialect, age, and intelligence-test performance in disadvantaged black children. *Child Development, 45,* 463–468.

Rabinow, P., & Sullivan, W. M. (1987). The interpretive turn: A second look. In P. Rabinow & W. M. Sullivan (Eds.), *Interpretive social science: A second look* (pp. 1–30). Berkeley: University of California Press.

Rakow, L. (1989). Information and power: Toward a critical theory of information campaigns. In C. T. Salmon (Ed.), *Information campaigns: Balancing social values and social change* (pp. 164–184). Newbury Park, CA: Sage.

Rakow, L. (1992). *Women making meaning.* New York: Routledge.

Rapoport, A. (1968). Foreword. In W. Buckley (Ed.), *Modern systems: Research for the behavioral scientist* (pp. vii–xxii). Chicago: Aldine.

Rees, A. M., & Schultz, D. G. (1967). Psychology and information retrieval. In G. Schecter (Ed.), *Information retrieval: A critical view* (pp. 143–150). Washington, DC: Thompson Press.

Resolution of the Administrative Council of the International Telecommunication Union. (1985, May). At the First World Telecommunications Development Conference, Arusha, Tanzania (pp. 1–15).

Reyes Matta, F. (1986). Analisis de formas [Analysis of forms]. In M. Simpson Grinberg (Ed.), *Communicación alternativa y cambio social* (pp. 362–373). Tlahuapan, Puebla, Mexico: Premia Editora de Libros.

Rice, R. E. (1980). The impacts of computer organizational and interpersonal communication. In M. E. Williams (Ed.), *Annual review of information science and technology* (Vol. 15, pp. 221–249). White Plains, NY: Knowledge Industry Publications.

Rice, R. E. & Atkin, C. K. (Eds.). (1989). *Public communication campaigns* (2nd ed.). Newbury Park, CA: Sage.

Rice, R. E., & Atkin, C. K. (Eds.). (2001). *Public communication campaigns* (3rd ed.). Thousand Oaks, CA: Sage.

Rice, R. E., & Paisley, W. J. (Eds.). (1981). *Public communication campaigns.* Beverly Hills, CA: Sage.

Ricoeur, P. (1970). *Freud and philosophy: An essay on interpretation.* (D. Savage, Trans.). New Haven, CT: Yale University Press.

Ricoeur, P. (1981). *Hermeneutics and human science: Essays on language, action, and interpretation* (J. B. Thompson, Ed. & Trans.). Cambridge, UK: Cambridge University Press.

Rieger, J. H., & Anderson, R. C. (1968). Information sources and need hierarchies of an adult population in five Michigan counties. *Adult Education Journal, 18,* 155–177.

Ritzer, G. (1992). Metatheorizing in sociology: Explaining the coming of age. In G. Ritzer (Ed.), *Metatheorizing* (pp. 7–26). Newbury Park, CA: Sage.

Robey, D. (1977). Computers and management structure: Some empirical findings re-examined. *Human Relations, 30,* 963–967.

Robinson, J. P. (1972). Toward defining the functions of television. In E. Rubinstein, G. A. Comstock, & J. P. Murray (Eds.), *Television and social behavior* (pp. 568–603). Rockville, MD: National Institute of Mental Health.

Rogers, C. (1961). *On becoming a person: A therapeutic view of psychotherapy.* Boston: Houghton Mifflin.

Rogers, E. M. (1976). Communication and development: The passing of the dominant paradigm. *Communication Research, 3* (2), 213–240.

Rogers, E. M. (1986). *Communication technology: The new media in society.* New York: Free Press.

Rogers, E. M., & Adhikarya, R. (1979). Diffusion of innovations: An up-to-date review and commentary. In D. Nimmo (Ed.), *Communication yearbook* (Vol. 3, pp. 67–82). New Brunswick, NJ: Transaction Books.

Rogers, E. M., & Kincaid, D. (1980). *Communication network analysis: A new paradigm for research.* New York: Free Press.

Rokeach, M. (1960). *The open and closed mind: Investigations into the nature of belief systems and personality systems.* New York: Basic Books.

Röling, N. G., Ascroft, J., & Chege, F. W. (1976). The diffusion of innovations and the issue of equity in rural development. *Communication Research, 3* (2), 155–170.

Rorty, R. (1979). *Philosophy and the mirror of nature.* Princeton, NJ: Princeton University Press.

Rorty, R. (1982). *Consequences of pragmatism.* Minneapolis: University of Minnesota Press.

Rorty, R. (1985). Habermas and Lyotard on postmodernity. In R. J. Bernstein (Ed.), *Habermas and modernity* (pp. 161–175). Cambridge, MA: MIT Press.

Rorty, R. (1991). *Objectivism, relativism, and truth: Philosophical papers* (Vol. 1). New York: Cambridge University Press.

Rosengren, K. E. (1989). Paradigms lost and regained. In B. Dervin, L. Grossberg, B. J. O'Keefe, & E. Wartella (Eds.), *Rethinking communication: Paradigm exemplars* (Vol. 2, pp. 21–39). Newbury Park, CA: Sage.

Rosnow, R. L. (1981). *Paradigms in transition: Methodology of social inquiry.* New York: Oxford University Press.

Rosnow, R. L. (1986). Summing up. In R. L. Rosnow & M. Georgoudi (Eds.), *Contextualism and understanding in behavioral science: Implications for research and theory* (pp. 303–310). New York: Praeger.

Rosnow, R. L., & Georgoudi, M. (1986a). *Contextualism and understanding in behavioral science: Implications for research and theory.* New York: Praeger.

Rosnow, R. L., & Georgoudi, M. (1986b). The spirit of contextualism. In R. L. Rosnow & M. Georgoudi (Eds.), *Contextualism and understanding in behavioral science: Implications for research and theory* (pp. 3–24). New York: Praeger.

Rotter, J. B. (1966). Generalized expectancies for internal versus external control of reinforcement. *Psychological Monographs, 80* (1), Whole No. 609.

Rotter, J. B, Chance, J. E., & Phares, E. J. (1972). *Application of a social learning theory to personality.* New York: Holt, Rinehart &Winston.

Ryan, S. M. (1985). *Parliamentary procedures: Essential principles.* New York: Cornwall Books.

Said, E. W. (1983a). Opponents, audiences, constituencies, and community. In W. J. T. Mitchell (Ed.), *The politics of interpretation* (pp. 7–32). Chicago: University of Chicago Press.

Said, E. W. (1983b). *The world, the text, and the critic.* Cambridge, MA: Harvard University Press.

Salmon, C. T., & Murray-Johnson, L. (2001). Communication campaign effectiveness: Critical distinctions. In R. E. Rice & C. K. Atkin (Eds.), *Public communication campaigns* (3rd ed., pp 168–180). Thousand Oaks, CA: Sage.

Sandman, P. M. (1987). Getting to maybe: Some communication aspects of hazardous waste facility siting. In R. W. Lake (Ed.), *Resolving locational conflict* (pp. 324–344). New Brunswick, NJ: Center for Urban Policy Research, Rutgers University.

Sandman, P. M., Weinstein, N., & Klotz, M. L. (1987). Public response to the risk from geological radon. *Journal of Communication, 37*, 93–108.

Sarbin, T. R. (1993). The narrative as the root metaphor of contextualism. In S. C. Hayes, L. J. Hayes, H. W. Reese, & T. R. Sarbin (Eds.), *Varieties of scientific contextualism* (pp. 51–65). Reno, NV: Context Press.

Sayer, A. (1992). *Method in social science: A realist approach* (2nd ed.). London: Routledge.

Schackle, G. L. S. (1974). Decision: The human predicament. *Annals of the American Academy of Political and Social Science, 412*, 1–10.

Schegloff, E. A. (1987). Between micro and macro: Contexts and other connections. In J. C. Alexander, B. Giesen, R. Munch, & N. J. Smelser (Eds.), *The micro-macro link* (pp. 207–234). Berkeley: University of California Press.

Schiller, H. I. (1978). Decolonization of information: Efforts toward a new international order. *Latin American Perspectives, 16*, 5 (1), 35–48.

Schramm, W. (1973). *Men, messages, and media*. New York: Harper and Row.

Schramm, W. (1983). The unique perspective of communication: A retrospective view. *Journal of Communication, 33* (3), 6–17.

Schutz, A. (1964). *Collected papers: Studies in social theory*. The Hague, Netherlands: Martinus Nijhoff.

Scolari. (1998). *Methodologist's toolchest* (Version 2.0) [Computer software]. Thousand Oaks, CA: Scolari, Sage Software.

Scott, R. A. (1967). The selection of clients by social welfare agencies: The case of the blind. *Social Problems, 14*, 248–257.

Sears, D. O., & Freedman, J. (1967). Selective exposure to information: A critical review. *Public Opinion Quarterly, 31*, 194–213.

Seeman, L. (1966). Alienation, membership, and political knowledge. *Public Opinion Quarterly, 30*, 353–367.

Seidman, S. (1986). Is there theoretical growth in sociology? *American Journal of Sociology, 92* (1), 164–168.

Servaes, J. (1986). Development theory and communication policy: Power to the people! *European Journal of Communication, 1*, 203–229.

Shah, H. (1996). Modernization, marginalization and emancipation: Toward a normative model of journalism and national development. *Communication Theory, 6*, 143–166.

Shannon, C. E., & Weaver, W. (1949). *The mathematical theory of communication*. Urbana: University of Illinois Press.

Shields, P., & Dervin, B. (1998). Telephone privacy: Residential user perspectives and strategies. *Media International Australia, 87* (May), 95–113.

Shields, P., Dervin, B., Richter, C., & Soller, R.E. (1993). Who needs "POTS-plus" services? A comparison of residential user needs along the rural-urban continuum. *Telecommunication Policy, 17* (8), 563–587.

Shingi, P. M., & Mody, B. (1976). The communication effects gap: A field experience on television and agricultural ignorance in India. *Communication Research, 3*, 171–190.

Shotter, J. (1986). Speaking practically: Whorf, the formative function of communication, and knowing of the third kind. In R. L. Rosnow & M. Georgoudi (Eds.), *Contextualism and understanding in behavioral science: Implications for research and theory* (pp. 211–227). New York: Praeger.

Sigman, S. J. (1990). Toward an integration of diverse communication contexts. In M. Burgoon (Ed.), *Communication yearbook* (Vol. 13, pp. 554–563). New Brunswick, NJ: Transaction Books.

Sjoberg, G., Brymer, R. A., & Farris, B. (1966). Bureaucracy and the lower class. *Sociology and Social Research, 50*, 325–336.

Slack, J. D. (1989). Contextualizing technology. In B. Dervin, L. Grossberg, B. J. O'Keefe, & E. Wartella (Eds.), *Rethinking communication: Paradigm issues* (Vol. 1, pp. 329–345). Newbury Park, CA: Sage.

Slack, J. D., & Allor, M. (1983). The political and epistemological constituents of critical communication research. *Journal of Communication Research, 33* (3), 208–218.

Smith, A. G. (1975). The primary resource. *Journal of Communications, 25* (2), 15–20.

Smith, D. E. (1990). *The conceptual practices of power*. Boston, MA: Northeastern University Press.

Sontag, S. (1966). *Against interpretation*. New York: Farrar, Straus and Giroux.

Sontag, S. (1982). Writing itself: On Roland Barthes. In S. Sontag (Ed.), *A Barthes reader* (pp. vii–xxxvi). New York: Hill and Wang.

Spitzack, C., & Carter, K. (1989). Women in communication studies: A typology for revision. *The Quarterly Journal of Speech, 73* (4), 401–423.

Spitzer, S. P., & Denzin, N. K. (1965). Levels of knowledge in an emergent crisis. *Social Forces, 44*, 234–237.

Splichal, S. (1987). "Public opinion" and the controversies of communication science. *Media, Culture, and Society, 9*, 237–261.

Stamm, K., & Grunig, J. E. (1977). Communication situations and cognitive strategies in resolving environmental issues. *Journalism Quarterly, 54* (4), 713–720.

Steinberg, C. (1985). *TV facts*. New York: Facts on File.

Stewart, J. (1978). Foundations of dialogic communication. *Quarterly Journal of Speech, 64*, 183–201.

Stewart, J., & Thomas, M. (1990). Dialogic listening: Sculpting mutual meaning. In J. Stewart (Ed.), *Bridges not walls: A book about interpersonal communication* (5th ed., pp. 192–210). New York: McGraw Hill.

Stohl, C. (1989). Understanding quality circles: A communication network perspective. In B. Dervin, L. Grossberg, B. J. O'Keefe, & E. Wartella (Eds.), *Rethinking communication: Paradigm exemplars* (Vol. 2, pp. 346–360). Newbury Park, CA: Sage.

Strassman, P. S. (1980). The office of the future: Information management for the new age. *Technology Reviews, 82* (3), 54–65.

Sugar, W. (1995). User-centered perspectives of information retrieval research and analysis methods. In M. E. Williams (Ed.), *Annual review of information science and technology* (Vol. 30, pp. 77–109). White Plains, NY: Knowledge Industry Publications.

Swain, M. A. (1993). Science has no business in the truth business. In S. C. Hayes, L. J. Hayes, H. W. Reese, & T. R. Sarbin (Eds.), *Varieties of scientific contextualism* (pp. 45–49). Reno, NV: Context Press.

Swanson, D. L. (1979). Political communication research and the uses and gratifications model: A critique. *Communication Research, 6*, 37–53.

Talley, M. A., & Peck, V. R. (1980). The relationship between psychological gender orientation and communication style. *Human Communication Research, 6*, 326–339.

Tardy, R. W., & Hayle, C. L. (1998). Bonding and cracking: The role of informal interpersonal networks in health care decision making. *Health Communication, 10* (2), 151–173.

Taylor, C. (1989). *Sources of the self*. Cambridge, MA: Harvard University Press.

Taylor, J. R. (1993). *Rethinking the theory of organizational communication: How to read an organization*. Norwood, NJ: Ablex.

Taylor, R. S. (1984). Value-added processes in document-based systems: Abstracting and indexing services. *Information Services and Use, 4* (3), 127–146.

Taylor, R. S. (1985). Information values in decision contexts. *Information Management Review, 1* (1), 47–55.

Tehranian, M. (1979). Communication and international development: Some theoretical considerations. *Cultures, 6* (3), 29–37.

Tehranian, M. (1982). Open planning: The uses of communications in participatory development. *Development and Peace, 3*, 60–70.

Tehranian, M. (1988). Information technologies and world development. *Intermedia, 16* (3), 30–38.

Tehranian, M. (1990). *Technologies of power: Information machines and democratic prospects.* Norwood, NJ: Ablex.

Tehranian, M. (1991). Is comparative community theory possible/desirable? *Communication Theory, 1* (1), 44–59.

Tehranian, M. (1992). Restructuring for peace: A global perspective. In K. Tehranian & M. Tehranian (Eds.), *Restructuring for world peace* (pp. 1–22). Cresskill, NJ: Hampton Press.

Textor, R. B. (1967). *A cross-cultural survey.* New Haven, CT: HRAF Press.

Theunissen, M. (1984). *The other: Studies in the social ontology of Husserl, Heidegger, Sartre, and Buber* (C. Macann, Trans.). Cambridge, MA: MIT Press.

Tichenor, P. J., Donohue, G. A., & Olien, C. N. (1970). Mass media flow and differential growth of knowledge. *Public Opinion Quarterly, 34*, 159–170.

Tichenor, P. J., Rodenkirchen, J. M., Olien, C. N., & Donohue, G. A. (1973). Community issues, conflict, and public affairs knowledge. In P. Clarke (Ed.), *New models for mass communication research* (pp. 45–79). Beverly Hills, CA: Sage.

Toffler, A. (1980). *The third wave.* New York: Bantam Books.

Tracy, K. (1989). Conversational dilemmas and the naturalistic experiment. In B. Dervin, L. Grossberg, B. J. O'Keefe, & E. Wartella (Eds.), *Rethinking communication: Paradigm exemplars* (Vol. 2, pp. 411–423). Newbury Park, CA: Sage.

Tracy, K., Van Dusen, D., & Robinson, S. (1987). "Good" and "bad" criticism: A descriptive analysis. *Journal of Communication, 37* (2), 46–59.

Tuchman, G. (1978). *Making news: A study in the construction of reality.* New York: Free Press.

Turner, B. S. (1989). Commentary: Some reflections on cumulative theorizing in sociology. In J. H. Turner (Ed.), *Theory building in sociology* (pp. 131–147). Newbury Park, CA: Sage.

Udell, J. G. (1966). Prepurchase behavior of buyers of small electrical appliances. *Journal of Marketing, 30* (4), 50–52.

Vakkari, P., Savolainen, R., & Dervin, B. (Eds.). (1997). *Information seeking in context.* London: Taylor Graham.

Van Driel, B., & Richardson, J. T. (1988). Print coverage of new religious movements: A longitudinal study. *Journal of Communication, 38* (3), 37–61.

Veroff, J. (1986). Contextual factors in the normal personality. In R. L. Rosnow & M. Georgoudi (Eds.), *Contextualism and understanding in behavioral science: Implications for research and theory* (pp. 147–167). New York: Praeger.

von Bertalanffy, L. (1968). *General systems theory: Foundations, development, and applications.* New York: Braziller.

Voos, H. (1969). *Information needs in urban areas: A summary of research in methodology.* New Brunswick, NJ: Rutgers University Press.

Wade, S., & Schramm, W. (1969). The mass media as sources of public affairs, science, and health knowledge. *Public Opinion Quarterly, 33*, 197–209.

Wagner, D. G., & Berger, J. (1986). Programs, theory, and metatheory. *American Journal of Sociology, 92* (1), 174–182.

Wallack, L. (1989). Mass communication and health promotion: A critical perspective. In R. E. Rice & C. K. Atkin (Eds.), *Public communication campaigns* (2nd ed., pp. 353–367). Newbury Park, CA: Sage.

Ward, S. A., & Reed, L. J. (Eds.). (1983). *Knowledge structure and use: Implications for synthesis and interpretation.* Philadelphia: Temple University Press.

Warner, E. S., Murray, A. D., & Palmour, V. E. (1973). *Information needs of urban residents* (Report No. OEC-0-71-455). Washington, DC: U.S, Department of Health, Education, & Welfare, Office of Education. (ERIC Document Reproduction Service No. ED 088 464)

Weber, M. (1963). *Max Weber: Selections.* New York: Crowell.

Webster, F., & Robins, S. (1986). *Information technology: A Luddite analysis.* Norwood, NJ: Ablex.

Weick, K. E. (1979). *The psychology of organizing* (2nd ed.). Reading, MA: Addison-Wesley.

Weick, K. E. (1995). *Sensemaking in organizations.* Thousand Oaks, CA: Sage.

Weimer, W.B. (1978). Communication, speech, and psychological models of man: Review and commentary. In B. E. Ruben (Ed.), *Communication yearbook* (Vol. 2, pp. 57–77). New Brunswick, NJ: Transaction Books.

Weyl, H. (1963). *Philosophy of mathematics and natural science.* New York: Atheneum.

White, E. C. (1987). *Kaironomia: On the will to invent.* Ithaca, NY: Cornell University Press.

White, R. A. (1987). *Progress toward a new world information and communication order: A Third World perspective.* Unpublished manuscript.

Willerman, L., Broman, S. H., & Fiedler, M. (1970). Infant development, pre-school IQ, and social class. *Child Development, 41,* 70–77.

Williams, R. (1976). Community. In R. Williams (Ed.), *Keywords: A vocabulary of culture and society* (pp. 65–66). New York: Oxford University Press.

Wilson, E. O. (1998). *Consilience: The unity of knowledge.* New York: Knopf.

Wilson, P. (1977). *Public knowledge, private ignorance: Toward a library and information policy.* Westport, CT: Greenwood Press.

Wilson, T. D. (1981). On user studies and information needs. *Journal of Documentation, 37* (1), 3–15.

Wilson, T. D. (1984). The cognitive approach to information seeking behavior and use. *Social Science Information Studies, 4* (2), 197–204.

Wittet, S. (1983). *Information needs of Southeast Asian refugees in medical situations.* Master's thesis, University of Washington, Seattle.

Wollheim, R. (1967). Naturalism. In P. Edwards (Ed.), *The encyclopedia of philosophy* (Vol. 2, pp. 448–450). New York: Macmillan.

Woodward, K. (Ed.). (1980). *The myths of information: Technology and post-industrial culture.* Madison, WI: Coda Press.

Woodward, W. (1993). Toward a normative-contextualist theory of technology. *Critical Studies in Mass Communication, 10* (2), 158–180.

Yankelovich, D. (1996). A new direction for survey research. *International Journal of Public Opinion Research, 8* (1), 1–9.

Yelsma, P. (1986). Marriage vs. cohabitation: Couples' communication practices and satisfaction. *Journal of Communication, 36* (4), 94–107.

Zaret, D. (1987). Statistical techniques and sociological theory. *Sociological Theory, 5* (1), 36–40.

Zweizig, D., & Dervin, B. (1977). Public library use, users, and uses: Advances in knowledge of the characteristics and needs of adult clientele of American public libraries. *Advances in Librarianship* (Vol. 7, pp. 232–253). New York: Academic Press.

Zukav, G. (1979). *The dancing Wu Li masters: An overview of the new physics.* New York: Morrow.

Author Index

Fugh-Berman, A., 91(*n*33), *359*
Furman, S.S., 24, *359*

G

Gabriel, M., 36, 39, 40, 42, 44, 138(*n*12), 207, 208, *357*
Gadamer, H., 116, 117, 118, 119, 120, 121, 122, 124, 125-126, 128, 134(*n*2), 138(*n*13), *359*
Galgan, G.J., 112(*n*1), *359*
Gallop, J., 85(*n*28), *359*
Galloway, J.J., 17, 20, 22-23, *359*
Galtung, J., 134(*n*2), *359*
Gandy, O.H., Jr., 48, 50, 51, 50(*n*3), 51(*n*5), 73(*n*4), 91(*n*32), 221(*n*13), 293(*n*1), *359*
Ganguly, K., 136(*n*6), *360*
Garfinkel, H., 116, *360*
Garzona, C., 31, 36, 37, 39, 40, 42, 43, 44, 45, 200(*n*6), 208, 223(*n*19), 228(*n*23), *356*
Gavin, W.J., 117, 123, 124, 128, 129, *360*
Geertz, C., 71(*n*1), 82(*n*18), 112(*n*1), 181(*n*10), 270(*n*2), 296(*n*5), *360*
Genova, B.K.L., 17, 40, 42, *360*
Georgoudi, M., 112(*n*1), 114, 134(*n*2), *360*, *370*
Gerbner, G., 83(*n*19), *360*
Gergen, K.J., 118, *360*
Giddens, A., 3(*n*1), 63, 71(*n*1), 79, 80(*n*14), 86(*n*29), 91(*n*33), 96, 102, 105, 117, 134(*n*1), 165(*n*1), 171(*n*6), 219(*n*6), 270(*n*2), 290(*n*12), 296(*n*5), 297(*n*6), 309(*n*3), 341(*n*1), *360*
Gitlin, T., 183(*n*17), 221(*n*9), 309(*n*3), *360*
Glasser, T.L., 183(*n*17), *358*
Godpodinoff, K., 112(*n*1), *366*
Goldberg, P., 91(*n*33), *363*
Goldhaber, G.M., 182(*n*15), *360*
Gonzales, A., 83(*n*21), *360*
Goodman, R.F., 309(*n*3), *360*
Goodwin, C., 182(*n*13), *360*

Gorney, R., 33, *360*
Gould, S.J., 137(*n*9), *360*
Gramsci, A., 77(*n*11), 119, *361*
Graven, H., 21, *363*
Greenberg, B.S., 17, 19, 21, 24, 40, 42, 197(*n*1), 202(*n*10, n11), *356, 360, 361*
Grossberg, L., 165(*n*1), *356*
Grunig, J.E., 24, 34, 39, 40, 42, 44, 45, 199(*n*4), 203(*n*14), 223(*n*19), 233, 254(*n*4), *358, 361, 372*
Grunig, L.A., 233, *358*
Guattari, F., 85(*n*28), *354*
Gurevitch, M., 24, 205(*n*17), *363*
Guttman, A., 48, 50, *361*
Guttman, N., 234(*n*1), *361*

H

Habermas, J., 57(*n*9), 71(*n*1), 81(*n*17), 86(*n*29), 102, 112(*n*1), 138(*n*13), 165(*n*1), 217(*n*2), 253(*n*3), 270(*n*2), 296(*n*5), 297(*n*6), 309(*n*3), 341(*n*1), *361*
Hachten, W.A., 179(*n*8), 309(*n*3), *362*
Hackett, R., 202(*n*10), *364*
Haight, L., 39, 41, 42-43, 199(*n*3), *362*
Halfpenny, P., 137(*n*9), *362*
Hall, E.P., 24, 36, 39, 40, 42, 44, 138(*n*12), 207, 208, *357*
Hall, H.J., 55, *362*
Hall, S., 71(*n*1), 77(*n*1), 104, 119, 165(*n*1), 183(*n*17), 290(*n*12), 296(*n*5), 309(*n*3), *362*
Hamelink, C.J., 179(*n*8), 309(*n*3), *362*
Hamlyn, D.W., 80, *362*
Haney, R., 36, *357*
Hanneman, G.J., 40, *362*
Harlock,, S., 31, 36, 37, 39, 40, 42, 43, 44, 45, 197(*n*1), 200(*n*6), 206(*n*20), 208, 219(*n*5), 223(*n*19), 228(*n*23), *356*
Harman, D., 50, 51, *363*
Harpring, J., 242, 245(*n*4), *356*
Havelock, R.G., 27, *362*

Subject Index